Contents

15 ID Project Facilities 359

16 Epilog 371

Job Aid List

Preface

I began teaching graduate courses in introductory instructional development (ID) as early as 1970. With experience, I went from a nagging doubt to a strong conviction that there were vital pieces missing in introductory ID texts. From my own thinking and from that gained in interaction with students and colleagues, I began to see factors which would suggest the value of a different kind of introductory ID text. The case for my writing this kind of text is directly related to the conclusions, below.

Conclusion One

introductory ID textbooks tend to ignore or to treat inadequately the relationships between ID processes and their supporting processes.

Most authors discuss *ID processes* (e.g., needs assessment, design, production, implementation) in detail, but only a few discuss *supporting processes*, and then discussion is usually limited to a single term like "management." In my practice as instructor, project manager, and consultant, I was stuck, again and again, by the interrelatedness and dependency of these two sets of processes, i.e., management, information handling, communication, resource acquisition and allocation, personnel matters, and use of project facilities. Logic and experience prompt me to think that all instructional developers, whether as project managers or as team members, require a basic understanding of these two sets of processes.

Once convinced of the value of my students learning the supporting processes, I began to incorporate different ones of the processes into my second level ID courses. This solution was less than satisfactory because I found it necessary to reteach much of the same material covered in the introductory course in order to properly relate the supporting processes to the ID processes. The obvious answer was to teach the two types of processes in one course, which eventually i did, both in a semester system and in a quarter system. Several generations of my graduate students and I found this to be effective. However, it was inefficient in another sense, because each time I adopted a new text, I had to supplement and integrate material over the supporting processes. This often meant significant revision in order to match up terminology and relevance to the particular ID model being used in a text. I think a single text, like this one, where the two sets of processes are carefully related takes care of that problem.

Conclusion Two

introductory ID textbooks should teach students both what to do, and how to do.

Most introductory ID texts focus most of their attention on *what* needs to be done, with limited attention as to *how* something is done. The how-to-do part of ID is accomplished through *techniques*, defined as "practical means for accomplishing specific tasks." It turns out that ID techniques are very hard to come by, which may explain why so few are found in introductory ID textbooks. The ones used in this text were searched out over several years, and most of them did *not* come from ID textbooks, but rather were found in several different professional literatures. Still other techniques, never in print before, were obtained through interviews with colleagues from ID and related fields. The majority of ID and supporting processes presented in this text are accompanied by one or more techniques.

Conclusion Three

there is enough time available in an average introductory ID course to teach the essential processes, and their concomitant techniques.

It is probably true that most instructors using traditional teaching methods do lack sufficient time to effectively teach all of the techniques necessary for the processes prescribed by ID models. However, I found there *was* sufficient time when my students were taught the techniques through self-instruction, followed by some practice and feedback in class. One of the unique features of this text is that it teaches the ID techniques through a largely self-instructional *job aid* format, thus enabling instructors to concentrate class time more on concept and process. Job aids have been used successfully in one form or another for many years. Until recently, they were used mostly by business and industry as a "quickie" teaching tool, and as a refresher for experienced instructional developers, faced with applying techniques grown rusty from lack of use.

Conclusion Four

a significant number of students who complete introductory ID courses will not necessarily take additional ID courses.

Many students taking introductory ID courses are getting their degrees in other fields, some of them related to ID, like vocational education and curriculum development. Other students come as experienced teachers from across a range of unrelated fields. Their reasons for taking an introductory ID course includes fulfilling an elective for their next degree, and/or to become a little bit knowledgeable in this area of educational technology in hopes it will make them better teachers. Still

other students may hold full time positions as instructional developers and trainers in business and industry training programs. Many in this last group have been pulled out of their jobs to teach some area in which they have expertise, with the sometimes questionable assumption that they also have expertise in developing and teaching such instruction. Many of these practitioners, who have acquired most of their ID skills through trial and error, hope that our courses may be a more efficient and effective way of gaining skills. They may or may not take more than one ID course. An introductory text like this could represent the best opportunity for these students to formally learn the relationships among ID and supporting processes.

Conclusion Five

only minimal effort is required of instructors and instructional developers to relate generic ID processes, supporting processes, and techniques to other ID models that they may prefer.

There is a strong tendency among educational technologists and others who develop instruction to tailor ID models to fit their respective interests. Sometimes this raises a concern about using texts that use a different ID model as its main organizer. While different ID models do vary in what they emphasize and how components are labeled, the ID components are not that different. One of the exercises I have often used in my classes is to have student teams use different ID models in developing *similar* projects. I perceived no major differences in the time taken, procedures used, or products, that could be attributed to a specific ID model.

Audiences

As one might guess from earlier comments, this text is designed to serve several audiences, including 1) graduate and undergraduate students in the fields of: educational technology, curriculum, and vocational education, 2) practicing instructional developers and other specialists associated with that group, and 3) teachers at all levels of training and education. The text should be useful *not only* to the novices of the ID field, but to the more experienced as well, by providing them access to the techniques accumulated here.

Mea culpa

I have attempted to present as unbiased a view of the ID and supporting processes as I could, partly through searching the literature, and partly by checking sources, facts and perceptions with others in the field. I also made faithful efforts to give credit where credit is due for the many ideas and techniques contributing to this work. I apologize in advance for any oversights.

Acknowledgments

Contributors to this work range from former teachers of mine and colleagues in educational

and training, to my many graduate students. I am particularly grateful to the professionals in educational technology and related fields who committed time to telephone and face-to-face interviews during my search for elusive techniques. I wish to express my appreciation to the reviewers: Gayle V. Davidson, University of South Alabama; John A Gretes, UNC at Charlotte; James D. Russell, Purdue University; and Jay C. Smith, University of Oklahoma. I also wish to thank Ms. Suzanna Brabant, Wadsworth editor, and her colleagues, who did so much to smooth the way for completing the manuscript and getting it published. Family members, too, played a significant role through their support and ideas, including my children, Linda Tilford, Karen Festa, Melanie Price, Larken Stedman, and Cass Daniel Gentry. My greatest gratitude is reserved for my wife, Nancy Beuthien Gentry, who provided constant support and encouragement. Of course, a final thanks must go to those many instructional developers who, over the years, have created, tested, and written about the many ID models, processes, and techniques that have helped ease our way.

CHAPTER 1

Instructional Development

A systematic approach to the design, production,
evaluation, and implementation of instruction

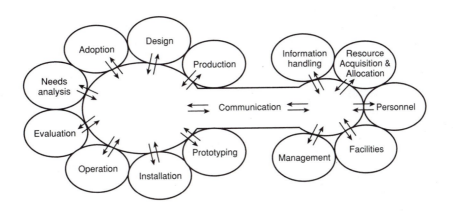

Learner Objectives

1. Differentiate between instructional development and educational technology.

2. Differentiate between instructional development processes and techniques.

3. Differentiate between development and support components.

4. Match example project tasks with components of the Instructional Project Development and Management Model.

5. Explain the major difference between projects and ongoing organizational activities.

6. Describe the purpose and form of job aids.

7. Recall definitions of major terms.

Introduction

Educators still have differences of opinion about what constitutes the essential processes necessary to carrying out instructional development. One reason has to do with confusion about the distinction between strategy (the *what* to do) and technique (the *how* to do). To carry out successfully the "how to do" of instructional development, there must be effective application of proven techniques. A **technique**, by definition, is a practical means for carrying out a specific task. A wide range of these techniques has evolved over the years, but, unfortunately, descriptions of them have been scattered among the literatures of several professions. One value of this book is the bringing together of *established* techniques relevant to accomplishing tasks in each of the processes of instructional development. By "established" is meant that either the technique has been published or it has been described and recommended to the author by two or more experienced instructional developers. In this text, techniques are presented in the form of **job aids**, which are teaching devices intended to be self-explanatory and self-instructional.

This book is designed to be used at two levels: It can be studied in detail by those beginning work in the field, or used as reference by those more experienced in instructional development and in related fields.

Relating Instructional Development to Educational Technology

Instructional development (ID) is a major activity of the field of educational technology. To paraphrase Galbraith's (1967) widely quoted definition of technology:

> **Educational technology is the practical application of scientific and/or other knowledge to accomplish given educational tasks.**

The "practical application" part is accomplished through techniques resulting from "scientific and/or other knowledge." The ID part of educational technology focuses on expertise necessary to take an instructional idea from inception to full implementation. According to Abedor and Sachs (1984):

> **Instructional development emphasizes those activities that deal directly with the systematic design, development, implementation, and evaluation of instructional materials, lessons, courses, or curricula in order to improve student learning or teaching efficiency** (p. 395).

There is some confusion of terms in the professional literature. Some authors use *instructional development* and *instructional design*, interchangeably, while others view them as having separate meanings. Here, instructional design will be considered one of the subsets of instructional development.

A valuable perspective of educational technology is to view everything as being made up of systems or subsystems. Simply put, a **system** is a set of components arranged to perform some wanted operation(s). Components of a system are also called *subsystems*, whereas "everything outside of a system that either affects the operation of the system or is affected by the system" is called the *supersystem*, or *environment* (Wilson and Wilson, 1965). By these definitions, an automobile can be looked at as a system, with its parts being its components, or subsystems, and the roads, other drivers, traffic signs, and traffic laws being its environment. As another example, management systems include components such as coordinating, monitoring, controlling, resource allocation, and motivating, which are arranged to enable a manager to guide personnel in completion of their tasks. Similarly, there are systems for accomplishing instructional development. Adopting the view that the ID process is also a system and part of a larger system helps remind the developer of the *interdependency* and *interrelatedness* of the components making up the system, and thus reduces the likelihood that important relationships will be overlooked.

An Instructional Development Model

Instructional development systems are often represented as graphic models. Over the years, numerous ID models have been promoted by different persons. For the most part these models are very similar. Their differences lie primarily in the emphasis placed on particular steps in the process of carrying out instructional development. There is currently no evidence that supports one model over another. Broadly defined:

> **An ID model is a graphic representation of a systematic approach, designed to facilitate efficient and effective development of instruction.**

Structurally, such ID models are made up of interdependent, interacting components. These components represent processes (*what* needs to be done) that are accomplished through application of specific techniques (*how* to do what needs to be done).

Figure 1.1 depicts a graphic representation of an ID model called the *Instructional Project Development and Management (IPDM) Model*. The fourteen components of the model serve as an organizer for this book. The components deal with essential processes for carrying out instructional development. For example, carrying out the processes of the *Needs analysis* component of the IPDM Model enables an instructional developer to determine what instruction *should be* developed for a targeted group. The needs generated by this process are easily restated as goals, which in turn guide the writing of specific objectives, one of the processes of the design component in this model. Each of the circles in the model represents a component relevant to carrying out the tasks of an instructional development project. The components on the left are specific to instructional development processes; the ones on the right are specific to managing those ID processes. Connecting the two sets of components is the communication component, which is also considered a support component. The arrows in the model

FIGURE 1.1 / Relationships among development and supporting components of the IPDM Model

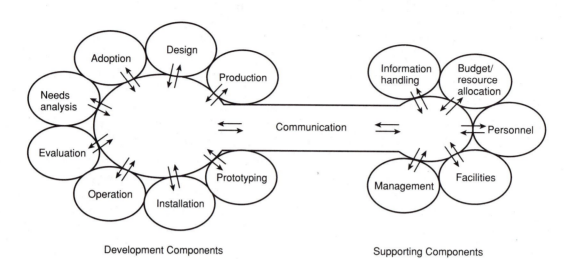

Development Components   Supporting Components

indicate that, as a system, each of the components generates and receives essential information from all of the other components.

There are several justifications for this particular model. First, the model helps present the ID process as more dynamic than do most other models. A person new to the field may assume, based on looking at some of the models, that instructional development is a *linear,* or step-by-step, process, which in fact is rarely so. To illustrate, an instructional developer might find him- or herself entering the instructional development process at any of the points, as represented by the components in the IPDM model. For example, the task of developing the instruction may be given to a person *after* the specific objectives have been set. Since specific objectives are normally developed during the *Design* process, the developer would not have been involved in either the *Needs analysis* process or the *Adoption* process. Continuing the example of specific objectives, it is not uncommon for these objectives to change several times as development of the instruction progresses.

Second, this model elaborates on the importance of the support components for the development components. An instructional developer finds the support components just as essential as the development components. Most models either give short shrift to how development and support components are related or may not show any relationship. Third, the IPDM model brings attention to the importance of sharing information. The arrows in the model indicate that each of the components may have important information needed by the other components. A brief meaning for each of the components of the IPDM Model, as presented in Figure 1.1, follows:

> *Needs analysis*—Process of establishing the validity of needs and goals for existing or proposed instruction, and of assigning priorities among them.

Adoption—Process of establishing acceptance of an innovation by decision makers, gatekeepers, and others affected, and of obtaining commitment of resources.

Design—Process of determining and specifying objectives, strategies, techniques, and media for meeting instructional goals.

Production—Process of constructing elements of a project, as specified in a design or as based on revision data.

Prototyping—Process of assembling, pilot testing, respecifying, validating, and finalizing an instructional unit.

Installation—Process of establishing the necessary conditions for effective operation of a new instructional product or process, when initially placed in a targeted system.

Operation—Process of effectively maintaining the continuing application of an instructional product and/or procedure, after its installation.

Evaluation—Process of collecting and analyzing data about and assigning values to an ongoing instructional unit, for enabling decisions on maintenance, revision, and/or elimination of its elements.

Management—Process by which resources are controlled, coordinated, integrated, and allocated to accomplish project goals.

Communication—Process by which essential information is distributed and circulated among those responsible for, or involved in, the activities of a project.

Information handling—Process of selecting, collecting/generating, organizing, storing, retrieving, distributing, and assessing information required by an ID project.

Resource acquisition and allocation—Process of determining resource needs, formalizing budgets, and acquiring and distributing resources.

Personnel—Process of determining staffing needs, hiring, training, assessing, motivating, counseling, censuring, and dismissing ID project members.

Facilities—Process for organizing and renovating spaces for design, implementation, and testing of elements of instruction.

Instructional development models such as IPDM guide the instructional developer in determining what processes need to be completed during the development of instruction, but they do not indicate how to accomplish them. ID processes are accomplished by applying *techniques*, which, as mentioned earlier are practical means by which tasks are carried out. A problem common to instructional developers is locating established, proven techniques for carrying out ID tasks. Information about established ID techniques is dispersed among several literatures, and even when located is often not in a form easily understood or applied by instructional developers.

A major function of this text is to relate ID processes to established, proven techniques for carrying out instructional development projects. A major premise of this book is that development of instruction, whether done by a teacher, a trainer, or an instructional developer, requires project management skills. Consider for a moment how projects differ from other organizational activities.

A project is a specific, finite task with a well defined set of predetermined outcomes.

Whereas most other management tasks are routine, and continue perhaps for the life of an organization, projects are ephemeral. They exist for a brief time and then are finished, and their remaining resources are switched to other organizational tasks. One of the functions of the IPDM Model is to provide a context for management of instructional development projects.

Job Aids

In the chapters that follow, selected techniques will be presented and taught through a job aid format that has proven effective and efficient.

A job aid is a formalized set of textual and/or graphical step-by-step directions for accomplishing a task through one or more techniques.

The step-by-step directions in a job aid may be in verbal or in graphic form, or both. One of the values of job aids is that they reduce the level of knowledge needed to apply a technique effectively, and thus the techniques can be taught more quickly than by traditional means. Traditional means usually demand a greater depth of knowledge. The formalized use of job aids has been more prevalent, to date, in the training programs of business and industry than in education. The "Gradual Disengagement" job aid illustrates one of many possible formats. This particular job aid is designed to teach an instructional developer a technique for withdrawing from a project in a way that reduces the likelihood of problems for the client.

Job Aid / Gradual Disengagement

Description   This technique is applied by the instructional developer concerned about the continued successful operation of an instructional unit, *after* implementation. Basically, it consists of the instructional developer's pulling him- or herself out of the client system a little at a time, as instructors and managers of the client system get familiar with the unit and develop the necessary expertise to continue delivering, maintaining, and improving the unit without the assistance of the developer.

Use Rationale   Instructional developers are sometimes unaware of the skill vacuum left behind in the maintenance of a newly developed instructional unit as a result of their withdrawal. By gradually, rather than abruptly, removing themselves and continuing to provide training of skills needed by the instructor, the developer increases considerably the likelihood of the unit's continued effectiveness, improvement, and, even, survival.

Critical Tasks

1. **Identify, minimally, the skills needed by an instructor to maintain and improve an instructional unit.** Ideally, the instructor will have been deeply involved in the creation of the

continued

Gradual Disengagement, continued

unit, and will have picked up a number of the skills from working with a developer sensitive to the need to leave behind a set of skills for maintaining and improving the unit. Examples of such skills are writing performance objectives, and matching objectives with their respective strategies, media, and test items.

2. **Develop a plan for training the instructor(s) during the unit's development and during gradual withdrawal from the project.** E.g., first make the instructor aware of the value of the necessary skills he or she lacks, then gradually impart skills by involving him or her in carrying out corrective and maintenance tasks during the development of the unit. During gradual withdrawal the developer may provide workshops at appropriate times, and be on call during the first year after implementation to assist with any problems related to the unit.

3. **Train the instructor(s).** As mentioned, if the developer and the instructor are working together, training can be done on an apprenticeship basis, with the instructor gradually developing the necessary skills and taking over responsibility for correcting and maintaining the instructional unit. See Figure 1.2.

4. **Gradually withdraw.** Often, as the client gains familiarity and understanding of the instructional unit, the withdrawal phase for the instructional developer may be speeded up. In those instances where the instructional development group is in the same organization as the training group, complete withdrawal is not necessary.

FIGURE 1.2 / Change in responsibility during instructional developer's gradual withdrawal from a project

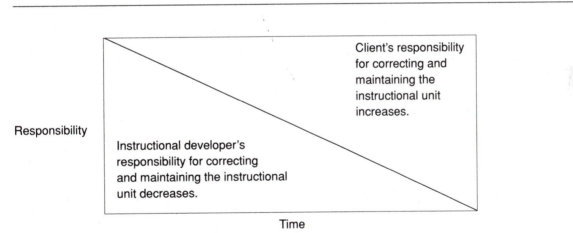

Client's responsibility for correcting and maintaining the instructional unit increases.

Responsibility

Instructional developer's responsibility for correcting and maintaining the instructional unit decreases.

Time

Reference

Havelock, R. G. (1973). *The Change Agent's Guide to Innovation in Education.* Englewood Cliffs, N.J.: Educational Technology Publications, pp. 136–139.

Another value of job aids is their use by instructional developers to refresh their memories of the steps for carrying out tasks that tend to occur infrequently.

The formats used with job aids vary considerably in the literature. However, for purposes of clarity and comparison, the format illustrated in the "Gradual Disengagement" job aid is used consistently throughout this text (although not all job aids will include figures).

Expectations

The components listed in the IPDM Model, and their related processes, should make sense as being important in carrying out an instructional development project. Job aids for carrying out aspects of each of these processes are taught throughout the text. However, there is no attempt at providing an exhaustive set of job aids for each component. The intent is to give the instructional developer access to a basic set of established, proven techniques through the step-by-step job aid format. The techniques presented here may not always be the most effective ones known for carrying out a process. In a number of cases, they are chosen because they are relatively inexpensive to carry out, do not require a high skill level, or can be carried out more quickly than other techniques.

Each of the next fourteen chapters focuses on a component of the IPDM Model. The chapters will vary in terms of the number of techniques presented, depending on the need. For example, the Design and the Management components are more extensively treated than other components because of the high dependence and complexity of those areas. Anyone who wants to go beyond the descriptions and explanations of the techniques presented can make use of the references listed at the end of each chapter and in the job aids. The final chapter of this text is dedicated to examining issues around the use of ID techniques and the need for continuing research on their effectiveness, efficiency, and relevance.

Summary

This chapter describes the structure of this text. The primary organizer is the *Instructional Project Development and Management (IPDM) Model*, which consists of fourteen major components. All of these components are viewed as necessary to the systematic development of instruction and to managing the development of instruction. This introduction to the instructional development model provides the reader with the understanding needed to put the various techniques into proper context. Thus, it is not necessary to read the chapters consecutively. Techniques, that is, the established means by which tasks are carried out, are tied to specific development and management processes. A job aid format is used to teach the techniques. The text is designed for use by both novices and experienced instructional developers. Reference is provided at the end of each chapter to enable more extensive study of topics.

References

Abedor, A. J., and Sachs, S. G. (1984). Faculty development (FD), organizational development (OD), and instructional development (ID): Choosing an orientation. In *Instructional Development: The State of the Art, II*, ed. R. K. Bass and C. R. Dills. pp. 394–403. Dubuque, Iowa: Kendall/Hunt.

Galbraith, J. (1967). *The New Industrial State*. Boston: Houghton Mifflin.

Gentry, C. G. (1980–81). A management framework for program development techniques. *Journal of Instructional Development* 4(2): 33–37.

Finnegan, G. T. (1985). Job aids: Improving employee performance in healthcare. *Performance and Instruction Journal* July: 10–11.

Lineberry, C. S., and Bullock, D. H. (1980). *Job Aids*. Englewood Cliffs, N.J.: Educational Technology Publications.

Nelson, J. J. (1989). Quick and dirty job aids. *Performance and Instruction Journal* 28(8): 35–36.

Taylor, R., and Doughty, P. J. (1988). Instructional development models: Analysis at the task and subtask levels. *Journal of Instructional Development* 11(4): 19–28.

Wilson, I. G., and Wilson, M. E. (1965). *Information, Computers and System Design*. New York: Wiley.

CHAPTER 2

Needs Analysis

Process of establishing the validity of needs
and goals for existing or proposed instruction,
and assigning priorities among them

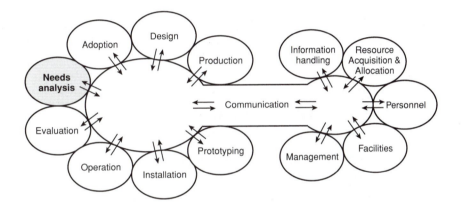

Learner Objectives

1. State major reasons for including needs analysis as part of the ID process.

2. Describe the general steps in the needs analysis process.

3. Differentiate between needs analysis and the other ID Model components.

4. Recognize rules restricting needs analysis.

5. List the two major purposes of needs analysis.

6. Relate needs and goals in the ID process.

7. Differentiate among the characteristics of needs analysis techniques: Delphi, Fault Tree Analysis, and Critical Incidence.

8. Recall definitions of major terms.

Introduction

There is a saying that "if you don't know where you're going, you shouldn't be surprised that you end up somewhere else!" Knowing where you are going in developing an instructional unit or program requires clear and unequivocal goals.

Major amounts of energy are lost to organizations when newly developed instructional units and programs suffer an early demise. Even worse is the case where instruction hangs on in a system long after its reason for being has passed. These two conditions occur regularly because educators, trainers, *and* instructional developers do not know how, or don't take the time to perform needs analyses. Techniques of instructional or curricular needs analysis serve three primary purposes: first, to identify within a system any discrepancy between what should be and what is; second, to restate those discrepancies as needs or goals; and finally, to prioritize the goals in terms of their relative importance to the operation of the system.

Over the years, a number of techniques have been devised for identifying changing conditions that affect our instructional systems, and for prioritizing their importance. Names used interchangeably for such techniques are *needs assessment*, and *needs analysis*. *Needs analysis* will be the preferred form in this text.

There is reasonable agreement across the professional literature on the meaning of *needs* and *needs analysis*. Simply stated:

Needs analysis is the process by which a system's needs and goals are identified, and priorities among them are decided.

A need is any significant discrepancy between a desired outcome and an observed outcome.

There, much of the agreement ends. An examination across the range of established needs analysis models show differences in what elements should and should not be included in such models. The literature also makes clear that needs analysis models owe their genesis to various discrepancy models of evaluation. That is, they are designed to discriminate between "what is" (the status quo), and "what should be" (the ideal).

There is a tendency to confuse graphic rendering of needs analysis *models* with needs analysis *techniques*. Most needs analysis models, whether graphic or verbal representations, serve only to relate the elements making up the model, and help clarify "what" needs to be done to carry out a needs analysis, as demonstrated by the Coffing Model (Coffing, 1977) in Figure 2.1, and the Kaufman model (Kaufman, et al., 1981) in Figure 2.2. To be effective, such models need to be accompanied by instruction on "how" (i.e., techniques) to carry out a needs analysis. Many of the techniques suitable for actually identifying needs and goals, are found under other labels, as well. The focus here is on "techniques" of needs analysis, and will only refer to needs analysis models for contextual purposes.

Why bother with needs analysis? It is not uncommon for the client and the instructional developer to disagree on the merits of a completed ID project. Often, such disagreement can be traced to an inadequate fix on a system's needs at the initiation of a project. A typical example is when a

FIGURE 2.1 / After Coffing's needs assessment model

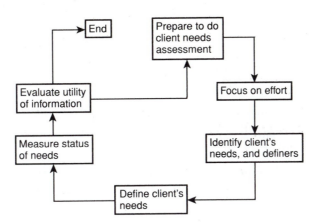

developer accepts a restricted view of what is needed by the system's students, based on what he or she is told by a single client, only to find out that the client's view is neither accurate nor the prevailing view of the other system members. Increasingly, instructional developers are taking the position of Burton and Merrill (1977, p. 21) that "needs analysis should be the first step in a systematic approach to the development of instructional materials for a course or training program."

FIGURE 2.2 / Graphic representation of the organizational elements model for needs analysis

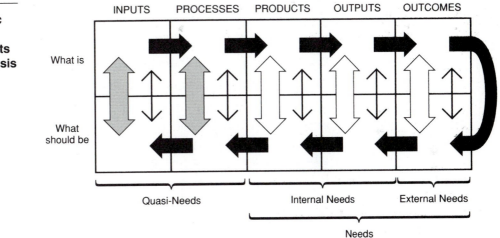

Thus, before taking responsibility for a proposed ID project, instructional developers could profit by answering to the question "What are the validated needs of the client system, relevant to the proposed ID project?" Where such information is lacking, an instructional developer may want to convince the client to sponsor a needs analysis or, if that fails, to consider withdrawing from the project, if he or she has that option.

Data used to identify the needs of a system may be either judgmental or objective or some combination of the two. For example, asking teachers, administrators, parents, and students what they think should be the major goals of their school to meet the needs of its graduates would result in data that is primarily "judgmental." On the other hand, if careful, systematic, on-the-job observations are made to determine the knowledge and skills actually used by employees, and those are compared with the knowledge and skills taught by the schools or training programs, any discrepancy between what was taught and what was required on the job could be viewed as "objective" data.

Inspection of the professional literature reveals some inconsistency and confusion about how needs are actually determined and about what is done with them after identification. Many needs analysis techniques require, as their first step, the identification of problems in the instructional system. According to Wilson and Wilson (1965):

A problem exists when someone desires a certain state of affairs and does not immediately know how to attain it.

In the next step of the process for carrying out a needs analysis, problems are translated into needs, and the needs, in turn, are translated into goals. According to Bushnell and Rappaport (1971, p. 212):

A goal is a general expression of intent, not limited in time or directly measurable.

In relation to the "what" and the "how" discussed earlier, goals are viewed as being the "why" of systems.

Others (Anthony, 1965; Cook, 1970) have tied the discrepancy between "what is" and "what should be" to the concept of *control*. For example, Cook perceives control as consisting of three steps:

1. *Problem identification:* Noting discrepancy or deviation between actual and expected performance.
2. *Problem analysis:* Determining the cause of deviation.
3. *Problem solution:* Developing and implementing a corrective action.

As can be seen, the first element is equivalent to the difference between "what is" and "what should be." Almost all models of planning, systems analysis, and accountability have some kind of a needs-sensing component built in; however, most of them are not prescriptively spelled out. Such models as Cook's appear to concern themselves with determining only the current needs of a system. However, organizations are finding it necessary to determine future needs, as well. With only slight modifications, most of the techniques suitable for determining current needs of a system can be used to determine future needs.

Needs Analysis Process

The following seven steps will act as a contextual frame for examining specific needs analysis techniques.

1. *Identify problems* (collect data to determine any "problems" or discrepancies within a target system's instructional program's processes or products).
2. *Validate problems* (determine whether problems identified are real problems or merely symptoms of problems).
3. *Formulate needs* (translate the problems into "needs" statements).
4. *Formulate goals* (translate needs into "goal" statements).

5. *Reconcile new and current goals* (combine new goals with a program's current goals in a single list, with duplicates removed).

6. *Validate reconciled goals* (have appropriate individuals or groups endorse the goals in the combined list).

7. *Prioritize goals* (have appropriate individuals or groups rank the validated goals in terms of their importance).

The product of many of the needs analysis models is a set of prioritized goals, so that perhaps the process should more properly be called "goal analysis" or "goal setting" rather than needs analysis! These, in fact, are common labels used among those who call themselves curriculum developers.

Once relevant goals are generated through needs analysis, the instructional developer would go on to other ID tasks in the IPDM Model, such as the following:

- Seek agreement from decision makers to incorporate the goals into the program (Adoption).
- Generate performance objectives from the goals (Design).
- Choose instructional strategies, techniques, and media for meeting the objectives (Design).
- Acquire and/or produce instructional materials (Production).
- Assemble a testable instructional unit (Prototyping).
- Try out and revise the prototype (Prototyping).
- Install the finished instructional package into the client system (Installation).
- Maintain the instructional package in the client system (Operation).
- Periodically assess the instructional package to decide whether to keep it as is, revise it, or eliminate it (Evaluation).

Many of the techniques relevant to determining a system's needs do not deal with all seven listed steps of the general needs analysis process. Therefore, the developer may have to use a combination of techniques in order to accomplish all of the steps. For steps 1 and 2, there is an extensive literature dealing with techniques of problem identification, validation, and solution that might be profitably related to the needs analysis process, should the reader desire to gain more depth.

While the needs certainly differ for instruction in an educational program, as opposed to instruction in a training program, one can easily see how the same processes used by one could be used by the other. As a practical illustration of the steps in the general needs analysis model, consider the case where the staff of a suburban high school discovered the following:

> Very few of our high school graduates who majored in business education are being hired into clerical jobs, and the majority of the ones that are hired are let go by the end of their probationary periods.

This could reasonably be viewed as symptomatic of a fault in the business education program of the high school. After validation, the problem could be refined to read:

Seventy percent of the business education majors graduating from our high school are unable to perform adequately the math operations necessary for the average clerical position for which they might be expected to apply.

For step 3, this problem could be restated as a need, through a minor modification:

The business education majors from our high school should be, or need to be, sufficiently competent to perform adequately the math operations necessary for the average clerical position that they might assume.

In turn, to satisfy step 4 of the needs analysis contextual frame, this need can be restated as a program goal:

The business education majors from our high school will be competent to perform the math operations necessary for the average clerical position that they might assume.

Step 5 of the general needs analysis process minimally requires that we take the goals resulting from the first four steps, match them with the current goals of our high school, and resolve any conflict among goals. After this, duplicates are thrown out and the remaining goals put into random order for later prioritization.

Commonly, step 6, the validation of goals, is accomplished by asking an appropriate group to indicate which of the goals on the list are appropriate for the school program. Similarly, for step 7, another group could rank the validated goals so that program developers would have a clear mandate about the order in which goals should be implemented, given that they hadn't previously been implemented. By the same token, instruction supporting invalid goals in the current program could be eliminated, and resources supporting them could be transferred to the implementation of validated goals. This example is certainly simplistic, and ignores the responsibility of determining a whole range of issues related to the goals, including the practicality of implementing the goals, whether some goals are incompatible with others, and whether they are short- or long-term in nature (Weiss, 1972). The goal issue becomes even more complex when an attempt is made to categorize them. Perrow (1961), as one of several early commentators on the categorization of organizational goals, lists five categories of goals: societal, output, system, product, and derived goals.

Some of these issues may require more expertise than is normally found in a sample of persons concerned with a particular school or training program. In such cases, special knowledge of external consultants might have to be called on. While recognizing this type of problem, it will not be dealt with here. Rather, the purpose here is to put needs analysis into an instructional development context and to present three needs analysis techniques that can assist instructional developers in arriving at validated, prioritized needs and goals.

There are many techniques that could be used for purposes of determining needs, and they range considerably in their adequacy, complexity, and cost. Most of them use some form of questionnaire, survey, or interview as their base instrument for collecting data, and they are subject to the criteria that research has determined as appropriate to such instruments, including how they are administered and how their data are interpreted.

The remainder of this chapter describes three separate techniques for carrying out the needs analysis process. While the techniques described are relatively simple, they are effective. They can also be adjusted to fit a wide range of conditions. In addition, they are sufficiently robust so that they can be used effectively with no more direction than is provided here, when such use is coupled with common sense.

Needs Analysis Techniques

The first technique described, the *Delphi Technique*, has a long and venerable history. Within its limits the Delphi Technique works very well. It is designed to be effective and efficient in capturing the best judgments of individuals and groups. Therein also lies its major shortcoming, in that it provides mainly judgments of need, *not* objective evidence of need. The second and third needs analysis techniques presented, *Critical Incident Technique* and *Fault Tree Analysis*, are designed to collect more objective data about the needs of a system, but they, too, have shortcomings. Nonetheless, any one of these three techniques, when used properly, has a high probability of generating valid needs for either educational or training systems.

The reader should be sensitive to the fact that many techniques presented in this text have multipurpose capabilities. That is particularly true of the Delphi Technique.

Delphi Technique

Dalkey and Helmer (1963) developed the Delphi Technique for the Rand Corporation in the early 1950s. The impetus for the development of the technique was to enable the government to predict (1) which American industries the Soviet Union was most likely to target, and (2) the number of atomic bombs the Soviet Union would be likely to send, in order to reduce the American industrial output by a prescribed amount. These predictions could then be used by Americans to determine appropriate preventative and countermeasures. Since that first application, the Delphi Technique has been used for thousands of projects where there was a need *to efficiently collect informed judgments and gain consensus about those judgments.*

The steps in the job aid that follows are after the excellent work of Delbecq, et al. (1975). These steps are common to most variations of the technique. Note that this job aid example begins, in step 1, with the assumption that the problem was unclear goals for the system. We could just as easily use the following as our first question:

> What are the major problems with academic programs designed
> to prepare instructional developers to work in industrial training
> programs?

This, of course, would have satisfied the first two of the seven general steps, listed earlier. However, in the Delphi example the problem has already been determined as:

Job Aid / Delphi

Description   Briefly, a Delphi is carried out by submitting a sequential set of questions, one at a time, to a group of experts who are anonymous to each other. After each question, the data generated by the group in response to the previous question is analyzed and then used to design the next question. Each round brings the experts closer to consensus.

Use Rationale   It is not uncommon for the client and the instructional developer to disagree on the merits of a completed instructional development project. All too often such disagreement can be traced to an inadequate fix on a system's needs at the initiation of the project. Thus, before taking responsibility for a proposed ID project, instructional developers need to determine what the validated needs are of the client system with which this ID project should deal.

Critical Steps

1. **Determine the initial question to be answered.** E.g., "What should be the goals of a master's program designed to produce instructional developers who will be working in business and industry training programs, where program candidates have had no previous formal training in ID?"

2. **Identify appropriate experts, and get agreement from them to participate.** E.g., directors of university ID programs, training program directors, and established instructional developers working in business and industry training programs.

3. **Send the initial question to the experts, and receive their responses.** E.g., by post, computer mail, or fax. Provide a return-addressed, stamped envelope. Ask them to respond by a reasonable date (2–4 weeks). Follow up on those who do not.

4. **Analyze the responses of the experts, and incorporate the responses into a question for the next round.** E.g., "Study the enclosed list of goals that you and others view as important for the training program, and rank them as to their relative importance."

5. **Again, analyze the experts' responses, and incorporate those data into the next question.** E.g., "The rankings made by you and others have been averaged for each goal and resequenced accordingly. Indicate why you would, or would not, agree with the new ranking for each of the goals."

6. **Again, after receiving the experts' responses, analyze them and use the data to form the next question.** E.g., "Note that the various explanations made by you and others as to why you did or did not change your rankings is placed next to the respective questions. Given these explanations, indicate why you would, or would not, now change the rankings of the goals."

7. **Repeat step 6 until you are satisfied with the ranking of the goals.**

References

Delbecq, A. H., et al. (1986). *Group Techniques for Program Planning: A Guide to Nominal Group and Delphi Processes.* Middleton, Wis.: Green Briar Press.

Linstone, H. A., and Turoff, M. (eds.) (1975). *The Delphi Method: Techniques and Application.* Reading, Mass.: Addison-Wesley.

We don't know what goals are most appropriate for the ID training program.

So we are able to skip the Identify and Validate Problem steps. Whether we should or not is a judgment call.

The determination of who should be queried as to the needs or goals of a system varies among models. For example, Kaufman (1977), in his taxonomy of needs, identifies two sources of the desired information, one source being the "external" community (Alpha), and the second source being persons "internal" to the system (Beta).

Although limited, some of the research on the use of the Delphi Technique is useful. Brown, Cochran, and Dalkey (1969) countered a previous rule that "only experts should be used in a Delphi." They found that "nothing of significance is lost by including less knowledgeable persons as long as there are *some* participants who are knowledgeable." Research by Sweigert and Schabacker (1974, pp. 8–12) resulted in four findings: (1) convergence of judgment increases with each round, with greatest convergence at the end of round two; (2) the minimum number of rounds necessary for convergence is two; (3) a reliable ranking of goals can be generated through Delphi; and (4) feedback of participants' own last responses tends to reduce the convergence of perceptions.

Critical Incident Technique

When Flanagan (1954) devised the Critical Incident Technique (CIT) back in the 1940s, it is doubtful he could have imagined all of the uses and misuses to which it would be put. Among the acceptable uses have been theory development (Leles, 1968), problem identification, and determining competencies necessary for a variety of positions (Rutherford, 1974). In defining this technique, Stano (1983, p. 4) states:

> In essence, the CIT involves the collection of real-world examples of behavior which characterized either very effective or very ineffective performance of some activity.

In discussing the principle advantage of CIT, Stano says (p. 4) that application of the technique:

> generates data which is based on actual behavior rather than on a particular researcher's inferences, hunches, stereotypes, and subjective estimates of what is important or necessary.

On the other hand, Flanagan (1954, p. 335) sees value in its flexibility:

> It should be emphasized that the Critical Incident Technique does not consist of a single rigid set of rules governing . . . data collection. Rather, it should be thought of as a flexible set of principles which must be modified and adapted to meet the specific situation at hand.

The sequential steps for carrying out the CIT are listed in the "CIT" job aid. The steps were adapted from Stano's work (1983).

The general needs analysis step missing in the CIT process is the prioritizing of generated goals. A variety of prioritizing techniques could be used for this purpose. Examples are the Delphi Technique and the Nominal Group process. The latter is presented in detail in Chapter 3.

Job Aid / Critical Incident Technique (CIT)

Description   The CIT involves the collection (from knowledgeable respondents) of real, rather than hypothetical, examples of behavior that are either very effective or very ineffective performance of some activity. The behaviors are categorized and summarized and then related to specific aspects of the system in question. The final list of behaviors can be restated as needs/goals required for the system.

Use Rationale   It is not uncommon for client and instructional developer to disagree on the merits of a completed ID project. All too often such disagreement can be traced to an inadequate fix on a system's needs at the initiation of the project. Thus, before taking responsibility for a proposed ID project, instructional developers need to determine what are the validated needs of the client system with which this ID project should deal?

Critical Steps

1. **State clearly the aim to be accomplished with the Critical Incident Technique.** E.g., "Describe any incidents witnessed *by you*, that illustrate the positive and/or negative aspects of the training of instructional developers for working in business and industry training programs."

2. **Select a sample of respondents who are in a position to observe relevant aspects of the system in question.** E.g., directors and faculty of ID training programs, their students and graduates, and employers of the graduates.

3. **Determine the instrument(s) for collecting the incidents from the respondents.** E.g., questionnaires, surveys, or oral interviews. In the latter, the interviewer questions the respondent and records the data on prepared forms.

4. **Formulate instructions to respondents:**
   a. State the aim unambiguously for them (e.g., "We would like you to write up any recent positive and/or negative incidents that you have personally witnessed that illustrate the level of competence of instructional developers being trained to work in business and industry training program development").
   b. Ask them to write the individual incidents on separate sheets of paper so that analysts will not confuse one incident with another.
   c. Convince respondents of their anonymity, so that they will respond candidly (e.g., "All data will be combined statistically, without reference to any respondent. Please answer the questions frankly").

5. **Collect the critical incidents.** E.g., use mail return or other means to collect questionnaires. There should be a minimum of fifty incidents.

6. **Sort critical incidents into common theme categories.** The process is analogous to a content or factor analysis; e.g., one theme could be the domains that incidents fall into: skills, knowledge, and attitudes that are relevant to ID in business and industry training program development.
   a. Translate each incident into a behavioral form, and sort them onto individual note cards (e.g., Incident: "The instructional strategies he chose didn't do the job!" Behavioral form: "Instructional developer was unable to match objectives with effective instructional strategies").

continued

Critical Incident Technique (CIT), continued

 b. Group cards together that contain identical incidents (if cards are concerned with the same behavior, they should be put in the same stack even though some are concerned with positive incidents and others are concerned with negative incidents).

 c. Break major groupings down into subcategories, when they are obvious (e.g., skills could be broken down according to the specific stage of development, i.e., needs analysis, design, prototype testing and revision, system installation, operation, or evaluation).

 d. Write simple-sentence summary statements for each of the categories and subcategories (e.g., for the subcategory of Design: Instructional developers wrote excellent objectives for all three domains but had difficulty in matching objectives to learning conditions, did not know how to cost out alternative instructional strategies, had good storyboarding skills, etc.).

 e. Optional: validate the combined behaviors (e.g., CIT facilitator could take the note cards and the summaries back to the generators of the incidents, or to another representative sample of respondents, to ensure that all behaviors have been interpreted correctly and that none have been left out).

 f. Compile a final list of behaviors that need to be included in the client system. (Usually, the lists are arranged by categories and subcategories of behaviors, followed by their summary statements.)

7. Restate the behaviors as system needs/goals. E.g., Behavioral form: "Instructional developer was unable to match objectives with effective instructional strategies; goal: students at the end of instruction are able to match objectives with appropriate instructional strategies.

Reference

Staño, Michael (1983). The Critical Incident Technique: A description of the Method. Paper presented at the Annual Meeting of the Southern Speech Communication Association. Lincoln, Neb., April 7–9.

Fault Tree Analysis

Fault Tree Analysis (FTA) is an operations research technique designed to identify undesired events that may negatively affect the operation of a system. Based on knowledge of such undesired events, FTA provides information for the redesign or monitoring of a system to prevent the undesired events from occurring. Any proposed changes for preventing the occurrence of undesired events can be interpreted as "needs" of the system. There is certainly an overlap between FTA and CIT, in the sense that the negative behaviors of CIT are similar to the undesired events of FTA. However, the undesired events of FTA can result from many sources, rather than from a single individual, as in CIT.

  There is some evidence that an analysis of undesired or failure-inducing events has an advantage over an analysis focusing only on events attributing to the success of an operation. Two of the reasons are: (1) failure-inducing events generate questions beyond those identified through success analysis; and (2) a group is able to come more rapidly to consensus on what caused a system to fail than on what caused success. According to Stephens (1973, p. 2):

Fault Tree Analysis is a technique for increasing the probability of success in any system by analyzing the most likely modes of failure which could occur within the system and then suggesting high priority avoidance strategies for those failure modes.

H. A. Watson, of Bell Laboratories, is given credit for originating the technique of Fault Tree Analysis (Fussell, et al., 1974). It was first used by Bell Laboratories in 1961, to evaluate the safety procedures of the Minuteman Launch Control System. The FTA technique was further developed and refined by a Bell Laboratory study team, and by researchers at the Boeing Company. Witkin and Stephens (1968) were the first to apply FTA to a major educational program. Stephens provided the technical expertise necessary to translate FTA from its industrial use to education. The technique, as presented here, was largely adapted from Witkin's and Stephens' interpretation of FTA.

The procedure for carrying out an FTA depends on a thorough knowledge of the target system. Therefore, to be effective in using FTA, the instructional developer must either know the target system intimately or have access to those who do.

The mechanics for performing an FTA are reasonably straightforward. According to Barker (1976, p. 8):

> The fault tree is constructed by showing the relationship between various kinds of events which could cause failure of the system. The relationships are symbolized by logic gates. The concept of logic gates is the heart of fault tree technology, and they are the factor which causes it to differ from other forms of analysis.

In this modification of FTA, only two primary types, AND and OR logic gates, are considered. Figure 2.3 graphically depicts two decision trees, one showing the use of the AND gate, and the other showing the use of the OR gate. In part a of Figure 2.3, the AND gate (i.e., the silo-shaped symbol) relates the critical undesired event A to the two undesired events responsible for producing it, B and C. The critical undesired event (CUE) will only occur as a result of both undesirable events, B *and* C. The CUE is *always* the topmost event in a fault tree. The OR logic gate, illustrated in part b of Figure 2.3 tells us that the CUE could result if either or both of the events B and C occur. Thus, with the OR gate, only *one* of the undesired events is necessary to cause the critical undesired event.

In essence, then, we are building a tree from the top down, beginning with the CUE. A fault tree will show the path of predecessor events leading to the CUE. Figure 2.4 presents a rudimentary tree that incorporates both AND and OR logic gates and the other symbols commonly used in FTA. This example shows only three levels of analysis, but a branch might run

FIGURE 2.3 / Decision trees showing use of AND and OR gates

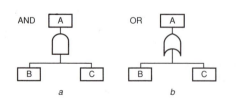

down as many as ten levels before reaching its terminal events. The fault tree in Figure 2.4 is read as follows.

1. The CUE (critical undesirable event) A can be caused by *either* undesirable event B *or* undesirable event C, as indicated by the OR gate.

2. The undesirable event B can be produced only by the *coexistence of* undesirable events D *and* E, as indicated by the AND gate.

3. The undesirable event C can be produced by *either* undesirable event F *or* undesirable event G, as indicated by the OR symbol that precedes undesirable events F and G.

FIGURE 2.4 / Decision tree showing the use of both AND and OR gates

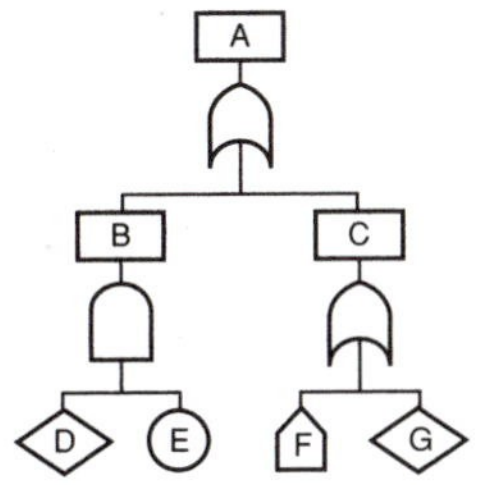

A number of symbols have been generated to build fault trees (Witkin and Stephens, 1968), but other than the AND and OR symbols, only five symbols are used in this adaptation of FTA:

1. The *rectangle*: used to state undesired events which result from at least two other AND or an OR logic gate. Rectangle events are always viewed as "output" events, since their causes, or "input" events are always identified.

2. The *rhombus* (diamond): used to show bottom or terminal events of a branch, which may *not* be broken down into further undesirable events, because:

   a. The event seldom occurs.

   b. The necessary information for further breakdown of preceding undesirable events is not available.

   c. There are other constraints (e.g., funds, time, expertise). However, given the removal of constraints, an event can be changed from a rhombus to a rectangle, thus indicating that additional analysis will be performed.

3. The *circle*: used to show terminal events of a branch, signifies an undesired event for which further breakdown into its causal events is unnecessary, for the purposes of the analysis.

4. The *house*: represents an undesired event that may occur often in the target system but will only have an effect on a succeeding event when it combines with some other undesirable event or events. It is also a terminal event.

5. The *delta or pyramid*: used to indicate the transfer of an undesirable event to another fault tree branch for continued breakdown into its causal events.

In Figure 2.4, the symbols used for undesired events D, E, F, and G indicate that they will *not* be broken down further. These *terminal undesired events* are indicated by the symbols rhombus, house, and circle. A major value of FTA is that if terminal undesired events can be identified and avoided, *their removal prevents any of the other undesired events in the higher levels of the sequence from occurring*, including the CUE. The diagram in Figure 2.5 (Barker, 1976, p. 17) illustrates a model for accomplishing the Mission Analysis. Moving from left to right are stated: the mission statement, a list of the functions required to complete the mission, and the tasks necessary to accomplish each function.

FIGURE 2.5 / A model for accomplishing the Mission Analysis

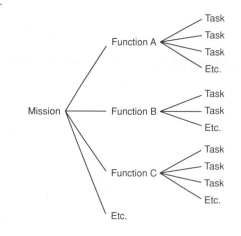

The necessary operational steps for completing an FTA are listed in the "Fault Tree Analysis" job aid. Again, a major value of FTA is that decision makers can concentrate their energies on the terminal or bottom events of the tree and ignore succeeding undesirable events, since these cannot logically occur if the terminal undesirable events have been avoided.

Job Aid / Fault Tree Analysis

Description   Fault Tree Analysis (FTA) is a technique designed to identify undesirable events that may negatively affect the operation of a system. The fault tree is constructed by showing the relationship between various kinds of events that could cause failure of the system. The relationships are symbolized by logic gates. Based on knowledge of such undesired events, FTA provides information for the redesign or monitoring of a system to prevent the undesirable events from occurring. Access to intimate knowledge of the target system is essential to carrying out a successful FTA.

Use Rationale   It is not uncommon for the client and the instructional developer to disagree on the merits of a completed ID project. All too often such disagreement can be traced to an inadequate fix on a system's needs at the initiation of the project. Thus, before taking responsibility for a proposed ID project, instructional developers need to determine what the validated needs are of the client system with which this ID project should deal. A major value of FTA is that decision makers can concentrate their energies on the terminal or bottom events of the tree and ignore succeeding undesirable events, since these cannot logically occur if the terminal undesirable events have been avoided.

continued

Fault Tree Analysis, continued

Critical Steps

1. **Define the Mission of the Target System.**
   a. State the current goals and/or objectives, of the system.
   b. State the restraints on the system, i.e., factors over which system managers have limited control.
   c. State the boundaries of the system, i.e., factors over which system managers have no control.

2. **Analyze the Mission of the System.**
   a. Identify the specific functions and tasks necessary to complete the mission, e.g., through *Task Analysis* techniques.
   b. Identify specific performance criteria that indicate accomplishment of the system mission.

3. **Identify Events Detrimental to the System.**
   a. Consider what possible undesired events might occur that could impede the satisfactory completion of the functions and tasks identified in the Mission Analysis; i.e., consider only major events, not all possible events.
   b. Write each event according to the model "Failure of *X* because of *Y.*" Here the suffix of an output undesirable event becomes the prefix of an input undesirable event; e.g., "Function *X* was performed improperly because task C was done inadequately."

4. **Complete a *Fault Hazard Analysis.*** Rank the undesired events to determine the Critical Undesired Event (CUE), that is, the event that can most seriously disrupt the system. The CUE is the event that is at the top of the fault tree.

5. **Draw the Fault Tree.**
   a. Use appropriate symbols.
   b. Answer the question "Given a specific CUE, what sequences of undesired events might take place that would trigger the CUE?" I.e., follow a deductive process of determining predecessor events, from the CUE at the top to the bottom, or terminal, undesirable events.
   c. Determine the predecessors for an undesirable event by asking "What are the immediate probable causes of this undesired event?" For each output (undesirable) event, represented by a rectangle, there should be at least two input events.
   d. Categorize undesired events as:
      (1) A *primary failure*, represented by a circle and needing no further breakdown.
      (2) A *secondary failure*, induced by the environment and represented by a rhombus or a rectangle, depending on whether additional predecessor events are to be broken out.
      (3) A *command failure*, where part of the system is ordered to fail, e.g., where an 18-year-old is not hired because of company policy requiring that hirees be 21, which doesn't speak to ability.
   e. Attempt to locate input, processing, and output failures for each event.
   f. Generate all predecessor events at the same level, before proceeding to the next level down. Go down to the level where you judge cause-and-effect relationships can take place. Bottom level will have terminal events depicted only by circle, rhombus, or house.
   g. Code undesirable events in the completed fault tree by level:
      (1) Level 1 is coded: A, B, C, . . . , Z

continued

Fault Tree Analysis, continued

    (2) Level 2 events (e.g., under event B) are coded: BA, BB, BC, . . . , BZ

    (3) Level 3 events (e.g., under event BB) are coded: BBA, BBB, BBC, . . . , BBZ

    (4) Level 4 events (e.g., under event BBA) are coded: BBAA, BBAB, BBAC, . . . , BBAZ

    (5) And so on.

As the analysis proceeds, similar or identical undesirable events will show up in different branches of the tree. These should be examined closely, particularly if they are expected to occur often.

6. **Validate the constructed fault tree.**

    a. Make sure that each rectangle states its event in failure terms.

    b. Study each terminal event, and determine whether it can be avoided or not. Consider whether it is possible to add AND gates.

7. **Categorize strategic or critical paths in the fault tree.** As: primary, secondary, and alternate branches, through expert opinion; e.g., use Delphi to get consensus as to the relative importance of the respective branches in causing the CUE.

8. **Rate the extent of occurrence for each terminal undesirable event.** E.g., rarely, periodically, frequently.

9. **Categorize the degree of rectification possible for each terminal event.** E.g., not rectifiable, difficult to rectify, easy to rectify.

10. **Translate terminal or bottom events into need statements.** E.g., bottom event: age restriction of 21 prevents hiring qualified people. Need statement: hiring age restriction should be lowered to 18.

11. **Prioritize need statements.** E.g., use Delphi or Nominal Group Process techniques.

12. **Report prioritized need statements, with supporting documentation, to appropriate decision makers.**

Reference

Witkin, Belle R., and Stephens, Kent G. (1968). Fault Tree Analysis: A Research Tool for Educational Planning. Technical Report No. 1. Alameda County PACE Center, Hayward, Calif. ERIC no. ED 029 379, October.

Summary

In this chapter, three established techniques for carrying out needs analysis were taught: Delphi, Critical Incident, and Fault Tree Analysis. The Delphi Technique may be used to get the best expert judgment of any system's needs. The Critical Incident Technique attempts a greater level of objectivity by tying needs to specific incidents observed during the system's operation. Finally, Fault Tree Analysis combines other techniques, including decision trees, Delphi, and Critical Incident Technique, to identify events that lead to a critical undesirable event that could negatively impact the operation of a system. Means for avoiding these undesired events can be stated as needs of the system. Each of the three techniques has its own strengths and weaknesses, but all have been validated as useful for determining needs of a system.

While it is the contention here that an instructional developer can adequately apply any of these three techniques with no more knowledge than is provided for their respective job aids, it is recommended that those desiring a greater level of expertise pursue the references, listed next.

References

Anderson, W. A., and Henry, R. C. (1980). Using needs analysis strategies for effective workshops. *Journal of Instructional Development* 4(1): 19–26.

Anthony, Robert N. (1965). *Planning and Control Systems: A Framework for Analysis.* Harvard University. Boston.

Barker, Bruce O. (1976). Fault Tree Analysis: Its implications for Use in Education. A Report Submitted Toward the Degree of Master of Education in Instructional Media. Utah State University. Logan, Utah. p.8.

Brown, B., Cochran, S., and Dalkey, N. (1969). *The Delphi Method II: Structure of experiments.* The Rand Corporation, RM-5957-PR.

Burton, J. K., and Merrill, P. F. (1977). Needs analysis. In *Goals, Needs and Priorities in Instructional Design.* ed. Leslie J. Briggs. Englewood Cliffs, N.J.: Educational Technology Publications.

Bushnell, D. S., and Rappaport, D. (1971). *Planned Change in Education: A Systems Approach.* New York: Harcourt Brace Jovanovich.

Coffing, R.T. (1977). "Client Need Assessment," from Zaltman, G. et. al (1977) *Dynamic Educational Change*, The Free Press. New York. p.190.

Cook, Desmond L. (1970). Management Control Theory as the Context for Educational Evaluation. A Prepublication draft of a paper that appeared in *Journal of Research and Development in Education* 3(4): 13–26.

Dalkey, N. C., and Helmer, O. (1963). An experimental application of the Delphi Method to the use of experts. *Management Science* 9: 458–467.

Delbecq, A. H., et al. (1986). *Group Techniques for Program Planning: A Guide to Nominal Group and Delphi Processes.* Middleton, Wis.: Green Briar Press.

Flanagan, John C. (1954). The Critical Incident Technique. *Psychological Bulletin* 51: 327–58.

Fussell, Jerry B., Powers, Gary J., and Bennetts, R. (1974). Fault trees: A state-of-the-art discussion. *IEEE Transactions on Reliability.* R-23 (April): 5–55.

Kaufman, R. A., et al. (1981). Relating needs analysis, program development, implementation, and evaluation. *Journal of Instructional Development* 4(4): 17–26.

Leles, Samual (1968). Using the Critical Incident Technique to Develop a Theory of Educational Professionalism: An Exploratory Study. *Journal of Teacher Education* 19: 59–69.

McKillip, Jack (1987). *Needs Analysis: Tools for the Human Services and Social Research.* Applied Social Research Methods Series, vol. 10. Newbury Park, Calif.: Sage.

Naisbitt, John (1984). *Megatrends: Ten New Directions Transforming Our Lives.* New York: Warner Books.

Perrow, Charles (1961). The analysis of goals in complex organizations. *American Sociological Review* 26(6): 855.

Rodriguez, S. R. (1988). Needs analysis and analysis: Tools for change. *Journal of Instructional Development* 11(1): 23–28.

Rossett, Allison (1982). A typology for generating needs assessments. *Journal of Instructional Development* 6(1): 28–33.

Rutherford, R. S. (1974). The Application of Critical Incident Procedures for an Initial Audit of Organizational Communication. Paper contributed to the International Communication Association Convention. New Orleans, April 17–20 (ED 698 624).

Stano, Michael (1983). The Critical Incident Technique: A Description of the Method. Paper presented at the Annual Meeting of the Southern Speech Communication Association. Lincoln, Neb., April 7–9.

Stephens, Kent G. (1973). Fault Tree Analysis: a management science technique for educational planning and evaluation. Technical Report Number 2. Alameda County School Department, Hayward, California. 36p.

Swiegert, Ray L., and Schabacker, W. H. (1974). "Delphi Technique: How Well Does It Work Setting Educational Goals?" Paper presented at AERA, Chicago. pp. 8–12.

Trimby, Madaline J. (1979). *Needs Analysis Models: A Comparison.* Englewood Cliffs, N.J.: Educational Technology Publications.

Weiss, Carol H. (1972). *Evaluation Research.* Englewood Cliffs, N.J.: Prentice-Hall, 26–35.

Wilson, I. G., and Wilson, M. E. (1965). *Information, Computers, and Systems Design.* New York: Wiley.

Witkin, Belle R., and Stephens, Kent G. (1968). Fault Tree Analysis: A Research Tool for Educational Planning. Technical Report No. 1. Alameda County PACE Center, Hayward, Calif. ERIC no. ED 029 379, October.

CHAPTER 3

Adoption

Process of establishing acceptance of an innovation by
decision makers, gatekeepers, and others affected,
and of obtaining commitment of resources

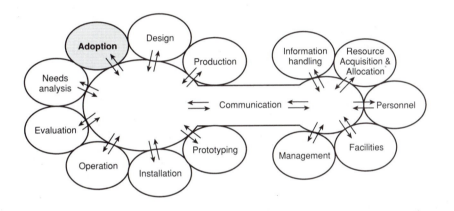

Learner Objectives

1. State rationale for using an ID Model adoption component.

2. Discriminate among the psychological stages that people go through before adopting an innovation.

3. List common factors that impede and encourage change.

4. Recognize the distinguishing characteristics of the adoption techniques presented.

5. Match techniques with the psychological stages that people move through before adopting an innovation.

6. Recall definitions of major terms.

Introduction

The preceding chapter dealt with processes and means for determining needs and goals for particular instructional systems. Once the goals have been determined, the person proposing the instruction will have to gain acceptance for the project from those persons in the system who control decision making and resource allocation, and from others whose work may be affected. In some cases, many of these same persons may have been involved with the decision to carry out the needs analysis and so may require little convincing during the adoption phase. But just as often, important persons with decision-making power may have been left out of the loop and must now be brought in, in a supportive way.

The skills for finding out what needs should be met in a system are very different from the skills for gaining support in meeting those needs. The first is concerned with *establishing facts about* a system, whereas the second is concerned with *changing* a system. While there may, indeed, be "no new thing under the sun," things *are* new to people, and it is people who will adopt or reject changes proposed for their systems.

The adoption component serves to guide instructional developers in gaining acceptance of an innovation, i.e., a new instructional process or product, from members of the client system or from some external funding group: staff members, because they must make the innovation work, and administrators and external funding groups, because they must provide resources and be responsible for what occurs in the system. There are two major types of innovations within a system: *internally developed* innovations and *externally developed* innovations. Innovations developed internal to a system are created by the members of that system with resources derived either internally or externally. In contrast, innovations developed externally, i.e., by persons outside of the system, may represent unfamiliar territory to staff and administrators, and may require different techniques to ensure adoption. By the same token, when an external instructional development team enters an organization, it too is in unfamiliar territory, and needs to determine quickly the relationships among its clients, particularly in terms of who communicates regularly with whom. The organization chart is not sufficient, because it does not speak to the informal communication network that operates in every organization. A useful technique for tapping into informal communication networks is Communication Network Analysis, presented in Chapter 7.

By definition, changes implemented in a client system affect other parts of the system. Such changes, while solving some problems, often create others. For example, changes usually require a shift in resources from one part of the system to another. This is likely to stimulate resistance on the part of those in the system who are detrimentally affected by the resource shift.

There are many documented instances in both education and training where failure to account for conditions necessary to client acceptance have resulted in delayed installation, cost overruns, and premature withdrawal of validated instructional packages. Examples of some of the factors impeding acceptance of change are: inertia, ambiguity surrounding the change, fear about one's ability to deal with the change, a lack of clarity about what the payoff is for the adopter, a lack of trust in the change agent, and a lack of consensus of the client group about the importance of the change. On the other hand, people make changes in their behaviors for many reasons, including those based on factual data, emotional appeals, political concerns, expediency, emergency conditions, readiness, and logic. The many reasons why individuals or groups resist or accept change is well documented in the literature on diffusion of innovation. Effectiveness in gaining adoption requires an instructional developer to have, minimally, basic knowledge of the change process as well as appropriate monitoring and intervention skills.

Adoption Process

Lewin (1947), Rogers (1962), Havelock (1973), and other authorities on change have noted that people go through distinct psychological stages before arriving at the point of adopting and integrating changes into their systems. Being able to tell which stage a client is in and what means are available to assist the client to the next stage of adoption is essential for the instructional developer. One version of these psychological stages includes: *unfreezing, appraising, trial, accepting/rejecting,* and *refreezing.* These stages and their respective processes are presented here as steps to gain adoption.

1. Assist clients and/or client system in *unfreezing* (process of selected clients, becoming aware of problems and becoming willing to consider potential solutions).

2. Assist clients in *appraising* proposed change (process of clients' assessing fitness of a solution, or of change, to their instructional problem, and of comparing it to other potential solutions).

3. Assist clients in *trying out* change (process of clients' piloting changes, or some subset of them, in their systems).

4. Assist clients in making *accept/reject* decision (process of clients' making go/no-go decisions about an innovation, based on the trial data).

5. Assist in *refreezing* the client system (process of stabilizing the target system until clients have successfully integrated the change or changes).

While the adoption process at this point in the instructional development model is concerned only with the first three stages, all five stages will be treated here and then referred back to in later chapters. The succeeding sections discuss each of the stages and present examples of job aids that are relevant to the stages.

Unfreezing

Inertia is one of the factors holding elements of a system in place. Staff and administrators of a system may be aware of a problem but not have the resources or leadership to do anything about it. Or they may not recognize that the problem is theirs or even that it is worth solving. Resistance to needed change may come from either staff or administration, depending on the circumstances and the personnel involved.

Educators and trainers, like members of other professions, tend to reduce cognitive dissonance in their work by routinizing everyday activities. Unfortunately, as these activities are reduced to routines, thinking about them is also reduced, and over time the activities may be accepted with little question, even though altered circumstances make questionable their continued operation. On those few occasions when questions *are* raised about the activities, adherents tend to assume a defensive posture.

Breaking clients out of this defensive posture is the function of the unfreezing stage. More precisely, the processes of the unfreezing stage are designed to: (1) raise client *awareness* that there is a problem with the status quo, and (2) raise client *interest* to the point of their being willing to examine potential solutions. These two aspects of unfreezing are looked at in the next two sections.

Awareness of the Problem   There are many ways to make clients aware of problems in their instructional systems, and of possible solutions to those problems. One way is through administrative decree, i.e., where staff members are told that a problem exists by their boss, who may also tell them which solution to apply. Unfortunately, a limitation of such authoritarian solutions is that interest or awareness persists only as long as administrative pressure is maintained; otherwise, interest tends to regress to some previous state, or worse. There are a number of more democratic means available to instructional developers for assisting clients to a point of more willing involvement.

One useful technique for breaking clients out of set patterns is the **Nominal Group Process (NGP)**. This well-researched technique (Delbecq et al., 1986) actually has multiple uses. The NGP is very effective in getting out of any group the best combined judgments about any subject in a short period of time. The design of the NGP technique is such that it pulls the best thinking out of all participants, including reticent or shy individuals. Further, its application reduces the influence of individuals who would tend to dominate discussion under more traditional methods. The technique's power and efficiency for pulling judgments and agreements from a group have been demonstrated many times. In one case familiar to the author, a college faculty had been trying, unsuccessfully, to come to agreement on a common set of objectives for their academic program for over three years. Using NGP they were able to get consensus in a little over three hours. While not all uses are as dramatic as this, the technique has proven effective over and over. It is widely used for many purposes besides the one described here.

Following the critical steps in the "NGP" job aid will enable an instructional developer to apply effectively the Nominal Group Process for purposes of creating awareness in clients of problems in their systems, and of possible solutions. In a manner similar to the way problems were derived, the Nominal Group Process can also be used to derive possible solutions from participants. An added advantage is that once members of a group agree that a problem exists, they become more receptive to looking at potential solutions.

Job Aid / Nominal Group Process (NGP)

Description In the Nominal Group Process (NGP) a facilitator submits a task to a group of six to twelve involved clients, who initially work independently in responding to a specific task (e.g., "to list factors causing our students to do so poorly on standardized math tests"). After they independently generate items in response to the task (about 10 minutes), the facilitator directs participants, in round-robin fashion, to state one of their responses to the task, in each pass, until all of their respective factors have been stated. The facilitator writes the factors on a flip chart. During this first phase, respondents are only permitted to ask for clarification of proposed factors. At the end of the first phase, the facilitator asks participants to rank the listed factors independently and anonymously on a special form. The rankings for each of the factors are added up by the facilitator and are used to show group rankings of the most important factors. During the second phase, group members justify why they may agree or disagree with this ranking of the factors, which provides new data for reassessing their relative importance. A final independent, anonymous ranking and weighting of the responses is then done by the group, and is again added for each of the factors. This provides a revised group ranking and weighting in terms of how much more important one factor is than another. These results are usually accepted by the client group as support for a working agreement on priorities.

Use Rationale A client group that is polarized on important issues relevant to processes of instructional development needs to resolve differences if progress is to be made. Working as a member of a group on an issue is in itself an involving process, which helps legitimize any problems recognized by the group. NGP, which is a very involving and efficient means of gaining the best judgment and consensus of a group, increases the likelihood of getting the individual members' best thinking on a problem, which tends to increase awareness not only of the problem but of many of its ramifications as well. A special advantage of the Nominal Group Process is that one can be completed in 3–4 hours, for most tasks.

Critical Steps

1. **Determine the initial question to be answered.** E.g., "Which elements of the manager training program on resource control need to be improved?"

2. **Identify appropriate respondents, and get agreement for them to participate.** E.g., sample of managers who have completed the instruction, and instructors currently teaching the course and/or ones who previously taught the course.

3. **Make sure the work space is set up appropriately.** See Figure 3.1. Note that the basic setup is repeated for multiple groups of six to twelve people.

4. **Seat groups of six to twelve respondents around tables.** Use a horseshoe arrangement, with a facilitator and a flip chart between the open ends of the horseshoe. See Figure 3.1.

5. **Present introductory statements and rules to the group.**
   a. *Introductory statements:*
      (1) Research has demonstrated that this technique works very effectively and efficiently when its few simple rules are followed.
      (2) This technique will enable you, as a group (six to twelve members in a group, each group with a facilitator) to identify and rank items relevant to your specific task.
      (3) The entire process should be completed in 3–4 hours. There will be a brief rest break toward the middle of the process.

continued

Nominal Group Process (NGP), continued

FIGURE 3.1 / Setup for a Nominal Group Process

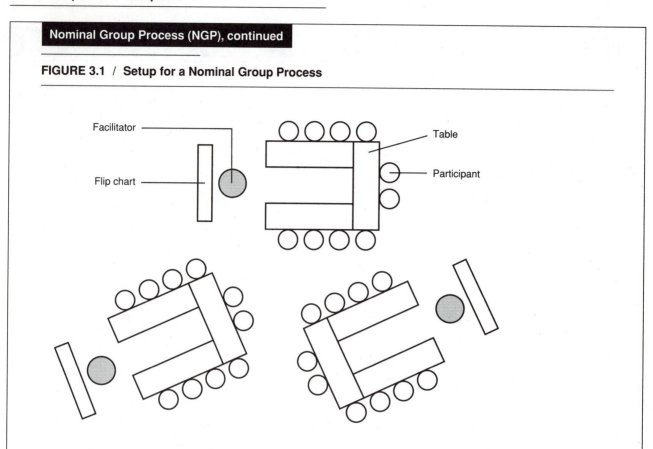

(4) The process is made up of four activities: (a) generating items in response to the task, (b) stating the items, (c) discussing the items, and (d) prioritizing the items.

(5) Different parts of these four activities will be done individually, and other parts will be done as a group. The job of the facilitator is to direct participants through these activities with a minimum of fuss.

(6) Answer any questions.

b. *Rules:* There are very few rules, but they must be adhered to strictly or the process will be neither effective nor efficient. One of the facilitator's most important tasks is to make sure that these few rules are followed. The rules are:

(1) Participants must attend the *entire* session. Their respective inputs are essential at different points.

(2) Participants may not speak to each other. They may speak *only* to and through the facilitator.

(3) Participants must begin and complete activities at the times designated by the facilitator.

(4) A participant may ask the facilitator for clarification of items, but may not otherwise comment on items put forward by other participants.

(5) Answer any questions.

6. Hand a response sheet to each participant. See an example of the response sheet in Figure 3.2. Tell the group members that they will have about 5–10 minutes to generate their list of items, and remind them that they are to generate their lists *independently*. Answer any questions.

continued

Nominal Group Process (NGP), continued

**FIGURE 3.2 / Example of a Nominal Group
Process task statement form**

NOMINAL GROUP PROCESS TASK STATEMENT FORM

Question for Participants:

What are the major objectives that should be met in a business ethics course?

Participants list objectives in the following spaces:

1. _____
2. _____
3. _____
4. _____
5. _____
6. _____
7. _____
8. _____
9. _____
10. _____
11. _____
12. _____
13. _____
14. _____
15. _____
16. _____
17. _____
18. _____
19. _____
20. _____

7. **Have participants begin the item-generating activity.** If people speak during this period, go to them and whisper the rule of no speaking. If they persist, invite them outside of the room and dismiss them if they will not agree to follow the rule. Ignore anyone who has stopped writing early. Group pressure will usually start them writing again.

continued

Nominal Group Process (NGP), continued

8. **Stop the item-generating activity when the large majority have stopped writing** (within 5–10 minutes). However, tell them that they can continue adding new items to their list, as they think of them, throughout the group listing process that follows.

9. **Have individuals begin the round-robin listing of the items that they generated.** Ask the first individual on the left of the facilitator to state one of his or her best items. The facilitator may need to restate the item for clarity and brevity. Write the item large enough for all to see on the flip chart. See Figure 3.3.

FIGURE 3.3 / Example of facilitator's flip chart

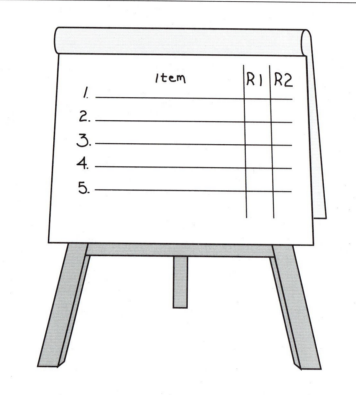

10. **Provide clarification on items, as needed.** Remind participants to direct their questions to you only. This reduces the threat of premature criticism, which could inhibit ideas. Once a question is raised, you may clarify the item or ask the originator of the item to clarify.

11. **Go to the next person, and continue the round-robin of stating, listing, and clarifying, until the group runs out of items.** As a flip chart sheet becomes full, tear it off and have an assistant or participant tape it on the wall so that all may continue to refer to the items.

12. **Pass blank ranking forms to each participant, and tell them to rank the most important items posted on the flip chart sheets.** Have them select three items when the total number of listed items is less than thirty, and five when the total is greater than thirty. Ask them to put the item number in the box in the upper right corner of the form, as shown in Figure 3.4. Tell them to place a 5 in the upper left box of the form for the most important item chosen, a 4 for

continued

Nominal Group Process (NGP), continued

FIGURE 3.4 / Example of participant ranking form

| 9 | ← First Ranking | Problem Number → | 33 |

Descriptor: _Writing test items_

| 3 | ← Final Ranking | Final Weight (%) → | 30 |

the next item, on down to 1. Tell them to bring their forms to the data table as soon as they have made their five choices. Tell them that they can take a 15-minute (variable) break as soon as they have given you their list of five ranked items.

13. **Record their rankings of the items on the facilitator data sheet.** Position yourself at the data table, and as they file by, record their respective rankings next to the item number on the data sheet. See Figure 3.5.

14. **Add the accumulated ranks for each item, and circle the highest-ranked items on the flip chart sheets.** Since participants are choosing different items to rank, there will be a spread of items beyond the five that any one individual ranks.

15. **Determine the items for which there is the widest disagreement.** Quickly analyze the responses from the facilitator data sheet, e.g., item 7 in Figure 3.5, for purposes of stimulating discussion in the next round.

16. **Begin the justification phase.** Remind participants they are to address their questions and answers *only* to you. To stimulate discussion, go over their accumulated ranks, as illustrated by the items circled by you on the flip charts, and ask why such wide disagreement. Also, ask them why they agree or disagree with the accumulated ranking of the items. Their respective responses on the items often provide other participants with new information and insights that will help them reassess their ranking of the items.

17. **Begin the reassessment phase.** Give each participant five blank ranking forms on which to reprioritize the items listed on the flip chart sheets. This time, however, not only should they indicate the item number and its rank but they should weight each of the items by assigning points in the lower right box of the form. Tell them that they can distribute 100 points, in multiples of 5 for easy adding, among the five choices, based on their relative importance. Again have them bring their results to the data table.

18. **Add up the ranks and weights for each item, and present the new prioritized and weighted list of items to the group.**

continued

Nominal Group Process (NGP), continued

FIGURE 3.5 / Example of facilitator data sheet

Problem Number	First Ranking	Second Ranking	Weights
1	5, 2, 3, 1, 4, 5,		
2			
3	5, 5, 5, 4, 3, 5		
4	2		
5	2, 1, 3, 2, 1		
6	1, 1, 4,		
7			
8	5, 5, 4, 5, 5,		
9	3, 2, 1, 4, 3,		
10	5, 5, 4, 5, 4, 5, 5,		
11			
12			
13			
14			
15			
16			
17			
18			
19			
20			
21			
22			
23			
24			
25			
26			
27			
28			
29			
30			

19. **Have the group agree on which of the prioritized items should be dealt with first by their system.** They will usually agree that the priority should match the top items in the last ranking and weighting of the items done by the group.

Reference

Delbecq, A. H., et al. (1975). *Group Techniques for Program Planning: A Guide to Nominal Group and Delphi Processes.* Middleton, Wis.:Green Briar Press, pp. 40–75.

Interest in Potential Solutions The bottom line for this stage is to get commitment of financial and other resources for the proposed change. For this to occur, those controlling resources must be convinced not only of a need but of the utility of the proposed means for meeting the need. There are many ways of stimulating client interest in potential means, once the need is recognized as valid for their system. Alternatives commonly used to drum up interest include having experts brought in to demonstrate solutions, and having individuals observe its application at a location where it is operating successfully.

Staff and administrators are more likely to become interested in an innovation if they can see it in operation, rather than considering it hypothetically. One of the names for this technique is *visitation*. A set of steps that tend to maximize the benefits of a visit are presented in the "Visitation" job aid. Care should be taken in using the technique, because a visit can backfire, resulting in a client less interested in an innovation after the visit than before. Usually, only staff and administrators who might be directly involved with the proposed innovation would be chosen to visit an innovation site.

Job Aid / Visitation

Description   A **visitation** is a carefully planned trip to some location to study some process or activity operating in another environment, usually for the purpose of determining the appropriateness of the process or activity for the visitor's location. An important contributor to the success of a visit depends on predetermination of factors to be examined and development of criteria for estimating the solution's potential for the visitor's location. It requires establishment of what will be seen during the visitation, and a schedule for maximizing the time. It requires scheduling events and interviews with knowledgeable people involved with the innovation at different levels of the organization to be visited.

Use Rationale   Reading about an innovation, or hearing about it, is a far cry from actually seeing it in operation and being able to question those running the system. Such observation permits the observer to relate realistically the important factors of the innovation to his or her own setting, a kind of mental trial of the system. It is said that "nothing persuades like a visit, and that nothing dissuades like a visit." It can be a powerful motivator to see a successful system in operation. By the same token, if the wrong parts of the system are being examined it may discourage possible adoption. Thus, it is important that careful orientation be done prior to the visit, careful scheduling of the events during the visit, and careful debriefing after the visit, if it is to have the maximum desired effect.

Critical Steps

1. **Establish the need for the visit.** Don't go to solve a nonproblem or a poorly analyzed one.

2. **Determine the appropriate sites for the visit.** Consider the distance factor, the similarity to the target system, etc.

3. **Get the client to agree to visit the site where innovation is in operation.** Orient the client to the major factors regarding the innovation, including its usefulness. Try to have the visitation at the client's convenience.

continued

Visitation, continued

4. **Arrange for release of the client for visitation.** This usually means planning ahead so that absence of the client doesn't create problems.

5. **Get agreement from site personnel for the visit.** Use mutual acquaintances for entry, or get someone to clear access to the visit, if you lack the necessary influence.

6. **Establish clearly specified objectives for the visit.** E.g., to understand what site personnel mean by *competency based instruction* [CBI]; to personally work through some of the CBI units; to observe selected seventh graders working through CBI units; to ask students who have completed the CBI units how they liked the program; to find out what the costs are to install such a program.

7. **Establish criteria to be applied to an innovation, during the visit, to determine if it meets the client's needs.** E.g., relevant for age group, affordable, congruent with community view and school policies.

8. **Brief the client prior to visiting the installation.** E.g., "You will see a competency-based instructional program designed to teach U.S. geography to seventh graders"; "Here are our reasons for the visit"; "These are the things we are looking for."

9. **Get agreement on who will be responsible for specific tasks during the visit.** E.g., who interviews who, who gets answers to which questions, who collects what materials.

10. **Schedule the visit with site personnel.** Include times with specific individuals. Visitors should reserve time in between contacts to correct notes from the last interview or observation, and to generate any new questions to be asked of the next contact.

11. **Send an abbreviated statement of expectations to the site.** Do this for each of the contacts to be interviewed or observed at the innovation site.

12. **Follow a plan during the visit.** The plan could include rules such as the following:
    a. Be on time.
    b. Refrain from being critical of the innovator or of the innovation (think of the innovation as the innovator's baby).
    c. Ask general questions of a specific contact, initially, to ensure that you are not curtailing innovator response, then get more specific in the latter part of meeting.
    d. Use planned times to correct and consolidate notes on the most recent contacts.
    e. Ask for examples of actual incidents to support any declarative statements made by site personnel about the innovation.
    f. Always ask each contact at the end of an interview, "What are the major problems that we should look out for if we adopt this innovation?"
    g. Meet periodically with other team members to share information and questions, so that they can be on the lookout for answers and corroboration of information.
    h. Be on the lookout for, and collect, program materials, especially those that site personnel have added to make the innovation work.

13. **Generate an initial report on the visitation.** Do it jointly with the clients, if they are willing.

continued

Visitation, continued

14. **Get additional input and recommendations from the client(s).** I.e., get their response to the initial report.

15. **Write and submit the final report with recommendations.** This should go to the appropriate decision makers, preferably under the client's name.

Reference

Jamison, D. (1988). *Guidelines for Setting up a Model Visitation Site for Demonstration of Collaborative Transition.* Sacramento, Calif.: California State Department of Education, Education Transition Center.

Appraising

During the appraisal stage, staff and administrators evaluate an innovation in terms of goodness of fit to their specific situation, and having established its fit, compare it to other available solutions.

Assessing Goodness of Fit   The "Visitation" job aid, presented here as an unfreezing technique, also serves to provide clients with data on how well the change might work in their respective settings. The assumption being that by *mentally* comparing and contrasting the relevant variables operating in the two systems, a reasonable conclusion can be drawn about goodness of fit of the change to the proposed system.

Comparing Alternative Solutions   Clients may have the option of choosing among two or more alternative solutions to an instructional problem. Here, variables like program objectives, cost, time, and benefit need to be considered. A time-tested technique that has proven useful for this purpose is *cost–benefit analysis.* This technique is often used interchangeably with *cost-effectiveness analysis,* although purists see a difference between the two. The job aid presenting cost-benefit analysis is not sufficient unto itself, in that other job techniques must be used in combination with it to complete some of the critical tasks. Cost–benefit analysis also gives system budgeters a clear idea of what the overall costs are, beyond the startup development costs.

Job Aid / Cost–Benefit Analysis (CBA)

Description   Cost–benefit analysis (CBA) is a technique designed to assist decision makers in identifying a preferred choice among possible alternatives. The CBA process uses the presentation of estimated quantitative and qualitative effects of proposed alternative solutions to provide a relatively objective means of comparison for a decision maker. By first establishing a comprehen-

continued

Cost–Benefit Analysis (CBA), continued

sive set of criteria and a format for data collection, the instructional developer can provide a common ground for evaluating dissimilar approaches. The CBA technique allows the inclusion of additional techniques, such as **force-field analysis (FFA),** which could aid in identifying benefits and liabilities of the alternatives. The CBA report would include statements of relevance, potential for acceptance, practicality, cost, time, and ease of installation.

Use Rationale   Evidence that a proposed innovation will have a positive impact on the target system is perhaps one of the strongest arguments for its adoption. The instructional developer greatly strengthens his/her chances of getting a particular solution adopted by providing a complete, unbiased cost–benefit analysis that quantitatively and qualitatively demonstrates its value over an alternative to the client system, saving time and/or money while still meeting system objectives.

Critical Steps

1. **Define the environment for which an alternative solution will be chosen.** Complete the following steps:

    a. Acquire a copy of the instructional objectives to be met. If not yet determined, you could use the *Nominal Group Process* technique with clients to generate objectives.

    b. List relevant characteristics of the target audience, from existing records and/or through tests and questionnaires.

    c. List possible constraints on making a change, e.g., budget, time, legal, institutional, environmental.

    d. Establish control values, e.g., acceptable ranges for costs, time committed, learner outcomes.

2. **Design the Analysis.** Complete the following steps:

    a. Determine criteria or standards, based on program objectives, used to compare alternative solutions; e.g., objectives are written in behavioral form, readability level will be for seventh grade.

    b. Identify costs and benefits for each alternative; e.g., vendors and users of alternatives will provide some. Use *PERT* to determine in-house estimates of costs of installation, use *Nominal Group Process or Force Field Analysis* to establish an internal view of benefits.

    c. Assess listed costs and benefits. Establish true costs by checking estimated *PERT* costs with experts and/or vendors.

    d. Establish the scope and dimensions of the analysis. Establish which elements will be evaluated on a quantitative basis and which on a qualitative basis.

    e. Determine the data to be collected, e.g., cost and time for completing all tasks in the installation, maintenance, and ongoing operation of the alternatives; benefits as perceived by experts, users, and clients.

3. **Collect the Data.** Use steps such as the following:

    a. Plan the data format. Databases, spreadsheets, and other matrices allow easy access to any part of the accumulated data, as well as rapid updating.

    b. Gather data from original sources when possible; through interview, questionnaire, observation.

    c. Record all sources of data for eventual CBA report reference.

continued

Cost–Benefit Analysis (CBA), continued

4. **Perform the Analysis.** Consider the following tasks:

   a. Estimate economic and quantitative values for the different alternatives. Summing data from *Program Evaluation and Review Technique* could be used.

   b. Include an analysis of noneconomic (e.g., social) and qualitative effects of each alternative. *Nominal Group Process* technique with in-system experts could be used.

   c. Structure the analysis to be as unbiased as possible; e.g., have two or more team members or teams do parallel, independent analyses.

5. **Organize and present the results.** Follow these steps:

   a. Arrange results to permit easy, rapid identification of the effects of the alternatives.

   b. Provide qualitative assessment of intangibles.

   c. Present all material in a format useful to the decision maker.

   d. Tailor your presentation to the special needs of your client, e.g., education, government, military, business or industry.

   e. Keep the cost–benefit analysis report, brief.

   f. Provide a report summary. Keep it to one page, if possible. You might use the *Eisenhower Brief* technique.

References

Goldman, Thomas A. (1967). *Cost-Effectiveness Analysis: New approaches in Decision Making.* New York: Praeger.

Prest, A. R. (1965). Cost–benefit analysis: A survey. *The Economic Journal* 75: 683–735.

Sassone, Peter G., and Schaffer, W. A. (1978). *Cost–Benefit Analysis.* New York: Academic Press, pp. 155–173.

Trying out

Occasionally, staff and administrators are ready to make a decision to accept or reject an innovation at the end of the appraisal stage but may find it necessary to try out the innovation at home before adoption can occur. Trying out an instructional change where it has not been previously tried is fraught with danger when the individuals or groups involved do not properly prepare. Because the system may not be geared up to serve the proposed change, many modifications and revisions, in both the change and the system, may be necessary for a successful trial. If modifications and revisions are not done in a timely manner, logistical problems arise that result in frustration for the innovator and for those giving and taking the instruction.

The technique of *pilot testing* has been long used for purposes of both tentative and permanent installation of an innovation in a new environment. In this text, *pilot testing* is distinguished from *prototype testing* (Chapter 6). Prototyping is limited, here, to testing newly developed instruction for its improvement and validation, while **pilot testing** is concerned with trying out a solution to see if it fits a specific environment. Although used for somewhat different purposes, they still have many processes in common.

Even when an innovation has proven successful in other, similar settings, there will still be problems idiosyncratic to a new setting, so that the processes of pilot testing are still valid. The "Pilot Testing" job aid is similar to those used by most educators to try out an innovation in a new setting.

Job Aid / Pilot Testing

Description   Briefly, pilot testing an innovation involves trying it out with representative members of a targeted group, under simulated or actual conditions, and evaluating the innovation's effects in terms of preestablished client needs. From this comes the necessary data for accepting the prototype as is, revising it, or rejecting it.

Use Rationale   There is often uncertainty on the part of a client about the validity of the claims for an innovation, particularly for *their* system, and a reticence to commit the necessary resources for full implementation before it is demonstrated that it will work in *their* system. A try out of the innovation, or some part of it, in the system permits the client to make judgments about the value of the innovation, without full resource commitment.

Critical Steps

1. **Establish objectives of the pilot test.** Get agreement from clients about what results are necessary to demonstrate value of the innovation for their system.

2. **Identify personnel to carry out the pilot test.** Ideally, the best adoption effect occurs when the client can be trained to carry out the pilot test, but it is not unusual for them to want someone else to run it.

3. **Get the support of decision makers.** You'll need the use of personnel, subjects, and facilities, all elements necessary to the pilot test.

4. **Find, develop, or modify instruments for collecting data during the pilot test.** E.g., observation guides, performance checklists, surveys, and tests.

5. **Develop a schedule for the pilot test.** Schedule personnel, activities, materials, equipment and facilities for pilot test. *Program Evaluation and Review Technique (PERT)* is a useful device for doing this.

6. **Train personnel to carry out the pilot test.** I.e., subject selection, classroom set-up, instruction, data collection, etc.

7. **Carry out the pilot test.** This can be done by doing the following:
   a. Conduct a walk-through, i.e., a dry run, using pilot materials and procedures in the client facility (to ensure that all elements necessary are accounted for and that all questions about procedures are answered).
   b. Assemble personnel and subjects in the facility at the agreed-on time(s), if possible, and include backup trainers and subjects in case of illness or no-shows.
   c. Have the trainer orient the subjects and answer their questions, establishing a friendly rapport, and introducing others (observers, evaluators, etc.) and explaining their presence.

continued

Pilot Testing, continued

    d. Complete a pretest of subjects by ascertaining the degree to which they have the necessary entry skills and knowledge, and the degree to which they already know the pilot material's content.

    e. Begin the activities of pilot testing. If the client is running the pilot, have an experienced trainer available, as backup, to help with unforeseen problems.

    f. Have observers periodically provide feedback to the manager and the trainer of the pilot on how well he or she is carrying out the pilot, including recommendations for adjustments in activities or procedures. This is usually done during breaks and between sessions for subjects.

    g. Complete pilot instructional activities.

    h. Complete the posttest of the subjects.

    i. Debrief the subjects to collect factual and attitudinal data from them. You could use the *Small-Group Formative Evaluation* technique.

8. Analyze all pilot test data, and draw conclusions. Conclusions should be in terms of the predetermined objectives of the pilot test.

9. Report the results and conclusions from the pilot test data analysis to decision makers.

Reference

Awad, Elias M. (1979). *Systems Analysis and Design.* Homewood, Ill.: Richard D. Irwin, pp. 95–96.

    Pilot testing is an element easily passed up, but there is evidence in support of using it for instruction that is controversial or previously untried in a client setting.

    A holding ploy that individuals opposing an innovation attempt to impose is to insist that new instruction not be tried out or implemented in a system until *all* of its modifications and revisions are complete. This is often done for self-serving reasons. For example, adoption of a change may require college faculty to spend more time on the job, reducing the time available for consulting for outside pay. If such individuals or groups have sufficient power to make their condition stick, it creates problems that may cause the innovation to be rejected. Additionally, if an innovation must have all of its bells and whistles before trial, the heavy resource draw on the target system may make decision makers chary about putting extensive resources into an innovation that may or may not be a success. One technique whose application can help to get past this argument is the *sunset law,* or *sunset review, technique,* which basically says we will give it a try, as is, brief or long, and then reassess it after a prescribed period of running time, a range of anywhere from 2 weeks to a year. This technique is described later in this chapter under "Accepting/Rejecting," where it is even more relevant.

    A second technique, which gets past the argument of the need to complete all revisions before implementing, is called **successive approximation**. This technique establishes what is necessary to implement the system initially, and then prescribes successive revisions of the system until it is up to original design specifications.

Job Aid / Successive Approximation

Description   Under strictures of insufficient time and resources, this technique justifies early implementation of instructional units while still in rough form, by recognizing the particular level of development at the time of implementation and by the planning of upgrading steps for the unrefined elements of the instruction, in successive teaching cycles.

Use Rationale   Because of demanding schedules and limited resources, it is not unusual for developers to implement instructional units at levels below that of which they are capable or below that which was specified by design. By applying the *successive approximation* technique, developers make provision for progressive upgrading of units that are incomplete or rough but that for different reasons need to be on-line before the instructional units come up to final design specifications. Plans resulting from this technique tend to allay the fears of those who are concerned about the quality of the instructional unit at the time of implementation.

Critical Steps

1. **Determine the desired level of development for each element of the unit.** E.g., the desired state of the unit's objectives might require that all objectives have statements of behavior, conditions, and performance criteria and that they be categorized by domain and placed in a behavioral hierarchy.

2. **Determine the current constraints on development for each element of the unit.** For example, available time and its constraints may only permit writing the behavior part of objectives by the time that the instruction is needed, and similar treatment of methods, media, and test items.

3. **Develop a schedule for progressive improvement of the unit.** Plan to add condition statements to each of the objectives by the end of the first cycle, and performance criteria by the end of the second cycle, etc. Similar plans could be made for methods, media, and test elements of the instructional unit.

4. **Get agreement on the schedule and commitment of resources for progressive improvement from decision makers.** Recognition of the need, and a clear plan for improvement of the unit over time, is often sufficient to allay concerns about the initial roughness of the instructional unit at implementation.

Reference

Gentry, C. G., and Johnson, C. (1973). Management of performance-based instruction. *AACTE Monograph:* 21–32.

Accepting/Rejecting

The decision to accept or reject an innovation, if left unattended by the instructional developer, becomes idiosyncratic to the individual staff member or administrator. But there are a number of techniques that can be used to structure these decisions more objectively. One such technique, called the *Decision Query* (Gilbert, 1978), has proven very effective under some circumstances. This particular technique is useful in getting staff and administration to reexamine a decision about adopting an alternative that is competing with the one preferred by the instructional developer. The technique guides the client to draw conclusions from data that demonstrate that the preliminary choice is not as desirable or useful as that proposed by the instructional developer. Willingness to go through the decision query technique requires trust and patience on the part of the client.

Job Aid / Decision Query

Description The change agent uses a data presentation method consisting of five to ten pages of relevant information in a special format, where the potential adopter is asked to respond serially, page by page, to an argument, and to select coded alternatives based on data provided on each page. Each of the responses is made by placing a check mark in a small, round hole next to the preferred alternative. All of the holes are registered with the next-to-last page (summation page) so that at that point the adopter can see how he or she has evaluated all of the different factors, and is then asked to make a selection based on this overall rating. The last page reveals the codes for the alternatives, which should demonstrate the superiority of the change agent's alternative, and the adopter is then asked to make a final commitment.

Use Rationale This is a good technique to use with potential adopters who have already decided or are leaning in favor of an alternative competing with the instructional developer's preference. Since the client personally makes the choices leading up to the final decision, it is a much better "unfreezing" device than telling the client about the differences or laying them all out at once. Most clients enjoy going through the exercise despite a certain amount of initial derision.

Critical Steps

1. **Determine the alternative that the potential adopter is currently favoring.** If it is not the desired alternative, complete task 2, below.

2. **Determine the factors that best differentiate the alternatives.** Search the literature, and question users of both alternatives. Compare the findings on the factors, and if, overall, they favor your preferred alternative, complete tasks 3–5 below.

3. **Write up query sheets for each of the factors** as shown in Figures 3.6–3.10. Position the response area so that the holes punched will register correctly on the summation sheet at the back. It is in these holes that they check their response.

4. **Work the potential adopters through the query.** Assure them that it will take only a few moments of their time and that their participation will get you off of their back. Set the condition that prevents them from looking ahead through the sheets. Point out that each sheet only takes a minute or two.

5. **At completion, attempt to get formal commitment to your preferred alternative from the adopter.** Individuals completing one of these are usually surprised. They may question the facts you have included, so be prepared to back them up.

continued

Decision Query, continued

FIGURE 3.6 / Response sheet 1

Read the following argument and check either Agree or Disagree, then follow the directions.

Argument: The more overtly involved adult students are in the instructional process, the higher will be their comprehension and retention of the subject matter.

Agree _____   **Disagree** _____

If you agree, read below; otherwise, go on to response sheet 2.

Research data on active learning

Instructional Strategy

	A	B
Comprehension	high	medium
Retention	high	low

Check hole that data favors

A	B	Neither
O	O	O

FIGURE 3.7 / Response sheet 2

Read the following argument and check either Agree or Disagree, then follow the directions.

Argument: Adult students are more likely to complete courses of instruction if they are able to take the instruction when and where it is most convenient to them.

Agree _____   **Disagree** _____

If you agree, read below; otherwise, go on to response sheet 3.

Research data on place and time effects

Instructional Strategy

	A	B
Place	high	low
Time	high	low

Check hole that data favors

A	B	Neither
O	O	O

continued

Decision Query, continued

FIGURE 3.8 / Response sheet 3

Read the following argument and check either Agree or Disagree, then follow the directions.

Argument: Adult students will be more likely to complete a course of study when they can study at their own pace and when their responses to the subject matter are appropriately reinforced.

Agree _____   Disagree _____

If you agree, read below; otherwise, go on to response sheet 4.

Research data on reinforcement and pace

Instructional Strategy

	A	B
Self-pacing	high	low
Reinforcement	high	low

Check hole that data favors

A	B	Neither
O	O	O

FIGURE 3.9 / Response sheet 4

Here is how you voted the strategies, based on research data.

Factor	A	B	Neither
Retention	X		
Place	X		
Time	X		
Self-pacing	X		
Reinforcement	X		
Etc.	X		

Check in one of the holes below which instructional strategy the research data favor overall (or check neither)

A	B	Neither
O	O	O

continued

Decision Query, continued

FIGURE 3.10 / Response sheet 5

The strategy you have chosen on the basis of research results has been checked by you below.

A   B   Neither
X

** Your final choice was?   A _____   B _____   Neither _____

A   Programmed instruction

B   Live lecture

Reference

Gilbert, T. F. (1978). *Human Competence*. New York: McGraw-Hill, pp. 198–206.

Accumulated information from peers may also have a strong effect on getting clients to adopt a particular solution. Another technique, called *force-field analysis*, also invented by Kurt Lewin, has proven very good at getting out the pros and cons for some proposed change and at assessing how they affect adoption of a change. This technique results in decisions about the risk involved in adopting a change, and can be carried out quickly.

Job Aid / Force-Field Analysis (FFA)

Description   Force-field analysis (FFA) can be used to generate and analyze forces that facilitate or hinder adoption of a proposed change. Participants generating the forces should be from the environment for which the change is targeted. The generated forces are ranked and then charted to give a graphic representation of their relative importance. The analysis consists of determining which of the facilitating forces can be maximized and which hindering forces can be minimized or eliminated. Based on this analysis, a decision may be made whether to go ahead or not.

Use Rationale   Instructional developers are constantly seeking means of involving clients in the process of decision making where change is concerned, because such involvement is more likely to lead to commitment to change. The FFA technique serves this purpose very well. Clients who proceed to generate and analyze forces hindering and facilitating a proposed change become deeply involved. But just as important, they become much more knowledgeable about the change as it relates to their system.

continued

Force-Field Analysis (FFA), continued

Critical Steps

1. **Establish the problem to be solved, and a solution (change) that will solve it.** The *Nominal Group Process* is a useful technique for garnering efficient group response and agreement about a problem and its solution. Even in those cases where administrators and/or specialists have made these decisions, FFA is effective in involving others and getting agreement, quickly.

2. **Devise both the question to which FFA participants will respond and the tailored materials masters for the FFA.** See Figures 3.11–3.13.

3. **Identify the FFA participants.** Participants should be members of the system targeted for the change. Their intimate knowledge of the system is necessary for generating realistic hindering and facilitating forces.

4. **Schedule personnel and facilities for the FFA.** A facilitator is needed to guide groups of three to five individuals, each with its own table, in a common work area. Any number of participants may take part; however, the larger the number, the more time required. Voice amplification and overhead projection equipment may be required for larger numbers of groups.

FIGURE 3.11 / Example of central question and participant response sheet

---

WORKSHEET A

"What forces affect the establishment in our elementary school of a course on human sexuality?"

Weight	*List of Facilitating Forces*
	(a)
	(b)
	(c)
	(d)
	(e)
	(f)
	(g)
	(h)
	(i)
	(j)
	(k)
	(l)
	(m)

continued

Force-Field Analysis (FFA), continued

5. **Divide participants into groups of three to five individuals, and assign half to generate forces hindering the adoption and half to generate forces facilitating it.** This division results in more diverse and original responses; otherwise, many of the hindering responses will be mirror images of the facilitating responses.

6. **Using worksheets A and B (see Figures 3.11 and 3.12), have the respective groups respond to the question of what facilitating and hindering forces affect the change's adoption.** The *brainstorming technique* is effective in doing this.

7. **Using the space to the left of the listed forces, have each team weight the effect of each.** They assign each force a value from the following scale: 1 = no effect, 2 = little effect, 3 = moderate effect, 4 = considerable effect, 5 = highest effect.

8. **Have each team choose five to ten of the most critical facilitating and restraining forces from their worksheets.** Choices are based on their weighting of the forces. There will be overlap of choices from group to group, but there will also be differences.

FIGURE 3.12 / Example of response sheet for participant listing of restraining forces and weights

---

WORKSHEET B

"What forces affect the establishment in our elementary school of a course on human sexuality?"

Weight		*List of Restraining Forces*
_____	(a)	_____
_____	(b)	_____
_____	(c)	_____
_____	(d)	_____
_____	(e)	_____
_____	(f)	_____
_____	(g)	_____
_____	(h)	_____
_____	(i)	_____
_____	(j)	_____
_____	(k)	_____
_____	(l)	_____
_____	(m)	_____

continued

Force-Field Analysis (FFA), continued

9. **Have each group graph its chosen forces on the FFA chart (worksheet C—Figure 3.13).** The respective groups will list the restraining forces on the left side and the facilitating forces on the right side. Then they simply draw an arrow to represent the weighting of each of the identified forces.

10. **Have the groups, in round-robin sequence, state one of their most important facilitating and hindering forces. This is repeated until all forces are listed.** The facilitator, or a clerk, enters the forces on an FFA chart, i.e., worksheet C, usually predrawn on a chalkboard or overhead transparency. The facilitator's task is to simplify and clarify responses and to eliminate duplicates.

11. **Using the completed FFA chart, have each group recommend means to enhance any facilitating forces, and to reduce the effects of any hindering forces.** The facilitator or clerk records the recommendations.

12. **Report the results of the FFA in terms of the feasibility of adopting the proposed change.** Often the report is sent both to participants and to administrators.

FIGURE 3.13 / Example of worksheet for graphically displaying forces

WORKSHEET C

Restraining Forces	5	4	3	2	1		1	2	3	4	5	Facilitating Forces
Example: Student apathy				←						→		Parent support
a												a
b												b
c												c
d												d
e												e
f												f
g												g
h												h
i												i
j												j
k												k
l												l
m												m
n												n

References

Bishop, L. J. (1976). *Staff Development and Instructional Improvement.* Boston: Allyn & Bacon, pp. 135–137, 320–321.

Erickson, S. M. (1981). *Management Tools for Everyone.* New York: Petrocelli Books, pp. 25–27.

Refreezing

Institutionalizing a change does not guarantee its persistence. To persist, the value of the change must be transmitted to succeeding generations of staff and administrators involved with the change, and this depends on selection, training, motivation, and performance of project staff, among other variables.

To increase the likelihood that a change will be accepted over the long term, decision makers must be able to defend the adoption logically and educationally, individuals responsible for maintaining the change need to feel reinforced, and the system's policies and procedures should support the change. The *sunset review technique*, presented in the nearby job aid, certainly doesn't accomplish all of these things, but it does provide an atmosphere for initial acceptance, as well as careful consideration of the fitness of the innovation over time.

Job Aid / Sunset Review Technique (aka Sunset Law Technique)

Description   The **Sunset Review technique** sets up the conditions under which an instructional unit will be reviewed at end of a set trial period, for purposes of determining if it should be continued as is, revised, or eliminated.

Use Rationale   Instructional developers recognize the need to stabilize the conditions required by a newly installed instructional unit. A critical time for most units is during the shakedown period, when the surfacing of logistical or other problems may cause a premature rejection of the unit. The setting of a more reasonable trial time—say, 2 years—tends to defuse critics not yet sure of a unit's value. There is, of course, a certain amount of risk if the unit doesn't demonstrate worth by the end of the more favorable trial period.

Critical Steps

1. **Get agreement on the date for the unit's sunset review.** Once begun, it will have to be played out regardless of the time required, but a minimum of 2 years for any significant change should be sought. Usually, a plea for a shakedown year followed by a test year is acceptable to critics. A common initial position, for purposes of negotiating, is 3 years.

2. **Get agreement on what will be evaluated.** Provide a list of specific aspects of your unit that you think are key to its effectiveness. Avoid ambiguous statements that can be broadly interpreted.

3. **Get agreement on the criteria to be used.** For each of the specific aspects of your unit, indicate a reasonable criterion of success. For example, 80% of the students must meet 80% of the objectives. Offer to provide test data yourself; if refused, offer a set of unit objectives with test items as a guide to developing the assigned evaluator's data-collection instruments.

4. **Get agreement on who will evaluate the unit.** Try to load the sunset review team with individuals you think are positive toward the innovation and/or objective in their judgments.

5. **Prepare for the sunset review.** Unless your unit has attracted a lot of attention, most of the former critics will have probably forgotten about the review. Less than 10% of planned sunset

continued

Sunset Review Technique, continued

reviews ever take place. But, as insurance, accumulate supportive unit data, hopefully favorable, for the reviewers and decision makers.

Reference

Silvern, L. C. (1972). *Systems Engineering Applied to Training.* Houston, Tex.: Gulf Publishing, pp. 10–17.

Many innovations fail because of a lack of thought about what is needed, minimally, to nourish them in the target system. Instances are numerous where individuals trained to run a system are promoted or move. Often the persons replacing them are not as well trained in an innovation, if at all, and are left to run it as best they can. In other cases, operation of such innovations is limited to leftover funds, if there are any.

Getting a fair trial for a new system depends partly on how well the policies and procedures of that system match up with the needs of the innovation. Plunkett and Attner (1989, p. 122) state that **policies** are "broad guidelines to aid managers at every level in making decisions about recurring situations or functions." These policies, if written down, are usually found in organization or policy manuals. However, many policies are not written down, and it may require some scouting around to determine what the prevailing policies are that relate to your project. For example, an organizational policy might be: "There shall be no sexual harassment in the workplace." One means of getting a closer match between the target system and the innovation is through the application of the *policy-setting technique.*

Job Aid / Policy Setting

Description The **policy-setting technique** guides a process for determining whether target system policies need to be deleted, added, or revised in order to accomplish the goals of a new instructional process or product. This is done by matching up goals, policies, rules, and procedures of the system as they relate to a specific proposal of change.

Use Rationale If the instructional innovation either being adopted or being tried out violates policy or is not included under existing policy, its likelihood of success is suspect. Thus, it may be necessary to trigger the policy-setting process to add, delete, and/or revise system policies. Changes in policies are usually followed by changes in rules and procedures of the organization.

Critical Steps

1. **Identify the change proposed for policy check.**

continued

Policy Setting, continued

2. **List the effects of the proposed change on the operations of the system.** E.g., causes shift in resources, reduces effectiveness of some other program element, increases output.

3. **List the needs of the proposed change to operate effectively.** E.g., resources, conditions.

4. **Determine the relevance of existing goals, policies, rules, and/or procedures for innovation.** Basically, it is a matter of sorting through the target system's documentation on the missions, policies, rules, and procedures and matching them against the needs of the innovation.

5. **Decide whether any changes in goals, policies, rules, and/or procedures are warranted.** This depends on whether they are expected to have an effect on the system mission. If yes, go to the next step; if no, go to step 8.

6. **Frame any changes needed in goals, policies, rules, and/or procedures.** Accommodate the proposed change within the system's missions criteria.

7. **Present the proposed changes in goals, policies, rules, and/or procedures.** Presentation is to the appropriate system committees for passage, modification, or rejection.

8. **Report the committee decision on acceptance or rejection of the proposed changes in goals, policies, rules, and/or procedures**.

References

Blake, R. R., and Mouton, J. S. (1969). *Building a Dynamic Corporation through Grid Organization and Development*. Reading, Mass.: Addison-Wesley, pp. 34–35.

Craig, R. L. (1976). *Training and Development Handbook*. 2d ed. New York: McGraw-Hill, pp. 2-6, 6-10, 6-11, 40-3, 40-4, 47-5, 47-6.

Janis, I. L., and Mann, L. (1977). *Decision Making: A Psychological Analysis of Conflict, Choice, and Commitment*. New York: Free Press.

Summary

A model set of processes for getting change to take place was presented. The steps of this model included the processes of unfreezing, appraising, trying out, accepting/rejecting, and refreezing. Techniques for these processes were presented in the form of job aids. An instructional developer who carefully follows the directions in these job aids can expect to be reasonably effective in the application of the techniques, without any further information. Clearly, further information in conjunction with practice would make that person even more effective. The job aids presented in this chapter are only a very few of the ones available, and they may vary in their usefulness depending on the task and the circumstances surrounding it. See the following references list for other techniques relevant to the adoption process.

References

Bennis, W. G., et al. (1976). *The Planning of Change.* 3d ed. New York: Holt, Rinehart and Winston.

Delbecq, A. H., et al. (1986). *Group Techniques for Program Planning: A Guide to Nominal Group and Delphi Processes.* Middleton, Wis.: Green Briar Press.

Doughty, P. L. (1979). Cost-effectiveness analysis trade-offs and pitfalls for planning and evaluating instructional programs. *Journal of Instructional Development* 2(4): 17–25.

Havelock, R. G. (1973). *The Change Agent's Guide to Innovation in Education.* Englewood Cliffs, N.J.: Educational Technology Publications, pp. 113–116.

Lent, R. (1979). A model for applying cost-effectiveness analysis to decisions involving the use of instructional technology. *Journal of Instructional Development* 3(1): 26–33.

Lewin, Kurt (1947). Frontiers in group dynamics: Concept, method and reality in social science. *Human Relations* 1(1): 5–41.

Plunkett, W. R., and Attner, R. F. (1989). *Introduction to Management.* 3d ed. Boston: PWS-Kent.

Rogers, Everett M. (1962). *Diffusion of Innovations.* New York: Free Press, pp. 81–86.

CHAPTER 4

Instructional Design

Process of determining and specifying objectives, strategies, techniques, and media for meeting instructional goals

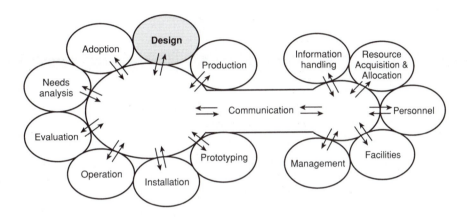

Learner Objectives

1. Sequence a randomly ordered set of design processes.

2. Discriminate among the three parts of a behaviorally stated objective.

3. Describe techniques relevant to accomplishing each of the steps in the design process.

4. Discriminate among cognitive, psychomotor, and affective objectives.

5. State a justification for building behavioral hierarchies.

6. Sequence a randomly ordered set of objectives into a behavioral hierarchy.

7. Explain the reason for writing test items before selecting instructional materials.

8. Discriminate among the characteristics of the six major types of test items.

9. Compare two established techniques for matching objectives with strategies.

10. Compare two or more techniques for writing instructional design specifications.

11. Differentiate between scripts and storyboards.

12. Recall definitions of major terms.

Introduction

The design process requires the interaction of two major elements: creativity and technique. Comparing the activities of an artist with those of an instructional developer helps to demonstrate this thesis. An artist's ability to mix oils to obtain desired colors is largely dependent on *technique*, but the selection of colors and the arrangement of the visual elements for a painting depend on the artist's *creativity*. Instructional designers, too, have their techniques. For example, they have techniques that enable them to develop instruction using media such as print, film, television, and computer. Technique goes a long way toward the development of new instruction, but the excitement and relevance of instruction depend on the level of imagination and creativity brought to the design process. The amount of skill and imagination brought to bear varies with the involved individual or individuals. Here is a second analogy: Most people can learn to perform techniques of word processing with skill, but to use their word processing skills in the production of a best-seller depends on the uniqueness of the plot and the creative selection and arrangement of words. In other words, creative design calls on a set of skills and abilities beyond those of technique. So it is that instruction may vary from useless to excellent, or from dull to exciting, depending on the tools available and the knowledge and imagination of the designer.

The design process, the most central of the processes discussed in this text, is the one about which the least is known, and of its two elements, i.e., technique and creativity, we know the least about creativity. Even so, we fail to apply many of the techniques that are known to affect the design process, and we do little to scout out individuals with a high level of creative potential to assist in these designs. While this chapter focuses on techniques of design and only touches on the creative aspects of design, the importance of the creative aspect of design should be kept in mind.

Instructional Design Process

While recognizing that design is not a linear process, one logical sequence of steps for carrying out **instructional design** is the following:

1. Collect entry-level data on the target audience (to determine characteristics, so that the instruction can be tailored to a specific audience).

2. Derive performance objectives from the established goals for the instruction (to provide clear guidance in selecting and arranging the elements constituting an instructional design).

3. Categorize performance objectives, and write any additional objectives (to ensure that all desired domains and levels of objectives are represented in the design, i.e., cognitive, psychomotor, and affective domains, and their respective levels).

4. Get agreement on the appropriateness of the performance objectives (partly to get support for the proposed instruction, but, also, to take advantage of client knowledge relative to the purposes and content of the instruction).

5. Establish a behavioral hierarchy of the performance objectives (to ensure that prerequisite learning takes place before succeeding learnings).

6. Write test items for each of the performance objectives (to ensure that tests are focused on objectives rather than on specifics of the content, strategy, or media).

7. Complete a task analysis, as guided by a set of performance objectives (this further breaks down objectives into the specific operations that must be performed by a learner to demonstrate competency).

8. Identify two or more alternative strategies appropriate to the instructional objectives (to help select the best strategy available and/or the most practical strategy, given existing resources).

9. Identify alternative print and nonprint media that can be used to present the instruction (be sure that the content and media selected fit the objectives and strategies).

10. Compare alternative strategies and media in terms of cost-effectiveness (such a comparison permits a more judicious choice in terms of the client's needs and resources).

11. Write specifications for the chosen instructional strategies and media (to guide personnel in acquisition and/or production of the required instructional elements).

There are a number of established techniques for carrying out each of these steps. Some of the techniques are superior to others. The application of these techniques requires some creative thought on the part of the designer. Each of these steps, and its respective job aids, is discussed in the following sections of this chapter.

Collecting Target Data

Collection of needs analysis data is, appropriately, the first step in the instructional development process. An important question that needs analysis assists in answering is: "Does the target group really need the proposed instruction?" But, given that they do need the instruction, the instructional developer also needs to determine: "What specific characteristics of the target group should be accounted for in the instructional design?" The collection of appropriate data about a target group is commonly determined through analysis of data from one or more of the following: expert opinion, achievement and aptitude tests, observations, interviews, and surveys. Some of the information needed is found from the needs analysis, that is, what most of the students need to learn that is not currently taught to them. But that information says little about the degree to which they have the necessary prerequisite information for starting a specific unit of instruction. A technique used to acquire data on the intended learners of the instruction in question is presented in the

"Learner Entering-Behavior Assessment" job aid. This technique assumes that a needs analysis has been previously completed and that its information can be made available.

Job Aid / Learner Entering-Behavior Assessment

Description   The instructional developer uses the proposed instructional goals, hopefully generated by a needs analysis, to extrapolate goals prerequisite to the new instruction. These prerequisite goals are critiqued by content specialists, and may be modified, depending on their reaction. Where available, the prerequisite goals can be compared to the goals of courses that would be prerequisite to the new course. At this point, the developer may decide the data of the subjectively derived goals, and their comparison, is sufficient for providing a reasonable estimation of whether the learners are likely to have the necessary prerequisite skills and knowledge, or the developer may go on and develop pretests and posttests for the instruction, test a representative sample of learners, and then make decisions based on this more objective data about student entering behaviors.

Use Rationale   A continuing fault of newly developed instruction has to do with "goodness of fit" for the intended audience. All too often, trainees entering new instruction lack, or are at too low a level of competence in, some essential knowledge or skill. While it is assumed that trainers will fill this gap through remedial work, much of the responsibility for closing these instructional gaps is left to the trainee. On the other side, some trainees find themselves having to sit through parts of the instruction they already know. Techniques like this one do not completely alleviate the problem, but they do significantly reduce its effects.

Critical Tasks

1. **Obtain the instructional goals proposed for the new instruction.** It is desirable that they come from a needs analysis report relevant to the proposed instruction, but it is more likely that they are educated guesses on the part of client and developer.

2. **Study the instructional goals for the new instruction, in order logically to generate prerequisite instructional goals.** Example of a goal for proposed instruction: to be able to find the causes of automobile engine malfunction. Example of prerequisite goals: understanding how the components making up an engine interact; understanding the concept of systematic problem solving.

3. **Verify and/or modify the newly generated prerequisite goals, based on the content experts' reaction.** Basically, the experts are asked what the immediate instructional goals are that would have to be met before learning the new goals, and how they compare to the ones logically generated.

4. **Check the content experts' opinions against records of a representative sampling of students.** Compare them against any school or training records that report on the level of attainment of the necessary prerequisite knowledge or skills for the new goals.

5. **If appropriate, regress to the next level of prerequisite goals, and repeat steps 3 and 4.** That is, it may be necessary to go even further back in the goal sequence to reach the entering level of the targeted students.

continued

Learner Entering-Behavior Assessment, continued

6. **Decide whether to go with the subjective conclusions of the developers and content experts or to gather more objective data.** For cost or time limitations, developers and clients may decide to base their entering-behavior decisions on the data accumulated thus far. Those wanting more objective evidence of learner entering behaviors would continue the next steps in this job aid.

7. **Acquire or generate performance objectives relevant to the prerequisite goals and for the new instructional goals.** These objectives will provide the data needed for generating tests over the level of knowledge and skill brought by entering students, and the degree to which they may already know the new subject matter.

8. **Acquire or generate test items relevant to the performance objectives.** Put these items into a testing instrument ready for administration. See the job aids on test construction later in this chapter.

9. **Test representative students to see if they have the necessary entering behaviors.** Test results will show both the degree to which students lack prerequisite behaviors and the degree to which they already have the competencies to be taught by the new instruction.

10. **Decide on the entering level of student knowledge and skill that the instruction should address.** If entering students lack some or all of the prerequisite knowledge and skill required for the proposed instruction, then additional instructional goals will have to be incorporated to cover these areas. Similarly, if they already have knowledge and skill relevant to some of the goals for the new instruction, those goals can be dropped.

Reference

Gentry, C. (1992) Assessing Learner Entering Behavior. Unpublished class handout at Michigan State University.

Entering behavior, particularly at the adult level of instruction, varies considerably. That is, learners' respective levels of knowledge and skill, relevant to any instruction, will likely differ in some important respects. This makes it difficult to avoid the twin pitfalls of using teaching materials for which students lack prerequisites and assigning teaching materials that students already know. Most instruction is directed toward a poorly defined middle group of students, with the assumption that the teacher or trainer will provide them with any remedial or accelerated materials or experiences needed. Clearly, there are other entering behaviors of students, besides those relevant to the instruction, that could be valuable to developing the instructional process, for example, the reading level range of the target group, or their preferred learning styles. The problem of designing instruction that can adjust effectively to the differences of learners in the same environment is one of the greatest challenges that instructional developers face. There are some who feel that the marriage of computer, video, and communication technologies may provide new and more effective means for tailoring or individualizing instruction for learners. This is an exciting area of experimentation and research for educators and trainers.

Writing/Deriving Objectives

Clear, precise performance objectives, preferably in a behavioral form, can provide a powerful guide to the design of instruction. Effective **behavioral objectives** include at least three elements: the *behavior* to be learned, the *conditions* under which the behavior is demonstrated, and the *degree* to which the behavior is to be learned. Some experts recommend including identification of the *audience*, or target group, at which the objective is aimed (e.g., fifth-grade science students), but that element is excluded from most objectives, probably for simplification purposes. The three elements of a behavioral objective can be demonstrated through a simple example:

> Given a standard bicycle, to ride the bicycle while pedaling in a sitting position for a distance of 300 yards on a flat surface without touching either foot to the surface, within a 3-minute period.

The distinction among the three elements making up a behavioral objective is not always clear. Consider the following breakdown of the example objective:

The behavior	To ride a bicycle
The conditions	Given a standard bicycle While pedaling in a sitting position For a distance of 300 yards On a flat surface
The standards	Without touching either foot on the surface while riding Within a 3-minute period

With this kind of explicit information, the instructional developer is very clear about what the instruction being designed is to accomplish, under what conditions, and how well it is to be accomplished. Note that performance objectives should always be focused on the learner, *not* on the instructor.

The use of behavioral objectives is particularly effective for developing instruction to teach cognitive and psychomotor knowledge and skills. However, most educators still have difficulty in effectively stating behavioral objectives for attitudes and values. Terms used interchangeably with *behavioral objectives* include *specific objectives* and *performance objectives*.

The "ABCD Approach to Writing Objectives" job aid teaches a set of steps through which designers can learn to write acceptable behavioral objectives. Instructional developers have found that when performance objectives are available to students as well as to the instructor, learning is more efficient.

Often, instructional developers will be asked to assist in the revision of training or educational programs. Initially, it may be very difficult to get the trainer or educator responsible for the instruction to write performance objectives, because they question the merit of doing so, feel that they lack the skills, and/or are too busy. Under these conditions, it may fall to the instructional developer to derive the performance objectives from the instructor's existing course materials. Test items used by the instructor provide a particularly good beginning point for deriving objectives. Test

Job Aid / ABCD Approach to Writing Objectives

Description   A process for writing behavioral objectives that are learner-centered and that focus on observable and measurable skills. Written objectives should specify: the Audience for the objective, the Behavior expected of the learner, the Conditions under which the behavior will be performed, and the Degree to which (how well) the behavior is to be performed.

Use Rationale   Instructors and learners need explicit statements that define for them the expected outcomes of instruction, and that help them to determine if and when those outcomes have occurred. They also serve as an important guide to the instructional developer in the design process.

Critical Tasks

1. **Identify a general goal for the instructional situation.** Example of goal: to be able to troubleshoot an automobile engine.

2. **Clearly specify the Audience for the objective.** This element is often omitted in behavioral objective statements. Example of audience: twelfth-grade auto shop students in urban public schools.

3. **Clearly specify the Behavior that will be the focus of the instruction.** Use a verb of observable and measurable behavior. An example would be: to identify any breakdown points in the electrical system of an automobile engine.

4. **Specify the Conditions under which the behavior will be taught and evaluated.** The teaching conditions should match the testing conditions. An example of conditions would be: given the appropriate tools, and an engine with a defective electrical system, while under instructor supervision.

5. **Specify the Degree to which proficiency in a behavior will be demonstrated.** Example: Correctly identify any defective electrical elements in an automobile engine, within a 30-minute period.

6. **Combine audience, behavior, conditions, and degree into one statement.** Example: Given the appropriate tools and an engine with a defective electrical system, eleventh- and twelfth-grade auto shop students, under supervision, will be able to identify correctly the defective element in the electrical system that prevents effective performance of an automobile engine, within 30 minutes.

References

Instructional Development Institute (1972). A mediated project funded by the National Special Media Institutes. Washington, D.C.: The Institute.

Kryspin, W. J., and Feldhusen, J. F. (1974). *Writing Behavioral Objectives.* Minneapolis, Minn.: Burgess, pp. 6–43, 50–80.

Mager, R. F. (1975). *Preparing Instructional Objectives.* Belmont, Calif.: Fearon, pp. 19–48.

items are usually easy to translate into performance objectives. The job aid on "Deriving Performance Objectives from Test Items" provides a common algorithm for deriving instructional objectives from test items.

Job Aid / Deriving Performance Objectives from Test Items

Description   Instructional developers first acquire copies of test items currently used by clients (e.g., educators or trainers) and then translate each test item into one or more performance objectives (initially writing only the behavior element, leaving out audience, condition, and degree elements). Then the client is asked to validate each behavior element and to add any missing behaviors the client thinks should be in the course. Any unvalidated behaviors that are listed are discarded, and behaviors covering any additions suggested by the client are written. Condition and degree elements are added to each behavior element to form complete performance objectives.

Use Rationale   It is often very difficult to get clients to write objectives, or even to work with an instructional developer in writing objectives for their courses, because of work priorities, lack of skill in writing performance objectives, or lack of conviction about their value. However, most clients *are* willing to react to performance objectives written by others, by agreeing or disagreeing as to whether the objectives are what was intended for their courses. This involvement generally leads clients to see the value in such objectives and eventually to write their own.

Critical Tasks

1. **Acquire copies of old and current course tests and answer keys from the client.** Assure the client that close security will be maintained over the tests.

2. **Code each test item with its own unique number.** For extensive or involved projects, this helps to keep track of the derivation of performance objectives as they go through their several revisions.

3. **Rewrite each test item as the behavior element of an objective.** For the client validation check that follows, the condition and degree elements in a performance objective are not needed, and only represent additional work at this point. As an example, for the following test item, you would generate only the behavior element of the performance objective.

   Test item: Demonstrate the steps, in correct sequence, for booting up a specific word processing computer program.

   Behavior element: To demonstrate the steps for booting up a specific computer word processing program.

   Performance Objective: Given an Apple IIe computer and the AppleWriter word processing program, to demonstrate the steps, in their appropriate sequence, for booting up the program, without error.

4. **Have the client validate the list of test-derived behavior elements.** Ask the client to check those behaviors he or she intended students to be able to demonstrate as a result of the instruction. For those unchecked, show the test item(s) from which they were derived to determine if you correctly interpreted them. The client will usually make corrections in your wording of objectives at this time, to better fit his or her professional perceptions and jargon.

5. **Ask the client to state any additional knowledge, skills, or attitudes for the course that are not represented in the list of behaviors.** Do not argue with clients, even though you may think their recommendations are already included, but be sure to clarify any additions.

continued

Deriving Performance Objectives from Test Items, continued

6. **Restate the client's additions as behavior elements, and integrate them into your list.** No serious attempt is made at sequencing behaviors, but it sometimes helps the client to make judgments about them when similar or related behaviors are grouped together.

7. **Ask the client to validate the revised list of behaviors.** The client will often think of additional desired behaviors at this point.

8. **Add condition and degree elements to each of the behavior elements to form complete performance objectives.** Add condition, e.g., "with an Apple IIe," "using AppleWriter," "with steps in sequence," and by adding the level or degree, e.g., "without error."

9. **Ask the client to validate the completed performance objectives.** This is a also good time to return the borrowed tests to the client, or to destroy them.

10. **Make appropriate changes, and submit a final set of performance objectives to the appropriate individual(s).**

Reference

Gentry, C. G. (1975). Procedure for Deriving Objectives from a Recalcitrant Client. Unpublished document written for Learning and Evaluation Services at Michigan State University. East Lansing, Mich.: the University, pp. 1–4.

Categorizing Instructional Objectives

Evaluators of instructional systems often find that the instruction in question is for teaching objectives not intended, or, conversely, that the instruction may fail to teach behaviors that were intended. The categorization of performance objectives according to instructional intent is crucial to the selection of appropriate instructional strategies and media. The "Bloom's Taxonomy" job aid is useful as a rough but efficient means for categorizing objectives. Taxonomies developed by Gagne and by Merrill (see the job aids "Gagne's Behavioral Hierarchy" and "Merrill and Goodman Strategy, and Media Selection Technique," later in this chapter) are also appropriate for assisting in the categorization of objectives.

Job Aid / Bloom's Taxonomy

Description Bloom's taxonomy, and those of his colleagues, Krathwohl and Ely, guide an instructional developer through the process of categorizing cognitive, psychomotor, and affective objectives according to the *Taxonomy of Behavioral Objectives*. The levels into which objectives of the cognitive domain fall are: knowledge, comprehension, application, analysis, synthesis, and evaluation. The levels for the psychomotor domain are: perception, set, guided response, mechanism, and complex overt response. The levels for the affective domain are: receiving, responding, valuing, organization, and value characterization. The objectives in question are compared to the definitions,

continued

Bloom's Taxonomy, continued

descriptions, and examples provided for the three domains and their levels, to determine into which categories they fall.

Use Rationale   There is a tendency among educators and trainers to choose objectives that are easy to write and to test. These fall mainly at the knowledge level of the cognitive domain, where the learner is asked to recognize or to recall knowledge specifics. However, the intent of a course may be to have students meet higher-level cognitive objectives or objectives that fall in the affective and psychomotor domains. Being able to discriminate the intent of objectives is important. Use of the taxonomy as a checklist is one means that improves the selection of instructional objectives.

Critical Tasks

1. **Acquire behavioral objectives for the target course.** These objectives may be newly written, already existing in the course, or obtained from someone else.

2. **Categorize objectives by domain, level, and example.** Check individual objectives against the definitions of the three domains and for their respective taxonomic levels, and compare the objectives in question with the example objectives, provided for each level:

   Cognitive-Domain Objectives: Objectives that require students to recall or recognize knowledge and to develop intellectual abilities and skills.

   a. *Knowledge-Level Objectives*—objectives that require learners to recall or recognize: (1) specifics and universals, (2) methods and processes, (3) patterns, (4) structures, and/or (5) settings.

   Example: to list the four rules of good test writing
   Example: to recognize the names of the American presidents
   Example: to recite the alphabet
   Example: to match the names of city government officials with their respective titles

   b. *Comprehension-Level Objectives*—when the learner is required to translate, interpret, or extrapolate.

   Example: to read a blueprint
   Example: to discriminate among warranted, unwarranted, and conflicting conclusions drawn from a body of data
   Example: to summarize a chapter in a book

   c. *Application-Level Objectives*—when a learner is required to solve a problem by selecting among and using techniques, principles, theories, and/or ideas.

   Example: to set up and use a contingency management program to motivate students
   Example: to explain the effect on the earth if the moon were to double in mass
   Example: to troubleshoot an electrical problem in an automobile engine

   d. *Analysis-Level Objectives*—when the learner is required to break down material into its constituent parts and to detect the relationships of the parts and the way they are organized.

   Example: to distinguish between facts and assumptions in a communication
   Example: to determine the major parts of an instructional system
   Example: to determine the assumptions underlying a political statement

   e. *Synthesis-Level Objectives*—where the learner is required to put together elements and parts so as to form a new whole.

   Example: to devise a theory to explain a phenomenon
   Example: to design an instructional unit according to specifications
   Example: to propose alternative ways of solving a problem

continued

f. *Evaluation-Level Objectives*—when the learner is required to make judgments on the basis of distinct criteria.

Example: to identify errors in a reasoned argument
Example: to critically assess religious beliefs
Example: to develop criteria for evaluating an instructional unit

Psychomotor-Domain Objectives: objectives that emphasize some muscular or motor skill, some manipulation of material and objects, or some act that requires neuromuscular coordination (Krathwohl, et al., 1964).

a. *Perception-Level Objectives*—objectives aimed at making a learner aware of objects, qualities, or relations through the senses.

Example: to identify different flavors through taste
Example: to recognize a problem with a running car engine, based on the sounds it makes
Example: to follow directions in assembling a computer

b. *Set-Level Objectives*—objectives aimed at assisting a learner in assuming a readiness for a particular kind of action.

Example: to be aware of the sequence of steps in troubleshooting an engine
Example: to assume a proper stance preparatory to bowling
Example: to have a disposition toward developing instruction

c. *Guided-Response-Level Objectives*—objectives aimed at assisting a learner to use criteria to self-evaluate the performance of an overt behavioral act, under teacher guidance.

Example: to perform a tennis serve as demonstrated
Example: to determine the best sequence of steps for cleaning a weapon through trial of several alternative sequences
Example: to imitate the process of titrating a solution

d. *Mechanism-Level Objectives*—objectives aimed at assisting a learner to apply and combine previously known responses to appropriate situations.

Example: to capture a swarm of bees
Example: to acquire a desired color by mixing paints
Example: to graft one variety of apple to another

e. *Complex-Overt-Response Level Objectives*—objectives aimed at assisting a learner to perform smoothly and efficiently a motor act that is considered complex because of the movement pattern required.

Example: to operate an automobile on a busy street
Example: to accurately sight in a rifle for increments of 50 yards up to 500 yards
Example: to perform advanced music on the piano

f. *Adaptation-Level Objectives*—objectives aimed at assisting a learner to alter motor responses when meeting demands of new, problematic situations requiring a physical response

Example: to develop a novel computer application by modifying skills already in the student's repertoire
Example: to devise a new tumbling routine by adapting routines already known
Example: to develop a piano composition by adapting one's existing playing skills and knowledge of music

g. *Origination-Level Objectives*—objectives aimed at assisting a learner to create new motor acts of manipulating materials out of current psychomotor understandings and skills.

Example: to create a new game requiring a psychomotor response
Example: to create a new technique for surgically removing a brain tumor
Example: to create a new method of muscle massage

continued

Bloom's Taxonomy, continued

Affective-Domain Objectives: objectives aimed at assisting a learner to change interests, attitudes, and values, and to develop appreciations and adequate adjustments.

a. *Receiving (Attending)-Level Objectives*—objectives aimed at assisting the learner to: (1) become aware of a situation, phenomenon, object, or stage of affairs; (2) be willing to tolerate a given stimulus, not avoid it; and (3) control one's attention so that the favored stimulus is selected and attended to, despite competing and distracting stimuli.

Example: to comply with school regulations
Example: to tolerate cultural differences exhibited by other groups
Example: to be sensitive to community mores

b. *Responding-Level Objectives*—objectives aimed at assisting the learner in willingly complying, responding, and finding satisfaction in response.

Example: to willingly comply with school regulations
Example: to accept responsibility for one's mistakes
Example: to enjoy writing letters to friends

c. *Valuing-Level Objectives*—objectives aimed at assisting the learner in accepting, preferring, and/or having commitment to a value.

Example: to maintain a desire to develop speaking and writing skills
Example: to assume responsibility for finding homes for stray animals
Example: to try actively to convince others of the importance of voting

d. *Organization-Level Objectives*—objectives aimed at assisting the learner to: (1) relate new values to values already held, and (2) bring values already held into an ordered relationship.

Example: to form judgments about the responsibility of the community to reduce pollution
Example: to develop rules for balancing recreation time against work time

e. *Consistency-of-Reaction-Level Objectives*—objectives aimed at assisting the learner to: (1) develop a persistent and consistent response to a family of related situations or objects, and (2) develop an internal consistency among encompassing objectives.

Example: to judge problems in terms of consequences rather than from dogmatic precepts
Example: to develop a consistent philosophy of life

3. **By inspection and judgment, determine whether there are appropriate and sufficient objectives written for each taxonomic category.** It may be appropriate to get the views of others involved in the instruction, about the appropriateness and sufficiency of objectives, by category.

References

Bloom, B. S. ed. (1956). *Taxonomy of Behavioral Objectives: Handbook I: Cognitive Domain.* New York: David McKay.

Krathwohl, D. R., et al. (1964). *Taxonomy of Behavioral Objectives: Handbook II: Affective Domain.* New York: David McKay.

Edling, J. V., et al. (1972). *The Cognitive Domain: A Resource Book for Media Specialists.* Washington, D.C.: Gryphon House.

Ely, D. P., et al. (1972). *The Psychomotor Domain: A Resource Book for Media Specialists.* Washington, D.C.: Gryphon House.

Validating Instructional Objectives

An important step in instructional design is getting agreement from the client about the validity of the modified or new list of instructional objectives. Failure to establish commitment to specific objectives prior to the final stages of design and even production is a common error made by instructional developers, one that often results in the client's later rejection of the instructional product or process. Many of the techniques for deriving objectives have the validation process built in (as in the "Bloom's Taxonomy" job aid), but many do not. Once objectives have been written, members of the client organization may be asked to apply a simple ranking technique, e.g., a five-point scale, to each of the objectives listed. The "Validating Instructional Objectives" job aid illustrates one such technique.

Job Aid / Validating Instructional Objectives

Description This technique is used to rank a list of instructional objectives in terms of their importance. The list is presented to appropriate members of the client organization who are asked to apply a five-point scale to each of the objectives, with 5 as the highest rating and 1 as the lowest. Their responses are compiled and added for each of the objectives. This gives a set of ranked objectives, where the higher the number the more important is considered the item. Respondents are then asked to indicate why they agree or disagree with the ranking of specific objectives. These data are compiled and returned to the respondents, and they are asked to rank the items a second time based on the data each has provided. Their responses are again compiled and added to give a final ranking of the objectives.

Use Rationale For a number of reasons, clients may vary in how they value some instructional objectives over others (e.g., personal preference). If consensus regarding their value is not obtained early in the process of design, the instructional designer may have to repeat much of the work, or in some cases lose the contract for developing the instruction.

Critical Tasks

1. **Acquire an established list of objectives.** E.g., either this can be done by techniques such as *Nominal Group Process, Brainstorming,* and *Deriving Objectives from Test Items,* the objectives may already exist, or they may have to be written.

2. **Format the list of objectives to include a five-point scale to the right of each objective.** This should include brief directions for respondents at the beginning of the list, e.g., "Rank each objective in terms of its importance by marking the number on the scale next to each item." See Figure 4.1.

3. **Identify the respondents.** This usually means administrators, teachers, students, and/or recognized experts.

4. **Have the respondents rank the objectives using the five-point scale.** This can be done by mail or with all of the respondents together. The latter requires clerical assistance to compile and add the responses for quick return, and a copy machine to provide them with compiled responses.

continued

Validating Instructional Objectives, continued

FIGURE 4.1 / Example of an objectives validation sheet

OBJECTIVES VALIDATION SHEET

Respondent _____

Project _____

Date _____

Directions: Rank each objective listed below in terms of its importance to the proposed introductory computer course by circling the number on the scale to the right of the objective that in your view best reflects the objective's importance. The scale values are:

5 = highest priority
4 = high priority
3 = medium priority
2 = low priority
1 = lowest priority

Objectives	*Rank*				
1. to define and relate bits, bytes, and words	1	2	3	4	5
2. to identify major inventions that improved computer software and computer hardware functions over time	1	2	3	4	5
3. to discriminate among the generations of computer hardware	1	2	3	4	5
4. to distinguish among the seven major types of software	1	2	3	4	5
5. to recognize common problems in the use of software	1	2	3	4	5
6. to list the individual components of an operating system and describe their purposes	1	2	3	4	5
7. to relate major types of applications software to operating systems	1	2	3	4	5
8. to select appropriate text entry, embedded commands, and immediate commands for specific word processing situations	1	2	3	4	5

5. **Sum the ranks for each objective.** This is often done on a larger sheet resembling the respondent's sheet, but with additional space so that all ranks for an item can be placed on the same line, for ease of summing.

6. **Place the sum of the ranks for each objective on a clean respondent sheet.** This is similar to the sheet given initially, but with a single column for the accumulated ranks to the right of each objective, followed by a third column for a summary of comments made for each objective. A copy is made of this for each respondent. See Figure 4.2.

7. **Respondents are asked to comment on any specific summed ranks with which they disagree.** The comments are written to the right of the respective objectives.

8. **The respondents' comments are summarized for each objective with whose ranking they did not agree.** Summaries are placed in the third column of the *Validation Summary Sheet.* See Figure 4.2.

continued

Validating Instructional Objectives, continued

9. **Respondents are asked to rerank the items based on the comment summaries.** People are willing to change their minds when they get new information, provided there is no danger of losing prestige or incurring punishment.

10. **Reranked items are compiled, and ranks are summed to form a new ranking.** This ranking is usually close enough to be accepted as satisfactory validation of the objectives by those whose agreement is important for the success of the endeavor.

FIGURE 4.2 / Example of a validation summary sheet

VALIDATION SUMMARY SHEET

Validator _____
Project _____
Date _____

Directions: Using the rankings from the *Objectives Validation Sheet*, add the ranks for each objective and place the sum under the Sum of Ranks column. Summarize the comments for each objective and write it under the Comment Summary column.

Objectives	Sum of Ranks	Comment Summary
1. to define and relate bits, bytes, and words	4	Should be ranked higher because it is necessary in order to understand what follows
2. to identify major inventions that improved computer software and computer hardware functions	37	
3. to discriminate among the generations of computer hardware	20	Ranked too high. Purpose of course is not to teach computer history
4. to distinguish among the seven major types of software	18	
5. to recognize common problems in the use of software	30	
6. to list the individual components of an operating system and describe their purposes	16	
7. to relate major types of applications software to operating systems	42	
8. to select appropriate text entry, embedded commands, and immediate commands for specific word processing situations	7	Ranked too low, since this is a major skill of students

Reference

Gentry, Cass (1977). Unpublished procedure generated for the use of instructional developers in the Learning and Evaluation Services of Michigan State University. East Lansing, Mich.: the University.

Sequencing Instructional Objectives

The major reasons for sequencing objectives (step 4 in the design process) are that some are prerequisite to others, or for the convenience or efficiency in developing similar parts of the instruction simultaneously. The "Objective Trees" job aid assists in the former, in that it is designed to demonstrate preceding, concurrent, and succeeding relationships among objectives. This basically tells the instructional developer which objectives should be learned before others, and which objectives can be learned at the same time, or concurrently. It is worth mentioning that the process of sequencing objectives will invariably stimulate the recognition of the need for other objectives not previously considered.

The placing of objectives in a hierarchy raises the question of how far down the hierarchy of objectives should extend. The rule is that the objectives are extended down until they match desirable entry behaviors of those accepted for the instruction, as demonstrated in Figure 4.3. This is a limit that design places on development. Students who do not have at least the designated entry behaviors would not be permitted to take the instruction.

Job Aid / Objective Trees

Description   **Objective trees** are used to hierarchically relate and to some extent generate objectives in terms of the desired ends of a project. Objectives and their relationships are portrayed graphically in the form of a tree, with the goal being at the top of the tree and levels of terminal and enabling objectives following in a hierarchy.

Use Rationale   In the design of any instructional system, important first steps are to determine the systems' outcomes as specific objectives and to show how goals and terminal and enabling objectives are related. In essence, the tree makes clear which objectives must be learned before others, and which can be learned at the same time.

Critical Tasks

1. **Identify instructional goal(s) for project.** This may result from a needs analysis or from value judgment, e.g., "to raise the reading level of elementary students by one grade." This goal is positioned at the top level of the tree.

2. **Generate an initial list of objectives.** E.g., can be done by other techniques, such as *Nominal Group Process, Brainstorming,* and *Deriving Objectives from Test Items.* Write the objectives on individual cards so that they can be shifted around within the tree. They should be congruent with the instructional goal.

3. **Extend the tree one level down from goal.** See Figure 4.3. Use the branching rule by asking: "What is the highest level of behavioral objective necessary for accomplishing the global goal?" This objective is usually called a *terminal objective.* Lines are drawn from the goal to the terminal objectives, which are listed horizontally below the goal on the tree. There may be more than one terminal objective per goal. A large sheet of paper will be needed, or objectives can be put on small pieces of paper and arranged on a flat surface.

continued

Objective Trees, continued

4. **Extend the tree to the next-lower level.** Ask the branching rule question for other levels of objectives: "What are the objectives necessary for accomplishing the objective(s) at the previous level?" Objectives from one level are connected by lines to the appropriate objectives in the next level. This is repeated until the lowest level desired is reached, i.e., at the predetermined entry level of the target students.

5. **Review the tree.** Check for missing objectives and/or any revision of objectives. Note which objectives must precede others. Note which objectives may be taught concurrently. Also, note duplicate objectives, so that instruction for them need only occur once. Make any needed modification in hierarchy.

6. **Have content and learning experts validate the tree.** Besides the potential of valuable comments, their participation lends credibility, which increases the likelihood of adoption by the clients.

FIGURE 4.3 / Example of a behavioral hierarchy

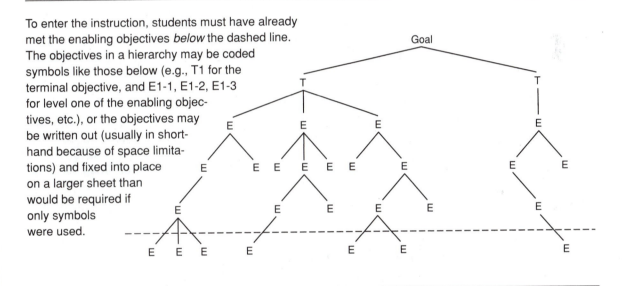

To enter the instruction, students must have already met the enabling objectives *below* the dashed line. The objectives in a hierarchy may be coded symbols like those below (e.g., T1 for the terminal objective, and E1-1, E1-2, E1-3 for level one of the enabling objectives, etc.), or the objectives may be written out (usually in shorthand because of space limitations) and fixed into place on a larger sheet than would be required if only symbols were used.

References

Delp, Peter, et al. (1977). *Systems Tools for Project Planning.* Bloomington, Ind.: PASTAM Publishers, pp. 49–54.

Granger, C. H. (1973). The hierarchy of objectives. *Harvard Review of Business.* March: 133–140.

Generating Criterion Test Items

Writing items for testing instructional outcomes is, of course, a production process rather than a design process, but carrying out that task at this point in the instructional development sequence solves a particularly plaguing problem. Instructional developers have found that if test items are written *after* content, strategy, and media decisions have been made, there is a strong tendency to test over the specific content, strategy, and media elements used at that time. This means that if any of these elements are changed (e.g., textbook, video), then the test items themselves must be rewritten, because the old items reflect the previous strategy, media, and/ or content. An example would be where a specific author or definition in a textbook is referred to in a test item. Since writing good test items is both difficult and tedious, it behooves instructional developers to keep relevant the ones they have, and they do that by writing the items to objectives rather than to content, strategy, or media.

The first job aid on generating criterion items focuses on "Multiple-Choice Test Item Construction." The multiple-choice item is a favorite in the testing arsenal; and when such items are established as valid and reliable, they prove to be effective for testing most types of learning.

Job Aid / Multiple-Choice Test Item Construction

Description   Basically, a **multiple-choice test item** contains a stem setting forth a problem, followed by a correct solution randomly placed among several foils or distractors. This procedure for writing multiple-choice test items has the writer follow a checklist of criteria that test item stems and distractors should meet.

Use Rationale   Some form of evaluation is required to demonstrate the effectiveness of the developed instruction to clients. Multiple-choice tests are considered one of the best types of objective tests for measuring a range of instructional outcomes. In addition, they are easy to correct; and when constructed to meet selected criteria, they are very effective. Also, since as a testing form they are in the common experience of most students, more student time is focused on answering the question rather than on figuring out the testing format.

Critical Tasks

1. **Acquire or write a set of objectives for an instructional unit.**

2. **Complete a table of specifications for test items** (see the example in Figure 4.4).

3. **Determine which of the test item specifications can be satisfied by multiple-choice questions.** For example, they should not be used where students need to show unique connections among ideas, nor should they be used, solely, when students are being tested on their ability to perform some specific process.

4. **Use incomplete statement stems when possible.** E.g., "An instance of a supply-type test item is the . . ." These are typically more concise and easier to write.

5. **Do not hesitate to change the number of distractors or alternatives used.** Most items have four or five alternatives, and the more you have the less chance of a student's guessing the right answer. There is no reason why each question should have the same number of alternatives.

continued

Multiple-Choice Test Item Construction, continued

FIGURE 4.4 / Example of a table of specifications showing the number of items needed for a test

Table of Specifications for a 60-Item Test on Weather Maps

Content Areas	Instructional Objectives				Total Items
	1. Knows Basic Terms	2. Knows Map Symbols	3. Knows Specific Facts	4. Interprets Weather Maps	
A. Air pressure	2	2	2	2	8
B. Air temperature	2	2	2	2	8
C. Humidity and precipitation	2	2	3	3	10
D. Wind	2	3	3	4	12
E. Clouds	3	2	3	2	10
F. Fronts	3	3	3	3	12
Total items	14	14	16	16	60

6. **State in the directions whether the student should choose the "best answer."** Best-answer items are used for more complex achievement tasks, but it is good advice to request the "best answer" for all multiple-choice items.

7. **Check to be sure that each item meets appropriate criteria.** Such as the following:

   a. A test item is specific to a specific objective.

   b. A single problem is stated in the stem in clear, simple language.

   c. The distractors and the solution are brief (use common wording in the stem).

   d. The stem is placed on the top line(s), with the alternatives below, one under the other.

   e. Numbers identify the stem of the item, while letters of the alphabet discriminate specific alternatives.

   f. The stem is stated in positive form, preferably.

   g. Negative wording in a stem is accentuated (by underlining or italicizing, e.g., ". . . do <u>not</u> include . . . ," or ". . . do *not* include . . .")

   h. Alternatives include only one correct or one most defensible answer.

   i. Alternatives grammatically and logically fit the stem and are approximately of the same length.

   j. Each of the alternatives would appear to be a likely answer to a guesser.

   k. The use of *all of the above* and *none of the above* is avoided.

   l. Verbal clues such as *never, all,* and *generally* are avoided.

   m. The construction of an item is varied so that it is not an exact repeat from a lesson or reading assignment.

   n. Correct answers are randomly assigned to different positions among the alternatives.

   o. Alternatives of an item are kept mutually exclusive.

8. **Have content experts critique the items to determine validity.** This will ensure that the test items are measuring what was intended. See Chapter 9.

continued

Multiple-Choice Test Item Construction, continued

9. **Try the test out on representative students, and revise accordingly.** This ensures that items communicate their intent clearly, and determines the reading difficulty of the items. To determine reliability, see the job aid on "Establishing Reliability of Instructional Tests" in Chapter 9.

References

Gronlund, N. E. (1973). *Preparing Criterion-Referenced Tests for Classroom Instruction.* New York: Macmillan.

Green, J. A. (1963). *Teacher-Made Tests.* New York: Harper & Row.

Sax, G. (1989). *Principles of Educational and Psychological Measurement and Evaluation.* 3d ed. Belmont, Calif.: Wadsworth Publishing Company. pp. 101–115.

Another commonly used type of test item is the *true-false item.* On the surface it would appear that true-false items would be easy to write, but test-wise students can guess with considerable accuracy, if giveaway cues are written into the items. The test-wiseness problem can be largely avoided if the procedures prescribed by the job aid on "Writing True-False Test Items" are followed.

Job Aid / Writing True-False Test Items

Description   This technique outlines the steps for generating effective **true-false test items**. These items consist of statements with some prescribed method of registering agreement or disagreement by the person being tested. Proper construction techniques, following several do's and don'ts, result in an efficient method of student evaluation.

Use Rationale   True-false test items are an effective and efficient tool for evaluating student achievement on the instructional content of a particular unit of study. This testing method exhibits greater efficiency in the utilization of time expended in construction and refinement of items. It can be administered relatively quickly, and scoring is completely objective. Comprehensive sampling of the content and objectives may be rapidly obtained.

Critical Tasks

1. **Obtain a list of performance objectives that are to be tested.** For effective test item writing these should be written in behavioral terms.

2. **Construct a table of specifications to ensure an adequate sampling of behaviors to be tested.** See Figure 4.5. This blueprint for selecting appropriate test items considers content, complexity, and the relative importance of each.

continued

Writing True-False Test Items, continued

FIGURE 4.5 / Table of specifications showing the number of items needed for a test

Table of Specifications for a 60-Item Test on Weather Maps

Content Areas	Instructional Objectives				Total Items
	1. Knows Basic Terms	2. Knows Map Symbols	3. Knows Specific Facts	4. Interprets Weather Maps	
A. Air pressure	2	2	2	2	8
B. Air temperature	2	2	2	2	8
C. Humidity and precipitation	2	2	3	3	10
D. Wind	2	3	3	4	12
E. Clouds	3	2	3	2	10
F. Fronts	3	3	3	3	12
Total items	14	14	16	16	60

3. **Consider limitations of this item format, and select objectives that are amenable to measurement with items of this type.** E.g., use items that test factual and comprehension levels of the cognitive domain.

4. **Follow prescribed rules when writing true-false test items for performance objectives.** The following rules are not exhaustive, but when followed they do result in effective true-false items.

   a. Be sure that each item is either absolutely true or completely false. It is difficult for the learner to know how to respond if part of the item is true and part of it false.

   b. Each item should possess only one central theme.

   c. Statements should be free from ambiguity, that is, clear, concise, grammatically correct, and explicit. Avoid unnecessary words and phrases that cause confusion.

   d. Negative statements should be avoided, e.g., "Hawaii is <u>not</u> the only state that does <u>not</u> have a common border with a neighboring state."

   e. Words such as "some," "few," and "many" should be avoided because these qualifying terms generally introduce true statements.

   f. Avoid irrelevant clues that indicate false statements, such as "all" and "none."

   g. Do not make false statements by taking a true one and adding "no" or "not."

   h. Try to make false statements about as long as true statements. This helps decrease guessing, since most true statements tend to be longer.

   i. Statements should not come directly from the textbook. This leads to memorization by students.

   j. Be sure items require more than common sense and logic to answer.

5. **Compile the items into a test format.** Provide clear directions to test takers. A test should contain approximately the same number of true statements and false statements. Avoid establishing a reputation for constructing tests that contain mainly true or mainly false items. This helps to prevent establishing a pattern among responses that can act as an unintended cue to test takers.

continued

Writing True-False Test Items, continued

6. **Write up a test answer key that can be easily used by others.** If alternative answers are possible, be sure to include these in the test answer key.

7. **Ask content experts to validate the test items.** Test validity asks whether a test measures what it was intended to measure. Ask content experts to identify weak items and to indicate how well items can be expected to discriminate between high and low achievers. See the job aid on "Establishing Content Validity for Instructional Tests," in Chapter 9.

8. **Check the reliability of the test items.** Reliability asks if a test is consistent in how it measures a specific skill or knowledge level. See the job aid on "Establishing Reliability of Instructional Tests," also in Chapter 9.

References

Marshall, Jon, and Hales, Lloyd (1972). *Essentials of Testing.* Reading, Mass.: Addison-Wesley, pp. 10–11, 68–75, 77–78.

Schoer, Lowell A. (1970). *Test Construction.* Boston, Mass.: Allyn and Bacon, pp. 108–116.

Tables of Specification like that presented in Figure 4.5 are useful for ordering design data so that they are clear to those who must carry out the production of the design elements. Simply stated, a **table of specifications** is a means for relating details of variables, usually in the form of a matrix and appropriate to the object or objects to be produced, that are followed to ensure that design criteria are met. Such tables can be set up for many other productions beyond test construction.

The job aid on "Constructing Short-Answer Test Items" teaches how to design *short-answer test items*. A major advantage in using short-answer test items is that they can be written quickly. These items, too, can be very effective, although they are often misused, as when the item is no more than a sentence out of a reading assignment, with a word replaced by a blank to be filled in.

Job Aid / Constructing Short-Answer Test Items

Description **Short-answer test items** represent an easy technique for writing factual-recall test items. Its advantage over true-false and multiple choice is that the student can't guess the answer if the item is well constructed. The form of the item is made up of unambiguous questions or statements, each requiring a brief answer to be written in an underlined blank space in the statement. Six rules are used to guide the test item developer through the process.

Use Rationale Short-answer items are easy to write and to use. Students supply their own answers in the blanks provided. This type of test item is especially appropriate where selection-

continued

Constructing Short-Answer Test Items, continued

type items (i.e., multiple choice, true-false, or matching) would make the answer obvious. When using short-answer (fill-in-the-blank) items, make sure they deal with appropriate learning outcomes (i.e., where students have to recall information, or where computational problems are used).

Critical Tasks

1. **Write the test item in the form of a direct question so that *only* a single brief answer is possible.** If upon rereading the item, it apparently can still be answered in several ways, then revise the test item.

2. **Rewrite a direct question in the form of an incomplete statement.** E.g., direct question: *What is another name for criterion-referenced test items?* Incomplete statement: *Criterion-referenced test items are also called _____.*

3. **Follow the rules when writing incomplete items.** Example rules are:
   a. Each test item should contain only one blank answer space.
   b. Place the blanks at the end of the statement.
   c. All blanks should be the same length.
   d. If the blank is preceded by the article "a" or "an," use the convention "a(n)."
   e. Arrange the blanks so that they are easy to score.
   f. Avoid verbatim textbook quotes.
   g. Design items so that answers respond to main points of the questions rather than to some minor aspects.

4. **Check for validity and reliability of test items.** See the job aids "Establishing Content Validity for Instructional Tests" and "Establishing Reliability of Instructional Tests," in Chapter 9.

Reference

Gronlund, N. E. (1988). *How to Construct Achievement Tests.* 4th ed. Englewood Cliffs, N.J.: Prentice-Hall, pp. 71–83.

Views vary about the value of *matching*, the next type of test item to be considered. In their favor, matching test items are relatively easy to write and to correct. However, their major use is to test the recognition of knowledge specifics, and thus they are of questionable value for testing outcomes higher in the cognitive domain and for the affective and psycho-motor domains.

The job aid on "Constructing Matching-Test Items" is a useful guide. This type of test is good for measuring recall and recognition at the knowledge level in the cognitive domain. Well-designed matching-type test items significantly reduce the chance of guessing the correct answer.

Job Aid / Constructing Matching-Test Items

Description Matching-test items are a special form of multiple choice. They are used to determine the ability of learners to identify relationships between items in two columns. A **matching-test item** consists of a stem that asks the question or gives a task, followed by two parallel columns (*premise* and *response*): an item in the *premise* column, through associated Arabic numbers or alphabetic letters, is matched with the correct item(s) in the *response* column. Depending on the particular matching test, a student can choose items in the *response* column once or more than once.

Use Rationale Matching-test items are relatively easy for the instructional developer to construct, although, like all test items, they should be assessed for their levels of validity (i.e., Does the item measure what was intended?) and reliability (i.e., Do the same-level students consistently get similar scores on the test?). As compared with multiple-choice item tests, matching tests can measure more related factual information in a smaller space, with less guessing.

Critical Tasks

1. **Determine the boundaries of the content or performance area to be tested.** Usually the test should not cover more than one unit of instruction, approximately 1–2 weeks of instruction. Final examinations would be an exception.

2. **Acquire or write instructional objectives in behavioral form.** Each behavioral objective should include statements of: the behavior to be performed, the conditions under which it is performed, and the standard of behavior that the performance must meet. The ABCD technique for writing objectives can be used as a guide for creating these.

3. **Construct a table of test item specifications.** As shown in the example in Figure 4.6, test items are cross-matched with content and objectives, which also gives the total number of items both for content and for objectives. Other techniques for determining the behaviors to be tested are *Bloom's Taxonomy,* and *Gagne's Behavioral Hierarchy.*

FIGURE 4.6 / Example of a table of specifications for a test

Table of Specifications for a 60-Item Test on Weather Maps

Content Areas	Instructional Objectives				Total Items
	1. Knows Basic Terms	2. Knows Map Symbols	3. Knows Specific Facts	4. Interprets Weather Maps	
A. Air pressure	2	2	2	2	8
B. Air temperature	2	2	2	2	8
C. Humidity and precipitation	2	2	3	3	10
D. Wind	2	3	3	4	12
E. Clouds	3	2	3	2	10
F. Fronts	3	3	3	3	12
Total items	14	14	16	16	60

continued

| Constructing Matching-Test Items, continued |

4. **Construct the test items according to criteria.** Such as the following:

   a. The test item stem is short and concise. It should address only one question.

   b. The matching columns are relatively short. This reduces unnecessary cognitive dissonance.

   c. *Response* columns are shorter than *premise* columns. There should be more responses than premises so that responses can't be determined through elimination of others. For a given question, all of its responses and premises should be on the same page, for ease of comparing. Set up conditions so that responses can be used more than once.

   d. Premises are placed in the left column. Use Arabic numbers to order them, e.g., 1, 2, 3.

   e. Responses are placed in the right column. Use alphabetic letters to order them, e.g., a, b, c.

   f. Each of the premises has one or more logical and correct response(s).

   g. The directions indicate the rule(s) for matching the items, e.g., whether responses can be used once, or more than once, for a premise.

5. **Write additional matching-test items, if needed, to determine adequately whether objectives are met.** Review the table of specifications.

6. **Ensure that model answers chosen for the test items are in agreement with the views of people knowledgeable in the field.**

7. **Establish the test's validity and reliability.** See the job aids on "Establishing Content Validity for Instructional Tests" and "Establishing Reliability of Instructional Tests," in Chapter 9.

8. **Revise test items, as appropriate.**

References

Gentry, C. (1987). Writing Multiple-Choice Test Items. Unpublished handout in class at Michigan State University, E. Lansing, Mich.

Gronlund, N. E. (1973). *Preparing Criterion-Referenced Tests for Classroom Instruction.* New York: Macmillan, pp. 16–37, 41.

Gronlund, N. E. (1981). *Measurement and Evaluation in Teaching.* New York: Macmillan, pp. 171–175.

Hopkins, C. D., and Antes, R. L. (1985). *Classroom Measurement and Evaluation.* 2d ed. Itasca, Ill.: F. E. Peacock, pp. 105–110, 149–155.

Sometimes, because of a lack of resources or time, student performance may have to be tested by objective test items (e.g., multiple choice, true-false) or even by subjective test items (e.g., essay, short answer). These are nowhere as effective as the use of performance checklists completed by an observer while the person tested is actually performing the skill or technique, preferably in a realistic setting.

Writing good *essay questions* has a high degree of difficulty, but correcting them is even more difficult. There is a common cynicism that the grade for an essay test will vary depending on who corrects it. However, if certain rules are followed such tests can reasonably be both reliable and valid, and they are capable of testing areas that other tests cannot do as

Job Aid / Generating Performance Test Items

Description   The purpose of performance items is to test skills, usually psychomotor or physical skills, in accomplishing specific tasks. **Performance test items** determine whether someone can directly apply specific skills in appropriate situations. These tests usually take the form of a checklist, where the evaluator checks off or grades appropriate items as the student performs them.

Use Rationale   It is important for learners to demonstrate not only that they know "what to do," but that they know "how to do" something, as well. This is particularly true for psychomotor skill objectives. Too often, the instructional developer develops tests for testing the "what" but not the "how," so he or she never really knows whether the instruction was effective or not. Performance checklists are used under real or simulated conditions while the skills are being performed, and will give a clearer reading on how well the student can perform a skill.

Critical Tasks

1. **Choose the performance skills to be evaluated.** Determine this through the *Nominal Group Process*, by observation, or through knowledgeable opinion.

2. **Each performance task should be broken down into its procedural steps.** E.g., through task analysis.

3. **Write each procedural step as a statement, followed by spaces for a scale and a comment.** See Figure 4.7.

4. **Check for the validity of the items.** Determine this through the *Nominal Group Process*, by observation, or through expert opinion.

5. **Write a set of directions for the evaluator who will be using the performance checklist.** These usually go at the beginning of the checklist and/or at points where items for a different skill begin. Here's an example of directions for a performance checklist:

   <u>Directions</u>: Observe students while they perform the set of skills explicit to this performance checklist. Circle the number on the scale that is most representative of their performance of each item, with 5 being superior, 4 being good, 3 being adequate, 2 being poor, and 1 being inferior. The steps they perform should usually match the ones in the checklist. Be sure to comment if they performed the steps out of sequence from what was expected. Also comment on any false starts for a step.

6. **Try out the performance checklist.** Use representative individuals who have already had training in the skills of interest. Carefully control for appropriate test conditions. They should match real-life situations as closely as available resources will allow. All learners should be tested under the same conditions, including any time constraints. A form of rater reliability can be established by having two or more evaluators use the checklist at the same time.

continued

well. The job aid on "Writing Essay Questions" teaches how to write effective essay test questions. If essay tests are not written and administered appropriately, they are of little value in assessing the degree to which learners have met objectives.

7. Revise the performance checklist, as appropriate.

FIGURE 4.7 / **Example of a performance checklist**

Change Agent _____

Evaluator _____

Date _____

Directions: Make certain your audiotape recorder is operating properly and that the microphone is placed so that it receives the least interference (air conditioner noise, etc.). Use the following five-point scale to indicate how well the change agent applies each of the persuasion principles during the meeting with the client. Be as objective as you can, and be prepared to support your observations. Justify negatives in the Evaluator Notes section. You should refer to the audiotape as needed. Feedback to the change agent is given immediately after meeting with the client. This form should be submitted within 24 hours.

a. excellent use
b. acceptable use
c. use needs improvement
d. very poor
e. principle not appropriate

Checklist of Principles to be Applied

_____ 1. Agent is convincing

_____ 2. Agent appears credible

_____ 3. Agent puts self in client's place

_____ 4. Agent gives client ample opportunity to explain

_____ 5. Agent assists client in clarifying client's position

_____ 6. Agent gives client opportunity to express feelings

_____ 7. Agent acts as sounding board

_____ 8. Agent provides information to client when requested

_____ 9. Agent begins by informing client of innovation's benefits

_____ 10. Agent approaches client in a friendly, natural manner

_____ 11. Agent presents an unbiased view of both sides of the issue

_____ 12. Agent presents major arguments first, if initial interest is low

_____ 13. Agent presents major arguments last, if interest is high

_____ 14. Agent states conclusions explicitly where arguments are not likely to be questioned

_____ 15. Agent lets client draw conclusions of the consequences if the arguments are unknown

_____ 16. Agent states arguments so that they don't conflict with group norms

_____ 17. Agent emphasizes acceptability of change to other clients

_____ 18. Agent points out common agreements with client

_____ 19. Agent uses logical argument with highly intelligent audience

continued

Generating Performance Test Items, continued

_____ 20. Agent uses emotional appeal combined with logic, as appropriate

_____ 21. Agent tailors communication to client's personality traits

_____ 22. Agent avoids highly controversial issues

_____ 23. Agent provides evidence for statements, when possible

_____ 24. Agent summarizes key points when closing

_____ 25. Agent repeats major points

_____ 26. Agent feeds in only one idea at a time

_____ 27. Agent gets feedback from client on each of his/her ideas

_____ 28. Agent gives client feedback to each idea

Evaluator Notes on Ineffectively Applied Principles

Reference

Green, J. A. (1963). _Teacher-Made Tests._ New York: Harper & Row.

Job Aid / Writing Essay Questions

Description   This technique is used for writing **essay questions**, items that test how well objectives from the higher levels of the cognitive domain (i.e., analysis, synthesis, and evaluation) are met. In an essay test, short questions or statements are posed about instructional content taught, in language that makes clear to the student what responses are being sought. Students are told the point value assigned each essay question and are given ample time to complete each. Before evaluating answers, to reduce bias, the instructor formulates an answer key covering the major points sought in the essay question(s).

Use Rationale   Essay items permit instructors to evaluate learning not easily measured by objective tests. The use of essay items discourages rote learning by requiring students to demonstrate their critical-thinking skills. Essay questions require students to compare, justify, contrast, compile, interpret, or formulate valid conclusions—all higher-order skills. Consequently, responses to essay questions give students the opportunity to display the highest range of cognitive knowledge and skills.

continued

Writing Essay Questions, continued

Critical Tasks

1. **Obtain a set of objectives for a unit of instruction.** Include both terminal and enabling objectives. Make sure the behavior is clearly and unambiguously stated in each objective.

2. **Categorize objectives in terms of level of learning, for cognitive, affective, and psychomotor domains.** See this chapter's earlier section on "Categorizing Instructional Objectives."

3. **Select only those objectives that measure higher cognitive skills of analysis, synthesis, and evaluation.** Lower- and middle-level objectives can best be measured through the use of objective-test formats such as multiple choice and true-false, or by observation.

4. **Construct a one- or two-sentence essay question for each objective. Use the following rules:**
   a. Clearly identify the responses and/or mental processes that are being assessed. Use specific terms such as *organize, relate, discuss,* and *formulate* to designate items appropriate to assessing desired responses, e.g., "Discuss the nutritional and psychological benefits of eating a variety of foods."
   b. Carefully word each item so that the student clearly understands the range of responses you are seeking. Phrase the question to give hints concerning the structure of the answer expected. This not only gives the student direction in responding but also provides a more reliable criterion for grading the accuracy of the response. Example: "Discuss three advantages and three disadvantages of both owning and renting a home."
   c. Clearly indicate the point value(s) for each essay question.

5. **Formulate a model response to each essay question.** This can be a written answer or can be put in outline form, giving major points to be dealt with for each essay question. This should be done before the test is administered. This set of answers is then used as a standard for uniformly evaluating the different responses from all students. It also serves as a check to make sure the question clearly indicates the range of acceptable responses.

6. **Have the essay questions and model written answers/outlines reviewed.** A content expert can determine their validity.

7. **Eliminate the practice of allowing students to select from among essay items those to which they prefer to respond.** Letting them choose allows students to respond to items they know best, but unfortunately may not accurately measure how well they can actually meet *all* objectives.

8. **Allow enough time for students to organize their answers.** This includes time to outline, write, edit, and rewrite.

9. **Provide written feedback on their responses, particularly for wrong answers.**

Reference

Coker, Donald R., Kilstad, Rosemarie K., and Sosa, Alonzo H. (1988). Improving essay tests. *The Clearing House* 61: 253–255.

Analyzing Learning Tasks

Using the earlier example of the bicycle behavioral objective can help explain how the technique of *task analysis* is related to, and goes beyond, a hierarchical listing of instructional behavioral objectives. Recall that the objective was stated as:

> Given a standard bicycle, to ride the bicycle while pedaling in a sitting position for a distance of 300 yards on a level surface without touching either foot on the surface, within a 3-minute period.

The tasks that a student would be involved in while learning to meet this objective go beyond the behavior stated in the objective. For example, a partial list of tasks that the learner would need to carry out to meet the objective are:

> Grasp the handle bars firmly, with the bike in an upright position.
>
> Place the left foot on the left pedal and push off with the right.
>
> Mount the bike by moving the right leg over the back of the bike so that you are seated.
>
> Place the right foot on the right pedal while coasting.
>
> Pedal by alternatingly pushing one pedal forward and down, then the other.
>
> Steer the bike by moving the handle bars so that the front wheel moves toward either left or right.
>
> Balance by shifting or leaning your weight either left or right.
>
> Stop by pushing down gently on a pedal when it is in the rear position.
>
> Hold the handles firmly while dismounting, by placing your left foot on the ground to stabilize the bike and moving your right leg over the back of the bike and to the ground.

As can be seen, both the objective and the tasks are relevant to the teacher who is responsible for assisting the learner to ride the bike, and both would be important in designing a bike-riding curriculum. The job aid on "Instructional Task Analysis" presents a procedure that is typical. Some instructional developers prefer to run their task analysis *before* writing specific instructional objectives, claiming that the tasks generated can more objectively point toward specific instructional objectives relevant to the instruction. The procedure used here is to work from needs to goals to

---

Job Aid / Instructional Task Analysis

Description   **Instructional task analysis** is a process of identifying, sequencing, and relating the tasks and subtasks that should be performed to meet learning objectives.

Use Rationale   Stating the desired outcomes (objectives) for learning is not enough. The instructional developer needs to know what tasks a learner best completes in the process of meeting the objective. Thus, it is necessary to identify and relate the tasks for meeting each objective.

continued

Instructional Task Analysis, continued

Critical Tasks

1. **Determine the tasks required to meet the behavioral objectives.** E.g., given a set of performance objectives, to ask content and learning specialists to specify, step-by-step, what learners do when they successfully meet each objective, or, alternatively, observe competent individuals meeting the objectives, e.g., time study technique, and list the steps they complete in that process.

2. **Sequence the tasks for all related objectives.** Begin with the tasks that must be accomplished first, and show the other tasks as being either preceding, succeeding, or concurrent in their sequence, e.g., Foshay's computer-program-debugging task hierarchy—see Figure 4.8. Where valid tasks do not relate to any of the objectives, write additional objectives for the instruction.

FIGURE 4.8 / Foshay's computer-program-debugging task hierarchy

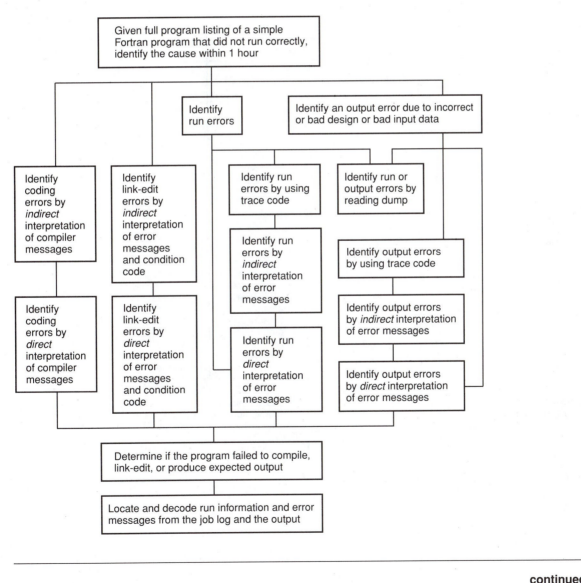

continued

Instructional Task Analysis, continued

3. **Complete task review.** Use people who regularly perform the tasks, to check out the combined sequence of tasks for all related behavioral objectives and to determine whether any tasks or their sequences could be usefully modified, i.e., expanded, collapsed, reworded, deleted, changed in descriptor, etc.

4. **Determine the appropriate learning strategy for each task.** E.g., use Carlisle's learning-strategy decision table to categorize tasks by strategy—see Figure 4.9.

5. **Apply the task analysis findings to generating design specifications for the instruction.**

FIGURE 4.9 / Carlisle's learning-strategy decision table

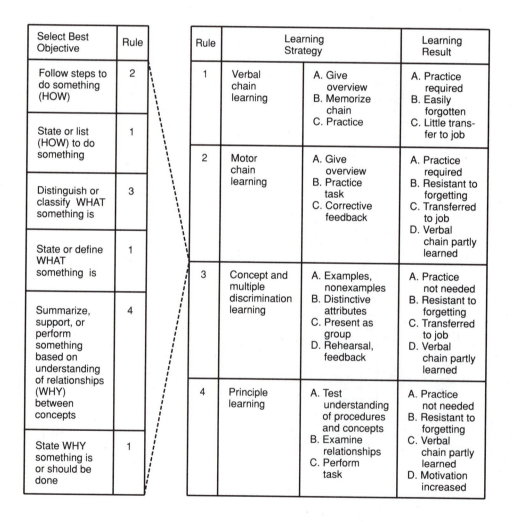

Select Best Objective	Rule
Follow steps to do something (HOW)	2
State or list (HOW) to do something	1
Distinguish or classify WHAT something is	3
State or define WHAT something is	1
Summarize, support, or perform something based on understanding of relationships (WHY) between concepts	4
State WHY something is or should be done	1

Rule	Learning Strategy		Learning Result
1	Verbal chain learning	A. Give overview B. Memorize chain C. Practice	A. Practice required B. Easily forgotten C. Little transfer to job
2	Motor chain learning	A. Give overview B. Practice task C. Corrective feedback	A. Practice required B. Resistant to forgetting C. Transferred to job D. Verbal chain partly learned
3	Concept and multiple discrimination learning	A. Examples, nonexamples B. Distinctive attributes C. Present as group D. Rehearsal, feedback	A. Practice not needed B. Resistant to forgetting C. Transferred to job D. Verbal chain partly learned
4	Principle learning	A. Test understanding of procedures and concepts B. Examine relationships C. Perform task	A. Practice not needed B. Resistant to forgetting C. Verbal chain partly learned D. Motivation increased

continued

Instructional Task Analysis, continued

References

Carlisle, K. E. (1983). The process of task analysis. *Journal of Instructional Development* 6(4): 31–35.

Davies, I. K. (1973). Task analysis: Some process and content concerns. *Audiovisual Communications Review* 21(1): 73–85.

Foshay, W. R. (1983). Alternative methods of task analysis. *Journal of Instructional Development* 6(4): 2–9.

Harmon, Paul (1983). Task analysis: A top-down approach. *Performance and Instruction Journal* 22(4): 14–19.

---

objectives and then to tasks. Either way, additional objectives and tasks tend to surface that otherwise would not if only objectives or only tasks were generated.

Two other techniques useful for deriving and sequencing tasks are the *Program Evaluation and Review Technique (PERT)* and *Analytical Flowcharting* (both presented in Chapter 10). PERT is a graphic system that enables the instructional developer to see the tasks in terms of whether they precede, succeed, or are concurrent with other tasks. One advantage analytical flowcharting has over PERT is that it can include alternative tasks where decision points arise.

Selecting Instructional Strategies

One of the most crucial tasks for the instructional developer is to select appropriate **instructional strategies** for the planned instruction. One important way of doing this is through the use of Gagne's learning conditions. A number of years ago, Robert Gagne wrote a book entitled *Conditions of Learning* (1965), and in it he listed eight major types of learning (signal, stimulus response, motor chaining, verbal association, discrimination, concept, principle, and problem solving). The second thing he did was to determine the necessary (essential) conditions for each of these types of learning to take place. For example, the conditions necessary to *stimulus-response learning,* include ensuring that there is (a) contiguity (closeness in time) between learned response and reinforcement, and (b) repetition of the stimulus situation, and that c) the terminating event results in reinforcement.

These learning types, with their associated conditions, have become important to the instructional developer as a guide to choosing appropriate learning strategies. The first step in the process would be to match the specific objectives for the proposed instruction to Gagne's learning types. Then note the conditions necessary to teach each objective. Potential instructional strategies would then be examined to make sure the necessary conditions were included.

The job aid on "Gagne's Behavioral Hierarchy" shows how instructional developers can use Gagne's learning types and conditions to determine the necessary conditions for their objectives, and how they can then match those conditions to the most appropriate strategies for the planned

Job Aid / Gagne's Behavioral Hierarchy

Description   This technique makes use of the taxonomy of learning types conceptualized by Robert Gagne, for purposes of determining appropriate and cost-effective strategies for teaching the objectives of an instructional unit. In the hierarchy, Gagne describes eight different types of learning. The hierarchy is divided into eight categories, the first four dealing with the simple acquisition of knowledge. The next four are more complex and require in most cases that a combination of one or more earlier categories be known.

Use Rationale   While instruction is far from being a science, educators need to make better use of theory and research based techniques that do exist for solving instructional development problems. Gagne's taxonomy is particularly powerful, in that it can be used to categorize performance objectives by *learning type*, and then to match them up with the attendant *learning conditions* necessary for the behavior. At that point, the learning conditions required can be matched with appropriate instructional strategies that meet the objectives and are cost beneficial.

Critical Tasks

1. **Acquire or develop a set of objectives for an instructional unit.**

2. **Place the objectives into the leftmost column of a matrix.** See Figure 4.10. The objectives will be compared to Gagne's learning types and conditions in columns 2 and 3. Column 4 lists selected instructional strategies that fit the conditions.

3. **Determine into which of the following learning types each of the performance objectives falls**:

   Signal learning—involuntary response to a signal, e.g., Pavlov's dog taught to salivate at the sound of a dinner bell, as a result of pairing the sound of the bell with food.

   Stimulus-response learning—voluntary response to a signal, e.g., pushing off of the starter block at the sound of the starter's gun.

   Motor-chaining learning—the linking of a series of stimulus-response motor behaviors, e.g., performing a predetermined sequence of steps in a tumbling routine.

FIGURE 4.10 / Example data matrix for performance objectives using Gagne's learning types and conditions

Objectives	Learning Type	Essential Conditions	Strategies
To correctly label a randomly ordered set of rocks	Discrimination	• Necessary chains learned • Stimuli presented one by one • Repetition between like stimuli • Correct response confirmed	• Practice • Feedback

continued

Gagne's Behavioral Hierarchy, continued

Verbal association learning—the linking of a series of stimulus-response verbal behaviors, e.g., memorizing the rules of etiquette.

Multiple-discrimination learning—choosing among a class of possible responses, e.g., identifying a cloud by its type.

Concept learning—classifying stimuli in terms of abstract characteristics, e.g., selecting from a group of geometric shapes, all which are oval.

Principle learning—combining two or more concepts to form a rule, e.g., "Liquids solidify when heat is removed from them."

Problem-solving learning—combining old rules into new rules, e.g., generating rules of fair play based on rules of jurisprudence.

4. **In the second column of the matrix, indicate which learning conditions are appropriate for each of the performance objectives.** This should be based on the conditions listed for each of the types, as follows:

Signal Learning Conditions

a. Contiguity of two stimuli, i.e., they must occur at about the same time.

b. Repetition of paired stimuli, e.g., the sound of a bell and the eating of food paired over several days.

Stimulus-Response Learning Conditions

a. Contiguity between learned response and reinforcement, i.e., the two occur at about the same time.

b. Repetition of the stimulus situation.

c. The terminating event should result in reinforcement.

Motor-Chaining Learning Conditions

a. Each individual stimulus-response (s-r) link must be previously learned.

b. Get the learner to reinstate the individual s-r links in the proper order.

c. Each s-r link must receive some kinesthetic feedback from the preceding response.

d. There is repetition for purpose of extinguishing residual incorrect connections.

e. The terminating act should lead to satisfaction, that is, a reinforcing state of affairs.

Verbal Association Learning Conditions

a. Each individual verbal s-r link must be previously learned.

b. Mediating connections between each verbal s-r link is previously learned.

c. Verbal s-r links are presented in proper sequence.

d. The learner actively responds, to generate kinesthetic stimuli that become part of the next succeeding link.

e. Provision is made for confirmation of the correct response.

Multiple-Discrimination Learning Conditions

a. Each of the motor or verbal chains to be discriminated must have been previously learned in isolation of the others.

b. The entire *set* of stimuli that are to be associated must be presented to the learner, one by one.

continued

Gagne's Behavioral Hierarchy, continued

   c. There is repetition to overcome generalization between similar stimuli.

   d. The correct terminal response must be confirmed or reinforced.

Concept Learning Conditions

   a. A set of verbal or motor chains that exhibit characteristics of the class must have been previously learned.

   b. Previously learned individual chains representative of the concept are presented in sequence, one at a time, so that unifying characteristics are clear.

   c. A *novel* stimulus situation is presented to ensure that the learner recognized the distinguishing characteristics.

   d. The response to *novel* instances of the concept is reinforced or confirmed.

Principle Learning Conditions

   a. Concepts that make up the principle were previously learned.

   b. The learner is aware of the expected terminal performance.

   c. Component concepts are invoked through instruction.

   d. Verbal cues for the principle *as a whole* are given.

   e. Verbal questions are given asking the learner to demonstrate the principle.

   f. There is contiguity between component concepts and verbal cues.

   g. There is immediate reinforcement when the terminal act is reached.

Problem-Solving Learning Conditions

   a. The learner recalls relevant principles previously learned.

   b. Contiguity of principles is used to solve a problem.

   c. The learner is informed of the goal of the activity.

   d. The learner must discover the *higher-order principle* without specific verbal help.

5. From a list of instructional strategies, select out those that are possible candidates, based on their containing the learning conditions necessary to the objectives. See Figure 4.11.

6. Compare alternative strategies in terms of time, skill, and cost factors. (*Cost-Benefit Analysis* is a common procedure for accomplishing the task. See Chapter 3.)

FIGURE 4.11 / Example list of instructional strategies

---

lecture	lab work
tutoring	homework
discussion	stimulation
practice	seminar
independent study	study groups
self-instruction	team work
individualized instruction	

---

continued

Gagne's Behavioral Hierarchy, continued

7. Select the cost-beneficial strategies fitting your circumstances for each of the objectives.
It is possible, in some cases, that one strategy will fit all of the unit objectives, but that is rare. More likely, a combination of strategies will be required.

References

Gagne, Robert M. (1965). *The Conditions of Learning.* New York: Holt, Reinhart & Winston.

Gagne, Robert M. (1970). *The Conditions of Learning.* 2d ed. New York: Holt, Reinhart & Winston.

Gagne, Robert M. (1985). *The Conditions of Learning.* 4th ed. New York: Holt, Reinhart & Winston.

---

instruction. Over the years there have been several editions of Gagne's important book. The job aid was written from an earlier edition, and although the learning categories have changed somewhat, all of the ideas are still relevant. (Note: there has been no attempt to update job aids in this and other chapters of the book to conform to more recent works, unless a technique has been significantly changed.)

Selecting Instructional Media

Media is a term that is somewhat confused in the literature and in the popular press. For our purposes, **media** will be defined as the means by which messages are communicated. An example of a medium (singular of *media*) would be a live teacher who uses voice and nonverbal expressions to present instructional messages to her class. She may also use other media as adjuncts to her instruction, including chalkboard, overhead transparency, filmstrip, slide/tape, film, and video. Another example could be the use of computer-assisted instruction, where the computer and its monitor serve to present electronically stored messages to the students. The computer program may include the capability of pulling messages from other media, such as laser videodiscs.

Instructional messages can be viewed as equivalent to specific instructional content. This means we are talking about the actual words or graphics used, whether presented by the teacher or a book. The words and the pictures in a book are the messages, or content, of that book. The covers, pages, and binding are the means for presenting the messages, or content. These make up the medium, or the means by which the message is delivered.

One of the more complete techniques for relating objectives to strategies and media is the strategy and media selection technique developed by Merrill and Goodman, an adapted version of which is presented in the job aid. The technique as presented here is considerably shortened from the original work, with some steps collapsed and others excluded. In their original version, Merrill and Goodman provide extended explanation, examples, and opportunities to practice.

Job Aid / Merrill and Goodman Strategy and Media Selection Technique

Description   This technique uses variations on the individual taxonomies of Bloom, Krathwohl, and Gagne. As a first step, instructional designers use a menu to categorize objectives as being in the cognitive, psychomotor, or affective domain. This decision routes users to one of three submenus, where they match the objective with the appropriate instructional strategy for that domain. Then they are guided through the process of writing an instructional strategy prescription, which includes the elements of presentation, practice, and evaluation. Finally, an additional submenu is consulted to make media decisions for the specific strategies chosen. A specific format is used for writing strategy and media prescriptions (see Figures 4.23 and 4.24).

Use Rationale   Often, design of instruction is done intuitively or learned from the designer's teachers. This frequently means use of the "shot-gun" approach, where everything that a designer thinks might work is included in the instruction. A more efficient approach is Merrill's and Goodman's technique for selecting instructional strategies and media. It is tied to a logical and testable scheme, well supported by what is known about the psychology of learning. Further, instructional designers are able to justify their decisions and are better able to find errors in the system once the instruction is implemented.

continued

Merrill and Goodman Strategy and Media Selection Technique, continued

Critical Tasks

1. **Match the objectives with their appropriate domains.** Use the Merrill/Goodman menu, i.e., Figure 4.12, to determine whether the objective is affective, psychomotor, or cognitive.

FIGURE 4.12 / Determining the appropriate domain for an objective

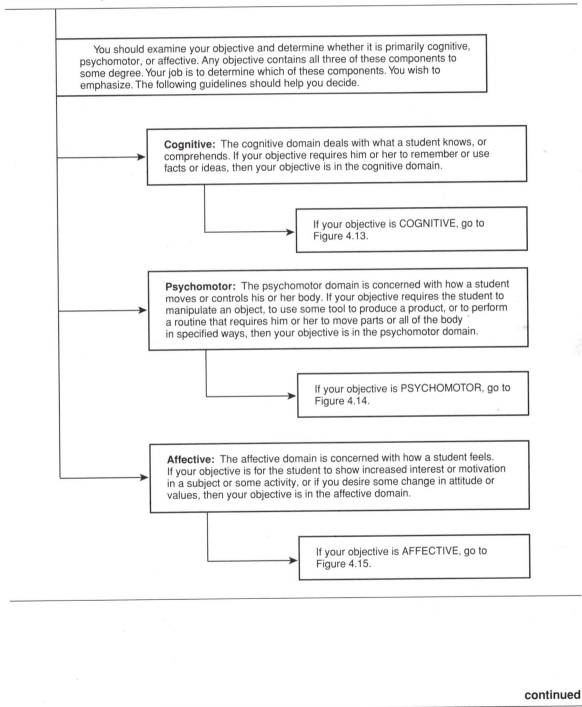

You should examine your objective and determine whether it is primarily cognitive, psychomotor, or affective. Any objective contains all three of these components to some degree. Your job is to determine which of these components. You wish to emphasize. The following guidelines should help you decide.

Cognitive: The cognitive domain deals with what a student knows, or comprehends. If your objective requires him or her to remember or use facts or ideas, then your objective is in the cognitive domain.

If your objective is COGNITIVE, go to Figure 4.13.

Psychomotor: The psychomotor domain is concerned with how a student moves or controls his or her body. If your objective requires the student to manipulate an object, to use some tool to produce a product, or to perform a routine that requires him or her to move parts or all of the body in specified ways, then your objective is in the psychomotor domain.

If your objective is PSYCHOMOTOR, go to Figure 4.14.

Affective: The affective domain is concerned with how a student feels. If your objective is for the student to show increased interest or motivation in a subject or some activity, or if you desire some change in attitude or values, then your objective is in the affective domain.

If your objective is AFFECTIVE, go to Figure 4.15.

continued

Merrill and Goodman Strategy and Media Selection Technique, continued

2. **Go to the appropriate submenu for a specific domain.** There is a submenu for each of the three domains that list the possible strategies for each domain and describe the acts and conditions for each. See Figures 4.13 through 4.15.

FIGURE 4.13 / Selecting the appropriate instructional strategy from the Cognitive domain

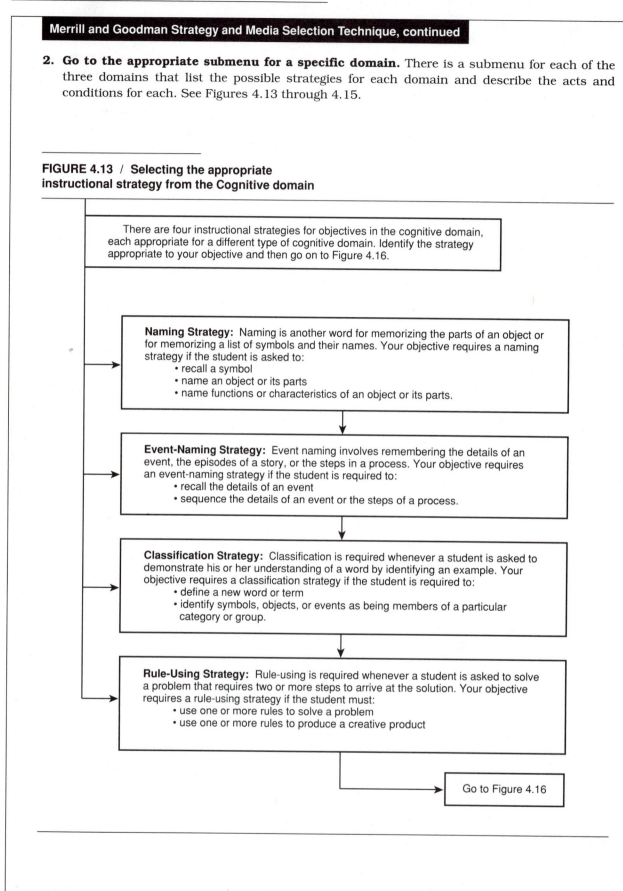

There are four instructional strategies for objectives in the cognitive domain, each appropriate for a different type of cognitive domain. Identify the strategy appropriate to your objective and then go on to Figure 4.16.

Naming Strategy: Naming is another word for memorizing the parts of an object or for memorizing a list of symbols and their names. Your objective requires a naming strategy if the student is asked to:
- recall a symbol
- name an object or its parts
- name functions or characteristics of an object or its parts.

Event-Naming Strategy: Event naming involves remembering the details of an event, the episodes of a story, or the steps in a process. Your objective requires an event-naming strategy if the student is required to:
- recall the details of an event
- sequence the details of an event or the steps of a process.

Classification Strategy: Classification is required whenever a student is asked to demonstrate his or her understanding of a word by identifying an example. Your objective requires a classification strategy if the student is required to:
- define a new word or term
- identify symbols, objects, or events as being members of a particular category or group.

Rule-Using Strategy: Rule-using is required whenever a student is asked to solve a problem that requires two or more steps to arrive at the solution. Your objective requires a rule-using strategy if the student must:
- use one or more rules to solve a problem
- use one or more rules to produce a creative product

Go to Figure 4.16

continued

Merrill and Goodman Strategy and Media Selection Technique, continued

3. **Match the objective with its appropriate strategy from the domain submenu.** E.g., in the cognitive domain submenu, the possible strategies are: naming, event naming, classification, and rule using.

FIGURE 4.14 / Selecting the appropriate instructional strategy from the psychomotor domain

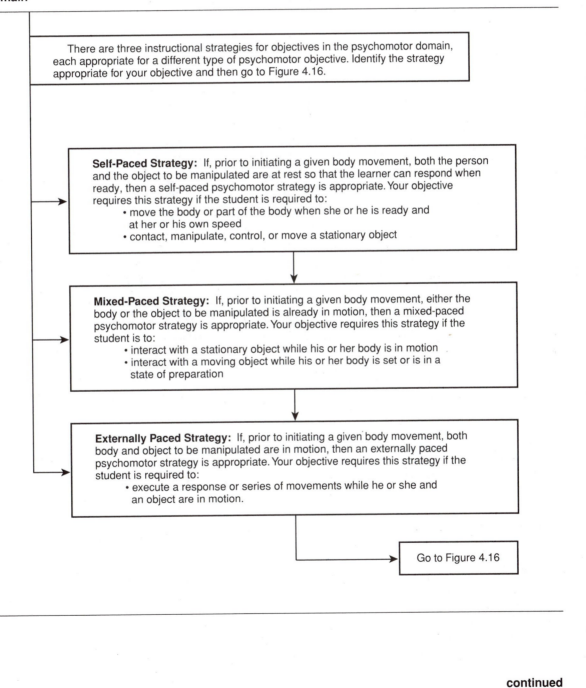

There are three instructional strategies for objectives in the psychomotor domain, each appropriate for a different type of psychomotor objective. Identify the strategy appropriate for your objective and then go to Figure 4.16.

Self-Paced Strategy: If, prior to initiating a given body movement, both the person and the object to be manipulated are at rest so that the learner can respond when ready, then a self-paced psychomotor strategy is appropriate. Your objective requires this strategy if the student is required to:
- move the body or part of the body when she or he is ready and at her or his own speed
- contact, manipulate, control, or move a stationary object

Mixed-Paced Strategy: If, prior to initiating a given body movement, either the body or the object to be manipulated is already in motion, then a mixed-paced psychomotor strategy is appropriate. Your objective requires this strategy if the student is to:
- interact with a stationary object while his or her body is in motion
- interact with a moving object while his or her body is set or is in a state of preparation

Externally Paced Strategy: If, prior to initiating a given body movement, both body and object to be manipulated are in motion, then an externally paced psychomotor strategy is appropriate. Your objective requires this strategy if the student is required to:
- execute a response or series of movements while he or she and an object are in motion.

Go to Figure 4.16

continued

Merrill and Goodman Strategy and Media Selection Technique, continued

FIGURE 4.15 / Selecting the appropriate instructional strategy from the affective domain

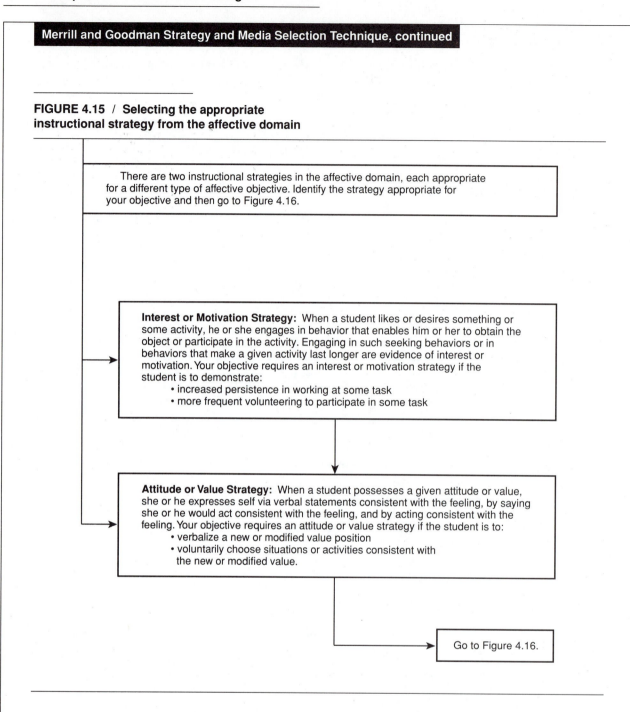

There are two instructional strategies in the affective domain, each appropriate for a different type of affective objective. Identify the strategy appropriate for your objective and then go to Figure 4.16.

Interest or Motivation Strategy: When a student likes or desires something or some activity, he or she engages in behavior that enables him or her to obtain the object or participate in the activity. Engaging in such seeking behaviors or in behaviors that make a given activity last longer are evidence of interest or motivation. Your objective requires an interest or motivation strategy if the student is to demonstrate:
- increased persistence in working at some task
- more frequent volunteering to participate in some task

Attitude or Value Strategy: When a student possesses a given attitude or value, she or he expresses self via verbal statements consistent with the feeling, by saying she or he would act consistent with the feeling, and by acting consistent with the feeling. Your objective requires an attitude or value strategy if the student is to:
- verbalize a new or modified value position
- voluntarily choose situations or activities consistent with the new or modified value.

Go to Figure 4.16.

4. **Study the three parts of a strategy prescription.** See Figure 4.16. These are: evaluation, practice, and presentation.

5. **Write the evaluation part of the strategy prescription.** See Figure 4.17. Describe the test format, the administration and scoring procedures, and any other special procedures.

continued

Merrill and Goodman Strategy and Media Selection Technique, continued

FIGURE 4.16 / Writing a strategy prescription

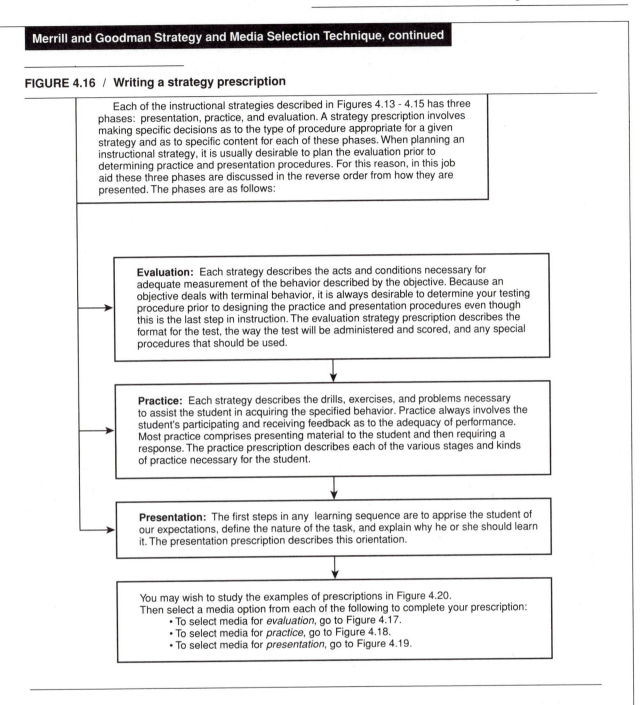

Each of the instructional strategies described in Figures 4.13 - 4.15 has three phases: presentation, practice, and evaluation. A strategy prescription involves making specific decisions as to the type of procedure appropriate for a given strategy and as to specific content for each of these phases. When planning an instructional strategy, it is usually desirable to plan the evaluation prior to determining practice and presentation procedures. For this reason, in this job aid these three phases are discussed in the reverse order from how they are presented. The phases are as follows:

Evaluation: Each strategy describes the acts and conditions necessary for adequate measurement of the behavior described by the objective. Because an objective deals with terminal behavior, it is always desirable to determine your testing procedure prior to designing the practice and presentation procedures even though this is the last step in instruction. The evaluation strategy prescription describes the format for the test, the way the test will be administered and scored, and any special procedures that should be used.

Practice: Each strategy describes the drills, exercises, and problems necessary to assist the student in acquiring the specified behavior. Practice always involves the student's participating and receiving feedback as to the adequacy of performance. Most practice comprises presenting material to the student and then requiring a response. The practice prescription describes each of the various stages and kinds of practice necessary for the student.

Presentation: The first steps in any learning sequence are to apprise the student of our expectations, define the nature of the task, and explain why he or she should learn it. The presentation prescription describes this orientation.

You may wish to study the examples of prescriptions in Figure 4.20.
Then select a media option from each of the following to complete your prescription:
• To select media for *evaluation*, go to Figure 4.17.
• To select media for *practice*, go to Figure 4.18.
• To select media for *presentation*, go to Figure 4.19.

6. **Write the practice part of the strategy prescription.** See Figure 4.18. This usually involves presenting material to a student that requires a response and feedback as to adequacy of response. This part describes the kinds of practice necessary for a student to reach competence.

7. **Write the presentation part of the strategy prescription.** Orient students as to what is expected, the nature of the task, and why it should be learned, and describe the media for teaching the task. See Figure 4.19.

8. **Place the strategy and media prescriptions in appropriate format.** See Figure 4.20.

continued

Merrill and Goodman Strategy and Media Selection Technique, continued

FIGURE 4.17 / Evaluating student performance

1. In the leftmost column, locate the learning strategy you previously selected. **2.** Consider how objects, still and motion pictures, audio media, and written materials can best be used alone or mixed. **3.** Repeat the process for "Providing for Student Practice" in Figure 4.18.

Learning Strategy	Objects	Still Pictures
Naming	To name an object or its parts, show real things or have students write or tell its name, its parts, or its functions.	If the object is inaccessible and can be adequately represented with still pictures, have students examine the pictures and write or tell names of the object, its parts, or its functions.
Event naming	If objects are a critical part of the event, display them and have students describe their relationship to the event or arrange them in sequence.	If an event can be presented via still pictures, provide a series for students to name, arrange in order, or use to illustrate relationships.
Classification	If the concept involves things, present students with a number of actual objects or models they haven't seen before and have them identify the class to which they belong.	If a concept can be represented with pictures, have students identify pictures of the actual object or event, and pictures of other objects or events. Pictures illustrate relevant attributes of the concept.
Rule using	If using the rule requires tools or production of some object from raw materials, provide students with the objects needed to show the rule or procedure.	If the application of the rule could be shown by pictures, ask students to select and arrange in sequence pictures showing the application of the rule.
Self-paced	When a student is to move his or her body or manipulate a still object, he or she must have suitable objects to perform with, under the conditions specified.	Still pictures are not usually appropriate for evaluation of this behavior. Photographs (especially polaroid) of the student's own performance may provide some feedback.
Mixed pace or Externally paced	Have the student perform with the required objects under the conditions specified in the objective.	Still pictures might be used for feedback, but are usually less effective than videotape or motion pictures.
Interest or Motivation	When assessing students' interest toward lone objects, observe their free choice, use, or study of certain type of objects, if available with other objects.	If still pictures could effectively display the object or situation of concern, have students rank in order of preference a series of still pictures of objects, events, or situations.

Motion Pictures	Audio Media	Written Words and Symbols
If motion is a critical feature or function to be named, show film clips of the object engaged in its function and ask the student to write or tell the name of the object, its parts, or its function.	If sounds are to be named, provide recorded or live sounds in different order than that practiced, and have the student name each sound. Recorded audio can be used to provide directions for assessing the use of other media.	If written words or symbols are to be named or associated with other words or symbols, or the students are asked to name a passage or symbolic statement, have students either write or orally recite the memorized material.
Since many events involve linkages or human actions, the best depiction is often a dramatization shown through motion picture or videotape. Present critical portions of such motion pictures for the student to identify or sequence.	If a key feature of an event is some type of sound, or if dramatic audio portrayal of events can provide critical information, have students name or sequence the event in recorded or live audio presentations.	If the event can be dramatized through the use of written words, provide students with written descriptions or narrations, and have them name the event, describe relationships, or order episodes in sequence.
If motion or time-space relationships are relevant attributes of a concept, have students view filmed examples and nonexamples of the object or event and then identify the examples.	If the concept is a sound or voice, or if critical attributes require dramatic portrayal, have students identify audio examples and like-sounding nonexamples.	If the concept is abstract or symbolic in nature, present written materials and descriptions and have students pick out the examples from a series that also includes nonexamples.
If rule use involves motion, have students view a short sequence of a motion picture and describe the use of the rule in the situation depicted. Actually using a rule usually provides for more adequate evaluation.	If rule use involves audio, play relevant audiotape, and have students identify the correct use of the rule. Actual use of a rule usually provides for better evaluation.	If the rule involves control of written or symbolic material, present a problem and have students apply appropriate operations to produce the answer or solution.
Motion pictures would be of value primarily for feedback. Videotape has advantage over motion pictures because of the more immediate feedback.	Recorded or live audio directions are often necessary to initiate evaluation. Recorded feedback may be useful to students.	Provide each judge with a checklist for evaluating psychomotor performance. Don't use written tests.
Motion pictures and videotape can provide valuable feedback for student.	Verbal cues are sometimes required to initiate action. Recorded feedback is sometimes useful.	Provide judges with a checklist for evaluating performance. Written tests usually are inadequate.
If motion pictures are effective in presenting an event or situation, have students view a film and then use interest scales to rate their interest in the event, situations, or behavior illustrated.	If the subject of the objective is either natural or man-made sounds, give students an opportunity to listen to a variety of tapes and records, including the subject of interest. Note the kinds of materials listened to.	If ideas you are concerned with are abstract, and words may be useful in assessing interest in them, have students use a scale to rate the statements and descriptions, to express their interest orally or in writing, or to sequence them according to interest.

continued

Merrill and Goodman Strategy and Media Selection Technique, continued

---

FIGURE 4.18 / Providing for student practice

---

1. In the leftmost column, locate the learning strategy you previously selected. **2.** Considering your objective and learning strategy, note how objects, still and motion pictures, audio media, and written materials can best be used either alone or in combination. **3.** Repeat the process for "Presenting Information" in Figure 4.19.

Learning Strategy	Objects	Still Pictures
Naming	If naming involves an object, parts of an object, or its function, make the objects available for repeated practice. Provide feedback to students.	If the object is inaccessible and can be shown by still pictures, provide unlabeled pictures for individual study. After students respond, give them the name so they can check their response. Provide repeated opportunities to name the pictures until the criterion is reached.
Event naming	If objects are important element of the event, make them available during practice to stimulate recall of episodes in the event or for practice in sequential arrangement. Provide feedback.	If episodes of an event or specific relationship can be effectively shown through still pictures, provide a series of pictures and have students practice arranging events and describing relationships between separate pictures, or have students order the pictures in the correct sequence of the event or process. Provide feedback.
Classification	If a concept consists of actual objects, supply a variety of both easy and hard examples for students to practice identifying.	If actual objects are inaccessible and if motion isn't required, still pictures could be used. Provide students with a series of pictures of the object or event along with a number of nonexamples.
Rule using	If the rule involves the use of objects, provide either objects necessary to practice the use of the rule or materials necessary to construct something using the rule.	If the rule can be illustrated with pictures, provide a series of still pictures calling for the use of a specified rule. Require students to apply the rule and to describe the steps they went through in using it.
Self-paced	Provide the required objects to be manipulated.	Display still pictures of the key points of the skill for students to use in analyzing and correcting their own performance.
Mixed pace or Externally paced	Use special objects to assist in simplifying the task and slowing its pace during initial practice. Final practice with required objects should be under real-world conditions.	Polaroid pictures may be used for feedback, or still pictures may be used to illustrate key aspects of the performance. Slow motion or stop action is usually better, if available.
Interest or Motivation	When developing interest in objects, display apt objects and models for each student. Provide written or taped descriptions.	If still pictures usefully depict the objects or events, provide a display of pictures dealing with the subject for individual study. Change display often.

Motion Pictures	Audio Media	Written Words and Symbols
If motion is an important feature of the object or parts of the object, provide film clips for naming practice. Repeated practice with feedback is essential.	If the objective calls for naming sounds, use audiotape or live sound, speech, or music. On audiotape, present sound, allow response time, then provide the correct name. Mix the order of sounds to reduce hidden hints.	If the objects to be named are written words or symbols, provide repeated practice with these words and symbols, in mixed order. Provide feedback.
If linkages between parts of an event are important, or if dramatization is needed, provide film clips and have students name the events depicted and describe the relationships to other parts of the event. Students should indicate the proper sequence of events. Provide feedback.	If sound is an important feature of the event, or if the event can be adequately shown by narration or dramatization, play an audiotape or make a live presentation. Have students name or sequence critical episodes. Provide feedback.	If an event can be adequately described by narration or dramatization, present such written materials and have students practice naming them or arranging the steps of the process in sequence. Provide feedback.
If motion is a relevant attribute or critical time-space linkages are involved, use film loops showing a variety of examples and nonexamples of the object/event.	If a type of sound is a critical attribute of the concept, provide audiotape with examples and nonexamples of sounds to be classified.	If a concept is abstract or symbolic, make available a variety of descriptions or symbol examples and nonexamples to provide classification practice.
If the application of the rule involves motion or takes place in real time, use motion pictures to present situations to students to analyze and describe specific application of the rule.	If the situation involves sounds that may be dramatically portrayed through audio, provide audiotaped situations requiring use of specific rules. Have students record dialog showing the correct use of the rule for a subject.	If the rule requires symbol manipulation, provide short, written situations or problems and have students apply the rule, listing the steps involved. They describe in writing a use of the rule in a specified situation.
Use videotape or motion picture to provide feedback.	Audio feedback, though less desirable than visual feedback, is better than no feedback at all.	Provide a checklist for students to use in practice, and remind them of key points for judging their skill level.
Normal- and slow-speed motion pictures and videotapes could be taken of performance to provide feedback to students.	Provide audio feedback with or in lieu of motion picture or videotape feedback. By itself, audio feedback is usually not sufficient.	Students use performance checklists so they can keep relevant cues in mind during practice.
Use motion pictures to show value and arouse interest in the subject. Let the students choose.	Use live or recorded resource people to raise interest in a subject.	To facilitate abstract writing, provide optional reading material.

continued

Merrill and Goodman Strategy and Media Selection Technique, continued

FIGURE 4.19 / Presenting information

1. In the leftmost column, locate the learning strategy you previously selected. 2. Considering your objective and learning strategy, note how objects, still and motion pictures, audio media, and written materials can best be used either alone or in combination.

Strategy	Objects	Still Pictures
Naming	If the objective specifies the naming of objects or parts, display the objects. The student names the objects, their features, and their functions.	If still pictures are used to present objects, display pictures and point to the objects or parts, name them, and describe their features and functions.
Event naming	Display objects connected with a specific event, explain how objects relate to it. Develop student interest in objects by describing and illustrating their use.	Display a series of still pictures showing the specific event, episode, relationship, or sequence. Provide names, and discuss the relationships and the sequence so the events occur as illustrated by the pictures.
Classification	If the concept is an object, display a variety of examples and nonexamples and point out relevant attributes.	If the concept is an inaccessible object or an event, display a series of pictures of the object or event while pointing out relevant characteristics.
Rule using	If the rule involves the use of an object, show the use of objects through the use of the rule, or demonstrate construction of something using the rule.	If use of the rule can be presented via still pictures, display a series of pictures showing the steps involved in using the specific rule. Also illustrate results of misapplying the rule.
Self-paced	While demonstrating a skill, point out the relevant cues and indicate performance criterion.	Project or display a series of still pictures showing key points of the skill. Make picture sets available with written or tape-recorded commentary for individual use.
Mixed pace or Externally paced	While demonstrating the skill in normal and slow motion, point out the relevant cues and indicate the criterion for performance.	Project or display a series of still pictures showing key points of the skill. Make picture sets available with written or tape-recorded commentary for individual use.
Interest or Motivation	If you are trying to develop interest in certain types of objects, display the objects in the classroom or take students to where the objects are located in the natural environment.	If still pictures can clearly illustrate the object or event, use them in class to illustrate a discussion in which you encourage interest in a particular thing or behavior. Make the pictures and an audiotape discussion available for individual student use.

Motion Pictures	Audio Media	Written Words and Symbols
If the object or part of the object is to be viewed in motion, show motion pictures or film clips while verbally naming objects or parts and describing their function and characteristics.	If an audio stimulus is to be named, present sound or voice and tell students its name and describe its characteristics.	If written words and symbols are to be named or associated with other words and symbols, provide the name or association while displaying the word or symbol.
If motion or a dramatic portrayal is required, used film clips showing specific events, episodes, linkages, or sequence. Also give names, descriptions, or sequence of steps.	If specific sounds are an important part of the event, use recorded or live presentation of required sounds. They should be presented as vividly as possible and with names and descriptions.	If the event would most efficiently be illustrated through written words, recount the event and provide statements that will motivate students to practice.
If motion is a relevant attribute of the object or if dramatic portrayal of the event is important, provide motion pictures or film clips for student viewing. Point to relevant features.	If sounds are relevant attributes of the concept, have students listen to either live or recorded examples of sounds and nonexamples. Point out differences between them.	If the concept is abstract and could adequately be presented with written materials, provide examples and nonexamples in the form of short, written descriptions or situations.
If application of a rule involves motion or is best shown in a dramatic situation, use film loops or sections of films to show the steps in applying the rule.	If the use of the rule could be shown with audio, then record conversations, using dramatic situations and/or descriptions that show use of the rule.	If the use of the rule involves mathematical or other symbols, provide short, written situations or problems showing step-by-step application of the rule.
Use stop action, slow motion, and normal speed, provide short film parts demonstrating the skill.	Point out key points, and offer performance tips during demonstration or viewing of still and motion pictures of the skill.	Provide descriptive materials for motivation, and make available performance checklists during the demonstrations.
Use films or film clips that have stop motion, slow motion, and normal speed while pointing out relevant cues and criteria.	During a demonstration or while using still or motion pictures to show the use of a skill, note the key points, and offer performance tips.	Provide checklists for students to use while they are observing the demonstration of the skill.
Locate one or more motion pictures showing an exciting example of the subject, and use it in class or make it available on individual-student basis.	Share your own excitement and that of resource people for the subject in class and on audiotape. If the subject is primarily audio, play recordings of materials as you discuss them.	If the subject is abstract and could be presented with written material, provide descriptions and examples for individual study.

continued

Merrill and Goodman Strategy and Media Selection Technique, continued

FIGURE 4.20 / Strategy and media prescriptions example for a cognitive objective

1. Write your *objective:*

   Audience: The junior high school science student
   Behavior: Will label clouds as being cirrus, stratus, cumulus, or nimbus
   Conditions: When shown actual cloud formations or pictures of them
   Degree: Be 100% correct on easy examples and at least 50% correct on more difficult
                 or ambiguous examples

2. The *domain* is: cognitive
3. The *appropriate strategy* is: classification
4. Write your *strategy prescription*:

Comments

Presentation

Objective: Tell the student he or she is going to learn to identify different types of clouds.

Show a set of four pictures, one of each type. Name each type. Show line drawings that emphasize relevant characteristics. List the characteristics of each type.

Explain how cloud types help with weather prediction.

Practice

Practice	Display	Feedback	Display
Picture	Picture	Drawing	Drawing

A set of 20 pictures, each of a different kind of cloud. Across the page a set of line drawings emphasizing the relevant features.

Response: Appropriate cloud type.

Directions: Name each type of cloud. Tell why the name is appropriate by pointing out distinctive characteristics. "After your responses, I'll show you a drawing to help you distinguish the features."

Evaluation

Display: Pictures of clouds (1-2-3-type)

Picture	Picture	Drawing	Drawing
1	2	3	4

(not used during class)

Response: Write name of cloud type.

Directions: You will be shown some pictures of cloud formation. Write the type of cloud pictured opposite the number on your answer sheet.

Criteria: The test should contain at least 12 pictures. Four of the items are very difficult to discriminate.

continued

Merrill and Goodman Strategy and Media Selection Technique, continued

5. Prescribe the media you will use:

Presentation

The teacher projects slides showing examples and nonexamples of each of the clouds listed. The use of two slide projectors at the same time would be helpful to show contrasting examples and non-examples. Project slides onto the chalkboard. Using chalk, trace the distinguishing characteristics on the chalkboard.

For individual study, students could view a slide set that presents a number of examples and nonexamples of each of the four types of clouds and then discuss the distinguishing characteristics. A number of slides of each cloud could also be provided for practice.

Practice

Allow students to work individually with slides and flat pictures of clouds. Slides could be numbered and then used with a printed key containing the name of each of the clouds so the students can check their identifications.

Evaluation

Present a series of 35mm slides of mounted flat pictures the student hasn't seen before. Use both easy and difficult examples. Have students write the names of each of the clouds on a response sheet.

Comments

35mm color slides would provide an inexpensive means of displaying high-quality color representation of clouds for prolonged study.

The use of the chalkboard provides a means of isolating relevant characteristics.

The audiotape would be used to direct attention to the distinguishing characteristics of the four types of clouds illustrated in the slides.

The one critical element here is to be sure the student hasn't previously viewed the pictures used.

Reference

Merrill, M. D., and Goodman, R. I. (1972). *Selecting Instructional Strategies and Media.* Washington, D.C.: National Special Media Institutes, pp. 2–13, 109–115, 138–139.

During initial development, some instructional developers prefer to use a "quick-and-dirty" technique that forms and tests a prototype that roughly approximates the final product. The formative testing of this rough prototype can make clear where the design specifications are in error. This process is repeated until an acceptable prototype emerges. The importance of using this technique lies in its capability of surfacing, early on, any problems that may need solving, or of making clear what additional elements need to be added to the instruction. If the instructional developer followed a set of finished design specifications, major problems or inadequacies might not be discovered until too late to make major changes without significant loss of time and/or extensive revision costs. The Rapid Prototype Development job aid provides direction for carrying out this technique.

Job Aid / Rapid Prototype Development

Description This technique is similar to other systematic design procedures, except its initial designs are considered tentative rather than final. Use of this technique assumes that the basic components needed to make up the trial prototype are available or that they can be rapidly generated in an acceptable form from existing materials. The initial establishment of the goals for the particular instruction is done with the usual care, but the determination of how to meet those goals at this point is more intuitively and experientially based than would be the case for more traditional ID models. The instructional designer, based on intuition and experience, draws up a design hypothesis for meeting the instructional goal, and rapidly brings together the components as a trial prototype. The trial prototype is tested (formative evaluation) to determine how viable it is, if at all. If viable, it is used; if not, a new design hypothesis is generated and a new prototype is rapidly created, tested, and judged for suitability. This continues until an acceptable prototype results.

Use Rationale Design is a very complex and unpredictable task, and the necessary knowledge for the most appropriate design is rarely available and never complete, so any design choice is going to be selective, subjective, and constraining. The usual procedure of systematic design models sets the design at the time it is completed, and it may not be until a year later that any products of that design are tested. Because of the resources invested by that time, it becomes very difficult to desert the initial design, so that practice limits revision to the existing design. Rapid prototype development avoids this problem by getting testable, trial prototypes developed quickly, with minimal commitment of resources.

Critical Tasks

1. **Complete the generation and prioritization of goals.** See the Needs Analysis component in Chapter 2.

2. **Generate a design hypothesis for the trial prototype.** Using your best judgment, generate a list of the elements to go into the rough instructional package, and determine how they may best be combined. You might use the *Brainstorming* technique among a sample of instructional developers to collect data.

3. **Retrieve and adapt any existing prototype elements.** Base this on the design hypothesis, e.g., instructional video segments, simulations, games, print material.

4. **Generate any elements still needed that don't currently exist.** These will usually be done at very low cost, in a rough but adequate form.

5. **Assemble prototype elements, based on the design hypothesis.** This usually requires the generation of some materials to interface the elements, e.g., student workbook or activity direction sheets.

continued

Rapid Prototype Development, continued

6. **Formatively evaluate the prototype.** Use two to five representative learners. The *One-On-One Formative Evaluation* technique works well. Keep careful notes on any problems arising, and jot down any solutions that occur to you.

7. **Analyze the data from the formative evaluation.** Study the problems and their possible solutions as they relate to the design hypothesis.

8. **Make a decision whether to continue with the current design hypothesis.** If evaluation is negative, repeat steps 2–7 until evaluation is positive. If results are mixed but require that some elements be modified, repeat steps 3–7. If evaluation is positive, go on to step 9.

9. **Generate detailed design specifications.** Base them on the results of the positive formative evaluation.

10. **Send the revised design specifications to the production unit.** They will produce polished elements for the instruction. Specifications could be in the form of storyboards, lesson plans, tables of specifications, etc.

Reference

Tripp, Steven D., and Bichelmeyer, Barbara (1990). Rapid prototyping: An alternative instructional design strategy. *Educational Technology Research and Development* 38(1): 31–44.

Completing Cost–Effectiveness Comparisons

Usually, there will be more than one strategy/media combination which is capable of delivering instruction satisfactorily for any one objective. There will always be resource constraints on the development of instruction, so at some point it is wise to see how well what has been designed fits budget realities. Usually, it will be necessary to make trade-offs among the variables affecting instructional development (e.g., between cost and time). A technique for comparing alternative instructional designs in terms of resource requirements is the *Cost–Effectiveness Technique*. This technique's description and job aid were presented in detail as Cost–benefit analysis in Chapter 3.

Formalizing Design Specifications

An architect's specifications for a specific housing design are called *blueprints*. Blueprints are sets of exact specifications that provide the information needed by the different artisans working on the various elements of the house. Similarly, an instructional designer must provide the necessary design specifications to those who will actually produce the instructional prototype. These specifications are provided in a number of different formats, depending on the particular instructional element. Examples of such formats are lesson plans, storyboards, scripts, and computer programming. Storyboarding and scripting are commonly used to provide production guidelines for instructional films and videotapes. Computer programming provides the specifications for computer-assisted instruction. Some instructional technologies, such as interactive videodisc instruction, may require the use of several different media formats. Other formats, such as those of storyboarding and scripting, are being combined to form new formats.

What follows is descriptions of several design specification formats that are commonly used by instructional designers. The first job aid presents a *preliminary type of design* that shows the relationships of important elements (objective, strategy, medium, and criterion), without the detail necessary for the final production of the instruction.

Job Aid / Objective-Strategy-Medium-Criterion Match

Description   The *Objective-Strategy-Medium-Criterion Match* technique is used to test the congruence of design elements in an existing instructional unit. It takes the form of a matrix, with the unit's objectives listed down the left side and strategies, media, and criteria for each of the objectives listed in the columns to the right of each objective. (This makes it convenient to check each element to see if it relates appropriately to the others in the instructional unit.) This matrix provides data for making decisions to modify, or not to modify, elements of the instruction.

Use Rationale   This technique enables the designer to see and relate central elements of the proposed instruction in a parsimonious way, making it less likely that essential content or media will be missed or that inappropriate content or media will be included. Instructional units change over time, or sometimes they become outdated because of new information or changes in the needs of the learners. This technique organizes the elements of instruction so that each can be analyzed in terms of its value to the instructional outcome.

Critical Tasks

1. **Collect the existing elements of the instructional unit currently being used by the instructor.** This usually consists of any written materials relevant to the course, including: syllabi, lesson plans, handouts, text, and tests.

2. **Draw the objective-strategy-medium-criterion matrix.** The matrix is usually drawn on $8\frac{1}{2} \times 11$-inch sheets of paper, with the objectives listed in the leftmost column, followed in turn by the other elements in their respective columns. Thus, for a particular objective, its strategies, media, and criterion items will all be in a line across the page, and easy to cross-relate. See Figure 4.21.

3. **Place the unit objectives in the leftmost column of the objective-strategy-medium-criterion matrix.** If the existing objectives are global or ambiguous, it will be necessary to rewrite them in behavioral terms. The objectives will be more useful if they are put in logical sequence.

4. **Place the strategies in the second column, immediately to the right of their respective objectives.** Strategies refer primarily to the mode of presenting information—e.g., lecture, assigned readings—and to the means for having the learners practice whatever is being taught, e.g., discussion, simulation, performing.

continued

Objective-Strategy-Medium-Criterion Match, continued

FIGURE 4.21 / Example of an objective-strategy-media-criterion matrix

Objective	Strategy	Media	Criteria
1. Seventh-grade science students will categorize a collection of randomly ordered rocks as sedimentary, igneous, or conglomerate, without error.	Lecture on the characteristics of rocks in the three basic classes. Students practice categorizing with instructor feedback. Evaluate students.	Slides of the rocks. Samples of numbered rocks before each student.	Test response sheet with key for three classes of rocks, with the right column having a list of the rock numbers, and a second column for the student to indicate the class of the rock.

5. **Place the list of print and/or nonprint media in the third column.** For a particular objective, this includes titles or descriptions of all of the nonprint media—e.g., transparencies, films, videos, slides, audiotapes—and print media, i.e., printed page.

6. **Place either the criterion items or their identifying numbers in the rightmost column.** Criterion items are synonymous with test items. Usually, the media and the criterion items are only referenced by number or by description on the matrix because of a lack of room, but they still must be carefully related to the objectives, just as were strategies and media.

7. **Check each of the objectives for congruence with its respective strategies, media, and criterion items.** They would not be congruent, for example, if discussion was the only strategy used to teach a psychomotor objective, such as "learning to type."

8. **Report any incongruities identified.** Usually these include one or more reasons why a relationship between or among elements is considered incongruent.

Reference

Gentry, C. G., and Johnson, C. (1974). *A Practical Management System for Performance-Based Teacher Education. PBTE Monograph,* Series 15, Washington, D.C.: American Association of Colleges for Teacher Education, pp. 31–35.

One of the oldest blueprints for instruction is the *lesson plan,* which, in the past, has been developed largely by the teacher or trainer using it. But over time, curriculum directors, publishers of textbooks, and instructional developers have increasingly provided these with their products. These institutional and commercially developed lesson plans have had mixed use by instructors, and those who do use them have modified them, often considerably. Because lesson plans provide reasonable detail about the elements of instruction and their relationships, they can be of good use to the producers of the elements of the instruction. The "Lesson Planning" job aid presents one of many forms for a lesson plan.

Job Aid / Lesson Planning

Description   A **lesson plan** is a formal design for a particular instructional segment. Lesson plans can range from single-page outlines to comprehensive instructor manuals. Specifically, a lesson plan guides the teacher in producing and delivering the instruction. A lesson plan relates learner outcomes to instructor and student activities for accomplishing the outcomes, and to resources required to support the activities. There is a wide variety of formats for lesson plans.

Use Rationale   The traditional use of lesson plans serves as a guide to the educator or trainer who delivers the instruction. But in addition, it has proven to be a very useful and inexpensive technique for organizing or arranging the elements of instruction when designing a prototype because it logically relates all of the elements and indicates where they fit in the sequence of instruction. Similarly, when in sufficient detail, it is useful to those who would produce the instruction.

Critical Tasks

1. **Generate or acquire an objective-strategy-medium-criterion match for the prototype.** This provides much of the data for the lesson plan.

2. **List, in their learning sequence, the specific objectives for the instruction.** These should be numbered consecutively, since that will serve as a code to relate the objectives to the activities of the lesson plan. The objectives should be stated in performance terms.

3. **List the in-class instructional activities according to the planned sequence of their occurrence.** The activities explicitly state the procedures followed, and, at least implicitly, reference the strategies used.

4. **List the out-of-class instructional activities according to the recommended sequence of their occurrence.** This can include any assignments of readings, papers, practice, etc.

5. **List and number, according to the sequence of their planned occurrence, any resources required.** This includes print and nonprint materials, equipment, special furniture or spaces. The numbers are used as a code to tie the resources to specific activities.

6. **In parentheses after each of the listed activities, write the codes for objectives, resources, and test items relevant to the activity.** The codes for objectives, resources, and test items give the teacher quick reference for each specific activity.

Reference

Gentry, Cass (1976). Lesson Planning Technique. Unpublished paper written for the Learning and Evaluation Center, Michigan State University. East Lansing, Mich.: The university, pp. 1–4.

An instructional production blueprint commonly used with instructional motion pictures, video, slide/tape, and filmstrip is the storyboard. **Storyboarding** is a technique for sequencing visual and audio elements as individual scenes. Each scene card provides the necessary directions for its production. See the "Storyboarding" job aid. Like many other ID processes, electronic versions of storyboarding are finding their way into use through computer software such as HyperCard.

Job Aid / Storyboarding

Description   Used in designing nonprint mediated instructional units, including those of film, video, slide/tape, and filmstrip. The instructional designer indicates both visual and audio messages on a card (e.g., 3 × 5, 5 × 7), for each scene, as well as the detail needed to produce them (e.g., closeup shot). The cards are placed in the desired sequence for the progression of the instruction. In the process of development, the cards can be easily resequenced, rewritten, added to, or deleted. The final product becomes a blueprint for producing the mediated unit. There are many variations on the theme.

Use Rationale   Design is a creative process where one idea may stimulate another, and calls for formats that permit easy modification. In addition, both the design and the production processes are often done jointly, which makes clear communication among designers, content and learning specialists, and producers essential. For instruction using media such as video, slide/tape, or film, the storyboard serves both of these needs admirably.

Critical Tasks

1. **Format storyboard cards for visual and audio messages.** Plain or lined 3 × 5 or 5 × 7-inch cards are commonly used, with a line drawn through the middle of each card and with the visual message placed on the left, the audio on the right. See Figure 4.22.

2. **Briefly describe the individual scenes on separate cards.** In the *first approximation* of the storyboard, it is more important to get the major ideas down than to be concerned with detail

FIGURE 4.22 / Example of a cell from a video storyboard

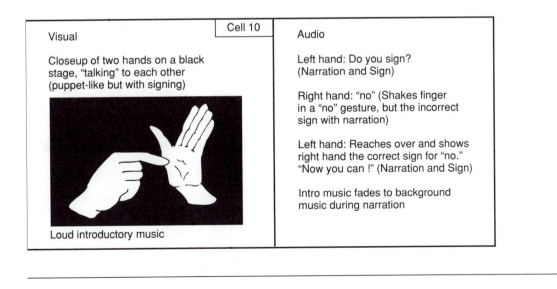

Visual

Cell 10

Audio

Closeup of two hands on a black stage, "talking" to each other (puppet-like but with signing)

Left hand: Do you sign? (Narration and Sign)

Right hand: "no" (Shakes finger in a "no" gesture, but the incorrect sign with narration)

Left hand: Reaches over and shows right hand the correct sign for "no." "Now you can !" (Narration and Sign)

Intro music fades to background music during narration

Loud introductory music

continued

Storyboarding, continued

and accuracy. Notes describing the visual and audio messages are jotted on the respective sections of each card.

3. **Arrange the completed cards in sequence.** This can be done on a table, or there are special storyboard card holders that can be hung on a wall that have individual pockets for each card.

4. **Check and revise the storyboard for continuity.** In the *second approximation*, the designer studies the cards, each a single cell or scene of the storyboard, to see if their sequence is logical and whether any scenes are missing, and fills in greater detail for both visual and audio messages. Each card or cell is given an identifying number showing where it fits in the sequence. See Figure 4.22 (Cell 10).

5. **Run an objectives/content/learning conditions check.** In the *third approximation*, modify the storyboard to make sure all objectives are included and unintended objectives are deleted. Check the content for accuracy and relevance. Make sure that appropriate learning conditions are set up for each objective, including reinforcement, repetition, and association. This is a good place to involve learning specialists, if available.

6. **Run a production check.** In the *fourth approximation*, make certain that any special directions for production staff are included on the cards, such as the type of shots or the kind of background music for a scene. This is also a good time to make sure that the narration written in the audio section of the storyboard cards is modified to fit the spoken mode rather than the reading mode.

7. **Run a final feasibility check, and revise as necessary.** In the *fifth approximation*, make sure that the product matches the expectations of others responsible for the unit or those who provide resources for its development. You may have to cut some elements because of cost factors. The storyboard is now ready to distribute to the production staff. Their input may cause further modification of the storyboard.

8. **Optional: Translate the storyboard from cards to standard paper sheet format.** Placing the storyboard on 8½ × 11-inch sheets of paper makes it more convenient for production personnel who will follow the storyboard in their work, and it also provides a more convenient form as a guide to users of the mediated instruction as well as a record of the storyboard. The record may be needed for future reference, in case this instructional mediated unit needs revision at a later time.

Reference

Kemp, J. E. (1963). *Planning and Producing Audiovisual Materials.* San Francisco, Calif.: Chandler, pp. 17–20.

Scripting has many similarities to storyboarding. In fact many of their respective characteristics have been incorporated into one another. However, **scripts** are usually more relevant for people who are acting parts and who need details about their lines, where to stand, and timing. Scripts usually contains few graphics, and when they do the emphasis is more on where characters are to be at a particular time on the set. What follows is a part of a video script used in an instructional program designed to teach hearing students to sign.

SCRIPT 5A: VIDEO SCENES DEPICTING JOE'S DREAM

CHARACTERS
JOE: Sam Lockridge
MOTHER: Sue Clark
DAD: Carl Gentile
FRIEND 1:   Kelly Wiles
FRIEND 2:   Fred Elmore
TEACHER: Arnold Brown
STUDENT 1:   Sara Belding
STUDENT 2:   Ellen Parker
STUDENT 3:   Joe Patten
STUDENT 4:   Mike Willis
STUDENT 5:   Jan Fells

PLOT ORIENTATION: *Purpose of these scenes is to give hearing students a sense of the effect of not being able to communicate with others. This is done by having a teenager, Joe, dream of awakening in a world where everyone signs (except him) and no one speaks aloud.*

SCENE ONE: (filmed in color and full sound)
Scene one opens with Joe seated on the floor and his two older sisters seated on chairs in a living room, watching television. There is a lot of environmental sound: the television, an open window, and background conversation of the sisters.

MOTHER: *(Calling son Joe from upstairs)* **JOE, LOOK AT THE TIME. YOU NEED TO GET TO BED. REMEMBER THAT DAD NEEDS TO LEAVE A LITTLE EARLIER IN THE MORNING TO DROP YOU OFF AT SCHOOL.**

JOE: *(Joe remains seated on the floor, lies down, and stretches out.)* **WHY IS DAD GOING SO EARLY, MOM?**

MOTHER: **HE HAS A MEETING. COME ON, LET'S GO. YOU WON'T BE ABLE TO GET UP IN THE MORNING.**

JOE: *(He stands up slowly and heads up the stairs. The environmental sounds slowly fade as he mounts the stairs.)* **OK, OK, I'M COMING. . . .**

SCENE TWO: (filmed in black and white, no sound)
Scene opens in Joe's bedroom, with morning light coming through the window. There are no environmental sounds. The mother walks in and awakens Joe by shaking him. Instead of speaking, she emphatically signs to him.

MOTHER: (in sign language) **GET UP! LET'S GO! MOVE IT! . . .**

Joe looks at her, rubs an eye, holds his head . . . very puzzled by her signing. He hops out of bed as his mother leaves, with his eyes on her back and a puzzled expression on his face.

SCENE THREE: (filmed in black and white, no sound)
Scene opens as Joe is coming down the stairs, still buttoning his shirt. He looks up to see his mother at the door pointing at his jacket, book and lunch bag on a chair.

MOTHER: *(signing emphatically)* **IT IS LATE. GET MOVING! YOUR DAD IS WAITING IN THE CAR.**

SCENE FOUR: (filmed in black and white, no sound)
Scene begins as Joe walks slowly out of the front door toward the car. He

sees two of his friends waiting up the street for the bus. He raises his hand to wave and shout hello, but stops midway and scratches his head. He sees that his friends, like his mother, are carrying on their conversation in sign language.

FRIEND 1: *(signing)* **DID YOU DO YOUR HOME WORK?**

FRIEND 2: *(signing)* **YEAH, ALL BUT MY COMPUTER ASSIGNMENT.**

DAD: *(with harried look on his face, signs to Joe)* **COME ON, GET IN THE CAR. WE NEED TO HURRY!**

They drive off, with Joe looking back in puzzlement at his friends.

SCENE FIVE: (The beginning is videotaped in black and white without sound, then changes to color video at end of scene)

Scene opens in the computer lab. As Joe enters he sees the teacher signing at a group of three students. He sees two other students signing and working on the computer. There are no environmental sounds. Totally bewildered, he goes to his computer console and sits down.

TEACHER: *(Signs to the class, giving instructions on an assignment)* **BOOT UP YOUR PROJECTS RIGHT AWAY. TRY TO COMPLETE THEM DURING THIS NEXT HOUR.**

STUDENT 1: *(asks a question in sign)* **WHEN IS THIS PROJECT DUE?**

TEACHER: *(signs)* **THE PROJECT IS DUE ON FRIDAY.**

TEACHER: *(The teacher signs another statement of instruction to the students, as he is turning to go to his desk.)* **IF YOU HAVE QUESTIONS, CHECK WITH ANOTHER STUDENT ON YOUR PROJECT TEAM.**

The students begin to work on the assignment, except for Joe, who doesn't know what is going on or what he is expected to do. He turns to a classmate.

JOE: *(speaks aloud, but no sound is heard)* **WHAT'S GOING ON?**

STUDENT 2: *(She signs at Joe.)* **WE ARE WORKING ON THE COMPUTER PROJECT.**

JOE: *(Looking very frustrated, Joe gets up from his desk and asks another student.)* **WHAT'S GOING ON?**

STUDENT 3: *(somewhat frustrated with him for mouthing words rather than signing, responds in sign language)* **WE ARE WORKING ON THE COMPUTER PROJECT.**

Joe spins around, holds his head, raises his arms out in confusion, plops down into the chair at the computer, and pounds the key on the remote control, which triggers a program to come up.

A closeup of his monitor shows an animated color graphic of hands displaying the sign for LINK. This title screen fades to an instructional screen that instructs the student how to make the sign for LINK. The camera focuses back on Joe (in black and white) as he fumbles his hands to create the sign for LINK. He makes the sign correctly (video scene turns to color), and he looks up to see a classmate returning the LINK sign to him. Joe shows excitement and understanding and turns to the computer to continue taking instruction from the program. He presses the key on the remote control and we see a closeup of the monitor showing the title of the program, "Basics of American Sign Language."

END OF SCENES DEPICTING JOE'S DREAM

Again, most instructional developers tend to use the storyboard to specify their designs for mediated instruction, but they freely add script elements to the storyboard.

Summary

Design is a process that is still more art than science. Instructional designers must have both a good knowledge of design techniques and the broader knowledge and imagination to apply the techniques creatively. This chapter has focused on a number of processes and concomitant techniques that assist in the design process. Processes discussed were: collecting data on the audience for the instruction; the writing, categorizing, sequencing, and getting agreement on performance objectives; deriving test items; running task analyses; selecting instructional strategies and media; costing alternative strategies and media; and developing design specifications for instruction.

References

Cantor, J. A. (1986). The Delphi as a job analysis tool. *Journal of Instructional Development* 9(1): 16–19.

Esque, T. J. (1988). Knowledge mapping: A multiple task analysis tool. *Journal of Instructional Development* 11(4): pp. 39–50.

Gagne, R. M. (1965). *The Conditions of Learning.* New York: Holt, Rinehart and Winston.

Gagne, R. M., and Briggs, L. J. (1974). *Principles of Instructional Design.* New York: Holt, Rinehart and Winston.

Jonassen, D. H., and Hannum, W. H. (1986). Analysis of task analysis procedures. *Journal of Instructional Development* 9(2): 2–8.

Simonson, M. R. (1979). Designing instruction for attitudinal outcomes. *Journal of Instructional Development* 2(3): 15–19.

Snow, R. E. (1977). Individual differences and instructional design. *Journal of Instructional Development* 1(1): 23–26.

Wilson, B. G. (1985). Techniques for teaching procedures. *Journal of Instructional Development* 8(2): 2–5.

CHAPTER 5

Production

Process of constructing elements of a project, as specified in a design or as based on revision data

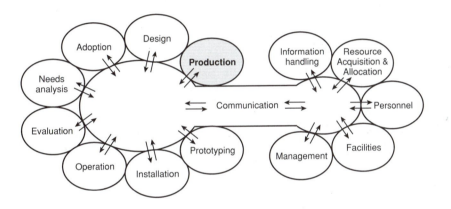

Learner Objectives

1. Justify the processes listed for the production component.

2. Interpret the elements of a specific PERT network for an ID project.

3. Determine probabilities for completing a project on time, given data from a specific PERT network.

4. Complete an ID PERT network, given the essential data.

5. Discriminate among tasks of pre-production, production, and post-production.

6. Match production techniques with appropriate processes and products.

7. Given a randomly ordered list of tasks for a production technique, order tasks in the appropriate sequence.

8. Recall definitions of major terms.

Introduction

Production units of instructional development systems are structured in many different ways. In some education and training organizations, a single individual may carry out all of the production processes, whereas in larger organizations there may be several separate divisions responsible for different types of production. For instance, separate divisions for instructional television, photography, and graphic production are common.

Production may involve original construction of instructional elements, revision of new instructional elements, or adaptive revision of existing instructional elements. In its way, production is one of the most exciting and creative parts of the instructional development process. It can also be one of the most difficult. Production personnel must take the skeletal frames provided by design specifications and turn them into functional products. Considering all of the tasks that have to be accomplished to turn a storyboard for video instruction into the final product gives an appreciation of the skills and knowledge production personnel must bring to the process. As would be suspected, there are many specialty areas supporting production. These specialties range from graphics, photographics, video, moving picture production, and construction of real objects all the way through to expertise in print media. And there are specialties within specialties. As an instance, in video production there are specialties in directing, audio and video recording, camera work, editing, and designing props, to name a few.

Like most other processes in instructional development, the production process is only partly linear. The process is dynamic, in the sense that many adjustments must be made during production of an instructional unit. For example, a modification in presentational format in one element may call for a modification in other elements of the product in order to maintain consistency. Although production is not a linear process, it is still useful to talk about the logical sequence of steps for producing instruction, as illustrated in the next section.

Production Process

To complete the production of an instructional unit, a production manager plus staff may need to consider all ten of the following steps.

1. Acquire design specifications for the instruction.
2. Complete a job work breakdown structure for the production project.
3. Divide large job work breakdown structures into subprojects, as appropriate.
4. Cost out production of subprojects.
5. Reconcile subproject production costs with management options and constraints (determine trade-offs, and get agreement from appropriate decision makers).

6. Assign subprojects (e.g., to individuals, production specialists, and/or production teams).

7. Subproject managers direct personnel in completing assigned production of elements.

8. Deliver production elements to the prototyping team.

9. Use any revised design specifications received from the prototyping team to modify instructional materials.

10. Deliver final production element masters to the prototyping team (or the masters may be stored with the production division to facilitate later mass production of the instructional unit, or for security).

Steps 7 and 9 are the ones directly concerned with the physical production of instructional elements, while the other steps focus on the immediate processes leading into and out of the physical production. The processes represented in this list have been divided into pre-production, production, and post production. The sections that follow will consider each of these, in turn.

Pre-Production

Acquiring Design Specifications   Design specifications are the detailed blueprints for producing the physical elements that make up an instructional unit. These specifications usually come to the production unit with orders for production. Design specifications vary considerably in format and detail. When they are drawn up by the same group that is to produce an instructional unit, communication about what was intended is usually adequate. However, when design specifications come from an outside group, they may be difficult for production personnel to interpret. Part of the reason for this is that different groups use different conventions in specifying a design. Even in-house, in cases where an organization's design and production units are clearly separated by structure and management, problems often occur in interpreting design specifications. For these reasons production personnel should spend time going through the specifications with the designers, to clarify intent. Design specifications are provided in several forms, through several techniques, including: *storyboards, scripts,* and *lesson plans* (all presented in Chapter 4).

Preparing Work Breakdown   Once the production teams have the design specifications, they need to determine the resources required to carry out all of the tasks necessary for meeting the specifications. A management technique that has proven particularly effective for this purpose is called the *Program Evaluation and Review Technique (PERT)*. A completed PERT provides an initial work breakdown structure that relates all of the project tasks to one another. The manager can then assign related clusters of the tasks for work by individual teams. (PERT is also discussed in Chapter 10 as a means of estimating the costs of proposed ID projects, in preparation for competitive bidding for the projects.) PERT is one of the most powerful techniques for the management of projects, and is an essential tool for any instructional developer. For this reason, considerably more explanation is given for PERT than for the other techniques.

PERT is successor and predecessor to several other networking techniques, e.g., Gannt, Critical Path Method (CPM), and Graphical Evaluation and Review Technique (GERT). The use of more elaborate versions of the technique, such as PERT/Time and PERT/Cost are considered too time consuming by many instructional developers. The majority of PERT users tend to adapt and simplify the technique. And that, in fact, is one of its major attractions: it can be used at several levels of sophistication with good effect. In more formal terms:

PERT is a systematic programming, timing, and costing technique for measuring, monitoring, and controlling the development of a project.

Operationally, PERT is a means of sequencing the order in which project activities or tasks can be most effectively and efficiently completed. Graphically this is presented through a network of events (circles) and activities (arrows) (Figure 5.1). The arrows in the figure represent project *activities* or tasks that must be completed. The numbered circles are called *events*, which indicate the beginning and/or completion of the project activities represented by the arrows. Unlike activities, events do not consume resources. Note that events 1 and 6 begin and end the project, respectively. Between these two events the activities and other events are ordered for maximum efficiency of development. Looking at the network, one can see that completion of activity A precedes the start of activities B, C, and D. In turn, activities C, E, and F must be completed before beginning activity G. It also shows that activities in paths B/E, C, and D/F can be done concurrently rather than one after another. Carrying out tasks concurrently rather than linearly often enables a developer to complete a project on a shorter schedule (this is especially important in those contracts where the developer is responsible for any time or cost overruns).

FIGURE 5.1 / Simple PERT network

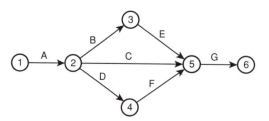

Key:
events (circles) = beginning and/or completion of tasks
arrows (letters) = specific tasks

It should be noted that the figures used here to illustrate PERT have vastly simplified networks. An average number of tasks for a real PERT would be around 200. Some complex PERT networks may deal with thousands of activities. PERT does a great job of keeping these tasks in perspective. A general rule of thumb used by developers says to apply PERT when a project contains twenty or more activities, and when the project's duration is expected to exceed one or more months.

Sometimes, it will be necessary to complete an activity in one path of the network before an activity in another path can be started. This relationship is represented by a dashed arrow, as shown in Figure 5.2. This is called a **dummy activity**, because neither time nor other resources are used. Note in Figure 5.2 that the times for each activity are placed below their respective arrows. The dummy activity arrow is drawn between events 3 and 5, and the 0 below the dashed arrow indicates that no time is used for this activity. The purpose of this dummy activity is to indicate that activity D in the upper path must be completed before activity H in the middle path can be begun. This device satisfies the need to show periodically a sequence relationship between activities on different paths without affecting time or resource estimates for the separate paths.

FIGURE 5.2 / PERT application using a dummy activity

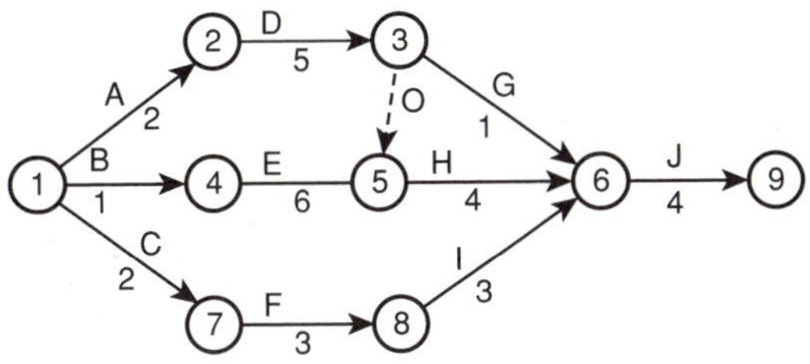

Key:
circles = events
arrows = activities
dashed arrows = dummy activity

With the exception of the dummy activity, time and cost estimates are made for each of the PERT network activities. Activity times are commonly specified in days, weeks, or tenths of weeks. The activities in Figure 5.3 are estimated in weeks (e.g., activity A takes 2 weeks to complete). The *longest* path (accumulated times) through the PERT network is called the **critical path**, which provides an estimate of how long the overall project will take. Usually, the client contracts for a specific delivery date for the finished project, and penalties may be levied in cases where deadlines are exceeded. Developers highlight the critical path in some way so that it can be more easily distinguished (e.g., a darkened or colored line may be drawn along the activities constituting the critical path). The critical path in Figure 5.3 is defined by the heavy line following the A–D–Dummy–H–J path in the network. If, by moving from one path to another via a dummy activity arrow, a longer or more time-consuming path is found, then that will also become part of the critical path. The accumulated times along this path (i.e., 2 + 7 + 0 + 4 + 4) indicate that 17 weeks is estimated as the minimum time necessary for completing the project.

A completed PERT will show not only the network but also a key that lets the developer know quickly which activities the letters represent in the network. Figure 5.4 illustrates a more formal expression of PERT, with the activities specified *by event* in a key below the network. The event numbers are used to reference the specific activities that each specific event begins and/or ends. For example, event 3 ends the RFP study (B), client research (C), and team assembly activities (D), and it begins the assigning tasks

FIGURE 5.3 / PERT application showing the critical path

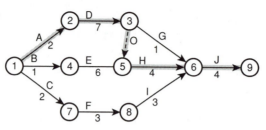

Key:
events (circles) = beginning and/or ending tasks
arrows = activities
dashed arrow = dummy activity
numbers = time, in weeks
letters = specific tasks

FIGURE 5.4 / An application of PERT for writing a proposal

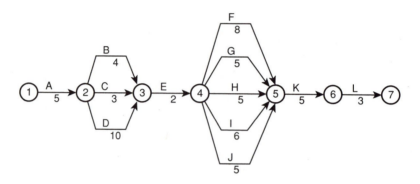

EVENTS
1. begin project, send for RFP (A)
2. receive RFP, begin RFP study (B), client research (C), team assembly (D)
3. end RFP study, client research, team assembly, begin assigning tasks (E)
4. end assigning tasks, begin planning implementation (H), design plan (F),
   production plan (G), evaluation plan (I), dissemination plan (J)
5. end implementation plan, design plan, production plan, evaluation plan,
   dissemination plan, begin writing proposal (K)
6. end writing proposal, begin submitting proposal (L)
7. end submitting proposal, end proposal writing project

activity (E). Note that the critical path for this project would follow activities A–D–E–F–K–L, since this is the path that would consume the most time. Accumulating the times required to complete each of the activities on the critical path (5 + 10 + 2 + 8 + 5 + 3) results in an estimated project completion time of 33 weeks.

The estimate of *expected elapsed time* (t_e) for completing each activity is based on three other time estimates, i.e., *optimistic time* (assuming everything goes without a hitch), *pessimistic time* (assuming that all likely problems will occur), and *most likely time* (best guess). These estimates are plugged into the following formula:

$$t_e = \frac{\text{optimistic time} + (4 \times \text{most likely time}) + \text{pessimistic time}}{6}$$

or

$$t_e = \frac{o + 4m + p}{6}$$

where o = optimistic time, m = most likely time, and p = pessimistic time.

Where possible, experienced individuals should be asked to estimate times and costs required for a specific task. Usually, staff members within an ID organization will have reasonable experience for estimating times for carrying out ID tasks, and they will have some idea about what their own time is worth. However, experience is often lacking in costing other aspects of ID activities. When such expertise is lacking, then homework must be done by contacting those who sell the necessary materials, equipment, facilities, skills, etc., for their current prices or fees. The accumulated times of the critical path and the accumulated cost estimates for all of the activities (plus a percentage increase in the final estimate of time and cost to protect against estimation error) will give a reasonable estimate of time and cost for completing an instructional development project.

In the past, project managers were discouraged from using PERT because of time-consuming and laborious data calculation and entry necessary to the process. For PERT to be effective, *it must be regularly recalculated* to show the effects of lost or gained time for activities, as well as shifts in resources. On most projects, revision occurs about every 2 weeks; on shorter projects, revision may need to occur more often. To illustrate the need for revision, suppose in Figure 5.4 that activities B and C were both completed a week early. This makes possible the shifting of personnel and resources that were originally budgeted for those 2 weeks to activity D, which in turn might enable the team to finish that activity a week or two early. This savings in time can positively affect the project's bottom line. There are usually several of these changes to be made at a time, and they in turn affect the time and resources of other activities. Ongoing manual recalculation of a PERT can take up a lot of time. However, with the advent of microcomputers, a large number of programmed management techniques for handling the calculations were developed. Besides easing recalculation, such computer programs can also table the information in a variety of useful ways beyond the network charts. For example, the programs can provide individual tables showing cash flow, and task and resource timelines. There are a number of these programs available (e.g., Dekker Limited's "Expert" has versions for the Apple II, Macintosh, and IBM PC and compatibles).

Figure 5.5 shows how the same PERT presented in Figure 5.4 appears when generated by Apple's MacProject PERT program. MacProject uses a format that places the activities or tasks in the nodes of the network, whereas the one in Figure 5.4 places the activities above the arcs (arrows) of the network, which makes the network much easier to read. In Figure 5.5, the finishing date for an activity is placed at the top right of the node. If a date has to be extended, all other subsequent dates in the network are automatically changed to reflect the added days. The dark line represents the critical path. Once entered, tasks, resources, costs and cash flow for the project can be pulled up in a tabular form whenever the user desires. (A job aid teaching the use of MacProject in developing a network is presented in Chapter 10.)

The "PERT" job aid here lists the major steps for using a manually developed PERT to estimate the times and costs required to complete the development of an instructional project.

FIGURE 5.5 / PERT network generated through MacProject

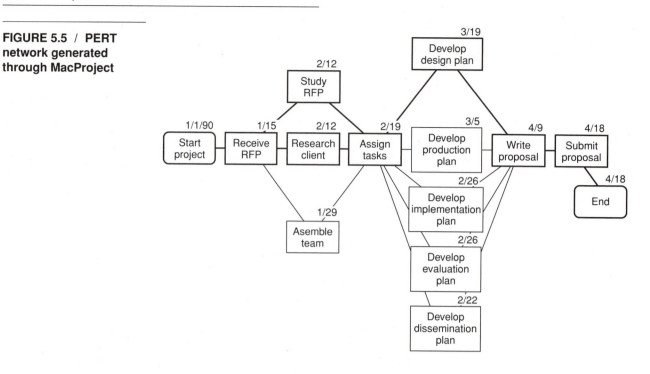

Job Aid / Project Evaluation and Review Technique (PERT)

Description This is a triple-threat technique that can be used at several levels for different purposes. It can be used for project cost analysis, task analysis, task scheduling, and resource management. It can be carried out manually or through a computer application program. The PERT technique requires that tasks be scheduled into a network as being preceding, succeeding, or concurrent with one another. The tasks may be analyzed as to resource requirements, including time, materials, equipment, facilities, and personnel. PERT identifies ways of allocating and re-allocating resources to maximize their use for the efficient completion of projects.

Use Rationale Individuals or groups contracting to complete instructional development projects often find themselves on thin ice because of inaccurate estimation of the resources necessary for projects. During instructional development, too many resources may be used to finish front-end requirements, to the detriment of later tasks. PERT is valuable because it reduces that risk at both levels, i.e., at the contracting stage, and during actual development. PERT also serves as an excellent means of communication among project members.

Critical Tasks

1. **Generate the set of tasks necessary to complete a project.** Use knowledgeable personnel who have had previous experience with similar projects. Use *Brainstorming* or *Nominal Group Process* techniques for generating the first round of tasks. Place tasks on individual 3 × 5-inch cards.

2. **Sequence tasks into a network, according to whether they precede, succeed, or are concurrent with other tasks.** Use the group that generated the task cards to sequence them, if possible. Use a large table or a space on the floor for sequencing the 3 × 5 task cards.

continued

Project Evaluation and Review Technique (PERT), continued

3. **Throw out duplicate tasks, and fill in any missing tasks revealed by the sequencing process.** Invariably, the initial generation of tasks will miss tasks necessary to the completion of the project. Their absence is relatively easy to spot during the sequencing process, because each of the activities must lead to others, and where there is no clear next activity or task, usually one is needed.

4. **Transfer the completed network from cards to sheets of paper for ease of handling and communication.** The tasks or activities are indicated by lettered arrows, and the beginning and completion points, or events, are indicated by numbered circles that connect arrows. See Figure 5.6.

FIGURE 5.6 / Simple PERT network

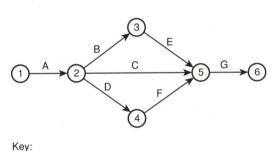

Key:
events (circles) = begining and/or completion of tasks
arrows (letters) = specific tasks

5. **Add dummy activities, as appropriate.** They are indicated by dashed arrows, using zero time and resources. Use where an activity in one path must be completed before an activity in a concurrent path can begin. For example, in Figure 5.7, activity H cannot be begun until activity D is completed. Note that the dummy activity between events 2 and 5 consumes no resources.

6. **Using event numbers, list the beginning and ending events at the bottom of the PERT network.** (This is for ease of reading the network. With the exception of the first and last events of the project, all events represent the completion of one task and the beginning of another. This information is stated after each event number, e.g., event 6 ends the writing of the proposal and begins the process of submitting the proposal. See Figure 5.8).

7. **Generate time estimates for each of the tasks.** Again, where possible, use knowledgeable personnel to do the estimating. Apply the formula for combining pessimistic, optimistic, and mostly likely times to get an expected elapsed time for the individual tasks:

$$t_e = \frac{o + 4m + p}{6}$$

Where t_e = expected elapsed time; o (optimistic time) is the expected time if everything goes without a hitch; p (pessimistic time) is the expected time if whatever can go wrong does; and m (most likely time) is the developer's best guess. Continue to add and/or delete activities, as appropriate.

continued

Project Evaluation and Review Technique (PERT), continued

FIGURE 5.7 / PERT application showing a dummy activity and the critical path

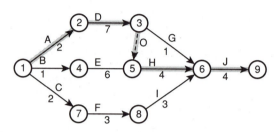

Key:
events (circles) = beginning and/or ending tasks
arrows = activities
dashed arrow = dummy activity
numbers = time, in weeks
letters = specific tasks

FIGURE 5.8 / An application of PERT for writing a proposal

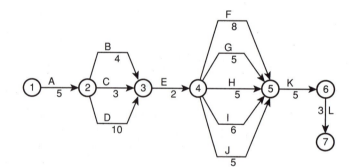

EVENTS
1. begin project, send for RFP (A)
2. receive RFP, begin RFP study (B), client research (C), team assembly (D)
3. end RFP study, client research, team assembly, begin assigning tasks (E)
4. end assigning tasks, begin planning implementation (H), design plan (F), production plan (G), evaluation plan (I), dissemination plan (J)
5. end implementation plan, design plan, production plan, evaluation plan, dissemination plan, begin writing proposal (K)
6. end writing proposal, begin submitting proposal (L)
7. end submitting proposal, end proposal writing project

continued

Project Evaluation and Review Technique (PERT), continued

8. **Determine the time required to complete the project by identifying the critical path through the network.** This is done by adding the expected elapsed times for all of the alternative paths through the network. The one consuming the most time is the critical path and tells the earliest date at which a project can be completed. See Figure 5.6.

9. **Generate cost estimates for each of the tasks.** Use knowledgeable personnel to provide pessimistic, optimistic, and most likely estimates for the cost of each task.

10. **Sum costs across all tasks to get direct costs of the project.**

11. **Break costs down according to line-item costs.** Most client budgets are of the *function-object* or *line-item* type, using general categories such as *salary* and *travel expense*. Usually, the instructional developer will have to present the costs in the client's budget format.

12. **Determine indirect, or overhead, costs.** If the instructional developers have to maintain their own plant and personnel they will need to include the mundane but necessary costs for electricity, rent, personnel insurance, etc. This can range from 20–60% of project cost.

13. **Determine the margin of profit, if you are a subcontractor.** This will depend on the market and organizational policies, but a range of 5–20% profit is common.

14. **Determine an acceptable safety margin for completing the project.** You need to recognize that PERT only provides a good estimate of the time required. Most instructional developers will add a 5–15% safety net.

15. **Divide the PERT network into sub-project size clusters, i.e., work breakdown structures, as appropriate.** (If the work is divided among different teams the manager needs to keep careful track of the time and resource expenditure for each. For example, computer programming and video production for an ID project would likely be carried out by different teams.)

16. **Revise every two to four weeks** (a major advantage of PERT is that by regular revision, resources can be switched, as appropriate, among the tasks, so that a project may be completed ahead of time, with fewer resources, and, thus, increase the profit margin.)

References

AECT Task Force (1977). *Educational Technology: Definition and Glossary of Terms.* Washington, D.C.: Association for Educational Communications and Technology, p. 267.

Evarts, H. E. (1964). *Introduction to PERT.* Boston: Allyn and Bacon.

Hussain, K. T. (1973). *Development of Information Systems for Education.* Englewood Cliffs, N.J.: Prentice-Hall, pp. 27–35.

Kaehler, C. (1984). *MacProject Program Users Manual.* Cupertino, Calif.: Apple Computer, pp. 41–56, 82–89.

PERT is very useful for adjusting activity times and other resources as a project progresses. Those unfamiliar with techniques such as PERT or CPM (critical path method) should realize that the application as presented here is an adaptation from far more complex and powerful techniques that may use a range of sophisticated formulae for purposes beyond those served by this text. For example, one formula applies concepts of the normal distribution to determine the number of workdays needed to increase the *chance* of finishing a project on time.

To illustrate, assume that the pessimistic time to complete a project is 140 days, the optimistic time is 70 days, and the most likely time is 110 days. When these figures are plugged into the expected elapsed time formula (t_e), presented earlier, they give an estimated time of 108 days to complete the project. Using this estimate we have about a 50% chance of finishing the project in 108 days. If instructional developers wish, they can determine the number of days needed to raise the probability of finishing on time to 68%, 96%, or 99%. The first step in doing so is to plug the pessimistic and optimistic time estimates into the following formula:

$$\sigma = \frac{p - o}{6} = \frac{140 - 70}{6} = 12 \text{ days}$$

When this information is in turn applied to the normal distribution curve, as shown in Figure 5.9, we can determine the number of days necessary to finish on time, for these three probabilities. Note the two rows of figures placed below the curve. The first row shows the standard deviations from the mean. The mean, in this case, would be our expected time of 108 days. Notice this number corresponds to 0 standard deviations.

FIGURE 5.9 / Probability of completing a project on time through MacProject

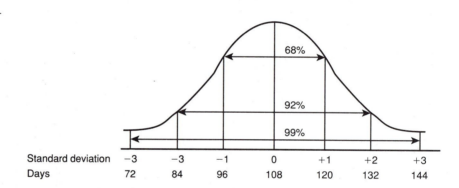

The sigma formula is used to determine the standard deviation, which will let us calculate how many days need to be added to 108 to determine a 68%, 96%, or 99% chance of finishing on time. In our example, the sigma formula gave 12 days as the standard deviation for a mean of 108 days. Note that at 1 standard deviation from the mean, there is a 68% probability that the project will be finished on time within 12 days either side of the mean, giving a range of 96–120 days. At 2 standard deviations there is a 96% chance, with a range of 84–132 days, and at 3 standard deviations there is a 99% chance with a range of 72–144 days. To be safe, instructional developers would pick the high numbers of each range. Thus, they would choose 120 days for a 68% chance, 132 days for a 96% chance, and 144 days for a 99% chance of completing the project on time.

Anyone interested in pursuing more sophisticated versions of PERT are invited to turn to some of the sources referenced in this job aid and at the end of this chapter. PERT is also presented in a slightly different form in Chapter 10, where it is used as a technique for costing out proposed projects, for bidding purposes.

The PERT technique presented in the preceding job aid assists reasonably well with pre-production steps 2, 3, 4, 5, and 6 of the production process listed at the beginning of the chapter.

Production

Even a small percentage of the production techniques relevant to print and nonprint instructional materials would easily fill several books. There is no intent to imply that the few techniques presented here would be sufficient for the production of any but a very basic instructional unit. The production skills needed to respond to the range of instructional designs could well consume the activities of several courses. In the larger education and training programs, specialists in the area of production carry out the instructional designs developed by others in their respective organizations.

To maintain the continuity of the instructional development model, a few production techniques are considered here. They are primarily of the low tech variety, favoring individuals with modest resources.

Optical Projection   Optical projection of instructional materials encompasses several different hardware systems, including overhead, slide, filmstrip, and video projectors. Becoming increasingly popular are newer optical projection systems designed to receive and project input directly from a computer.

The most common projector available in education and training programs is the **overhead projector**. This projector is used to project the image on a transparent acetate sheet onto a screen located above and behind the presenter. Some critics have labeled this system as nothing more than a glorified chalkboard, but it has decided advantages over the chalkboard. First, the information can be prepared some time prior to the need, and the same material can be stored and reused over and over again. Second, its use enables the presenter to face the audience throughout the presentation or lecture. Of course, on the negative side, the bulb can burn out at a crucial moment! There is a plethora of techniques for designing and producing overhead transparencies. A few common techniques for producing transparencies are presented in the nearby job aids.

Job Aid / Producing Overhead Transparencies

Description   Instructional **overhead transparencies** are made with clear acetate sheets and used with an overhead projector to project images onto a screen. The process of producing a transparency includes: establishing design specifications, generating lettering and graphic elements, completing an opaque master, reproducing the master on acetate, and framing the transparency.

Use Rationale   Transparencies are applicable when you wish to prepare inexpensive, easy-to-use materials ahead of when you will be doing the instruction. Transparencies can be used with different-size groups in a lighted room. They are easy to store, and assist the instructor in controlling the pace of the presentation.

Critical Tasks

1. **Receive the specifications for the transparency.** These vary in their sophistication and completeness, but each transparency should be limited to a single idea, concept, or comparison.

2. **Check the lettering specifications.** The designer should have specified key words and short sentences; seven lines per transparency with seven words per line, maximum. Lettering produced by a standard typewriter is too small.

3. **Check the graphics specifications.** You should *not* have so much information as to be cluttered or confusing. Keep it simple, low on detail.

4. **Rough-out an opaque layout of the transparency to show the relationship between the lettering and the graphics.** Place the graphics by dividing the transparency into thirds, vertically and horizontally. The graphics go where the lines intersect. Remember that the finished master should have everything within a space limited to $7\frac{1}{2} \times 9\frac{1}{2}$ inches so that it will fit in a standard cardboard or plastic transparency frame.

3. **Design the lettering format.** Use block lettering. Use bold capitals for headings with smaller, upper- and lowercase letters for information, and avoid lettering vertically.

4. **Draw or acquire the graphics for transparency.** You can promote audience attention through the use of lines, arrows, and boxes. Include color for emphasis.

5. **Produce the finished transparency master.** An alternative to manual means is to use computer word processing and graphics software to produce a master, and then to use a laser printer for copying onto clear or colored acetate.

6. **Decide whether or not to mount the transparency.** Some instructors prefer their transparencies unframed. A transparency frame is usually made of cardboard or plastic, with a $7\frac{1}{2} \times 9\frac{1}{2}$-inch rectangular opening through which the transparency can be seen. See Figure 5.10.

7. **Mount the transparency on a frame.** Commercially produced frames are available. The transparency acetate is mounted by placing the frame face down, then aligning the transparency acetate face down on the frame and affixing the outside edges of the transparency to the frame with masking tape. See Figure 5.10.

continued

Producing Overhead Transparencies, continued

FIGURE 5.10 / Mounting a transparency acetate onto a frame

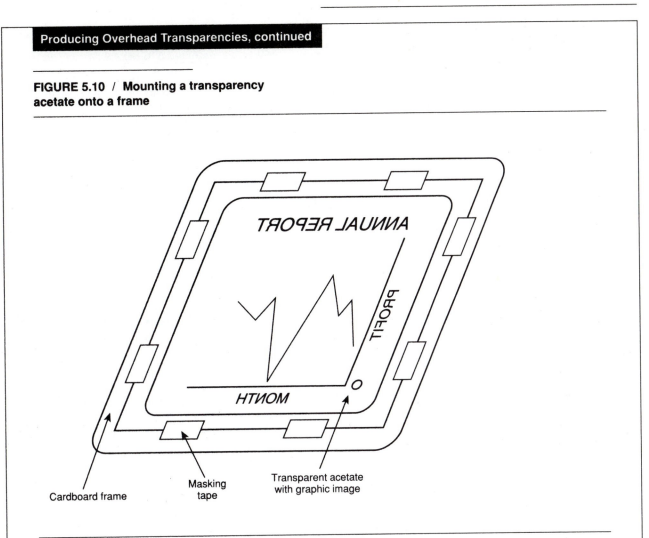

Cardboard frame

Masking tape

Transparent acetate with graphic image

References

Beaseley, Augie E., and Palmer, Carolyn G. (1987). *Ways to Improve Visual Communication* (ED 310 726). Charlotte, N.C.: Charlotte Mecklenburg Public Schools.

Beaseley, Augie E., and Palmer, Carolyn G. (1987). *Production Fever—Catch It!* Charlotte, N.C.: (ED 310 726). Charlotte Mecklenburg Public Schools.

3M Co. (no date). *How to Prepare and Present Better Meeting Graphics.* St. Paul, Minn.: 3M.

Locatis, C. N., and Atkinson, F. D. (1984). *Media and Technology for Education and Training.* Columbus, Ohio: Charles E. Merrill.

While the most common overhead transparencies are made up of one sheet of acetate, there are advantages of combining more than one sheet for some instructional purposes. These are called **overlay transparencies**. A major reason for their use is so that presenters can reveal different parts of the visual information as they proceed while still taking advantage of the base transparency. The nearby job aid teaches the process for constructing overlay transparencies.

Job Aid / Transparency Overlay Production

Description   Overlay transparencies are constructed with registered overlaying sheets, which permit information to be revealed in stages while still showing the information revealed in the previous stages. One such use would be in a discussion comparing sales figures to production costs over a period of time.

Use Rationale   Instructional presenters, like good magicians, know that they will have greater effect if they reveal information at appropriate times rather than all at once. It is more interesting that way, and it doesn't tend to overload the viewer.

Critical Tasks

1. **Determine the information to be put on a transparency.** E.g., to selectively reveal the organ systems of the human anatomy.

2. **Acquire or produce base image and related images on separate opaque sheets.** The base image is the one to which all other parts will attach and relate. For example, the base image might be the outline of a person, while the related images would be the separate organ systems, i.e., circulatory, musculature, skeletal, etc.

3. **Transform the opaque images into transparency masters.** There are a number of processes available, including the thermofax process. Another technique rapidly gaining in popularity is the use of computer word processing and graphics software to produce a master, which is then sent to a laser printer for copying onto clear or colored acetate.

4. **Mount the base image acetate on a frame.** See Figure 5.11. Commercially produced frames are available. The transparency acetate is mounted by placing the frame face down, then aligning the transparency acetate face down on the frame and affixing the outside edges of the transparency to the frame with masking tape.

continued

Transparency Overlay Production, continued

FIGURE 5.11 / Mounting a transparency acetate onto a frame

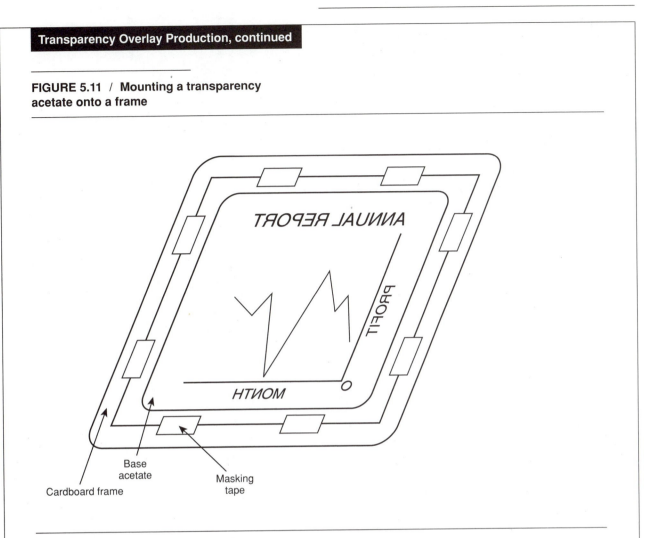

Cardboard frame

Base acetate

Masking tape

5. **Turn the framed image face-side up.** Decide how the overlay(s) will be presented. If the order is sequential, all overlays can be mounted on the same side. If more flexibility in presentation order is wanted, up to four overlays can be mounted onto different sides of the frame.

6. **Attach overlay 1, being sure that it is in proper register with the base transparency.** Use professional silver mylar hinges or masking tape to hold the overlay image in place, as shown in Figure 5.12. (The example overlay has numeric information that the presenter wants to show later.) You may also need to trim the overlay on the opposite side from the hinges in order to attach another overlay. This assumes two overlays. If you are using three or four overlays, other sides of the overlays may need to be trimmed.

7. **Attach other overlays in same manner until all are attached.**

continued

Transparency Overlay Production, continued

FIGURE 5.12 / Base transparency with one overlay

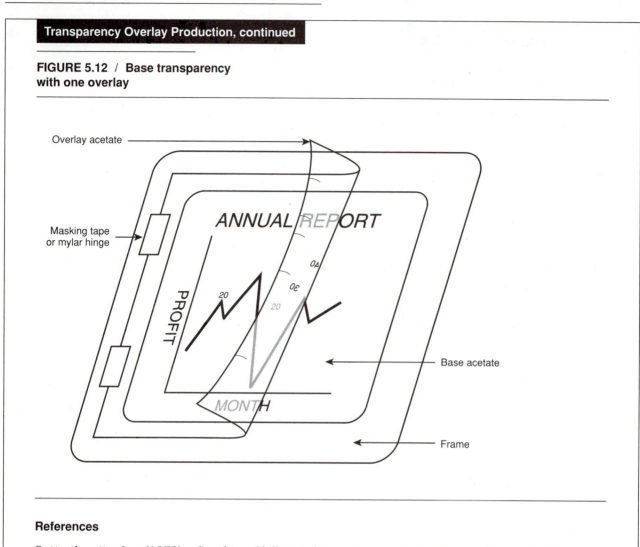

References

Satterthwaite, Les (1972). *Graphics: Skills, Media, and Materials.* Dubuque, Iowa: Kendall/Hunt, pp. 139–140.

Minor, Ed, and Frye, Harvey R. (1977). *Techniques for Producing Visual Instructional Media.* New York: McGraw-Hill, pp. 212–215.

There are a number of techniques for forming a master for a new transparency. Transparencies are usually made from opaque masters. The verbal and graphic information on a master could, of course, be hand printed and drawn, but often a more professional-looking transparency is desired. One way of making a professional-looking transparency master that employs words and numbers is through the *Dry-transfer letter* technique.

A major cost in making a master for overhead transparencies is the charge for creating their graphics. For one-of-a-kind graphics, the use of professional graphic artists is usually desirable; however, there is a large body of graphic material available from existing journals and other documents that can be tapped into. Educators and trainers who wish to make use of these graphics have an obligation to get permission from the owners

Job Aid / Dry-Transfer Lettering

Description   Most visual media (charts, graphs, transparencies, etc.) employ words as well as figures. A relatively easy way of placing letters on the various visual media is with *dry-transfer lettering* (also referred to as *press-on* or *rub-on lettering*). The dry-transfer letters are made of carbon and wax printed on plastic, acetate, or polyethylene carrier sheets. These letters can be transferred to nearly all dry surfaces by rubbing over the back of the translucent carrier sheet (on which the letters are affixed) with a dull-point pencil or ballpoint pen. Special stylus-type instruments are also available for this purpose.

Use Rationale   Dry-transfer letters are ideal for giving a professional look to charts, graphs, maps, diagrams, posters, exhibits, signs, bulletin boards, captions for photographs, television title cards, overhead projection transparencies, silk-screen artwork, and publications. Since only the letter comes off the carrier sheet, there are no edges to create unwanted lines on the surface to which the letter is applied.

A limitation of dry-transfer lettering is that if the letters are to look professional, they must be precisely placed. Poor placement should be avoided, because once the letters are affixed, their position is difficult to change. However, they can be removed with judicious use of the sticky side of a piece of masking tape.

Critical Tasks

1. **Acquire the required dry-transfer letter sheets and the base transparent acetate sheet onto which letters will be transferred.**

2. **Draw a line on a sheet of white paper and place the paper under the base transparent acetate sheet.** A sheet of ruled paper can be placed under the acetate as a guide for placing the letters.

3. **Arrange in sequence the letters for the first line so that both letters and words appear to have equal or uniform spaces between them.** This visual spacing will have a more natural look than would exact, equally spaced distances between letters. For example, if one word ends and the next one starts with a narrow letter, e.g., *I* or *T*, position them a little closer than words that end and begin with broader letters, e.g., *O, W*.

4. **Count up the letters and spaces between the words in the first line.**

5. **Make a pencil mark on the white paper under the acetate at the center point of the line of letters.**

6. **Position the middle letter at the center point on the carrier sheet.**

7. **Rub a finger over the letter to form contact between the carrier sheet and the surface. Then rub the letter with a burnisher.** E.g., a dull-pointed pencil, ballpoint pen, or similar blunt instrument. Rub until the letter changes color. Burnish any thin lines and/or edges. Be careful not to tear the carrier sheet with the burnishing instrument. Do not press too hard, or you may cause cracking or chopping of the letters.

8. **Peel or lift the carrier sheet away from the artwork, carefully.**

continued

Dry-Transfer Lettering, continued

9. **Working from the left of the middle letter, apply other letters in a similar manner.** Then repeat to the right until all the letters are in place.

Reference

Minor, Ed, and Frye, Harvey R. (1977). *Techniques of Producing Visual Instructional Media.* New York: McGraw-Hill, pp. 110–158.

---

of the graphics, or to limit their use to fair use standards of the copyright law. One technique that takes advantage of existing graphics in magazines whose pictures are printed on clay-coated paper is called the *color picture lift process.*

Job Aid / Color Picture Lift Process

Description   This technique is used to create overhead color transparencies from pictures in magazines. Only pictures printed on clay-coated paper can be used, such as *Time, Life,* and *National Geographic.* Another limitation is that the magazine picture is destroyed in the process; thus, only expendable pictures should be used. The picture is first bonded to a sheet of adhesive-backed acetate, and then soaked in cool water. When the paper is peeled away from the acetate, the ink from the picture adheres to the acetate. The transparency is then swabbed with damp cotton to remove any clay residue. After drying the transparency thoroughly, the inked surface can be protected and made more transparent by spraying it with clear plastic. The transparency can then be mounted in a transparency frame, after which it is ready for use.

Use Rationale   This method of transparency production is relatively inexpensive. The picture transfer process allows the instructor to make magazine pictures into transparencies that can be easily seen by an entire classroom. This method allows direct transfer of the picture to overhead media in a simple, direct manner. These transparencies can then be used alone or to enhance other instructional media. Most education and training systems have overhead transparency projectors.

Critical Tasks

1. **Select the picture for mounting.** Only pictures printed on clay-coated paper will work. Test for the clay coating by rubbing a moist finger on the page margin. A weak, white chalky residue can be seen on the finger if the paper is clay-coated.

2. **Bond a sheet of clear, adhesive-backed acetate to the face of the picture.** Shelf-paper will serve this purpose well, but lamination machine film works best.

3. **Rub the bonded picture and acetate with a roller (e.g., rolling pin) to get a tight seal.** Otherwise, air bubbles may distort the picture.

continued

Color Picture Lift Process, continued

4. **Soak the picture and acetate in cool water for several minutes.** This weakens the hold that the paper has on the inks making up the picture. The clay between the ink and the paper dissolves, thus allowing the inked image to transfer to the acetate.

5. **Peel the paper away from the acetate, leaving the inks making up the picture on the acetate.** If the paper does not peel easily, return to soaking it for a few more minutes.

6. **Gently swab the picture side of the acetate with a damp cotton ball.** This removes any remaining clay residue on the ink. This chalky substance should be completely removed for best projection results.

7. **Place the transparency on a flat surface and allow it to dry thoroughly.** Otherwise, the acetate may wrinkle, giving a distorted picture.

8. **Spray a clear plastic on the ink side of the transparency.** This preserves the picture and makes it more transparent.

9. **Mount the transparency on a standard transparency frame.** These come in several sizes, but $8 \times 9\frac{1}{2}$-inch is most common.

References

Brown, J. W., Lewis, R. B., and Harcleroad, F. F. (1973). *AV Instruction: Technology, Media and Methods.* 4th ed. New York: McGraw-Hill, pp. 130–131.

Kemp, J. E., and Smellie, D.C. (1989). *Planning and Producing, and Using Instructional Media.* 6th ed. New York: Harper & Row, pp. 208–209.

A relatively inexpensive and quick means of copying an opaque master to acetate is through a Thermofax machine, which uses heat-sensitive transparent film onto which the image of the master is "burned." These machines are still very prevalent in education and training institutions.

Job Aid / Thermal Overhead Transparency Production

Description This easy-to-use technique can quickly produce an overhead transparency. After making or acquiring an opaque transparency master, choose a thermal film of the desired color, place the master face down against the thermal film, and run the combination through a Thermofax copy machine. Depending on the type of acetate used, this will produce a black or a colored transparency (single color per sheet). Then mount the transparency and store the master.

Use Rationale This procedure is very quick and inexpensive, and many schools and training departments have the copy equipment and material.

continued

Thermal Overhead Transparency Production, continued

Critical Tasks

1. **Produce or acquire the transparency master.** E.g., use carbon pencil or India ink to trace a desired picture from a book or journal, or obtain commercially produced masters. Photocopies make good masters, but use each master only once.

2. **Select the most appropriate thermal film.** E.g., black line on clear film, black on color acetate, or color line on clear film. The black line on clear film is least expensive and most easily obtained.

3. **Place the transparency film on the master with the thermal side toward the image side of the master.** Do this by positioning the notch in the film to the upper right-hand corner.

4. **Run the combined pieces through the Thermofax.** Adjust the dial setting on the Thermofax copier if the transparency is too light or too dark. Large, solid dark areas do not reproduce well with this method—centers of solid areas tend to be too light.

5. **Repeat steps 3 and 4 until an acceptable transparency is produced.**

References

Satterthwaite, L. (1977). *Graphics: Skills, Media, and Materials.* 3d ed. Dubuque, Iowa: Kendall/Hunt.

Kemp, J. E. (1963). *Planning and Producing Audiovisual Materials.* San Francisco: Chandler.

Rapidly replacing the heat process for making transparencies are the more modern dot matrix, ink jet, and laser printers, some of which can give multiple colors to transparencies. These printers can copy an image onto a transparent sheet almost as easily as printing on a page.

Video Production Video is a more expensive medium for instruction, but very popular in both education and training. A high cost in producing instructional videos is the creation of their graphic elements. ID project managers are constantly searching out techniques for reducing these costs. Existing computer programs often contain graphics. Many times, these graphics could serve other purposes than those for which they were originally designed. For example, some computer graphics might serve as elements in a video production. A technique for "lifting" images from a computer monitor screen to videotape is described in the job aid on "Videotaping Computer Monitor Images."

Of course, an alternative to videotaping a computer graphic as proposed in the job aid is to print a copy of the graphic from the computer and then videotape the printed sheet, just as the artist-rendered graphic is normally taped in video production. A problem with using a graphic printout from a computer is capturing the use of color in the computer graphic. Currently, most available printers either copy in black and white or have very limited color capabilities. Of course, copyright proprieties pertain to computer materials as well.

Job Aid / Videotaping Computer Monitor Images

Description   A video camera is used to videotape images from a computer monitor screen. A video camera, on a tripod and connected to a videotape recorder, is focused on a microcomputer screen presenting a graphic image. The software images to be videotaped could be single graphics and/or animated graphics.

Use Rationale   Single and animated graphics are costly and time-consuming to produce. This technique allows for videotaping materials previously generated by a microcomputer. Once videotaped, images can then be edited like any other videotape and arranged into the desired sequences for instructional purposes.

Critical Tasks

1. **Set up videotaping equipment.** Connect the video camera to the recorder, and insert a blank tape into the video recorder.

2. **Attach the video camera to its tripod.** You need a steady base to record a clean image.

3. **Power up the video camera, recorder, and computer.** See their respective manuals.

4. **Display a graphic image on the computer monitor.** This can come from any compatible software.

5. **Focus the video camera.** The image on the computer monitor screen must be sharp in the camera viewfinder.

6. **Zoom the video camera in as close as possible, and refocus the image on the screen**.

7. **Shift the tripod back until the camera viewfinder is filled by the computer screen.** Placing the camera as far away from the computer screen as possible while the image still fills the viewfinder reduces screen distortion.

8. **Darken the room completely.** This will cut out ambient light that might reflect from the monitor screen, and it will make the monitor image brighter for recording. Because of the difficulty of finding rooms with light control, this technique is often done at night.

9. **Check and adjust the camera focus through the viewfinder so that the image of the monitor screen is sharp.** The entire computer screen should be visible without showing the surrounding edges of the monitor. Adjust the distance, again, and refocus, if required.

10. **Record the video sequences by switching video recorder into *record* mode.** Use *pause* to stop recording when booting up new pictures or animations to be videotaped.

11. **Edit the videotape as desired.** See the job aid on "Videotape Editing."

Reference

Norwood, N. S. (1989). *Integrating Elements: Creative Approaches to Video and Computer Imagery in Education*. Minneapolis, Minn.: Intermedia Arts Minnesota.

Both print and nonprint instructional materials require *editing* to improve them for purposes of communication and parsimony (workbooks, class handouts, film, video, slide/tape, filmstrip, etc.). The "Videotape Editing" job aid presents a relatively simple procedure for editing one of the nonprint media: videotape.

Job Aid / Videotape Editing

Description   The editing of videotape involves identifying and mapping scenes found on existing videotape(s) that will serve an instructional designer's purpose. Once identified, the scenes are electronically assembled according to design specifications, usually via a script or storyboard. The major elements required are a script, editing equipment, and an equipment operator. The equipment consists of two monitors and two interconnected video decks (source and recording monitors and decks), with appropriate video and audio connections, and an audio monitor to listen to the audio portion of the videotapes. The operator locates the scenes to be edited and uses the video editing controller to edit according to the storyboard specifications. The particular type of editing presented in this job aid is called *insert control track editing.*

Use Rationale   Seldom is it possible to videotape what is desired in a single pass. In fact, to ensure that the best scene is captured, several shots of the same scene and elements of the different scenes may have to be edited and assembled together to produce the desired product. In addition, program developers will usually specify special effects, including fades, graphics, change in speed, and music, which must be done after the initial or post-production videotaping.

Critical Task Sequence

1. **Acquire all relevant unedited videotapes, storyboards, and scripts for the finished videotape.** Storyboards are detailed, sequenced, graphic and verbal descriptions of visual and audio elements planned for a videotape. A script gives detailed lines used to narrate or portray a role.

2. **Preview and prepare to code the unedited videotapes.** Give each videotape its own name or number to facilitate easy location of segments. Create a *tape log* for each videotape, which briefly describes each scene, listing IN and OUT times and any visual or audio cues. See Figure 5.13.

3. **Use the storyboard/script to help establish the location of the IN and OUT points on corresponding videotape segments.** Write these IN and OUT points and the running time for each segment into the editor's tape log as you search out the individual segments during source video playback. Video recording and playback equipment counts time in seconds of play as a videotape is run so that any particular part of the tape may be tied to a specific time. These times are used to mark the IN and OUT points for each scene. See columns 4 and 5 in Figure 5.13.

4. **Estimate the total running times to be used in the final version of the videotape.** Add up the running times of each of the segments on the editor's tape log. This will tell roughly how long the videotape should be for the recording deck.

5. **Connect the videotape recording monitors and source decks to each other and to the editing console.** The source deck will play the unedited videotape, and the recording deck will record the edits onto a new videotape. Schematics for connecting the three are included in the manuals for the equipment.

continued

Videotape Editing, continued

FIGURE 5.13 / Example of an editor's videotape log

VIDEOTAPE LOG

Tape No. _____ Page: _____ of : _____

Series:_____ Program: _____

Date: _____ Project Name: _____

Storyboard Cell No.	Cut No.	Description/ IN-OUT Cues	Counter/Timer IN OUT	Running Time	Comment
		IN: OUT:			
		IN: OUT:			
		IN: OUT:			
		IN: OUT:			
		IN: OUT:			
		IN: OUT:			
		IN: OUT:			
		IN: OUT:			
		IN: OUT:			
		IN: OUT:			
		IN: OUT:			

KEY/COMMENTS: G — useable material   C — cutaway material
               NG— material unuseable   + — material to be used

continued

Videotape Editing, continued

6. **Using the recording deck, record "color black" onto an unused videotape on which the unedited segments will be laid.** This is done by recording without any incoming visual or audio signal.

7. **Select the first scene to be edited.** Determine this from the tape log.

8. **Set the videotape in the recording deck to the appropriate IN point.** This is the point at which you will begin recording the first segment from the unedited videotape. Press buttons RECORD/ENTER.

9. **Set the videotape in the source deck to the appropriate IN point.** This will be the beginning point of the videotape segment that will be transferred to the recording deck. Press buttons SOURCE/ENTER.

10. **Press buttons AUTO/EDIT on editing controller.** The editing controller will then automatically synchronize the recording and source video decks so that their IN points match as the two videotapes begin to roll.

11. **Press the END button when the predetermined OUT point for the source videotape is reached.** This will cause the two decks to pause.

12. **Select the other scenes from the source videotape(s), in sequence, according to the storyboard and the tape log, and repeat steps 7–10.** Do this until all edited scenes have been recorded on the new videotape.

13. **From this finished videotape (master) make review copies for critiquing or testing.** Use the master only for further editing or for making copies. Store the master under cool, dry conditions.

References

Sony Corporation. (1980). *RM-440 Automatic Editing Control Unit Operation Manual.* Tokyo: Sony, pp. 8–17, 22–23.

Slide/Tape Production   Another popular means of presenting instruction is through the combination of slide film and audiotape. This combined system requires an audiotape playback unit that is in synchronization with a slide projector. Not all slide projectors and audio playback units have the synchronization capability. The use of the slide/tape medium results in a less spontaneous presentation than would a slide presentation with a live narrator, but it provides a far more consistent presentation, and one that can be viewed over and over by the learner without an instructor being present. A disadvantage in developing instruction on slide/tape is that if a change in narration or sequence of slides is wanted, it will be necessary to renarrate and/or reprogram the sequence. Many self-instructional labs in education and training programs around the country use this medium. The popularity of the slide/tape system lies partly in the ease of software production and in the availability of production and projection equipment.

Job Aid / Slide/Tape Program Production

Description   Once objectives and strategies have been established through the design process and a slide/tape has been chosen as the means of instructional delivery, a storyboard or script is generated that specifies visual and audio details for each slide. Photographs are shot on location or from existing pictures, and graphics are acquired or produced. Then slide film is used to shoot the graphics and photographs. The exposed slide film is sent to a lab, where the film is processed and mounted on slide frames (usually 2 × 2). After the mounted slides are returned from the lab, they are placed in a slide tray in the order specified by the storyboard. Appropriate audio is acquired or produced (narration, music, special sounds, etc.) and then synchronized for automatic play with the slides.

Use Rationale   Slide/tape programs are far cheaper to produce than are video programs. The equipment for playing slide/tape instructional programs is readily available in most education and training settings. Slide/tape instruction can be designed to fit group or individual use.

Critical Tasks

1. **Receive the specifications for the slide/tape instructional program.** I.e., the storyboard and/or script.

2. **Check the storyboard for accuracy.** Use the following criteria:
   a. The central idea is clearly expressed and the topic limited.
   b. The degree to which the program is to be motivational, informational, or instructional is clear.
   c. The important characteristics of the target learners have been accounted for in the design.
   d. The audio matches exactly with the visuals.
   e. The design specifications match with production realities, e.g., budget, completion date, facilities and equipment, length.

3. **Select other staff, if needed, to assist with the preparation of visual and audio materials.** E.g., graphic artist, photographer, narrator, talent.

4. **Prepare a photo shot list, clustering those visual scenes to be shot in the same locale.** Place the concomitant number from the individual storyboard cells in parentheses next to the shot directions, for easy reference to the storyboard.

5. **Schedule the shooting of clustered visual scenes.** It is wise to visit the location, check the facilities, and gather any props prior to the shoot date. It is also important to get a signed release from the person(s) in charge of shoot locations.

6. **Acquire or produce the art work, including titles, illustrations, graphs, and charts.** Using an 8 × 12-inch format for artwork saves time and money, because it is equivalent to the 35mm slide ratio of 2:3.

7. **Photograph the scenes and/or the pictures and artwork.** Usually it is wise to take additional pictures if you're uncertain about exposure or about what will fit best. Pictures and artwork are usually photographed by a camera on a tripod using a special closeup lens. Have all slides in a horizontal format, if possible.

continued

Slide/Tape Program Production, continued

8. **Keep a log sheet of all pictures taken.** This record will be useful while assessing picture quality and content, and for reshooting scenes.

9. **Have exposed film processed and mounted as slides.** There are many excellent film processing labs.

10. **Select from among the returned slides.** You can use a manual slide sorter to sequence slides and to eliminate poorer slides in favor of better ones.

11. **Place the slides into the slide projector tray(s).** Use the predetermined sequence dictated by the storyboard.

12. **Project the slides onto the type of screen planned for the system's use, and check them for quality.** Reshoot any slides not meeting specifications.

13. **Modify any written narration or captions to get the best fit for the final sequence of slides.** Use criteria that require conversational style and short sentences and avoids the use of undefined technical terms.

14. **Record any audio elements of the slide series.** Usually, it is wise to find a good voice for narration, even at additional cost.

15. **Program the slide/tape equipment so that the audio playback and visual playback are synchronized.**

16. **Assess the completed product.** Use the following criteria:

    a. The flow should be smooth from one slide to the next.

    b. The narration should facilitate continuity and support visuals.

17. **Summatively evaluate the slide/tape program to establish program validity.** Pretest, instruct through slide/tape, and posttest a group of representative learners, to determine if the instruction has the desired effect.

References

Kemp, J. E. (1980). *Planning and Producing Audiovisual Materials.* New York: Harper & Row, pp. 56–59, 63.

Kemp, J. E., and Dayton, D. K. (1985). *Planning and Producing Instructional Media.* New York: Harper & Row, pp. 38, 55–57, 196–206.

Bishop, Ann (1986). *Slides: Planning and Producing Slide Programs.* Rochester, N.Y.: Eastman Kodak, pp. 16, 90, 116–124.

There is a plethora of graphic and photographic material available in a wide range of journals and other print media. Often, permission can be obtained from the owners of these pictures to reproduce them for instructional purposes. The job aid on "Photocopying Print and Nonprint Material" presents the process steps drawn from Robert Beacon's excellent work, and were slightly modified to fit the job aid format used here. The

Job Aid / Photocopying Print and Nonprint Material

Description The procedure outlined here lists the step-by-step operations for production of successful slides and pictures of copy material. If the results are consistently too dark or too light, adjust the lens opening or exposure accordingly. If they are inconsistent, check your meter and camera. If the problem is still not solved, consult an expert.

Use Rationale Anyone using photography in a media center for instructional or motivational purposes will find it necessary sooner or later to make copies of print or nonprint materials, either for projection as slides or for pictures for display purposes.

Critical Tasks

1. **Gather the necessary equipment and materials for copy work.**

   copy stand
   film for slides or pictures
   lights that color match the film
   camera
   supplementary lenses, if needed
   gray card

   light meter
   cable release
   bubble level
   lens tissue
   glass sheet, 9 × 12-inch, nonreflecting copy material

2. **Load the camera with film.** Clean the lens with lens tissue only. Ordinary tissue can scratch valuable lenses.

3. **Set both meter and camera at the proper ASA number.** The number can be found for each film on the film roll or cassette or on the box it comes in.

4. **Mount the camera on the copy stand.** Make sure that it is level, pointing perpendicularly down to the copy. Use a bubble level if one is available. Shooting copy at even a slight angle will produce distortion.

5. **Attach the cable release to the camera.** Its use will minimize camera movement at the moment the shutter is released.

6. **Place the copy material on the copy stand.** Place a glass sheet over the material if there is need to keep it flat. Adjust the lights so that there is no glare or unwanted reflections; they should be at an approximate angle of 45 degrees to the copy. Focus.

7. **Measure the light falling on different parts of the copy material with the light meter.** For best results, the meter should show the same amount of light falling on all parts of the picture. Adjust the lights to eliminate glare and reflections that may arise through moving the lights. If the copying is done outdoors, it should be done in the shade, away from any structure that might reflect a strong color. Changes in lighting are accomplished by moving the copy stand.

8. **Refocus the camera on the copy as sharply as possible.** Use f8 or smaller whenever possible. This will minimize focusing error, especially with closeup lenses. Recheck the focus and the gray

continued

increased availability of good 35mm cameras, and the ability of fast film to take pictures under low light levels, is making the shooting of slides for instructional purposes more and more popular.

Photocopying Print and Nonprint Material, continued

card reading whenever the camera, lights, or copy stand are moved. When an exposure of 1/60 second or more is required, the copy stand must be very steady, for a small vibration will cause the slide or picture to lose its sharpness of image.

9. **Frame the copy in the viewfinder.** It should appear exactly as it is to appear as a slide or picture.

10. **Place a gray card on the copy stand as though it were the material to be copied.** Take the exposure reading for this card. The light-meter reading will usually be more accurate if taken from the gray card than if the reading is taken from the copy material itself. If your camera isn't automatic, read the values for exposure and f-stop on the meter or through the built-in meter of the camera, and set your camera.

11. **Release the shutter.** Slowly squeeze the cable release.

12. **Advance the film, and begin again with the next exposure.**

References

Beacon, Robert (1973). How to use a copy stand. In *The School Media Center: A Book of Readings*, ed. P. L. Ward and R. Beacon, pp. 196–198. Metuchen, N.J.: Scarecrow Press.

Audiotape There is a tendency to downplay the use of audiotape in instructional programs, but evidence supports its use in many applications. A common use by students is to record the lectures of their instructors.

Audiotapes have been used by educational institutions and sold commercially as self-contained instruction for many topics, including language instruction. They are also used to guide students through lab experiments. The heyday for the use of such tapes occurred in the 1960s and '70s, although considerable use is still being made of them. A major application in laboratory settings was Samual Postlethwait's Audio-Tutorial System at Purdue University, begun in the early '60s. It is currently headed up by Dr. Robert Hurst. This system uses audio instruction as the major guide to students as they learn freshman botany and biology. It still has from 700 to 800 students going through the courses each semester. The student is tutored through a great variety of learning activities, which, in Postlethwait's words (Postlethwait et al., 1969, pp. 11–12), may require:

> doing an experiment, the collecting of data from the demonstration materials, reading short segments from his text or appropriate journal article, making observations through the microscope, filling in diagrams, charts or appropriate blanks in his study guide or laboratory manual, viewing sections of films, and other kinds of learning activities suitable to the topic under consideration.

His instructional audio system is integrated with live lectures, lab work, study guides, and small group meetings. Postlethwait's system is basically a centralized system, with the student going to the laboratory to receive audio instruction. However, other audio instruction programs, such as the elaborate audio teaching program at Ohio State University, called Dial Access Information Retrieval System (DAIRS), provides access to learners at a number of different locations around campus, including student dorms and the library. Students can also dial in from their homes and receive the instruction. In 1991, there were over 17,000 uses of the system. Pennsylvania State University has a similar system. Examples of public school systems that have actively involved themselves in the use of instructional audio systems are found in Beverly Hills, California, the Oak Park School District in Illinois, and the Abington School District near Philadelphia.

Advantages of using audiotape include: (1) the ease of recording audio stimuli, (2) the availability for immediate playback, (3) the many public school and university libraries that have collections of audiotapes that can be checked out, and (4) the ease of synchronizing audiotapes with other materials, including slides and workbooks. An important advantage is that almost every school and home has cassette audiotape record and playback units.

After audiotape sounds are recorded, it is usually necessary to edit them for instructional purposes. This can be done electronically or manually. Unfortunately, manually splicing the narrow tape on cassette audio tapes is not too practical. The alternative is to make a quality dub (copy) of the original tape to an open-reel audiotape. The nearby job aid presents a practical technique for manually editing and splicing audiotapes using open-reel audiotape systems.

Job Aid / Audiotape Editing and Splicing

Description This is a process for deleting, adding, and/or arranging segments of an audio recording or recordings. Basically, the editor finds the spots where changes needs to be made in a tape or tapes, cuts them, and then splices them together to form a new master. The fundamental skills required for editing and splicing audiotape is not complex and can be mastered with knowledge and practice.

Use Rationale Often, new or existing instructional audiotapes may need to be shortened or combined with segments from the same tape or other tapes.

Critical Tasks

1. **Preview the target audiotape or tapes on an open-reel audiotape recorder.** If several changes are to be made, list the individual segments to be edited. Prepare a cut list, with exact words just before and after each cut, e.g., before: "... go to the store"; after: "Sure, I'll be glad to go."

2. **Replay the audiotape, and stop as close to the first cutting point as you can.**

3. **Pinpoint the exact spot to be cut by moving the tape manually back and forth across the playback head of the open-reel audiotape recorder.** You can hear the sound sufficiently to judge where to mark.

continued

Audiotape Editing and Splicing, continued

4. **Carefully mark the cutting points on the tape.** Use a small, indelible felt pen and mark gently on the tape over the playback head, on the back or shiny side of the tape. Don't use grease pencil, because it leaves a glue residue that damages the head of the tape recorder.

5. **Cut the tape or tapes at one or more of the cutting points.** Use a single-edge razor blade and a tape splicing block, as shown in Figure 5.14, and then cut and splice by completing the following tasks:

   a. Place one piece of audiotape, shiny side up, firmly in the middle channel of the splicing block so that it barely reaches beyond the cutting groove.

   b. With the cutting groove as a guide, trim the end of the tape with the razor blade. It is preferable to use a new blade to avoid tearing the tape.

   c. Repeat the steps a and b from the other side of the splicing block with a second piece of audiotape. If there will be several cuts, keep the audiotape segments carefully ordered so as not to confuse which is which. Use numbered pieces of splicing tape placed on the end of each piece of audiotape for this purpose. The numbers are keyed to a splice list showing their new sequence. Also, draw a small arrow on the splicing tape to show the running direction of the audiotape.

   d. Repeat the same procedure for all tape segments. You will then have a set of marked audiotapes ready to be spliced.

   e. Use a 1-inch piece of splicing tape to weld together the first two matched cut ends of audiotape segments. It should be unnecessary to trim the sides of the splicing tape since they are bought to size.

   g. Repeat for all marked audiotape segments.

FIGURE 5.14 / Audiotape splicing block

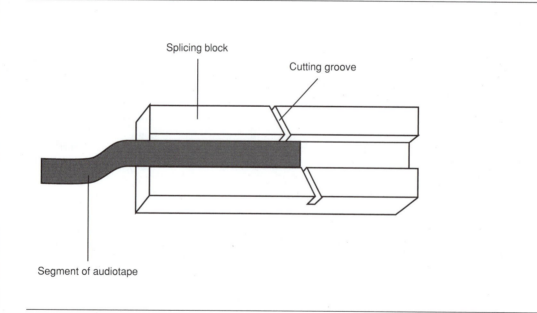

Splicing block

Cutting groove

Segment of audiotape

---

6. **Quality dub (copy) or remaster the edited tape.** Always use new tape for dubbing, or at least erase old tape. Keep original edited tape as the master for making copies. If sound levels are

continued

Audiotape Editing and Splicing, continued

different from one piece of edited tape to another, it may be necessary to ride gain on the level meter on the tape recorder.

References

Kemp, J. E., and Smellie, D. C. (1989). *Planning and Producing, and Using Instructional Media.* 6th ed. New York: Harper & Row, pp. 156–157.

Minor, E., and Frye, H. R. (1977). *Techniques of Producing Visual Instructional Media.* New York: McGraw-Hill, pp. 110–158.

Motion Pictures   Despite the advent of video for instruction, instructional moving pictures, because of numerous film libraries and the wide proliferation of 16mm projection equipment, are still very much in use. A common problem in using instructional motion pictures is having the film break during instruction. The repair or splicing of the film is a simple procedure requiring limited skills and hardware. Further, as education and service programs continue to accumulate their own instructional films, there is a need to edit them so that they better fit the objectives of the instructional unit. Some of the same skills of splicing a broken film can be used in editing existing films to better fit specific instruction.

Job Aid / Motion Picture Film Splicing

Description   This technique is part of the process for editing a motion picture, where segments of the original footage are cut, deleted, and/or resequenced to better fit the objectives the film is to meet. Splicing is the technique necessary for welding the edited pieces back into one continuous roll of film.

Use Rationale   Whether in the editing process of instructional film production or simply for repairing a broken instructional film, anyone who regularly uses the motion picture medium will have occasion to use the splicing technique to connect pieces of film in order to make the film operational.

Critical Tasks

1. **Bring together materials and equipment.** Film, cement, and splicer—see Figure 5.15.

2. **Position the first piece of film on the sprockets, from the right.** Set the film on the front sprocket pin of the bottom right jaw of the splicer, with the emulsion or dull side up.

3. **Lock the film in place.** Lower the top right-hand jaw and close the far right-hand clamp. See Figure 5.16.

continued

Motion Picture Film Splicing, continued

FIGURE 5.15 / Film splicer

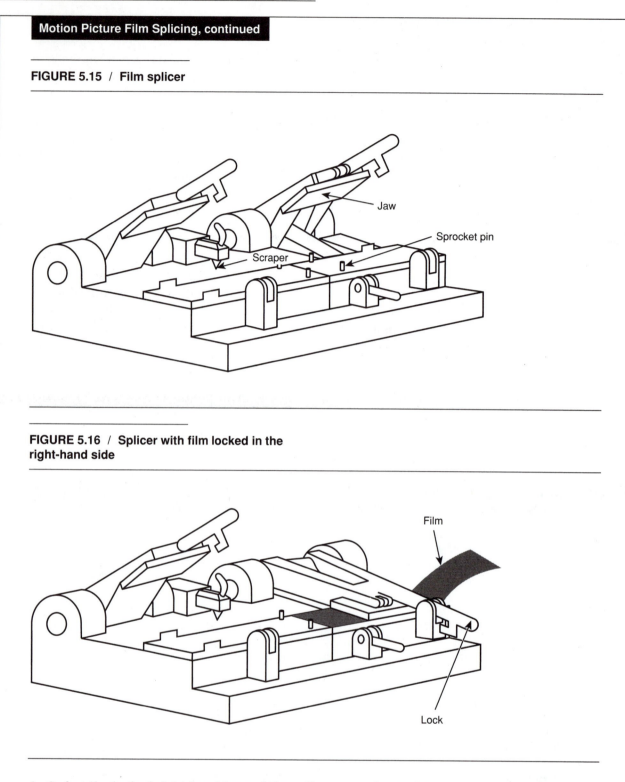

FIGURE 5.16 / Splicer with film locked in the right-hand side

4. **Swing the locked right-hand jaws of the splicer up and out of the way.** The first piece of film, untrimmed, is still clamped in place. See Figure 5.17.

5. **Position the second piece of film.** Set it on the front sprocket pin of the bottom left-hand jaw of the splicer, with the emulsion (dull) side up.

continued

Motion Picture Film Splicing, continued

FIGURE 5.17 / Splicer with film locked on the right-hand side and out of the way

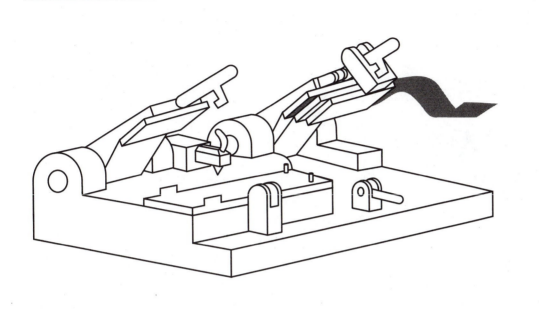

6. **Lock the second piece of film in place.** Lower and secure the clamp of the upper left-hand jaw of the splicer so that it holds the film in place.

7. **Trim the ends of both pieces of film.** Lower the right jaws of the splicer, then again swing the right-hand jaws of the splicer up and out of the way, with the first piece of film still clamped in place.

8. **Remove the emulsion.** Pull the scraper forward and down, and carefully scrape toward the rear. Repeat until all of the emulsion is removed from the leading edge of the left-hand piece of film, down to the clear film base.

9. **Brush away any deposits or dust from the scraped film edge.** Such particles tend to weaken the effect of the cement if left on the film.

10. **Apply film cement.** Apply a very thin coating of cement to the exposed film base, and quickly go to the next step before the film can dry.

11. **Quickly lower the right-hand piece of film into place.** Lower the clamped jaws of the right-hand section of the splicer with its piece of film, which brings the two pieces of film together, the one on the right slightly overlapping the other. Then secure the middle clamp. See Figure 5.18.

12. **Raise the top left-hand jaw out of the way.** This permits the cement to dry faster, making a cleaner bond.

13. **Time the cement drying for a period of 5–10 seconds.** This permits the cement to harden.

continued

Motion Picture Film Splicing, continued

**FIGURE 5.18 / Splicer with film locked
on both sides**

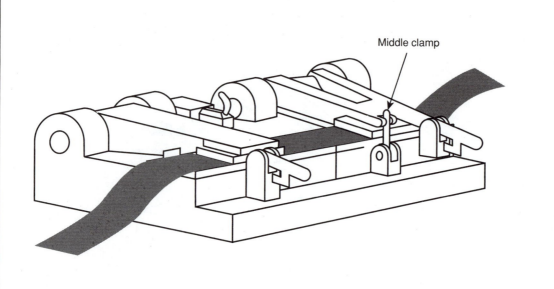

Middle clamp

14. **Remove the spliced film carefully.** Unclamp both the right-hand and left-hand upper jaws of the splicer, and gently remove the spliced film.

15. **If the splice fails to hold, check for process errors.** Such as:
    a. The film cement is too old (appears thickened).
    b. All of the emulsion was not scraped off.
    c. The film was weakened by excessive scraping.
    d. The film was removed before the cement had set.
    e. There was faulty alignment of the splicer sprocket pins or the pressure clamp.

    Note: If the film has been protected with a coating of *Photogard*, the bottom piece of film on the right will not stick to the cement. To solve, raise the clamped jaws of the right-hand side with the trimmed film so that you can see the bottom edge of the film. Use a razor blade to scrape away the Photogard down to a clear or frosted base. Brush away loose particles. Continue at step 11.

16. **Repeat the entire process as necessary.**

Reference

Kemp, J. E. (1963). *Planning and Producing Audiovisual Materials.* San Francisco: Chandler, pp. 139–144.

Post-Production

Prototype Assembly, Revision, and Delivery In step 8 of the production process, personnel turn the instructional elements that they have produced over to those running the prototyping component (dealt with in the next chapter). This is not just a matter of passing the baton on to the next runner, but requires careful consultation with those who will do the final assembly, testing, and polishing of the instruction. This is particularly important for agencies where production and prototyping are separately managed. Each additional layer of bureaucracy impedes communication among those involved and increases the chance of error. Again, meeting with persons responsible for the prototyping and relating the products with the design, will short circuit many potential problems.

The same rule pertains to receiving revision specifications from prototyping (step 9). A careful walk-through of the specifications so that both parties are in agreement will save much time and frustration later, by reducing misinterpretations.

The products of the final revision of the combined production elements are called **masters**. There should be more than one set of masters, preferably stored at different locations. Months and even years of effort have gone up in smoke because of careless handling of masters. An important rule is to use masters only to make copies. Masters should be stored under conditions that promise the least deterioration. For best results, there should be a formal plan and formal responsibility for storing and protecting them.

Summary

This chapter discussed the processes involved in taking design specifications and transforming them into actual products that, with assembly, can be used in the classroom. The Program Evaluation and Review Technique (PERT) was described as an effective means for identifying, costing, and timing the production process. Examples of job aids were presented or referenced for each of the steps in the production process. Job aids for nonprint production included those on overhead transparencies, audiotapes, videotapes, and slides.

References

Anderson, R. H. (1983). *Selecting and Developing Media for Instruction.* New York: Van Nostrand Reinhold.

Bishop, Ann (1986). *Slides: Planning and Producing Slide Programs.* Rochester, N.Y.: Eastman Kodak.

DeLuca, S. M. (1991). *Instructional Video.* Boston: Focal Press.

Gray, Bill (1976). *Studio Tips for Artists and Graphic Designers.* Englewood Cliffs, N.J.: Prentice-Hall.

Matkowshi, B. S. (1983). *Steps to Effective Business Graphics.* San Diego, Calif.: Hewlett-Packard.

Piper, Amy J. (1990). An Analysis and Comparison of Selected Project Management Techniques and Their Implications for the Instructional Development Process. Unpublished dissertation. East Lansing, Mich.: Michigan State University.

Postlethwait, S. N., et al. (1969). *The Audio-Tutorial Approach to Learning.* Minneapolis, Minn.: Burgess.

Romiszowski, A. J. (1974). *The Selection and Use of Instructional Media.* New York: Wiley.

Ward, P. S., and Beacon, R. (eds.) (1973). *The School Media Center: A Book of Readings.* Metuchen, N.J.: Scarecrow Press.

CHAPTER 6

Prototyping

Process of assembling, pilot testing, respecifying, validating, and finalizing an instructional unit

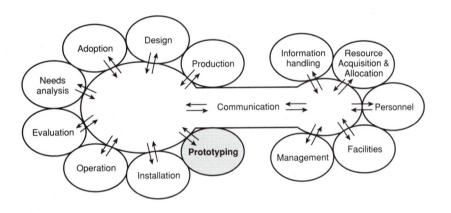

Learner Objectives

1. Differentiate between an instructional prototype and a completed instructional package.

2. Differentiate among the functions and characteristics of formative and summative evaluation.

3. Relate the concept of *interface* to the effectiveness of an instructional prototype.

4. Given a randomly ordered list of the steps in the prototyping process, to place them in the appropriate sequence.

5. Match prototyping tasks with appropriate techniques.

6. Recall definitions of major terms.

Introduction

Instructional prototyping, as found across the literature, ranges from a few processes to many processes. Often, it is treated as part of the production process. However, the functions of prototyping, as described here, are limited to assembly and testing of an instructional unit, and generation of revision and marketing specifications.

A prototype is a functional version of an instructional unit, usually in an unfinished state, whose effectiveness and efficiency can be tested.

Prototypes are assembled from instructional elements that have been generated and/or acquired by personnel of a production unit.

The function of the prototyping component, as presented in the ID model used here, is to guide instructional developers through the processes of combining elements to form a testable and finished instructional unit. Based on the test results, prototyping personnel would then generate specifications for any needed revision and send them back to production. After the production personnel have returned the revised material and the materials have been integrated into the instructional unit, prototyping personnel may need to retest the unit to determine whether the revision brought the instruction up to specifications. Once the revised materials meet criteria, the prototyping unit is responsible for generating fine-tuning specifications for making the instructional package marketable. These specifications are then sent to production or some other agency for final revision to form a **product master**. Copies made from this product master would be sent to installation teams and clients. In cases where mass production is indicated, the instructional unit is contracted out to external production and marketing agencies.

Prototyping Process

Operationally, the prototyping process has the following steps:

1. Receive the prototype elements from the production team.
2. Check the elements received against the design specifications, and reconcile any discrepancies found with the design and/or production teams.
3. Design the interfaces for assembling the prototype elements.
4. Assemble the prototype elements into a testable instructional unit.
5. Generate directions for staff or others carrying out the formative and summative evaluations of the prototype.
6. Identify representative subjects to be used in the pilot testing of the prototype.
7. Complete a formative evaluation of the prototype (which may be carried out several times at different stages of prototype development).

8. Analyze the formative-evaluation data, and report any instructional specification recommendations to the design or the production unit, as appropriate.

9. Sequence and integrate the revised elements provided by the production team into the prototype by repeating steps 3–8, as necessary, until the instructional prototype performs satisfactorily.

10. Generate specifications for any marketing refinements, and send them to the design and/or production units, as appropriate.

11. Receive the revised instructional elements from production, and upgrade the prototype to an instructional unit product master.

12. Set up conditions for summative evaluation, carry it out, and report the results.

13. Submit the finished instructional unit product master to the appropriate agency for mass production and marketing.

The very fact that groups responsible for design, production, and prototyping are working separately makes it likely that some errors will be made in performing their respective processes. To control for error, the sequence of actions carried out separately by larger ID teams require more checks than would be necessary for individual or small-team efforts. Quality control is enhanced for both large and small ID groups by following sequentially ordered processes such as those just listed. The following sections deal with the specifics of the thirteen prototyping processes and their concomitant techniques.

Analyze Specific Prototyping Tasks

In a sense, steps 1 and 2 of the prototyping process are roughly analogous to receiving the parts of a prefabricated house from the manufacturer. To successfully assemble it, a builder must have plans and directions (specifications) and an inventory of all of the elements making up the house, and sometimes it is important to have information about the wishes and expectations of the people for whom the house is being assembled. Similarly, plans for a finished instructional prototype and characteristics of the target audience and location are studied, and the prototype elements received are compared against their design specifications to ensure that all of the design elements are accounted for and come up to predetermined criteria. *Task analysis* and *PERT* are two techniques that can assist in the identification and analysis of prototyping tasks.

Assemble Prototype Elements

Steps 3 and 4 of the prototyping process are concerned with determining appropriate relationships among the instructional elements and forming a testable instructional unit. A major concern with prototype development is the context into which the prototype is to fit. Usually, a prototype will become part of other instruction and must be designed so that it complements and works with that other instruction. This includes agreements on the meaning given to terms used in the prototype and its larger system, as well as how the prototype fits logistically within the rest of the instructional system. If these kinds of factors are left unattended, the prototype's effectiveness, and even survival, may be suspect. There is an assumption that these concerns will be dealt with by the design component and will be highlighted in the design specifications. Even when that is true, what works on paper is not necessarily what works as a prototype. A prototype may work well in a lab setting but not work well when installed in the target location. The recall of new automobiles is a classic example of this problem.

These types of problems can be looked at profitably from a system point of view. By definition, a **system** is a set of components arranged to perform some wanted operation(s). The components of a system are also called its **subsystems**. For example, a workshop is a system that facilitates the acquisition of specific knowledge and skills by its participants. Some of its subsystems are facilitator, instructors, students, materials, equipment, and instructional facility. **Interfaces** are the common boundaries between components of a system. These components interact and operate effectively together, by sharing essential information across their common boundaries.

One technique for relating the components of a system is called **interface analysis**. This technique is supported by general systems theory, which looks at all organized entities as systems made up of interdependent subsystems, or components working together toward a common purpose. For example, the automobile component of a transportation system depends on its own components (motor, transmission, drive shaft, wheels, electrical system, and so on) operating together to enable it to function properly. The automobile, in turn, must interact with components of a larger system (e.g., other drivers, roads, traffic signs, traffic rules). Each of these components has information that is essential to the functions of the other components. This information must travel across common boundaries, i.e., interfaces, between components. Sometimes these interfaces are closed to the passing of information. For instance, a defective gear shift will not permit the driver to inform the car which gear to mesh with the drive shaft. A defective turn signal does not warn the drivers behind. In these examples of a **closed system**, the boundaries, or interfaces, between some components of the system were closed to the passing of essential information needed for effective operation. The degree to which interfaces form an **open system**, that is, permit the flow of essential information between the components of the system, has a large effect on the system's effectiveness.

The concept of closed and open systems extends beyond things mechanical. Social systems may be closed to information. For example, many nations at different times in their history have closed their borders to foreigners and prevented their citizens from traveling, thus preventing the ready exchange of information with the rest of the world.

The Instructional Project Development and Management (IPDM) Model, depicted in Figure 6.1 is another example of a system that depends on the open exchange of information across component interfaces. The arrows in the figure are a symbolic way of representing the flow of essential information between the components. Without this information, those responsible for carrying out the processes of the components would be severely hampered in meeting their charge. For example, imagine the effect if design personnel did *not* share information with production personnel.

FIGURE 6.1 / Exchange of essential information among IPDM components
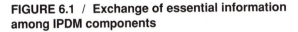

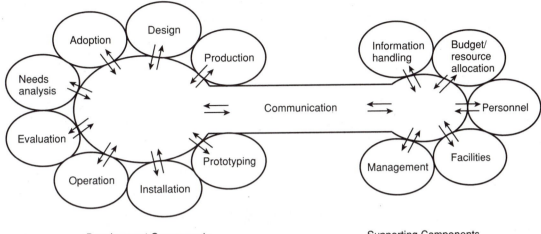

A major task of managers is to identify the information necessary for the effective interaction of the individual and collective components of their instructional systems, and to make sure the component interfaces are open to sending and receiving essential information. The *interface analysis technique* has been effective in identifying that information. A job aid for this technique is presented in Chapter 11.

Assembly of a prototype may be a simple or a complex process, depending on its instructional strategies, media, and/or procedures. As a simple example, suppose that the principal prototype elements in an elementary science unit on energy include a 10-minute videotape, eight overhead transparencies, an instructor's manual, and a student workbook. Assembling these elements into an instructional unit would be relatively simple. In fact, all of the directions needed could be included in the manual and the workbook. Curiously, even for units easy to assemble, directions for doing so are often left to guess work. Needless to say, assembly of a prototype for a course, or for several interacting courses, would be much more complex and thus would have a higher potential for error.

Many of the interface defects overlooked by the designers of an instructional unit can be spotted by persons doing the formative and the summative evaluations, *if* they are told what to look for.

Formatively Evaluate Prototype

An instructional prototype should be assessed at various stages of completion (steps 5–7 of the prototyping process). In practice, this testing ranges from an informal check of particular elements to the application of sophisticated psychometric techniques. While it is certainly desirable to empirically test the prototype, the cost, time, and other resource requirements usually discourage it. However, practitioners have found that having as few as two or three representative members of the target audience work through early versions of the prototype, one at a time, will catch the large majority of any problems.

The advantage of testing instructional elements as they are completed is that any errors found in the preceding elements can be avoided in the development of succeeding elements, thereby reducing the costs of revision. Some instructional developers have enough confidence to wait until the entire prototype is completed before doing formative testing, gambling that there will be few revisions required. This is seldom recommended, except in the use of *rapid prototype development* (see Chapter 4), which deliberately does the prototype quick-and-dirty before testing, as an alternative to more costly development. A very cost-effective technique is presented here in the "One-on-One Formative Evaluation" job aid.

Job Aid / One-on-One Formative Evaluation

Description   **Formative evaluation** serves to identify design flaws *during* the process of instructional development rather than after completion of its development. Thus, not only can the data from this technique can be used to correct the parts being tested, but any flaws discovered in initial development can be avoided in later development. There are many versions of the formative-evaluation technique. The basic scheme of the one-on-one version is focused on self-instructional products: The evaluator observes one student at a time, carefully, while they are actually being taught by an early draft of the prototype. The evaluator questions the student as he or she progresses through the instruction. The process may be repeated three or more times, with a new student each time. When available, students of different ability levels should be tested.

Use Rationale   All too often, instruction is developed in a finished form before serious evaluation is carried out. When flaws are discovered, developers and clients are faced with the expense of revising materials that were costly to get in finished form in the first place. As a result, revisions are made reluctantly, and the instruction often is continued in its flawed state. Formative evaluation uses early draft prototype materials and is thus considerably less expensive. Despite the limited number of students put through this version, most of the flaws found through more sophisticated procedures are also found using the one-on-one formative-evaluation technique.

Critical Tasks

1. **From the prototype data, complete an objective-strategy-medium-criterion match for the instruction.** The data from this technique serve as reference material for organizing the data collected while doing a formative evaluation. See Chapter 4.

2. **Organize the prototype materials.** Usually, these are ordered into a sequence based on their use by the student, so that the materials may be delivered efficiently to the student during the formative-evaluation process.

3. **Schedule student(s) to take the instruction.** The students will go through the instructional unit one at a time. They should be representative of the population at which the instruction is aimed.

4. **Orient the student(s) to the task.** You need to ensure their cooperation, usually by indicating that it is the instruction that is suspect rather than their personal abilities.

continued

One-on-One Formative Evaluation, continued

5. **Observe, question, and record data as a single student proceeds through the instruction and testing.** Note whenever the student appears to have difficulty, e.g., makes errors, doesn't know what to do next, and, through questioning, determine the possible reasons for the problems, and record them. See Figure 6.2.

6. **Specify what changes you think have to be made to correct the specific problems.** E.g., changes in vocabulary, strategy, adding or deleting content or media, varying sequence of activities.

7. **Specify any changes in the ID practice.** This avoids similar problems in the instructional segments yet to be developed.

8. **Deliver the recommendations to the appropriate personnel.**

FIGURE 6.2 / Data collection instrument for one-on-one evaluation

---

DATA COLLECTION GUIDE FOR FORMATIVE EVALUATION

Evaluator: _____

Subject: _____

Date: _____

Package: _____

Directions: After each observation connoting a problem in the instruction, complete the following sections, before having the student continue.

Observation 1

a. Problem:

b. Possible cause:

c. Possible correction:

Observation 2

a. Problem:

b. Possible cause:

c. Possible correction:

References

Baker, E. L., and Alkin, M. C. (1973). Formative evaluation of instructional development. *AV Communication Review* 21 (winter): 389–418.

Bloom, B. S., Hastings, J. T., and Madaus, G. F. (1971). *Handbook on Formative and Summative Evaluation.* New York: McGraw-Hill, pp. 117–138.

Lawson, T. E. (1974). *Formative Instructional Product Evaluation: Instruments and Strategies.* Englewood Cliffs, N.J.: Educational Technology Publications, pp. 93–95.

An interesting variation on the "One-on-One Formative Evaluation" job aid is to add an **oral protocol**, in which the student is asked to talk his or her way through the instruction, so it will be clear what the student is thinking as he or she makes decisions and responses. This obviously puts an artificial constraint on learning that is different from what would happen under normal classroom conditions, but it is often worth the loss, particularly in the early stages of formative evaluation, because of the insights gained into how the instruction affects student understanding and decision making.

Other instructional developers prefer to run several individuals through the instruction at the same time, to establish a broader and more representative database In their formative evaluation. They use a small-group testing format as described in the "Small-Group Formative Evaluation" job aid.

Job Aid / Small-Group Formative Evaluation

Description   A sample of approximately ten to thirty subjects is drawn from the target population. Procedures are used to collect all the relevant information whose interpretation would suggest ways the instructional materials could be revised. After the subjects are pretested, they are put through the instruction. Then they are administered posttests and attitude questionnaires. Finally, they are put through an oral debriefing. The data are analyzed, and a report is generated recommending modifications in the instructional unit and in instructional development processes. It is desirable to perform small-group formative evaluation two to three times during instructional development of course-size instructional units. More repetitions may be required for assessing the development of larger projects.

Use Rationale   Instructional development is costly and time-consuming. The checking of the effectiveness of instruction while it is in development lets the developer know if the right procedures are being followed and how functional the instructional materials and processes are to that point. In addition, such evaluation can help determine the need for remedial, review, and enrichment materials. Because a small group can better represent the target population, the data gathered make a better indicator of likely student response to the instruction than do the data from the one-on-one technique.

Critical Tasks

1. **Complete or acquire a draft of the prototype to be tested.** Assemble the materials and equipment. Train the assessment personnel and instructors involved. Arrange for facilities. Assemble and validate any tests used prior to, during, and after instruction.

2. **Sequence the instructional materials and tests.** Put them in the order in which they will be presented to the subjects, for more efficient implementation.

3. **Select an appropriate subject sample.** If possible, choose the subjects from the target population. A random selection of ten to thirty students from the subject pool is preferred.

4. **Choose a facility for the prototype trial.** The facility conditions should be typical of those under which the instruction and testing would normally take place.

continued

Small-Group Formative Evaluation, continued

5. **Schedule the instruction and evaluation.** Adequate time should be arranged for required testing as well as instructional activity.

6. **Orient the subjects and instructors to the trial.** Establish rapport with the learners: explain that a new set of instructional materials has been designed and that their responses and comments are important for the improvement of the instruction. Provide any necessary training to instructors, including a walk-through of the instruction.

7. **Pretest the subjects.** Test to establish entering behaviors and the degree to which they are knowledgeable about the instructional content.

8. **Carry out the instruction.** Serve as an aide to the instructor, when needed. Get the instructor and the student past any unforeseen problems. Monitor them to make sure the instruction is done as planned. Note any discrepancies.

9. **Administer the posttest.** Test to establish the degree to which the subjects have mastered what was taught.

10. *Optional:* **Administer an attitude questionnaire.** Test to determine how the subjects felt about the content, the instruction, and the testing.

11. **Carry out an in-depth debriefing of the subjects.** E.g., use a modified *Nominal Group Process* (Chapter 3). First the subjects are asked to write a list of any defects or problems related to the instruction. Then the debriefer writes their items on a flip chart so all can see, followed by a discussion of each item.

12. **Carry out an in-depth debriefing of the instructors.** Walk them through the instruction, asking them to comment on content, objectives, testing, strategies, media, and instruction. Given a flaw, ask them how they would fix it.

13. **Analyze and synthesize the data from the evaluation.** E.g., use the *Objective-Strategy-Media-Criterion Matrix* (Chapter 4) to organize the data. Draw conclusions. Generate specifications for correcting any defects.

14. **Generate a report of the results of the evaluation.** Summarize and record the various types of information gathered during the evaluation for revision of the instructional prototype. Use effective methods to record the learners' performance, e.g., a test item analysis table. Indicate the time required for learners to complete various components of the instruction. If necessary, recommend a second evaluation after materials and procedures have been modified.

References

Baker, E. L. (1984). Evaluation dimension for program development and improvement. In *Instructional Development: The State of the Art, II*, Dubuque, Iowa: Kendall/Hunt.

Gagne, R. M., and Briggs, L. J. (1974). *Principles of Instructional Design.* New York: Holt, Rinehart and Winston, pp. 232–236.

Most times it is necessary to get permission from parents and schools to use students for the testing of instruction through formative evaluation. Most universities have a human-subjects policy that requires getting permission from the appropriate office to use college subjects. Business and industry are also moving in the direction of formally controlling access to subjects, when they permit access at all. The permission forms themselves are idiosyncratic to the particular organization. Figure 6.3 gives an example of such a form for participants.

FIGURE 6.3 / Example of a consent form for video talent

CONSENT FORM

I agree to participate in a project that will use an interactive videodisc to teach signed English phrases and is directed by Drs. Gentry, McLeod, and Stewart of Michigan State University, East Lansing, MI 48824 (517/voice/TDD: 355-1837). I understand that my participation in the project is entirely voluntary and that I have the right to decline to participate or discontinue participation at any time during the project without penalty.

The purpose and the nature of the project have been explained to me. I understand that my interaction with the interactive videodisc will be assessed and that the results will be published in academic journals and other methods of publication, and presented at education meetings and lectures. My understanding is that in all publications, complete anonymity will be maintained and that the publications will not mention my real name.

I understand that I may ask questions at any time during the project. In the unlikely event of any injury as a result of this project, no reimbursement, compensation, or free medical care is offered by Michigan State University.

Signature _____

Name _____

Date _____
          (Please Print)

Data Analysis for Revision

Once formative evaluation data are received, efficient analysis will depend on how the data are formatted (step 8). We have just recommended the use of the *Objective-Strategy-Medium-Criterion Matrix* as a means of organizing the evaluation data. Another effective technique of formatting data is described in the "Material Revision Analysis Matrix" job aid. This job aid was adapted by Josephine Csete, a graduate student at Michigan State University, from a matrix presented in Dick and Carey's excellent book *The Systematic Design of Instruction.*

Correction and refining of a prototype is an ongoing process throughout its development. Some revisions can be done by the prototyping team, such as dropping out an unneeded element or simple editing; but for most other problems, those responsible for formative testing would provide data on weaknesses and send those data to the design unit, which would revise the specifications and send them on to the production team, which would in turn revise and send the revised product to the prototyping unit. The

Job Aid / Material Revision Analysis Matrix

Description   In using the Material Revision Analysis form, the designer provides information on four factors: (1) components being evaluated, (2) problems identified, (3) potential changes, and (4) evidence (including sources) to justify changes. Information to complete this form is derived from previously completed formative-evaluation data and relevant instructional objectives.

Use Rationale   Use of the matrix will slow the designer from making premature decisions. The form requires analysis of each component and evidence for justifying any change. Such a matrix also increases the degree of consistency across evaluators reporting on the same instruction.

Critical Tasks

1. **Gather the necessary resources.** These include documents such as test data and observations of students using the materials, notes and remarks students made on the materials, and information taken from attitude questionnaires.

2. **List all the components being evaluated in the leftmost column of the Materials Revision Analysis form.** See Figure 6.4. These components will vary with your chosen instructional design plan. As noted in the attached example, common components include motivational introductory material, entry-behavior items, pretest on the instructional objectives, materials content, embedded tests, posttest, and attitude questionnaire.

3. **In the next two columns, list problems identified and the potential changes to solve those problems.** Note that for some components no problems will have been identified; however, you may still choose to suggest a possible change for even further improvement. For each identified problem, list at least one possible change.

4. **In the final column list the evidence used to justify the change.** Make sure that all evidence includes the source, usually from the resources gathered in step 1, and that there is always more than one source of evidence.

FIGURE 6.4 / Materials Revision Analysis form

Component	Problem	Change	Evidence and Source
Motivational introductory material	None	Perhaps add another example story to the material.	Students reported enjoying illustrative story and understanding the purpose for the unit (attitude questionnaire). All groups reported wanting to read more example stories on the questionnaire and in the debriefing session.
Entry-behavior items	None	None	1. Items did identify students who would have difficulty with the first lesson (comparison of entry-behavior scores and posttest scores).

continued

Material Revision Analysis Matrix, continued

Component	Problem	Change	Evidence and Source
			2. The test fits the time frame. 3. Students understood the vocabulary level OK. 4. Question format OK.
Pretest on instructional objectives	None	None	1. The pretest did separate students who knew the materials from those who did not. 2. Vocabulary level OK. 3. Time frame OK. 4. Question format OK.
Materials content	1. Instruction on punctuation (5.8 and 5.9) was not needed by any students.	Potential removal of punctuation objectives from the lesson.	Observe any problems with the use of periods to close imperative and exclamatory sentences in subsequent lessons—this may provide a foundation here.
	2. Entire lesson was not needed by students who mastered pretest.	Possibly have high-ability students begin with Lesson two.	Five students did not need the lesson (pretest, embedded test, posttest, attitude questionnaire).
	3. Entry-behavior skills and sentence-writing skills were not mastered by some members of the group.	Develop a set of remedial materials for these students to cover entry behaviors as well as provide more practice in writing sentences.	1. Four students had difficulty recognizing complete sentences, subjects, and predicates (pretest). 2. Four students had difficulty writing sentences (posttest, objective 5.11).
	4. Students lost focus on story writing in the lesson on sentences.	Add stories from which students can classify declarative sentences. Have students write declarative sentences for given stories.	Debriefing session and questionnaire
Embedded tests	Predictive validity (embedded items did not indicate eventual problems on posttest for same items)	Insert embedded test items on recognizing complete sentences and on writing sentences into materials a distance from the instruction and examples.	Embedded test items functioned well in the materials, but they did not predict the students who would have difficulty on the posttest. This may be related to the students' ability to mimic sentences in the embedded tests (embedded and posttest scores).

continued

Material Revision Analysis Matrix, continued

Component	Problem	Change	Evidence and Source
Posttest	None	None	1. The test did identify students having difficulty with objectives 5.10 and 5.11. 2. Time OK. 3. Question format OK. 4. Vocabulary OK (posttest data).
Attitude questionnaire	None	None	1. Did detect dissatisfaction with high-ability students with lesson. 2. Information corroborated the correct level of difficulty for students with prerequisite skills. 3. Information from students without the prerequisites (guessing) was corroborated with test data.

Reference

Dick, W., and Carey, L. (1990). *The Systematic Design of Instruction.* 2d ed. Glenview, Ill.: Scott-Foresman, pp. 260–287.

---

exception to this procedure would be in those instances where the production unit had misread the original design specifications; in which case, the data on the problem would be sent directly to the production team for correction. Usually, the formative-evaluation report would include appropriate sections of the original design specifications, with the problem areas pinpointed and referenced to the details in the report.

Combine, Sequence, and Test Revised Elements

Step 9 of the prototyping process, i.e., sequence and integrate revised elements, is basically a repeat of steps 3–8, except that the modifications are focused on revising an *existing* prototype.

Summatively Evaluate Prototype

Summative evaluation is *not* done primarily for purposes of finding out what is wrong and correcting an instructional package but rather to provide evidence to prospective adopters about its value to teach what it proposes to teach. Truth be told, many ID groups do not do formative evaluations, and only discover problems when testing the fully installed system. Sometimes, problems that surface after installation are of a magnitude where the product must be recalled and revised, usually at considerably more expense than doing the formative evaluation and revision prior to installation. More often, the product does not undergo the major revision indicated, but its use will depend on patchwork corrections by the developers and on instructors' ingenuity to get past the problems. Not a desirable condition.

There are a number of different summative-evaluation techniques available to the instructional developer. They range widely in their costs and in the skills necessary to carry them out. The "Summative Evaluation" job aid presents a typical technique, covering prototyping process steps 14 and 15, one that is effective for most ID projects.

Job Aid / Summative Evaluation

Description This is really a collection of techniques designed to assess the overall relevance, effectiveness, and efficiency of a completed instructional unit. The report resulting from such an evaluation will provide in-house decision makers with the data they need to decide whether to continue the unit as is, modify it, drop it, and/or replace it. External decision makers depend on the summative-evaluation data to make adoption or rejection decisions. Therefore, the validity and the reliability of the data-collecting instruments are critical. It is desirable to have the evaluation set up and carried out by individuals not involved in the development of the instruction, to reduce bias.

Use Rationale The effectiveness of most instructional units is determined through judgments rather than through empirical test as are decisions to drop or modify an instructional unit. There is a real need for objective information that tells educators and trainers whether or not an instructional unit does what it is supposed to and whether it does it consistently. Summative evaluation serves that purpose.

Critical Tasks

1. **Study the available descriptive, instructional, and management materials of the unit to be evaluated.** This familiarity will enable you to discuss relevant variables with decision makers.

2. **Determine any variables for which data are needed by decision makers.** That is, data on variables of effectiveness, relevance, and efficiency in a unit as they affect the behaviors of targeted learners. Relevance asks the question "What is the evidence that the unit's content *should be* learned?"

3. **Acquire or develop valid and reliable instruments for collecting the data.** This involves a whole set of evaluation techniques, including those of test item writing.

4. **Determine a statistical design for treating the evaluation data.** The design spells out the appropriate configuration of experimental and control groups needed.

5. **Identify and schedule teachers and students to carry out and to take the instruction.** Make sure the students fit the design in terms of numbers and variables such as entering behaviors, gender ratios, achievement levels. The teachers should be competent and trained in giving the instruction.

continued

Summative Evaluation, continued

6. **Select and train any data collectors who will be assisting the evaluators.** If there are several groups, or if some of the groups meet at the same time, there will have to be more than one person collecting data at different points.

7. **Collect data on the entering behaviors of target learners.** This is usually done through pretests that include items on what students need to know in order to begin the unit, and what they already know that is taught by the unit. Pretest data will be compared later with posttest data to determine gains.

8. **Collect interim progress data on target learners.** This is usually done for instructional units that last for a month or more, so that the evaluator can be more certain of when a particular defect occurred. It is not usually collected unless the data are expected to be used to modify the unit. Usually this is done with objective test instruments.

9. **Collect exiting data on target learners.** Usually this is done with traditional posttests of an objective nature. However, it is common also to collect student attitudinal data toward the unit.

10. **Collect exiting data from the instructors.** This includes interview data on the effectiveness, relevance, and efficiency of the unit from the instructors' perspective, and also for confirming, correcting, or explaining evaluator observations, such as instructor deviation from the instructional plan.

11. **Apply statistical and judgmental analysis to the appropriate data.** Be careful not to combine empirical data with observational data.

12. **Draw conclusions from the analysis, and generate recommendations.** Make clear any connections between the purpose of a particular part of the evaluation, the empirical and subjective data, the statistical treatment, and the analysis, with the conclusions and recommendations drawn.

13. **Place the analyses, conclusions, and recommendations into a report for decision makers.**

References

Fitz-Gibbon, C. T., and Morris, L. L. (1978). *How to Design a Program Evaluation.* Beverly Hills, Calif.: Sage

Worthen, B. R., Sanders, J. R. (1973). *Educational Evaluation: Theory and Practice.* Worthington, Ohio: Charles A. Jones.

The report of the summative evaluation should be submitted to design component personnel if there are any serious flaws in the instructional unit. Otherwise, the results will be given to the marketing group to incorporate into their brochures and other information as evidence of the validity of the instructional package.

Make Marketing Refinements

A test prototype is usually rough as compared to the final version or master of an instructional package. The final version will be expected to meet additional criteria beyond those of effectiveness, efficiency, and relevance. These criteria may serve cosmetic needs, including certain bells and whistles expected by clients who may buy the package. As examples, the final version might require that cleaner graphics for the videotape element be produced and edited in, professional labels be affixed to different parts of the instructional package, and superior frames be used for overhead transparencies. The design may also require a professionally made container, or containers, for packaging the instruction. Often, brochures or other advertisements will be developed to enhance the package's marketability. Different versions for different hardware and software may be developed at this time.

What follows is a marketing checklist consisting of questions whose answers help make more certain that appropriate steps are taken in the marketing process. The response to these questions could lead to a modification of some of the prototype specifications, which would be sent to the production unit. Upon receipt of the revised elements from production, the prototyping unit would do final assembly of the instructional unit product master.

Instructional Product Marketing Checklist

Advertising factors

1. Are there needs analysis data, expert opinion, of summative-evaluation evidence available that supports marketing the instruction?

2. Are the target audiences for the product clearly identified?

3. Has the retail price been determined?

4. What advertising strategies will be used?

Profitability factors

5. What is the estimate of the number of units that could be sold?

6. How does the cost of producing the product affect the desired or required profit level?

7. How long before revision or replacement of the product will be necessary?

Factors affecting client acceptance

8. To what degree will the instructor-training requirements be expected to affect sales of the product?

9. To what degree will the program's requirement for special equipment affect expected sales of the product?

10. To what degree do warranty conditions affect client acceptance?

11. To what degree will delivery and replacement turnaround time affect client acceptance?

Packaging factors

12. What would be the most cost-effective packaging of the instructional product?

13. What are the trade-offs among alternative means for distributing the product?

Submit Finished Product Masters

After the summative evaluation is completed and any final modifications are made, the finished product masters are returned to the Production unit. Using the masters, production personnel would then produce copies of the instruction for marketing or sales, upon demand. As mentioned earlier, mass production and marketing of the final product may be contracted out to external agencies.

Summary

This chapter presented the concept of prototyping, i.e., the process of assembling, evaluating, respecifying, and finalizing an instructional unit. Prototyping begins where production ends, and ends where installation begins. The use of interface analysis was discussed as an effective means for identifying the information necessary for the required interaction of the individual and collective elements of a prototype instructional unit. The problems related to carrying out formative and summative evaluation were discussed, and techniques for performing the evaluations were presented. This was followed by techniques for analyzing evaluation data. The last section looked at aspects of marketing the completed instructional product.

References

Bloom, B. S., et al. (1971). *Handbook on Formative and Summative Evaluation of Student Learning*. New York: McGraw-Hill.

Chinien, C. (1990). Paradigms of inquiry for research in formative evaluation. *Performance and Instruction* 29(9): 26–29.

Dick, Walter (1980). Formative evaluation in instructional development. *Journal of Instructional Development* 3(3): 3–6.

Gooler, D. D. (1980). Formative evaluation strategies for major instructional development projects. *Journal of Instructional Development* 3(3): 7–11.

Greer, M. (1989). Reproduction and distribution. *Performance and instruction* 28(4): 40–48.

Lantz, K. E. (no date). *The prototyping methodology*. Englewood Cliffs, N.J.: Prentice-Hall. Referenced in Tripp, Steven D., and Bichelmeyer, Barbara (1990). Rapid prototyping: An alternative instructional design strategy. *Educational Technology Research and Development* 38(1): 35.

Smith, P. L., and Wedman, J. F. (1988). Read-think-aloud protocols: A new data-source for formative evaluation. *Performance Improvement Quarterly* 1(2): 13–22.

Trimby, M. J., and Gentry, C. G. (1984). State of ID systems approach models. In *Instructional Development: The State of the Art, II,* ed. R. K. Bass and C. R. Dills, pp. 80–93. Dubuque, Iowa: Kendall/Hunt.

Weiss, E. A. (1978). Prototype development of a self-instructional program in media selection. *Journal of Instructional Development* 1(2): 25–29.

CHAPTER 7

Product Installation

Process of establishing the necessary conditions for effective operation of a new instructional product or process when initially placed in a targeted system

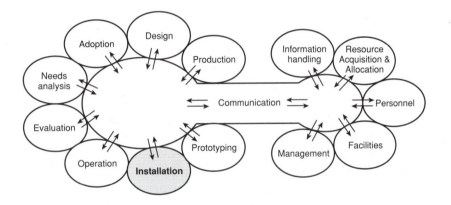

Learner Objectives

1. Given a randomly ordered list of the steps in the installation process, to place them in the appropriate sequence.

2. Recognize tasks that are normally carried out in the Installation process.

3. State conditions that inhibit installation of instructional products and processes.

4. Match processes of installation with appropriate techniques.

5. Describe the techniques recommended for the installation process.

6. Recall definitions of major terms.

Introduction

The moment of installation can be hazardous for a new instructional process or product. Organizations, whether educational or training, tend to resist intrusions not complying with their established policies and procedures. Unfortunately, many of the formal policies and procedures of organizations are not always clearly stated, and may be subject to much misinterpretation, particularly for an instructional developer coming from outside the system. This problem is compounded by the fact that some enforced policies and procedures have evolved informally and may be unwritten. More to the point, if the appropriate policies and procedures for installing a new instructional product into an established organization are not followed, the product may be rejected by the client. The problem is somewhat analogous to that of getting a donor heart to take hold successfully in a recipient. The body's natural defense mechanisms must be restricted until the organ has integrated with the surrounding tissue. To this end, medical science continues to develop and apply a variety of techniques. So it is with the introduction of instructional products into education and training systems.

There are reasons why installation of instructional products and processes is so difficult. One reason has to do with there seldom being enough resources in educational or training systems to satisfy the continuing demands of its members. As a result, individuals and groups within organizations are constantly competing among themselves for limited resources. If advocates for specific instructional products and processes are unable to get sufficient resources allocated for their effective operation, then those products and processes are likely to operate unsatisfactorily, or may even fail. A second reason has to do with the need to train instructors in the use of new instructional products or processes. If there are no policies or resources supporting such activities, then instructors may have to train themselves, and their frustration at this process can result in ineffective teaching or the early demise of the instruction. The scheduling of a new course poses another potential problem, in that its assigned meeting time may put the course in direct conflict with existing required courses, making it difficult for targeted students to attend. The process of installation is fraught with problems like these, and instructional developers must be wary if their products and processes are to persevere.

Installation Process

The tasks for carrying out instructional product installation are closely related to those of the adoption component (Chapter 3), and many of the same techniques for gaining adoption are useful for installing new instruction. Tasks necessary to the installation process, include:

1. Get agreement to support a new product or process from organization decision makers and gatekeepers.

2. Identify others in the target system who will be affected by the product's installation.

3. Convince others affected by the product's installation of its value.

4. Make sure that supporting structures required by the product are in place (e.g., policies, procedures, evaluation, and maintenance).

5. Make sure that the resources required by the product or process have been formally allocated.

6. Identify system personnel who will be teaching or managing the ongoing operation of the instructional product.

7. Provide training for teachers and/or managers (build training into the product, where possible).

8. Establish access to the appropriate instructional facilities for operation of the product's first use.

9. Support the instructors and managers during the first uses of the product in the client system.

Obtaining Decision-Maker Agreement

Whether operating from within a system or from without, agreement from those who are responsible for the target system is a necessary prerequisite to installation of any instructional innovation. Aside from the biases resulting from the all-too-human tendency to protect territory or from the negative effects of uncertainty, administrators and staff *do* have a legitimate responsibility to protect the system from inappropriate intrusions that may disrupt formal operations or leach away resources. Most of the decision makers and gatekeepers in a system can be readily identified through the system's organizational chart. Other decision makers, who possess *informal* leadership status, are not so easily identified, particularly by outsiders. The influence of informal leaders may be due to any number of factors, including professional knowledge, control of external resources, social prestige, or even charisma. One of the techniques that has proven reliable in identifying individuals and groups possessing informal influence in a system is called **Communications Network Analysis** (presented later in the chapter). The same technique can be used to determine who, besides the obvious persons, will be affected by the proposed innovation. It is the not-so-obvious ones that may cause serious difficulties for a program down the line.

Once all of the significant players are known, they need to be involved in such a way that their attitudes and contributions relative to the innovation being installed are positive. The "Product and Process Acceptance" job aid presents a technique for approaching agreement with administrators and staff on acceptance of changes within their system.

Depending on the circumstances, other techniques may be used to convince decision makers and gatekeepers of the value of installing new products or processes. Among these are *Needs Analysis* (see Chapter 2) and *Visitation, Decision Query, Cost–Benefit Analysis,* and *Sunset Review Technique,* all of which are elaborated in Chapter 3.

Job Aid / Product and Process Acceptance

Description   This is a set of logical steps for procuring agreement to permit entry of a product and/or process into an established organization. It requires identification of system policies and procedures, and of system decision makers and gatekeepers. Decision makers are those responsible for directing the activities of organizational members, while gatekeepers are those who control the system's resources. The needs of installing a product or process are matched against relevant policies and procedures, followed by the preparation of a formal plan. Agreement is reached through acceptance of a plan.

Use Rationale   As a general rule, administrators, along with their staffs, have the option and the power to accept or reject innovations entering their organizations. So logic alone dictates that an instructional developer should always get agreement to proceed from this formal authority. Too often when this authority is ignored or overlooked, new products are summarily done away with, despite their potential value to that system. Thus, it pays to find and use the built-in mechanisms of the organization that control acceptance of new products.

Critical Steps

1. **Acquire and study relevant parts of the organization's policies and procedures.** All formal organizations have a set of policies and procedures that members of the organization are expected to adhere to, although the names of such documents vary from organization to organization.

2. **Make an initial list of the *relevant* policies and procedures.** E.g., all modifications of the curriculum must be agreed to by the curriculum committee. All recommendations for course changes sent to the curriculum committee must go through the department chairperson.

3. **Check the list for accuracy and completeness with a knowledgeable administrator of the system.** Invariably, your list will fall short because of jargon used or because of special interpretation placed on some policies and procedures. In addition, some of the policies may be unwritten, and learnable only through trial and error or, preferably, through knowledgeable members of the system.

4. **Determine whether the installation of your product or process violates any of the organization's policies or procedures.** Again, it is useful to have knowledgeable members of the organization assist you in checking against this need.

5. **Facilitate any policy or procedural change as may be necessary or practical.** Refer to the *Policy Setting* technique in Chapter 3.

6. **Provide a formal plan for following the policies and procedures.** This is simply a statement of the project objective(s) and a listing of the relevant policies, followed by a brief description of the procedures that support the policies.

7. **Have administrators and staff critique the plan.** Again, some assumptions will prove wrong, so this is a crucial step. Minimally, the plan should be passed by administrators and staff that are directly affected by the installation of the product or process.

8. **Make any revisions necessary to an acceptable plan.**

continued

Product and Process Acceptance, continued

9. **Complete formal acceptance by system decision makers and gatekeepers.** These individuals can be identified through the organizational chart of a system. To identify those holding *informal* power, use the *Communications Network Analysis* technique. Depending on the organization and how much is at stake, acceptance can be formalized through one or more means, ranging from an oral agreement to a signed memo to a formal contract.

10. **Make certain that all those involved with the installation are aware of the policies and procedures.** Go over the policies and procedures plan with affected parties.

Reference

Gentry, Cass (1987). Gaining Organizational Acceptance of an Innovation. Unpublished document.

Identifying and Persuading Others Affected

It is assumed that the interests and needs of a traditionally powerless member, i.e., the student, have been adequately considered during needs assessment. Others affected by the installation of a new instructional unit could include managers, instructors, clerical staff, and service units of the target system. There are many reasons for resistance toward an instructional innovation, including the belief of individuals that the product's acceptance will rob their own projects or courses of resources, or because its acceptance may violate what they think is appropriate for their system. Usually, it is not too difficult to identify those who may be affected: simply look at their organizational and logical relation to the new instruction.

Once aware of who they are, an innovator can make certain that each gets the necessary information for making positive judgments about the new instruction. However, a major difficulty is determining their relationships with others who are not so obvious in the system but who may be able to positively or negatively affect the installation. For example, an affected party who is also a golf partner of a board member may drop a word that affects your project. The "Communications Network Analysis" job aid presents an efficient technique assisting in identification of, and determining relationships among, these people.

Job Aid / Communications Network Analysis

Description   This technique enables an outside instructional developer entering an organization to determine very quickly who is communicating with whom. A simple questionnaire listing everyone's name is used, along with a frequency scale to collect information on how often the people on the list speak to one another. These data are then graphed to show the communications relationships. From an analysis of the graph, conclusions can be made about who the best people are to get information from or to distribute information among fellow group members. It also assists the instructional developer, to some degree, in determining which individuals need what information.

continued

Communications Network Analysis, continued

Use Rationale   People are always surprised, when they see the results of this technique, at discovering with whom individual members of an organization communicate or do not communicate. Communication in an organization can be critical, particularly for instructional developers coming from the outside. A misunderstood statement could easily get back to someone who is in a position to affect a project's success.

Critical Steps

1. **Establish the need to identify the informal communication patterns for members of an organization.** This is especially useful for external instructional developers coming into an unfamiliar organization.

2. **Get permission and establish guidelines for using the analysis.** When administrators see the results, they will want to use them to clear up any communication problems. Get agreement that results will not be used by them, so that staff won't be alienated from the developers.

3. **Place all of the members' names on a data-collection form.** See the Group Communication Questionnaire in Figure 7.1.

4. **Members independently indicate the frequency of communications contact with other members.** This is done on their respective copies of the questionnaire, using the frequency scale at the top of the form.

5. **Determine the scale level cutoff for strength of relationship.** For example, you may decide that you only want to include communications contacts that are "often" or "very often," i.e., 4 and 5, ignoring contact frequencies indicated by 1, 2, and 3, i.e., "never," "seldom," and "occasionally."

**FIGURE 7.1 / Example data-collection instrument
for Communications Network Analysis**

GROUP COMMUNICATION QUESTIONNAIRE

Your Name: _____

Directions: This questionnaire is being used to get a reading on the level of communication among members of your organization. Please indicate how often you communicate with the individuals listed below, through writing and/or speaking, by placing the appropriate number from the following frequency scale after each name (ignore your own name). For example, if you speak to Mr. Barton only "occasionally," then you would place a 3 in the lined space after his name. Please give your completed questionnaire to Mr. Harrington by 5:00 PM this coming Friday. If you have any questions about the questionnaire, speak with Mr. Harrington. Thank you.

Frequency Scale

1. Never
2. Seldom
3. Occasionally
4. Often
5. Very often

continued

Communications Network Analysis, continued

1. William Barton _____	16. Abner Warren _____
2. Horace Elwood _____	17. George Galen _____
3. Janet Coffee _____	18. Gene Dayton _____
4. Edward Faust _____	19. Heneretta Dugay _____
5. Harley Young _____	20. Lawerence Wells _____
6. Brian Wallington _____	21. John Fist _____
7. Susan Smith _____	22. Able Harrington _____
8. Jeanette Wynte _____	23. Henry Arnt _____
9. Donna Dorowski _____	24. Lucy Bell _____
10. Ernest Billingsley _____	25. Thomas Hutson _____
11. Kurby Hyatt _____	26. _____
12. Anne Haliburton _____	27. _____
13. Laura Ye _____	28. _____
14. Herbert Fox _____	29. _____
15. Wilma Denton _____	30. _____

FIGURE 7.2 / Example of data accumulated from Communications Network Analysis questionnaires. The numbers, keyed to the names on the questionnaire, reflect only who spoke to whom, not the frequency.

1. 2, 7, 16	16. 14, 17, 18, 19, 21
2. 1, 3, 5, 6	17. 16, 18, 19
3. 2, 4, 5, 6, 13, 17	18. 16, 17, 19, 20
4. 3, 5, 6	19. 14, 16, 17, 18, 20, 21, 25
5. 2, 3, 4, 6	20. 14, 17, 18, 19, 21, 24, 25
6. 2, 3, 4, 5, 9	21. 14, 16, 19, 20, 25
7. 1, 8, 9, 11, 12	22. 10, 15, 23
8. 7, 9, 11, 12	23. 10, 15, 22
9. 6, 7, 8, 11	24. 20
10. 15, 22, 23	25. 19, 20, 21
11. 7, 8, 9, 12	26.
12. 7, 8, 11	27.
13. 3	28.
14. 11, 14, 16, 19, 20, 21	29.
15. 10, 22, 23	30.

6. **Accumulate the data, by person, on a common form.** See Figure 7.2. The numbers on the form are keyed to the numbers next to the names on the questionnaire.

7. **Graph the selected relationships.** See Figure 7.3. Use numbered circles, keyed to the names on the questionnaire, and draw lines between the circles where a communication link exists. A little practice is required to get the groups to fall out as nicely as they do in the figure. As you draw a line to show communication between two people, draw an arrow head on the end away from the person claiming communication. Then check the other person, and if that person agrees, draw a head on the other end of the arrow, showing a confirmed communication link. Sometimes people will claim a link when none exists.

continued

Communications Network Analysis, continued

FIGURE 7.3 / Example of a graph of a communications network

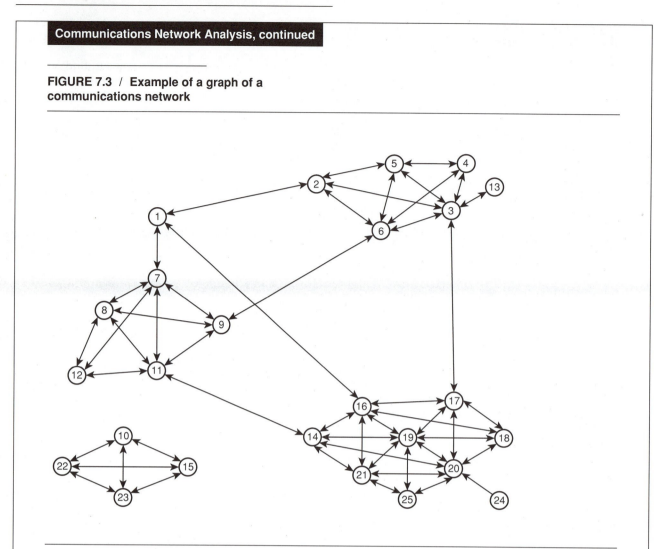

8.   **Analyze the relationships among members.** Identify the following.

   a. *Groups.* Three or more members who have at least three mutual communication links, as indicated by the arrows connecting them. There are four groups in Figure 7.3: groups 10-15-22-23, 7-8-9-11-12, 2-3-4-5-6, and 14-16-17-18-19-20-21-25. Persons 1, 13, and 24 are not members of a group.

   b. Any *bridge links*. Persons who are members of two different groups. In Figure 7.3, there are three bridge links: 6–9, 11–14, and 3–17.

   c. Any *liaisons*. Persons who have contact with more than two different groups. Person 1 in Figure 7.3 is an example.

   d. Any *isolates*. Persons who have one or *no* contact with other members. In Figure 7.3, 13 is a *confirmed* isolate, in that 3 agrees that they communicate; 24 is an *unconfirmed* communication link, in that 20 says he does not talk to 24. An arrow with only one head indicates an unconfirmed link, while an arrow with two heads indicates a confirmed link.

   e. Any *isolate groups*. Groups that do not communicate with other groups. In Figure 7.3, group 10-15-22-23 is an isolate group.

continued

Communications Network Analysis, continued

9. **Check conflicts.** When one person professes to communicate and the other denies it, find out from the first person what was communicated, and then ask the second person if it is true. Often, the person will then remember, and it is appropriate to change the data and graph to reflect that.

10. **Compare the communications network analysis results with organizational chart expectations.** See Figure 7.4. Based on this chart you would expect that the CEO would speak to her or his chairpersons and that each chairperson would speak with her or his staff members and in turn that members of a department would speak to one another. The lines drawn on the figure show who speaks with whom. Note that our expectations are not confirmed in some cases.

FIGURE 7.4 / Example of an organizational chart. The lines drawn around names show communication links found in the Communications Network Analysis.

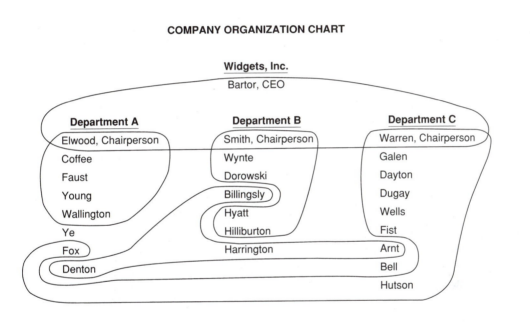

COMPANY ORGANIZATION CHART

11. **Generate a report based on the analysis.** Obviously, the information under item 8 would be included, as well as members' interpretation in terms of the project. The liaisons and the bridge links can be excellent sources of information as well as distributors of information, assuming they buy what you are selling. They need to be cultivated carefully, for they can be very helpful. Also, when a member will not respond to you, cultivating someone who regularly communicates with the member may provide a way to get to that person. Often, from a pragmatic view, the developer is wise not to put much energy into isolated individuals or groups, since they have little influence with the majority. This is particularly true in the early stages of a project. Finally, a developer should make a point of giving very clear information to a person who is a communication link with an individual who could seriously affect the project, i.e., gatekeepers and decision makers.

continued

Communications Network Analysis, continued

12. Send the report to appropriate decision makers.

Reference

Gentry, Cass, and Decker, Betty (1987). *Communication Network Analysis.* Self-Instructional Slide/Tape. East Lansing, Mich.: Michigan State University Marketing Division.

The process by which system members learn of their involvement with a new process or product has, historically, been haphazard. Some do not learn about their involvement until it is a fait accompli. Many a workshop has begun with members having less than 24 hours' notice of their participation. Such careless planning has created attitude problems having little to do with the merits of the proposed instruction. Regardless of when members become aware, they begin a process of assessment of the change as it may relate to them. Instructional developers rightly fear assessment or evaluation of a new product or process by members of the target system because of the misunderstandings often accompanying the process. Curiously, it is not the evaluation process itself that instructional developers need fear, but rather what *criteria* are applied in making judgments about the innovation. Too often, individuals apply criteria having little to do with the qualities of the innovation itself. For example, a common error is made when system members incorrectly compare the new process or product to existing ones, when their operation or purpose is significantly different. An important advantage can be gained if target members can be convinced to apply the appropriate criteria when assessing an innovation entering their system. See the job aid on "Encouraging Criterion-Based Assessment of Entering Innovations."

Job Aid / Encouraging Criterion-Based Assessment of Entering Innovations

Description This technique requires the developer to generate clear criteria for assessing an instructional product or process, and then to get agreement from individuals in the system (who may affect the innovation's success) to use the criteria when assessing the innovation.

Use Rationale A continuing problem suffered by instructional developers and change agents generally results from misunderstandings of individuals involved in the installation and ongoing operation of a new product or process. Lack of pertinent information can cause individuals who would otherwise be supportive to throw up road blocks against a change.

Critical Steps

1. **Identify a new instructional product or process about to be installed.** Choose ones likely to be evaluated by those affected, either casually or formally.

continued

Encouraging Criterion-Based Assessment of Entering Innovations, continued

2. **Generate a criterion-based instrument to be used to assess the product or process.** Complete the following tasks:

   a. At the beginning of the assessment document, provide headings, a general statement of assessment purpose, and directions to the assessors. Directions should include how to use the assessment instrument and where to return the completed assessment.

   b. Include a brief description of the product or process, to orient members.

   c. List the specific objectives to be met by the product or process.

   d. List appropriate criteria under each objective.

   e. Have each criterion followed by a five-point scale, to be completed by the assessors.

3. **Identify individuals in the system whose assessment could positively or negatively affect the installation of the innovation.**

4. **Modify the criteria, based on an estimate of possible concerns these individuals might have relative to the innovation.**

5. **Have affected individuals complete the criterion-based instrument.** See Figure 7.5. It is desirable to know who has responded to the instrument, but as a first step it may be wise to have them respond anonymously.

FIGURE 7.5 / Sample of a criterion-based assessment instrument

---

ASSESSMENT OF HEALTH 412: PREVENTION OF AIDS

Name: _____

School: _____

Date: _____

Explanation: The course that you are assessing was designed to provide high school juniors and seniors with basic knowledge and skills for avoiding infection with AIDS. Those responsible for the course are very interested in having your judgments about how well the course materials and procedures meet the indicated objectives, with an eye to modifying or supplementing the materials based on feedback from the professionals in MacComber High School.

Directions: Below are listed the specific objectives that this course hopes to meet. Based on your perusal of the course materials, indicate on the five-point scale following each of the criteria under an objective your judgment of how well the course will meet each objective. For those items for which you assigned a value of 2 or less, please write a brief statement of why you think the course has difficulty in this area (in the space directly below the criterion item). Please complete each of the items and return this document to Mr. Harless, the assistant principal, in room 117, by Friday, May 8, 1988.

Course Objective 1: to list the major means by which the AIDS disease is transmitted.

	Poor			Good	
Criterion a: Factual support	1	2	3	4	5

Comment: _____

---

continued

Encouraging Criterion-Based Assessment of Entering Innovations, continued

	Poor				Good
Criterion b: Scientific support	1	2	3	4	5

Comment: _____

_____

Course Objective 2: to list the major means for preventing the transmission of AIDS.

	Poor				Good
Criterion a: Comprehensive	1	2	3	4	5

Comment: _____

_____

	Poor				Good
Criterion b: Motivation	1	2	3	4	5

Comment: _____

_____

Course Objective 3: to list the major means of treating the AIDS disease.

	Poor				Good
Criterion a: Comprehensive	1	2	3	4	5

Comment: _____

_____

_____

6. **Receive and analyze data from completed instruments.**

7. **Disseminate the results of member assessment, if needed or if appropriate.** The assumptions are that if appropriate criteria have been applied, then the results of the assessment will be positive, and that it will be confirming and reinforcing to the clients to see their general agreement to that effect. If legitimate problems surface, then they should be recognized and addressed.

Reference

Gentry, Cass (1989). Gaining Organizational Acceptance of an Innovation. Unpublished document.

Many of the same Chapter 3 techniques used to convince organizational decision makers and gatekeepers can be used effectively with individuals and groups involved in installation.

Establishing a Structural Base

Structure is the framework of expectancies and limits controlling a system's processes, more specifically, an organization's forms, procedures, and rules.

When the structure is restrictive in terms of the needs of an innovation, the innovation's effectiveness will be reduced. For example, a course might require that students use school equipment (e.g., tape recorder, camera, telescope, calculators) outside of the school for school purposes. If the school has a hard-and-fast policy of *not* permitting equipment to leave the premises, this would affect the course. Making certain that the structural base necessary for innovation is in place can be accomplished through a number of means, depending on the target. The *policy setting* technique (see Chapter 3) is relevant to part of this task. The *product and process acceptance* technique presented earlier in this chapter is also helpful in establishing structural changes in a system.

One of the structures affecting the success of instructional installation is the budget structure. Most organizations budget in two ways: (1) for ongoing operations, and (2) for temporary operations. It is far preferable that the innovation be listed under the budget heading for ongoing operations. Support of temporary operations is the first to go at the onset of hard times. In order to protect an instructional innovation, it is necessary for the installer to become familiar with the types of budgeting used by the organization in which the innovation will be placed. The process of budgeting and concomitant techniques are discussed in some detail in Chapter 13.

Commitment of Resources

Lip service for a project by an administrator does not always result in the assignment of resources. The best indication of support is when the need is recognized in the formal budget of the system. If that is not possible, it is wise to devise and submit a formal list of needs and their necessary schedule of allocation. Sometimes administrators promise to support a project without being aware of its real costs. Later, when they *do* understand how these real costs impact their budgets, they may lose enthusiasm for supporting it. Providing administrators with the formal list of resources needed and their allocation dates will give them a clearer idea of what they are supporting. Of course, it is good sales technique to convince administrators of the value of the product to the system, *before* presenting the costs.

Identifying Instructional Delivery Personnel

There are many variables that can negatively affect the installation of new instruction. One is the caliber of personnel recruited to deliver or manage the instruction. A teacher or trainer who doubts the value of the new instruction or who has been assigned to deliver the instruction under protest can negatively affect the instruction in very subtle ways. Of equal concern is the level of competence of members of the instructional delivery staff. When lacking sufficient competence, their errors can reflect poorly on the instruction, and may make it difficult to maintain. Therefore, it is desirable to find competent staff who view the new instruction as valuable and effective for its avowed purpose. An important way of coming by staff competent in delivery of the new instructional unit is to involve them in the development of the instruction. Their assistance in the instruction's development enables them to acquire knowledge and skills important to its later delivery. And further, just being involved contributes to their buying in to its importance. Of course, their involvement also consumes the time and energy of the instructional developer. Thus, a trade-off or a compromise between the status quo and what is ideal is often necessary.

Training Instructional Personnel

Usually, when new instructional units or programs are put in place, some training of instructional managers, instructors, and lab personnel will be necessary. This is done under a variety of techniques, e.g., *oral walkthrough, regressive assistance* (this chapter), and *peer teaching* (see Chapter 14). These training periods are usually brief, with limited follow-up by development personnel. The result is that the ground covered in training is usually not done at the desired depth; and because it is delivered over such a short time, much is forgotten by the time what was taught is to be applied.

A means of partially solving this problem is to provide training of instructors *within* the instructional package. For example, textbook publishers have for years provided instructors' manuals as a means of training instructors in a book's new constructs and on techniques of instructional method. Similarly, designers of computer applications (e.g., spreadsheets, word processing, graphics, database) increasingly include self-instructional modules and help functions to train users in these applications. The former are notorious for being of limited value; however, the latter are proving reasonably effective, and have great promise. The combination of computer-assisted instruction with expert systems is considered by many to be a significant breakthrough in self-instructional systems (McLaughlin, 1992). These systems operate by rules and make use of databases to respond to a learner's need. Such training systems can act almost like human tutors. When the client system will not or cannot provide adequate training for users of these new systems, a solution would be to build the training into the product or process.

For the moment, the major responses to training needs of instructors taking on a new course are no training or some form of learn-on-the-job through advisement or through brief apprenticeships with experienced instructors. One technique that has proven effective is presented in the job aid on "Regressive Assistance," in which a novice assists the experienced instructor in the first round, they team-teach in the second round, and the experienced instructor assists the novice in the third round. From that point on, the novice would be on his or her own.

Job Aid / Regressive Assistance

Description   This technique presents the logical steps in preparing novice instructors to take responsibility for all of the activities involved in running an instructional unit. Basically, the instructor-trainee begins by observing and assisting an experienced instructor in teaching the

continued

Regressive Assistance, continued

course in the first cycle, team-teaches the course during the second cycle, and teaches all in the third cycle, with some assistance from the experienced instructor.

Use Rationale   When teachers assigned to teach a course lack proper preparation, they will be less successful than those properly prepared to teach it.

Critical Tasks

1. **Identify a course where a novice instructor is assigned to take over a course.** This will be a course with which he or she has limited knowledge and experience.

2. **Get agreement from affected administrators, the experienced instructor, and the novice instructor on the use of this technique for training the new instructor.** This may take some convincing, because its use ties up an experienced instructor for two to three cycles of the course. Demonstrating the negative effects of not using such a technique is one way of convincing administrators. You may have to revert to the *Oral Walk-Through* technique as an alternative to this technique. (See later this chapter.)

3. **Meet with the administrator, the experienced instructor, and the novice instructor to discuss their respective roles in the process.**

4. **Have the novice instructor assist the experienced instructor in delivering the course during the first cycle through the course.**

5. *Optional:* **Have the experienced instructor and the novice instructor team-teach the course during the second stage.**

6. **Have the experienced instructor assist the novice instructor in the next cycle of the course.**

7. **Have the novice (replacement) instructor deliver the instruction alone during the next cycle.** The experienced teacher should be on call for advisement purposes.

8. **Assume that, by now, the not-so-novice instructor is capable of delivering the instruction during future cycles without further assistance.**

Reference

Shaplin, J. T., and Olds, H. F. (1964). *Team Teaching.* New York: Harper & Row.

The *oral walk-through* technique is a stop-gap technique at best, but it is much superior to no training at all. It basically involves an experienced instructor (often it may be the instructional developer in this role) going through the instructional materials and procedures verbally, with demonstration and extra explanation. This is done at a rapid pace, so conditions must be set up so that the novice instructor gets maximum benefit from the training. The "Oral Walk-Through" job aid teaches the technique.

Job Aid / Oral Walk-Through

Description   This technique is a quick, semiadequate means of preparing an instructor to take over a new course. It is used as a last resort when there are no resources for more serious training. The basic idea is to have an experienced instructor go through the materials, in the order they will be taught, with the novice instructor. Questions by the novice instructor are attended to, and more difficult procedures are demonstrated by the experienced instructor. Explanation of most of the materials is done verbally. When time allows, difficult teaching tasks are practiced with feedback from the experienced instructor. The time for walk-throughs may vary from 2 hours to 2 days.

Use Rationale   Instructors assigned to teach a new course who lack proper preparation need to be prepared for teaching the course. When resources for training are limited, instructors can be brought to a more desirable stage of preparation via a walk-through, although this is far from an ideal means. But, however limited is this training, it will result in less frustration and fewer criticisms of instructors than if they were to begin teaching the course cold.

Critical Tasks

1. **Identify a condition where a novice instructor is assigned to take over a new course.** This will be a course with which he or she has very limited knowledge and experience.

2. **Get agreement from administrators, an experienced instructor, and the novice instructor to use the technique for training the new instructor.** Administrators will usually go along, because they recognize the need for training and because there is relatively little cost involved.

3. **Discuss their respective roles with the administrators, experienced instructor, and novice instructor.** Roles: The administrators free up the experienced and novice instructors, and provide a facility for the training. The experienced instructor goes through the materials in the order to be taught, explaining and demonstrating the instruction. The novice instructor attends to the training and asks questions on those sections not clear.

4. **Schedule the training.** Preferably, this is in a location where interruptions are minimal, because of the concentration required. A large worktable for spreading out materials is desirable. Also, whatever equipment that will be used should be available, e.g., overhead projector, chalkboard.

5. **Acquire and sequence all instructional materials.** Sequence materials in the order in which they would normally be presented to the intended students. When appropriate, place materials in three-ring binders for both the experienced instructor and the novice instructor. This assists in control of what may be extensive materials, and makes sure both experienced and novice instructors are looking at the same information at the same time.

6. **The experienced instructor begins the training by asking the novice instructor to play two roles.** One, as the new instructor, and two, to behave as they would expect their new students to behave during instruction. These two perspectives will assist the novice instructor in perceiving the majority of problems he or she might have as the instruction unfolds.

7. **The experienced instructor also assumes two roles during the training.** The instructor moves in and out of roles as trainer of the novice instructor and as instructor of intended students, as appropriate, to make the functions of procedures and materials clear.

continued

Oral Walk-Through, continued

8. **The experienced instructor varies the speed of presentation.** When procedures or materials are straightforward, the instructor moves rapidly, fielding questions as they occur. For more difficult items, the instructor takes time to explain and/or demonstrate.

9. **The novice instructor explains/demonstrates his or her way through the instructional materials and procedures.** Corrections are made by the experienced instructor as the novice instructor proceeds.

10. *Optional.* **The experienced instructor makes him- or herself available for questions at a later date.** By telephone and appointment, but only during the novice instructor's first teaching cycle with targeted students.

11. **Assume that the novice instructor is now capable of satisfactorily delivering the instruction during future cycles.** This comes with steady improvement through self-correction of errors made while delivering the instruction.

Reference

Gentry, Cass (1970). *Instructor's Manual for "Diffusion of Innovations" Game.* Instructional Development Institute. Washington, D.C.

Establishing Appropriate Facility for Product Delivery

Depending on the instructional process or product, its effectiveness could depend on its being operated in the appropriate environment. (Chapter 15 deals in more detail with the design, renovation, and organization of instructional facilities. The famous saying that "Mark Hopkins on one end of a log and the student on the other is classroom enough" would get some argument today. Research has demonstrated that environmental aspects, such as a classroom's air conditioning, lighting and acoustical levels, seating, and even color scheme may affect the learning process. Some of the instructional techniques where the spaces in which they are used may affect learning include lecture, small-group instruction, peer teaching, tutoring, self-instruction, and laboratory instruction.

Modern education is periodically criticized for its egg-crate approach to instructional facility design. The "ticky tacky boxes" in which we install teachers and students, are an offshoot of the conveyer belt mentality of the Industrial Revolution, which tended to treat people as replaceable parts rather than as human beings. Such a design is cost efficient, and it serves a need for teacher and administrative control of student movement and activity. However, it seriously neglects human factors. In the 1960s and '70s there was a considerable movement toward a different design of learning spaces that ranged from the very practical to the bizarre! Robert Sommer in his excellent book *Personal Space* (1969) lays out many of the concepts and arguments relevant to views of architectural innovators, including some of those of Frank Lloyd Wright, who insisted that "form should follow function." More recently, there have surfaced several terms adopted to discriminate between the older architecture that treats people as objects and the new architecture that is guided by human needs. One such area of study is called *ergonomics*. According to Ellington and Harris (1986):

Ergonomics is the application of anatomical, physiological, and psychological knowledge and principles to the study of the relationship between people and all aspects of their activities.

Work and learning environments, with their concomitant equipment and tasks, were part of the foci for ergonomics. For example, the *open classroom*, or school-without-walls, design was tried out in a number of schools, with very mixed results. The walls between classrooms were removed so that teachers and students from the same floor or section of a school building could see each other. Carpeting was used to reduce auditory distraction. Teachers who were not convinced of the value of this innovation, very quickly began to form new walls, using filing cabinets, movable chalkboards, and any other innovative means to regain at least visual privacy. In other open classrooms, architects provided sound-proofed, toadstool-like pods standing on pedestals 6 feet above the floor, for purposes of individual study. They proved to be wonderful places for taking naps!

For a while, *classrooms without windows* garnered the attention of educators. This innovation, with its absence of windows, not only permitted maximum use of classroom walls, but it removed the distraction of outside stimuli. In addition, this condition provided the instructor with maximum light control for the use of projected materials. Such classrooms were also easier to heat since much heat loss in traditional classrooms is through the windows.

The initial success of *electronic language laboratories* caused them to be adapted to a variety of other academic areas, including science and social studies, again with mixed results. These labs consisted of individual work stations where a learner would don a headset and listen to audio tape language instruction, usually with the assistance of a workbook. In the more expensive setups, the teacher or manager of the language lab could monitor the progress of individuals from his or her central console.

Distance education has waxed and waned in the United States over the years, under such labels as *correspondence study* and *home study*. But as Daniel Granger (1990, p. 45), director of the Center for Distance Learning of Empire State College, State University of New York, points out: " 'Distance learning' as a term associated with new technologies offering a full-fledged alternative to classroom education got its biggest boost internationally with the founding of the British Open University in 1969." To date, the British Open System has graduated over 60,000 students with respectable college degrees. James Hall, Empire State College president, claims that "distance learning is the fastest-growing instructional pattern in the world." Distance learning is more prevalent in countries like Japan, China, Thailand, Singapore, Pakistan, India, Israel, and Brazil than in the United States. China's Central Television University is the largest in the world, with over 800,000 students enrolled. In this country the number of students per program is comparatively low, but there are a number of distance-learning programs that are proving themselves, including those at Empire State College of New York, Governors State College of Illinois, and Nova University in Florida. Nova's distance-education program uses an on-line computer system for their students, who are spread over the United States. They have over 400 masters and doctoral students in their distance-education program. The only times students come to campus are for two 1-week-long institutes. Students study from textbooks and study guides, with the on-line component serving to provide assignments and for exchange of messages among themselves and with their instructors.

In most other education and training programs, more pedestrian concerns are looked to by those installing instruction, such as "Does the instructor have basic control over lighting, acoustical, and temperature variables? Are there adequate electrical outlets? Can seating of students be varied to facilitate different instructional modes?" Chapter 15 presents processes and techniques used in adapting and controlling instructional facilities to the benefit of learners.

Client Staff Support After Implementation

In practice, the instructional developer's degree of responsibility to the client during the first instructional cycle of a product or process after installation varies from complete to none. The usual case is for the instructional developer to stay with the instructor for only a few class periods, and then fade out of the picture. Reasons for this early withdrawal are many; a new project making demands, no resources to pay for developer time, or a lack of understanding of how crucial the first cycles are to the continuing success of the instruction.

The delivery of *all* instructional packages, no matter how detailed or how well designed, are open to interpretation. This means that decisions could be made and are made counter to the original intent of the instruction, and that these decisions could eventually bring the value of the instruction into question. It is seldom necessary, or desirable, for developers to withdraw their help abruptly from target personnel. One reason for continuing support is that developers themselves are rarely clear about just how dependent personnel are on the developer in carrying out the instruction. To leave abruptly may create serious problems for personnel when they lack crucial competencies previously performed by the development staff. Serious problems for them at that time may cause problems later for the developer in terms of getting future projects with a dissatisfied client. A useful means for ensuring a successful transition of responsibility is through the *gradual disengagement* technique, as presented in Chapter 1.

Ideally, given that instructor training, course and facility scheduling, acquisition of instructional materials and equipment, and the registration of a sufficient number of the desired student population have all been completed, the major tasks of the instructional designer will be those of monitoring instructional delivery and management as a troubleshooter, fine-tuning the instruction, and providing backup for the instructors as they go through the cycle. Another important function they perform is providing feedback to members of the client organization who have been involved in the development of the instructional unit, such as teacher-trainers, curriculum specialists, and administrators.

Summary

The moment of installation of a new product or process is a critical one for its success. It is here that many projects are vulnerable because of the uncertainty that arises. A list of nine steps was presented that can facilitate successful installation of an innovation. Most of the techniques referenced for installation are techniques presented in other sections of this book, particularly in Chapter 3 on adoption of innovations. The processes of adoption and installation have much in common.

References

Ellington, Henry, and Harris, Duncan (1986). *Dictionary of Instructional Technology.* New York: Nichols.

Gentry, Castelle (1977). Management of Teacher Education Programs. *Teacher Education and Special Education Journal* 1(1): 45–57.

Granger, Daniel (1990). Open universities: Closing the distances to learning. *Change* vol. 22(4).

Havelock, R. G. (1973). *The Change Agent's Guide to Innovation in Education.* Englewood Cliffs, N.J.: Educational Technology Publications.

Knirk, F. G. (1979). *Designing Productive Learning Environments.* Englewood Cliffs, N.J.: Educational Technology Publications.

McLaughlin, Timothy (1992). Combining Expert Systems and Optical Data Storage Technologies in Computer-Facilitated Learning: Implications for Institutional Technology. Unpublished dissertation. East Lansing, Mich.: Michigan State University.

Sommer, Robert (1969). *Personal Space: The Behavioral Basis of Design.* Englewood Cliffs, N.J.: Prentice-Hall.

CHAPTER 8

Ongoing Operation

Process of effectively maintaining the continuing application of an instructional product and/or procedure after its installation

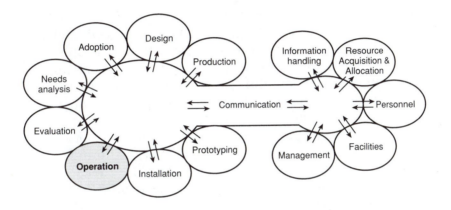

Learner Objectives

1. List and describe at least two techniques for finding and correcting problems in ongoing instructional systems.

2. Discriminate between preventative and regular maintenance of ongoing instructional systems.

3. Relate troubleshooting to monitoring and maintenance.

4. List common problems with integrating new instruction into ongoing systems.

5. List the conditions necessary to integrate new instruction into ongoing systems.

6. Recall definitions of major terms.

Introduction

While considerable resources may be expended in the development of an instructional product, it is common that, once the product is installed, instructional developers leave the product to pretty much sink or swim on its own. For example, prior to installation, time and energy are usually spent in training those initially responsible for managing and delivering the instruction, but relatively little is spent afterwards. As these initial managers and presenters of the new instruction transfer to other assignments, their replacements find few or no resources available for their training. Replacement personnel are often reticent about asking for assistance, and tend to muddle along as they attempt to train themselves in a product's use. Often, they will modify instructional elements to fit their own experience or to conform to resources available, which may do violence to the integrity of the instructional package. Flaws resulting from poor training of instructors may result in early elimination of a course.

Instructional programs tend to undergo curriculum revision on a sporadic basis as courses are added, modified, and/or deleted. The selection of which courses to drop out of the curriculum in order to make room for new courses represents a moment when ongoing courses may be challenged, and rightly so. However, if there are no advocates for a particular course, or if advocacy is weak, a course may be dropped despite its value to student or society.

These are but two examples of the many problems that may besiege the ongoing operation of an instructional unit. A formal plan for maintaining instructional units supported by resources with clear lines of responsibility seems a necessary condition for continuing effective instruction.

Ongoing Operation Process

Tasks important in maintaining ongoing instructional products and processes in a curriculum include the following.

1. Periodically monitor the effectiveness and relevance of instructional units (e.g., programs, courses, workshops).

2. Carry out preventive maintenance, regular maintenance, updating, and replacement of instructional units.

3. Establish and maintain an appropriate resource level for instructional units.

4. Train replacement personnel to manage/deliver ongoing instructional units.

5. Establish conditions necessary to making recently added instructional units integral to the overall instructional system rather than as supplemental or temporary additions.

Monitoring an Instructional Unit

The products and processes of instructional units are subject to the general systems principle of **entropy,** which rules that all organized entities tend to disorganize, unless maintained. More simply, this means man-made processes and procedures tend to deteriorate if not furnished appropriate and timely maintenance. This is true for any system, whether it be a highway, a small business, a marriage, or an instructional package. Thus, once an instructional package or unit is installed in a target system, it must be monitored regularly in order to find and correct any defects that occur, before problems are created for the learners taking the instruction.

Usually, it is assumed that the instructor or trainer responsible for presenting the instruction is also responsible for monitoring it. However, resources are seldom assigned to a specific course or element of a course, which means that an advocate is needed to compete for resources, usually on a problem-to-problem basis. More often, when defects surface, instructors tend to act as a bridge to get learners past the defect. However, as these defects accrue, it becomes more and more difficult to deal with their effects. Change of instructor, or assignment of multiple instructors, further compounds the problem. Eventually, if a sufficient number of problems related to the course come to the attention of decision makers, they may decide to eliminate the instruction.

The most desired state for protecting an ongoing instructional product or process is to follow a *preventative maintenance* routine, where problems can be anticipated and dealt with *before* they create difficulties for the learner or the instructor. For this state to occur requires some formalization of the responsibility for monitoring the continued effectiveness, efficiency, and relevance of the instructional product or process. One technique proven useful for monitoring instructional units is described in the job aid on "Key Indicator Management."

While man-made things do tend to break down, they can also be repaired. Valuable, indeed, are those individuals who are effective in spotting the cause of a breakdown and who correct it. In some cases, such

---

Job Aid / Key Indicator Management (KIM)

Description KIM is a technique for continuous monitoring of a course or program once it has been put into effect. It uses graphics (e.g., charts, tables, drawings) to give a quick indication of how a program is operating (see Figures 8.1 and 8.2). To do this, a target goal is selected and a report format created to show progress, or a lack thereof, for that goal over a specified time period.

Use Rationale Ongoing actions need to be monitored. This technique allows the individual in charge of implementing a program to monitor it by concentrating on a given indicator rather than watching every aspect of the entire operation. This technique can provide continuous feedback on how well a system is working. If the indicator is not on target, then a further, more-specific investigation can be made into the operation. This technique can be used to watch over a program on a temporary or a permanent basis.

continued

Key Indicator Management (KIM), continued

Critical Tasks

1. **Identify the operation or function to be monitored.** E.g., math instruction for seventh graders.

2. **Determine the items to be used as indicators of successful instruction.** Indicators should be based on the goals and objectives of the program, in order to reflect whether or not success is being achieved, e.g., student attitude toward the math instruction.

3. **List or establish levels of success for each indicator.** This involves establishing acceptable levels of performance for determining if an objective is being met, satisfactorily; e.g., 80% of a sample of representative students finishing a unit will report, anonymously, that they enjoyed and appreciated the instruction and would recommend the course to others.

4. **Determine how to measure these indicators and display the results.** See Figure 8.1. Select the format to be used to communicate the progress, or lack thereof, made toward the target.

5. **Establish the measurement details.** This involves stipulating how the data will be gathered and interpreted, setting up a timetable, making daily and/or weekly reports, etc. E.g., measure attitude through a brief, unsigned response to a short questionnaire at the end of instruction, asking students about their level of enjoyment and appreciation of the course, and willingness to recommend the course to others.

6. **Prepare the report, and review the levels achieved against the levels desired.** This allows someone to analyze the progress of an operation at a glance, to tell if things are on track or if discrepancies are occurring that need to be examined further.

FIGURE 8.1 / An example of a key indicator management report focusing on students' attitude toward math instruction

---

KEY INDICATOR REPORT

Attitude Indicator: Dislike for math instruction seems to be a major reason for students doing so poorly in the subject.

Data for all seventh-grade math classes:

Indicator	Measure	Target	This Month	Year to Date	Past Year	Range over Past 12 Months High	Low
Attitude toward math	Student reponse to attitude survey	80% positive	84.1%	64.4%	34.7%	89.7%	43.7%

Result: Target for this month was met, but not for year-to-date target. Need to isolate data in terms of specific teachers, and make sure each has adopted the changes mandated.

---

continued

Key Indicator Management (KIM), continued

FIGURE 8.2 / An example of a key indicator management report designed to promote the goal of efficiency (adapted from Plunkett and Attner, 1989)

KEY INDICATOR REPORT

Timing Indicator: The time it takes to process an order serves as an indicator of both efficiency and lead time needed to meet reliable promises to customers.

Data:

Indicator	Measure	Target	This Month	Year to Date	Past Year	Range over Past 12 Months	
						High	Low
Order entry	Customer order processing time (in days)	3.0	4.1	4.4	4.7	5.7	3.7

Result: Targets for this month and for year to date have not been met. Need to either change system or promise 5-day processing time.

References

Janson, Robert B., (1980). Graphic indicators of operations. *Harvard Business Review*, 58(6): 165–66.

Plunkett, Warren R., and Attner, Raymond F. (1989). *Introduction to Management*. Boston: Kent, pp. 387–389.

persons are called *troubleshooters*. A troubleshooter is someone, who, because of knowledge, skill, and talent, is able to ferret out causes of system breakdown and then to determine appropriate solutions. While monitoring may be a means of early identification of a problem **troubleshooting** is a means by which a problem can be analyzed and resolved. In a sense, this is a less fancy and more limited term for *problem solving*. Problem solving and troubleshooting certainly have much in common. Usually, problem solving is considered more scientific in its approach than is troubleshooting. The *scientific method* is one of the early systematic procedures followed in the troubleshooting of systems.

The basic procedures of troubleshooting, whether performed by a physician, a mechanic, or an instructional developer, are to: (1) recognize that a problem exists in a system, (2) examine the system for symptoms of the problem, (3) consider possible causes of the problem, (4) try out corrective procedures for the most likely causes, and (5) repeat until the problem is solved.

Figure 8.3 shows an excerpt from a troubleshooting guide sheet found in a *Time/Life* repair manual (1989, p. 369). Its purpose is to guide a troubleshooter in correcting a problem. In this case, it is directed at

FIGURE 8.3 / A section of a troubleshooting guide sheet for correcting an audiocassette tape recorder problem

Symptoms	Possible Causes	Procedure
No display lights, no sound	Recorder unplugged or off	Plug in and turn on recorder
	No power to outlet, outlet faulty	Reset breaker, or replace fuse
	Power fuse blown	Test and replace fuse
	On/off switch faulty	Test and replace on/off switch
	Faulty power supply	Take recorder to professional
	Faulty circuit board	Take recorder to professional
Has display lights but no sound	Controls set incorrectly	Adjust recorder controls
	Audiotape torn or jammed	Splice tape
	Receiver faulty	Troubleshoot receiver
	Drive belt loose or broken	Service drive belts
	Play/record head faulty	Test and replace head
	Play/record switch dirty	Clean switch
	Play/record switch faulty	Replace switch
	Capstan motor dirty	Take recorder to professional
	Capstan motor faulty	Take recorder to professional

determining the cause of and correction for a problem with an ailing audiocassette tape recorder. Note (1) that the leftmost column lists the symptoms flagging a problem, (2) that these symptoms lead to possible causes, as listed in the second column, which in turn lead to (3) the procedures for correcting the problem, as listed in the right-hand column. So, for example, if the symptoms are *no display lights come on, and there is no sound,* one of the possible causes might be that the *power fuse is blown.* To correct that for cause, the troubleshooter would *test the power fuse, and replace it,* if it is blown. If it is not blown, then the troubleshooter would test the next most likely cause. While instructional technologists usually deal with problems a bit more esoteric than the one depicted in the figures, their troubleshooting procedures are not that different. The "Troubleshooting" job aid presents one version of a useful technique.

Job Aid / Troubleshooting

Description   Troubleshooting is a technique both for finding the cause of a problem and for correcting it. This technique presents a process for systematically checking out the possible causes of the problem, beginning with the most likely cause, continuing to the least likely. Troubleshooting also has a strong intuitive aspect. In addition, its successful application requires a fairly intimate knowledge of the system being examined, and experience in solving such problems.

Use Rationale   Problems ranging from the trivial to the complex occur in instructional systems. Searching out the causes of these problems and correcting them efficiently is important for maintaining the flow of learning. Troubleshooting skills have proven very helpful in this regard.

continued

Troubleshooting, continued

Critical Tasks

1. **Identify the instructional unit having a problem.** E.g., a course in general high school math.

2. **Collect data on events leading to the problem.** Determine what symptoms or events triggered the concern for the course, e.g., complaints from teachers of courses for which this one is prerequisite.

3. **Describe the effects of the problem.** E.g., 10% of the new class are having great difficulty in meeting objectives in succeeding courses.

4. **List possible causes.** E.g., (a) the general high school math course is poorly taught, (b) the advanced high school math courses are poorly taught, (c) both general and advanced courses are poorly taught, (d) students are not applying themselves, (e) tests are poorly constructed.

5. **Sequence the causes from most likely to least likely.** This should be based on logic, experience, input from those involved, external expertise if needed, and whatever data are available.

6. **Choose the most probable cause.** E.g., because the teachers of the advanced math course used valid pretests that indicated that students entering the advanced course lacked some of the basic math skills and concepts, assume that the problem lies with the introductory or general math course.

7. **Analyze elements of the instructional unit relevant to the probable cause.** E.g., through inspection of instructional materials and procedures, interviews of teachers and students, observation, and/or testing.

8. **Select a solution to the problem, based on experience and data, and try it out.** Alternative solutions may have to be considered. If there is more than one possible solution, the *Cost-Effectiveness* technique may help in deciding which solution to choose.

9. **Repeat steps 5 through 8 until the problem is resolved.** There may be times when other expertise should be brought in. Good troubleshooters recognize their limits.

References

Gentry, Cass (1989). Trouble-shooting. Part of unpublished paper entitled Instructional Problem-Solving. 12 pages.

Time/Life Books (1989). *Complete Fix-It-Yourself Manual.* New York: Prentice-Hall.

Suggestion Box and *Walking About* (see Chapter 10) are other techniques that have proven useful for monitoring programs for purposes of spotting potential and existing problems. *Suggestion Box* is a technique for capturing anonymous reports of problems (and sometimes solutions) from system personnel, usually in written form. *Walking About* is a technique used by managers when they visit different parts of their domain without prior notice to personnel, to observe and to discuss problems and possible solutions as seen by the personnel.

Maintaining Instructional Units

Most education and training institutions have as a part of their organization specific units responsible for preventative maintenance and regular maintenance of their program's instructional products, processes, and equipment. Unfortunately, they are usually underfunded. **Maintenance** refers to the servicing, repair, and general upkeep of a system. The quality of maintenance units in educational and training organizations, and access to them, varies considerably. Usually, maintenance units are reactive in nature; i.e., they are triggered only when something stops working or is working incorrectly. This means that the instruction in question may be down for a period while the maintenance unit gets around to repairing it, causing frustration on the part of both instructors and learners.

Despite the failings of formalized maintenance units, those responsible for the continued effectiveness of the instruction should find out how their organization's maintenance unit operates and what its limitations are, so that contingency plans can be set up to deal with anticipated problems with the instruction. The job aids on "Maintaining an Instructional Unit" and "Course Maintenance Checklist" use checklists as a means of: (1) determining what maintenance should be done, and (2) ranking maintenance needs in terms of their criticality.

Job Aid / Maintaining an Instructional Unit

Description   A manager of instruction selects from a checklist the most frequent and/or most likely problems with an ongoing instructional unit. The manager then *predetermines* how those problems will be handled if and when they occur so that there is the least disruption of the instructional process. This includes documenting and distributing the information to responsible persons. The problems identified may require *preventive maintenance* (which is concerned with heading off potential problems), *maintenance* (which is concerned with the servicing, repair, and general upkeep of an instructional system), or *updating* (which is concerned with installing newer or revised versions of the instruction).

Use Rationale   Instructional managers who wait until problems arise with their instruction before considering how to deal with potential problems may find that the instruction is disrupted for an unnecessary length of time, exacerbating the initial problem.

Critical Tasks

1. **Acquire an instructional maintenance problem checklist.** See Figure 8.4.

2. **Select the problems from the checklist that are likely to occur for a specific instruction.** This could vary depending on the conditions affecting the instructional unit.

3. **Add any other problems to your list that you think might occur.** The list is neither comprehensive nor exhaustive, so you may see additional problems that need attending.

4. **After each problem on your list, indicate one or more ways the system normally handles such problems.** Include contact people and their telephone numbers as well as prices for the maintenance, and the contact personnel who are responsible for approving the correction.

continued

Maintaining an Instructional Unit, continued

FIGURE 8.4 / Instructional maintenance problem checklist

COURSE MAINTENANCE CHECKLIST

Instructor: _____
Course: _____
Date: _____

Directions: Read the following items, and check those that are not satisfactory. Write NA after the item when it is not appropriate to the course in question.

Preventive Maintenance

1. Are there enough copies of instructional materials available? _____
2. Has space and time for instruction been formally scheduled? _____
3. Have any space- and time-scheduling conflicts been resolved? _____
4. Has instructional hardware been formally scheduled? _____
5. Have new instructors been assigned? _____
6. Have new instructors been trained in the use of the new instruction? _____
7. Have course evaluation procedure dates been determined? _____
8. Has responsibility for evaluating the course been assigned? _____
9. Other: _____

Maintenance

1. media software

   a. Have service checks on print materials been completed? _____
   b. Have service checks on nonprint materials been completed? _____
   c. Have service checks on computer programs been checked? _____
   d. Are any of the printed instructional materials damaged? _____
   e. Are any of the nonprint instructional materials damaged? _____
   f. Are any of the computer programs damaged? _____
   g. Other: _____

2. media hardware

   h. Have service checks on hardware been completed? _____
   i. Was hardware delivered to the classroom on time? _____
   j. Is backup hardware available in case of breakdown in class? _____
   k. Are there sufficient electrical outlets for hardware? _____
   l. Is there sufficient light control for optical projection? _____
   m. Other: _____

Updating

1. Do newer or revised versions of software need to be installed? _____
2. Do newer or revised versions of programs need to be installed? _____
3. Do newer versions of hardware need to be installed? _____
4. Other: _____

continued

Maintaining an Instructional Unit, continued

5. **Make the list available to all those responsible for the instruction.**

6. **Set up a schedule for periodically repeating and updating steps 1–5.**

Reference

Gentry, C. G. (1975). Maintaining an Instructional Unit. Unpublished document written for Learning and Evaluation Services at Michigan State University. East Lansing, Mich.: The University, pp. 1–4.

A second technique proven effective for periodic (yearly) checking on the state of an instructional unit is presented in the "Course Maintenance Checklist" job aid.

Job Aid / Course Maintenance Checklist

Description This checklist was designed to assess and rank individual training courses on a yearly basis. The prelude of the checklist is used to collect historical and administrative data. Then fifteen areas are rated (e.g., course length). Criteria are provided for each item, with a space for comments. A five-point scale is used, with 1 as adequate and 5 as inadequate. Zero is used when an item is inappropriate for the course being evaluated. These ratings identify courses ranging from those most in need of maintenance to those needing little or no maintenance.

Use Rationale Keeping a course current is an ongoing problem for training centers. Courses do deteriorate, becoming less relevant and effective. This is particularly true for content areas where technology is changing rapidly. If trainees are to be prepared adequately for their jobs, then the curriculum must be valid and reliable.

Critical Tasks

1. **Rate all items on the checklist using the five-point scale.** See Figure 8.5. On the scale, 1 indicates adequacy, 5 indicates inadequacy, and 0 indicates an item is not appropriate for this course.

2. **Sum all response numbers for the items.** Enter the sum under Total Score.

3. **Use the total score to rank the course.** Determine the course rank from the table at the bottom of the last page of the checklist. A score of 46 or higher means the course needs significant revision.

4. **Factor in any other inputs before making a final decision.** Such as those mentioned at the end of the checklist, e.g., redevelopment costs.

5. **Make revision decision.**

continued

Course Maintenance Checklist, continued

FIGURE 8.5 / Checklist for determining the level of maintenance needed by a course

COURSE MAINTENANCE CHECKLIST

This checklist is a performance aid to help you evaluate the condition of the courses at your training center. It is designed to serve as a document that should help you rank your various courses.

Course Evaluator _____

Date of Evaluation _____

Course Name _____

Course Number _____

Course Was Developed by _____

Initial Development Date _____

Revision Date(s) _____

Number of Times Course Has Been Taught, Ever _____

Number of Times Course Was Taught Last Year _____

Total Number of Students Who Have Taken Course _____

Number of Students Who Took Course Last Year _____

Formal Follow-up and Evaluation of Course Accomplished? Yes _____ No _____ If Yes, Date _____

Rate each of the following items on a scale from 1 (Adequate) to 5 (Inadequate). If the item is not applicable, e.g., no course problem, select 0. Circle the appropriate value. For items rated 3 through 5, explain the exact discrepancy in the comments section. For example, if you rate the Instructor Guide as inadequate, state the specific inadequacy, such as "Lacks sufficient examples in units 2 and 3."

1. The length of the course is:

   Inadequate   Adequate   N/A   (Evaluation Criteria: Do all students finish the course? Are
   5   4   3   2   1   0   some units too long or short? Does the course pace seem too
                                              fast or too slow?)

   Comments: _____

   _____

   _____

2. The Instructor Guide is:

   Inadequate   Adequate   N/A   (Evaluation Criteria: Is the technical content complete? Is the
   5   4   3   2   1   0   document organized? Is the format easy to follow? Are the
                                              directions clear?)

   Comments: _____

   _____

   _____

continued

Course Maintenance Checklist, continued

3. The student materials (text, workbook, handouts, etc.) are:

Inadequate				Adequate	N/A
5	4	3	2	1	0

    (Evaluation Criteria: Are student materials complete? Do they look professionally produced? Are they easily read? Do students refer to them?)

    Comments: _____

    _____

    _____

4. The multimedia used in the course are:

Inadequate				Adequate	N/A
5	4	3	2	1	0

    (Evaluation Criteria: Are the multimedia sufficient? Do the multimedia enhance the learning? Are they appropriate? Are the multimedia aesthetic?)

    Comments: _____

    _____

    _____

5. The course objectives (overall and unit) are:

Inadequate				Adequate	N/A
5	4	3	2	1	0

    (Evaluation Criteria: Are objectives clear and concise? Do they stress key points? Do they help preorganize the material?)

    Comments: _____

    _____

    _____

6. The course tests (pretest and unit tests) are:

Inadequate				Adequate	N/A
5	4	3	2	1	0

    (Evaluation Criteria: Are these tests in existence? Are they sufficient? Are there quantitative criteria for scoring the tests? Do they measure required skills and knowledge?)

    Comments: _____

    _____

    _____

7. The exercises in the course are:

Inadequate				Adequate	N/A
5	4	3	2	1	0

    (Evaluation Criteria: Are the exercises sufficient? Are they challenging and meaningful? Can they be evaluated?)

    Comments: _____

    _____

    _____

continued

Course Maintenance Checklist, continued

8. The course mode (instructor-led vs. self-instructional) is:

   Inadequate   Adequate   N/A   (Evaluation Criteria: Is an instructor available? Is there an on-
   5   4   3   2   1   0   site demand for the course? Can the course be converted to
                                                 self-instructional mode?)

   Comments: _____

   _____

   _____

9. The technical content of the course represents the current state of the art:

   Inadequate   Adequate   N/A   (Evaluation Criteria: How long has the course been taught?
   5   4   3   2   1   0   How recently has it been revised?)

   Comments: _____

   _____

   _____

10. The teaching strategies used in this course are:

    Inadequate   Adequate   N/A   (Evaluation Criteria: Does the course provide for student
    5   4   3   2   1   0   practice and evaluation? Are students *involved*? Does
                                                 learning take place?)

    Comments: _____

    _____

    _____

11. The organization of the course is:

    Inadequate   Adequate   N/A   (Evaluation Criteria: Does the course flow smoothly? Are
    5   4   3   2   1   0   lessons and units integrated?)

    Comments: _____

    _____

    _____

12. The case problem(s) used in this course is (are):

    Inadequate   Adequate   N/A   (Evaluation Criteria: Is the number of case problems
    5   4   3   2   1   0   adequate? Do they relate to the students' work experience?)

    Comments: _____

    _____

    _____

continued

Course Maintenance Checklist, continued

13. Student interest and motivation in the course is:

Inadequate			Adequate		N/A	(Evaluation Criteria: Do students react positively to the course? Do students seem enthusiastic in class?)
5	4	3	2	1	0	

Comments: _____

_____

_____

14. Student feedback on the course indicated the course is:

Inadequate			Adequate		N/A	(Evaluation Criteria: Are the student feedback summary data positive? Are the student comments positive?)
1	2	3	4	5	0	

Comments: _____

_____

_____

15. The value of this course to students' job needs is:

Inadequate			Adequate		N/A	(Evaluation Criteria: Do students need this course to do their jobs? Does the course provide them with the required skills and knowledge to do their jobs?)
5	4	3	2	1	0	

Comments: _____

_____

_____

Please add any additional comments not covered by this checklist. _____

_____

_____

Total the values on the scale that you selected for each item. Total Score _____

The following table will give you an estimate of course revision needs.

Score	Action
15 or less	Course requires no revision
16–30	Course requires minor revision
31–45	Course requires revision
46–60	Course requires significant revision
61–75	Course requires major revision

Other factors that should be considered when determining course revision requirements are:

1. Student demand for course
2. Redevelopment cost
3. Criticality of skills and knowledge taught
4. Anticipated life of the course

Reference

Martinez, Charles F. (1980). Course maintenance: The problem and solution. *Educational Technology.* 20(12): pp. 12–21.

Maintaining an Appropriate Resource Level

That there are seldom enough resources to go around in an organization is a well-accepted truism. Under such circumstances, it logically follows that there will be competition for limited resources in most, if not all, organizations. This implies that if units of a program are to succeed, there needs to be advocates that will fight for a just share of limited resources. A second truism is that when everyone is responsible for an instructional unit, no one is! Given these "truths," the needs of an instructional unit will be haphazardly met unless there are clear procedures for determining a unit's ongoing operational needs and a specific advocate assigned who knows the organizational procedures that control the resources. To convince others about the continuing value of the unit, advocates of instructional units should be versed in change techniques, as well.

Knowing the procedures by which resources are allocated and accessed is particularly important for advocates of a unit. In these processes lie power, which is usually guarded jealously by an organization's hierarchy. In most organizations, the processes of resource acquisition and allocation are spelled out to staff only in a general way, while knowledge of details and the rules governing allocation tend to be reserved to managers and other administrators of the system. However, with a little effort, the details of a budget, relevant to an instructional unit, can be ferreted out. For example, the budgets of public-supported institutions are usually open to public inspection, although the fact is not widely advertised. Often, college and university budgets are kept on reserve in an institution's library, and may be examined on request by members of the public. The annual reports of business and industry are also not difficult to access, and they usually contain enough information to make clear the type of budget being used by a company.

Even though a course may be recognized in the economic flow of an organization, the resources are seldom sufficient to accomplish all of the things that advocates would like. For those willing to do the investigative homework, there are almost always excess funds in a system. One technique that is useful for obtaining excess funds is called *Proactive Requisitioning*. This technique takes advantage of the fact that sooner or later most organizations get in the position where they must spend money in a hurry, to prevent losing it in future budgets. This is usually the result of some deadline imposed from without, whether from a funding agency or through a policy that requires that unexpended funds in departmental budgets be returned to the general fund at the end of the fiscal year. The return of unspent resources to the general fund is not usually rewarded by the administration. In fact, those with budget control see such returns as evidence that a department can get by on less, and they tend to cut budgets accordingly. Needless to say, project managers and department heads go out of their way to get these moneys spent rather than let them go back to the general fund. Operating on the principle that "opportunity favors the prepared mind," the "Proactive Requisitioning" job aid formalizes a process for seizing the brief moment when such funds are available.

Job Aid / Proactive Requisitioning

Description   This technique consists of steps that personnel can follow to take advantage of those sporadic moments during a year when money surfaces that must be spent although the organization has no immediate plan for spending the funds.

Use Rationale   A serious problem for instructional managers is getting the necessary resources to maintain their instructional units. This means that when resources are inadequate, the units tend to deteriorate. To prevent unit deterioration, managers may have to use unorthodox methods to obtain funds.

Critical Tasks

1. **Determine and list the ongoing resources required by your instructional units.** E.g., materials, personnel, training, space, scheduling.

2. **Prioritize the items in terms of their relative importance.** So that you are in a position to negotiate without making snap decisions about what is important.

3. **Estimate the costs of resources needed, and when they are needed.** Most of these cost data can be found in the system, but some might need to be sought through vendors.

4. **Get copies of the organization's requisition form.** These vary in content and format with the organization.

5. **Determine the categories used in the organization's budget.** The budget itself may not be available, but no one objects to staff knowing the formal budget categories, e.g., travel, salaries, communication.

6. **Predetermine the formal budget categories into which your required resources would fall.** There may be more than one place in the budget where items would fit.

7. **Determine the paper trail that a requisition follows.** Ask a smart secretary to explain where it stops at points in the process, what is checked, and who has what responsibility for passing it on at that time.

8. **Determine the types of allocation authority and procedures in the organization.** Including budgeting systems such as contingency funds, no-budget budget. Also, whether particular resources requested have to be put out for bid or can be bought directly from a vendor by you.

9. **Fill out preparatory, undated copies of requisitions in anticipation of need and opportunity.** E.g., end-of-year dumping of money so next year's budget won't be cut.

10. **If categories covering your unit's need are not in the budget, petition to include them.** There are formal procedures for changing almost anything in an organization, but it may take some digging to find the procedure and the means.

11. **When the opportunity arises, submit one or more requisitions.** This should be to individuals in appropriate units of the organization.

continued

Reference

Gentry, C. G. (1966). Opportunistic Requisitioning. Unpublished document prepared for staff of the media center at the University of Maine. Orono, Maine: the University.

Training Replacement Personnel

Managers and instructors move on from one job or activity to another, which necessitates that replacement personnel be brought in to take over their old responsibilities. As mentioned earlier, assignments may be dumped in the laps of replacement personnel without providing them with the necessary training. Techniques for the training of personnel are presented in detail in Chapter 14. The *Regressive Assistance* technique, described in Chapter 7, is also one that has proven effective for training personnel in both installation and ongoing operation phases.

Integrating Instructional Units into System

Unmonitored, unadvocated instructional units tend to lose the resources and the esteem of the system in which they operate. They tend to hang out in limbo rather than being viewed as a valued part of the overall system. How does an instructional unit become integrated into the parent system after installation? Clearly, the unit must have value to the members of that system. The unit's value to the system is not always obvious, and even when obvious it may be competing for resources with other instructional units viewed as equally valuable. So an advocate may find it necessary to demonstrate a unit's value over and over as adjustments are proposed to the curriculum. How is that done, practically? It is easier to demonstrate value when the unit is clearly prerequisite to some required instructional unit or if it teaches some skill or knowledge that is applied directly on the job. It is most difficult when there is no clear tie to other courses in the curriculum. More specifically, the following conditions are important for integrating an ongoing instructional unit or program into the parent organization:

1. There is a competent instructor and/or manager (person or persons knowledgeable about the subject matter of the instructional unit and trained in the delivery of the instruction).

2. There is a dedicated advocate assigned to look out routinely for the unit's interests (through contacts with appropriate decision makers and gatekeepers).

3. The instructional unit is viewed as valuable by those who are involved with it (including curriculum specialists, instructors, managers, and students).

4. The instructional unit is included as a cost item (directly or indirectly) in the organization's budget.

5. The instruction is scheduled at intervals convenient for student attendance (does not conflict with other required courses, and follows appropriate prerequisites).

6. The instruction clearly serves a purpose for the curriculum of which it is a part (is either prerequisite to or provides successor knowledge for other units of related instruction).

To illustrate their importance, consider item 3. One means of meeting this condition is to build a written documentation file, that supports the instructional unit in question. This includes lists of specific instructors, students, and potential employers who depend on the instruction, with testimonials citing the value of the course to them. Means for accomplishing each of the five other conditions are discussed at different locations in the text.

Summary

Instructional units left to operate with insufficient resources tend to deteriorate and lose their effectiveness, and in many cases are prematurely eliminated. A range of techniques is recommended for supporting ongoing instruction, including monitoring the unit, maintenance of software and hardware, maintaining the resource level, training replacement personnel, and integrating the instructional unit into the parent system. One of the most important conditions necessary for a unit's continuing operation is the designation of a dedicated advocate who can speak for its needs.

References

Bass, R. K., and Dills, C. R. (1984). *Instructional Development: The State of the Art, II.* Dubuque, Iowa: Kendall/Hunt.

Cleland, D. I. (1990). *Project Management: Strategic Design and Implementation.* Blue Ridge Summit, Penna.: TAB Professional and Reference Books.

French, W. L., and Bell, C. H. (1978). *Organization Development.* 2d ed. Englewood Cliffs, N.J.: Prentice-Hall.

Perrow, Charles (1986). *Complex Organizations.* 3d ed. New York: Random House.

Plunkett, W. R., and Attner, R. F. (1989). *Introduction to Management.* Boston: PWS-Kent.

CHAPTER 9

Ongoing Instructional Unit Evaluation

Process of collecting and analyzing data about, and assigning values to, an ongoing instructional unit, to help in making decisions on maintenance, revision, and/or elimination of its elements

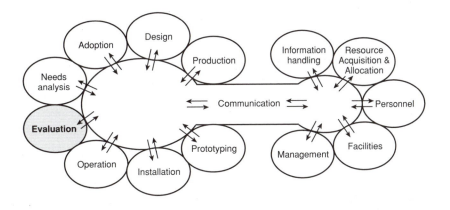

Learner Objectives

1. Discriminate between the *deterioration cycle* and the *improvement cycle* that instructional units may go through over time.

2. Relate needs analysis and cost-effectiveness to the evaluation process.

3. Describe and justify the use of the Stake technique for evaluating an ongoing instructional unit.

4. Discriminate between test *reliability* and test *validity*.

5. Describe one or more techniques for training test administrators.

6. Recall definitions of major terms.

Introduction

Depending on the particular client organization, instructional developers may or may not be involved in the very important processes of ongoing evaluation and revision of courses. After installation of an instructional unit, most instructional development project teams either are disbanded or they go on to other projects. When evaluation of ongoing instructional units does occur, it is usually carried out by client personnel, and it tends to be sporadic and inconsistent. This casual view of when and how evaluation is done is being replaced by a growing recognition of the importance of subjecting ongoing courses to periodic, formal evaluation, and that those responsible should be knowledgeable in the techniques of empirical evaluation. The practice of timely evaluation and revision of instructional units significantly extends the unit's longevity. This chapter provides instructional developers with the basics needed to carry out evaluation of ongoing instructional units. Even when instructional developers do not themselves carry out such evaluations, they can use this knowledge to help clients set up the necessary conditions for evaluation to take place.

Evaluation is a process everyone talks about but that few do well. The major reason for evaluation's not being done well seems to be due to a lack of evaluation skills and/or a lack of interest on the part of school and training personnel. There are certainly good reasons why ongoing instructional courses are dropped. But, unfortunately, with the absence of empirical evaluation data, decisions about courses are made primarily on a subjective basis. Sometimes courses lose support because those in control want to redirect a course's resources to projects in which they hold greater interest. In other cases, courses die because of their being incompetently taught. From another perspective, there is some truth in the charge that simple inertia enables too many courses to hang on long after they lose their value. Courses also stay beyond their time due to support by individuals or groups who are emotionally linked to the subject matter or courses, regardless of their value to the learner or society. These conditions persist primarily because neither the advocates of courses nor the administrators of the parent organizations have sufficient hard data to enable them to support or deny the value of the courses in their curricula. Most decisions are based on prevailing experience and opinion, and on "happiness" indices, i.e., the typical one- to two-page response sheet asking students how they liked it.

The process of acquiring and analyzing hard data on effectiveness, efficiency, and relevance of existing courses is called *ongoing instructional evaluation*, the basic purpose of which is to provide information that will facilitate decision making for those responsible for the instruction.

Instructional units are much like any other product, in that they, too, are affected by the ravages of time. As mentioned in the previous chapter, all man-made products and processes are subject to the principle of *entropy*, which states that organized entities tend to disorganize. Whether the system considered is an automobile or the road it runs on, or whether it is an instructional product or the organization using it, all systems are subject to the effects of entropy. In other words, all artificial systems tend to deteriorate. To slow down the deterioration of an instructional product, or to improve the product, requires an input of energy (resources). For an automobile, entropy might be counteracted by the replacement of a spark plug. For a highway, it might mean the filling of potholes or drawing white lines along its sides as guides to motorists during periods of poor visibility. In an instructional unit, entropy might be counteracted by replacing outdated information with up-to-date information. In every case, collection of data on a system is necessary to come to appropriate decisions about it. Such data are often collected through evaluative techniques.

When should an ongoing instructional unit be evaluated? Some instructional developers maintain that the revision of instruction is, itself, an ongoing task, even after an instructional unit has successfully met summative-evaluation criteria. Three of the reasons put forth are: (1) instruction is never developed as well as it should be and could be, (2) the information in a unit may have become outdated, and (3) the content needs of a specific group change over time. If these reasons are valid, it makes sense for evaluation of a unit of instruction to continue as long as the unit is in operation. Practically, it is difficult to get that kind of commitment from instructional system managers.

There appears to be a negative cycle operating in the development process that almost ensures early failure of instructional products and processes. This cycle, as depicted in Figure 9.1, graphs the different ID stages in terms of the resources spent over time. Line segment A in the figure represents the instructional design stage, where considerable energy is expended. Line segment B represents the installation stage of the instruction. Note that less energy is being used in the installation stage than in the previous stage. As they complete their tasks, many of the staff, and supporting resources, are pulled off to other ID projects. Appropriately, the developers who remain focus on working with those personnel and conditions of the target system that support the installation process. Line segment C represents the initial period of ongoing operation of the instruction. It is unusual that the operational activities of the unit are provided the resources that would maximize instruction. In fact, it is more usual that less and less energy is provided in support of the system as time goes on. When the energy input gets below that required by the unit's design, as in the later stages of ongoing operation (line segment D), the unit begins to deteriorate at a more rapid rate. Eventually, enough deterioration occurs that someone decides to scrap the instructional unit and start over, as illustrated by the second stage in Figure 9.1. This cycle may be repeated over and over, with concomitant loss of resources. Only rarely is serious revision considered for an ongoing course in its early stages of deterioration. As more than one critic has complained, "There is never time enough to do a job right, but there is always time to do it over."

Possible reasons for the deterioration in stages C and D are many. Initially, during development (A) and installation (B) a lot of resources are used to bring instructors up to speed so they can do a good job of delivering the instruction. As a result, in its early operation (C), instruction is delivered pretty much according to plan. However, because of the normal processes of change in a system (e.g., job shifts, hiring, firing, and retirement), the original instructors may have to be replaced. When new instructors are assigned, they are usually given a very cursory introduction to the instruction, often with no more than a casual offer of "let me know if you need help!" As new instructors begin teaching the units, they may find

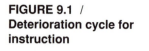

**FIGURE 9.1 /
Deterioration cycle for
instruction**

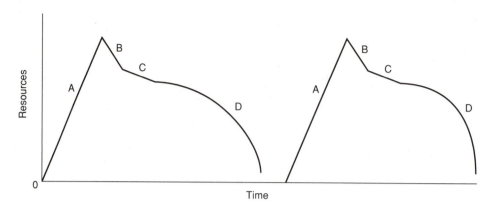

themselves unsure of the value of some elements of the instruction, or they may feel incompetent to teach particular elements. So they may either do a poor job of teaching the element or, given the autonomy that often falls to instructors, replace an element with something they think is more important, not realizing that they have dropped out something crucial to the instructional system.

Deterioration of the original instruction may also occur as a result of an across-the-board budget cut, where loss of revenue limits purchases to less effective supporting materials and equipment. Instructional material that becomes outdated also counts toward deterioration. A more specific example of a deteriorating effect is the failure of the instructional support service to deliver projection equipment on time. As a result, learners may miss an essential piece of mediated instruction. Eventually, the level of deterioration reaches a point (D) where there is enough dissatisfaction that either serious revision is initiated or, more likely, the instruction is scrapped and the cycle begins all over again.

A more desirable cycle for improvement of instruction is presented in Figure 9.2. Here we see a similar outcome up through the operational stage (C). If, during this stage, evaluative data are regularly collected regarding the instruction's effectiveness, efficiency, and relevance, a plan based on an analysis of the data can be formed for periodically revising the instruction, as illustrated by the repeating ABC cycles in the figure. Assuming that administrators can be made to see that revision of the instruction at this point is less costly than scrapping the instruction and starting over, resources will be made available for beginning the next cycle of development, installation, and operation. This process would be repeated periodically, not only to ensure that deterioration does not reduce the instruction's effect, but, in fact, to steadily improve its effect.

A concise meaning of evaluation tends to escape educators and trainers. A simple but effective way of looking at **evaluation** is to think of it as a means of detecting discrepancies between what exists and what is desired. If the criterion of effectiveness for a course is for it to teach, minimally, 80% of the course objectives, to 80% of a representative group, its effectiveness can be determined by evaluating the students before and after their taking the course, and comparing the results against the 80/80 standard. This should reveal any discrepancies between what was intended and what actually occurred.

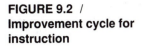

**FIGURE 9.2 /
Improvement cycle for
instruction**

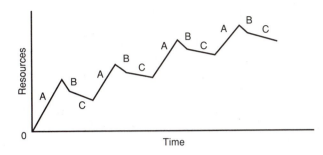

Evaluation comes in many guises. *Needs analysis*, for example, is a technique that can be used to establish the instructional needs of a particular group of students. This can be viewed as seeking to identify the discrepancy between what students are being taught and what they should be taught. Thus, needs assessment can be viewed as a form of evaluation. *Cost-effectiveness* is another form of evaluation that is used to compare two or more alternative instructional systems in terms of their respective costs and capabilities in successfully teaching the same objectives. Knowledge of the discrepancies between the two, in terms of how well they perform on certain variables, assists in making the choice between the two.

The saying that "when everyone is responsible for a process, no one is" is certainly true for the evaluation process. Most testing of learner achievement is seldom carried out consistently in any coherent, systematic manner. Part of the reason for this is that organizational responsibility for evaluation is seldom clear-cut. One of the most important steps toward ensuring that effective evaluation of ongoing instructional units take place is for the host organization to formalize processes, responsibilities, and resource support for an evaluation subunit.

Instructional Unit Evaluation Process

Here are steps important to the process of evaluating an ongoing instructional system:

1. Identify an existing ongoing instructional unit or course whose value is in question.
2. Get agreement to evaluate from those responsible for the instruction in question.
3. Organize for handling evaluation data.
4. Acquire, modify or generate an evaluation instrument, including directions for its administration.
5. Establish the validity and reliability of the evaluation instrument(s).
6. Schedule and carry out the evaluation.
7. Analyze the data and report the findings to appropriate decision makers.

Identifying the Evaluation Target

There is a saying: "If it ain't broke, don't fix it!" This makes a great deal of logical sense, but not always practical sense. *Broke* is a relative term. Its meaning could range from "partly ineffective" all the way up to "inoperative." Most educators and trainers have had limited preparation in recognizing early symptoms pointing toward deterioration of an instructional package, when saving a unit may very well depend on early identification of its problems. To use a medical analogy, early diagnosis of a disease improves considerably the chances of patient survival. Some systems have a predetermined schedule for checking on the health of a program. Such periodic assessments are similar in intent to the annual physical exam. All too often, serious assessment doesn't take place until there is an emergency, which may be too late to salvage an instructional program. Entropy will have had its way for too long. A much-preferred procedure is to provide data early enough that decision makers can be proactive, rather than reactive, to problems with the unit.

Periodic scheduling of evaluation for instructional systems is certainly desirable, but problems may also occur during the periods between evaluations. Some problems can be spotted early through less objective techniques, such as *Walking About* (see Chapter 10), where the elements of an instructional system are observed somewhat randomly, or through the *Suggestion Box* technique, which provides voluntary input from instructors and students (see Chapter 10). Just as a doctor checks for symptoms of illness, the instructional manager keeps on the lookout for signs or telltales that suggest problems in instruction. These telltales may come in the form of complaints made by instructors or students or a drop in student enrollment, or they may come from employers of a program's graduates.

Obtaining Agreement to Evaluate

There are times when getting agreement for an evaluation is no more difficult than identifying those affected or responsible and asking for consent. But other times it may be necessary first to lead individuals through recognized stages of adoption, i.e., unfreezing, appraisal, trial, accept/reject, and refreezing. Evaluation of courses is threatening to both teachers and trainers, especially when the evaluation is imposed externally. Chapter 3 presents several job aids useful for moving personnel through the stages necessary to obtain agreement, or at least to allay fears (e.g., *Nominal Group Process, Visitation*). The inspection of a client system's organizational chart will show the *formal* relationships among members, and techniques such as *Communications Network Analysis* (Chapter 7) are useful for identifying the *informal* connections among key individuals within a system. After identifying these individuals, other techniques, such as *Force-Field Analysis* (Chapter 3), can be used to collect facts and opinions about potential negative and positive outcomes of carrying out the evaluation (e.g., defensiveness of instructors who have bought into the instruction, question of priorities for spending a limited budget). These data can be used to write separate memos to each of the groups concerned, to alleviate any dissatisfaction or concern on their part. Examples of sources of such data are student comments, instructor concerns, community views, and specialist or expert opinion.

Those responsible for the instruction may ask for cost information for the proposed evaluation. An instructional developer should be prepared to provide, on demand, tentative budget and time-line estimates. See Chapter 13 to review techniques for writing budgets.

Organizing for Handling Evaluation Data

A number of evaluation models and their respective techniques were discussed in Chapter 6. While the models there were focused on formative and summative evaluation, there is much overlap among those and other evaluation models. The model used here for evaluating ongoing instruction, adapted from Stake's Contingency Model of Evaluation, is presented in the "Modified Stake Evaluation Management Technique" job aid.

Job Aid / Modified Stake Evaluation Management Technique

Description   This technique combines elements from Stake's and Provus's evaluation models with interpretations from Nelson's work. The technique provides a matrix for organizing, analyzing, and communicating evaluation data. In the Descriptive Matrix of Stake's model (see Figure 9.3), the first column lists the classes of information needed for the evaluation (i.e., entry conditions, instructional methods, and learning outcomes). Information is recorded in the second and third columns of the matrix on what was intended for instruction and what was actually observed. The second section of the descriptive matrix is concerned with specifying discrepancies between intents and observations, and their causes, for each class of information. The technique requires that both the congruences across columns of the matrix and the contingencies among the rows of the matrix be reconciled.

Use Rationale   Everyone agrees on the importance of periodically evaluating instruction, and they may also agree on how often to evaluate, but seldom do the evaluators have the knowledge or skills to list the kinds of data to be collected, based on evaluation and psychometric principles. Stake's technique requires the collection of data at the time the instruction is implemented (the intents of the instruction), which is the time when it is most readily available. The evaluation at the end of the instructional cycle deals with the same elements, and thus does not impose artificial or unrealistic standards. These findings may then be used by decision makers to decide whether to retain the instruction as is, revise it, or eliminate it.

Critical Tasks

1. **Collect and record course intents data in the matrix.** See Figures 9.4 and 9.5. This action is done at the beginning of the instructional cycle for a unit. Students' entry-level data and instructional setting and strategies data may be taken from the requirements section in the instructor's manual, the course description, and the student syllabus.

continued

Modified Stake Evaluation Management Technique, continued

FIGURE 9.3 / Modified Stake Evaluation Model

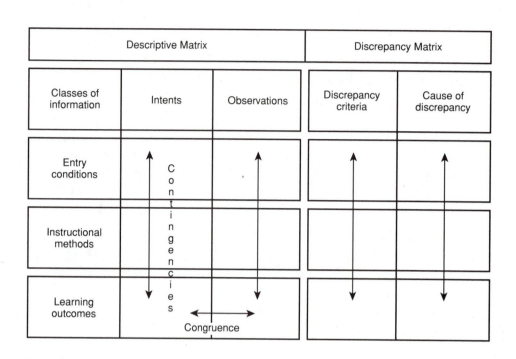

2. **Collect and record observations data in the matrix.** See Figures 9.4 and 9.5. Data are collected at different points during the instructional cycle for the unit: entry-conditions data on students are usually taken from entry tests and pretests at the beginning of an instructional cycle, data on instructional settings and strategies are collected throughout the cycle by matching strategies and activities against the resources provided, whereas learning outcomes are collected through posttests after the instruction is completed.

3. **List any discrepancies among *contingent* elements.** See Figure 9.3. This looks to see if there is a mismatch across entry conditions, instructional methods, and learning outcomes.

4. **List any discrepancies among *congruent* elements.** See Figure 9.3. This looks to see if what was intended is significantly different from what was actually observed for each class of information.

5. **List the cause(s) for each discrepancy to the degree known.** See Figures 9.4 and 9.5. Additional research may be necessary to determine the causes for certain discrepancies.

6. **Report evaluation data, discrepancies, and discrepancy causes to decision makers.** Obviously, the evaluation is not over, because the decision makers will then apply their own standards to the data in the report.

continued

Modified Stake Evaluation Management Technique, continued

FIGURE 9.4 / Example of a completed descriptive matrix

	Intents	Observations
Entry conditions	1. Completed 7th-grade math 2. At grade-level reading ability 3. Can compute area of rectangle	1. All completed 7th-grade math 2. 20% are at 4th-grade reading level, 20% at 10th-grade reading level 3. 60% able to compute area of rectangle

Procedures	1. Slide-tape
	2. 16mm film
	3. Manual
	4. Workbook
	5. Tutoring (individually by teacher)
		1. Two examples not understood by 40% of class
		2. Not available—not received in the mail
		3. (a) Instructions unclear
		   (b) Relationship between manual and workbook not understood by 25% of class
		4. (a) Instructions on Problems 3, 12, 15, 26 not clear
		   (b) Content jump from Problems 11–12 too great; need more examples—80% of students not able to cope
		5. No time for individual work

Learner outcomes	1. Compute area of triangle 2. Apply formula for computing area of triangle to four different types of triangles	

FIGURE 9.5 / Second example of a completed descriptive matrix

	Plans	Observations
Entry conditions	1. Student will want to learn about community groups. 2. Student will not be able to list in order the basic steps for forming a community action group. 3. Film will arrive on time.	1. All twenty students responded that they wanted a class on community action groups. 2. Students could not list more than three steps needed to form a community action group. 3. Film arrived on time.
Strategies and media	1. Show film "Solving Community Problems Through Community Action." 2. List ten steps randomly on chalkboard for organizing action group. 3. Number steps according to class direction. 4. Give proper ordering on worksheet, illustrating how each step is implemented.	1. Showed film. 2. Listed all twelve examples of improving the community that were shown in the film. 3. Each student gave at least one additional example of how a community action group improves its own community.
Learner outcomes	1. Student will be able to develop an outline for organizing a community action group, using at least eight of the ten steps stated in the film.	1. Each student gave at least three examples in written form describing how each example could be used to improve the community using eight or more steps.

continued

Modified Stake Evaluation Management Technique, continued

References

Nelson, Frank (1970). *Evaluation for Instructional Development*. Washington, D.C.: National Special Media Institute, pp. 36–41.

Provus, Malcolm (1971). *Discrepancy Evaluation: For Educational Program Improvement and Assessment*. Berkeley, Calif.: McCutchan.

Stake, R. E. (1967). The countenance of educational evaluation. *Teachers College Record* 68: 523–540.

Collecting data using the Stake technique is not sufficient in itself. Responsible individuals must not only have access to the data but must have among them other *information-handling* skills as well. The processes of **information handling** include selecting the kind of information needed, collecting the information, interpreting and organizing it, arranging for its storage and retrieval, distributing the information, and assessing the information's impact on a targeted system. Consider the following example of information handling in the case of evaluating an ongoing instructional science unit.

Selection: data on the effectiveness of General Science I

Collection: data collected from learners through a multiple-choice test and attitude inventory; from the curriculum director, science department chair, and science teachers (through structured interviews)

Organization: All data organized according to the evaluation objectives. Multiple-choice data tabled, using t scores and z scores; attitudinal and interview data collated and assessed by three expert judges. Data reported as outcomes for individual elements of the instructional units, followed by recommendations from the test administrator based on test, attitudinal, and interview data

Storage: Data entered into an electronic database system used according to predetermined key terms

Retrieval: access through key terms by designated personnel only

Distribution: circulated only to designated personnel, and following predetermined criteria for reporting results and recommendations to school personnel and the public

Assessment: Effectiveness of information for administrators in making decisions to leave instruction as is, modify it, or eliminate it is determined by interviews with decision makers

Processes and techniques relevant to information handling are discussed in greater detail in Chapters 10 and 12.

Preparing the Evaluation Instrument

The procedures for drawing up a table of specifications for an evaluation instrument are presented in Chapter 4. A table of specifications provides a reasoned guide as to how many and what kind of items are needed to test students over specific instructional objectives.

Test items generated for this type of evaluation instrument would be no different than those discussed in Chapter 4. The reader is referred to the section on generating test items, where job aids for writing different forms of test items are presented (multiple choice, true-false, matching, short answer, essay, and performance checklist). Once items are written, they need to be ordered into a desired test format, which may include clustering similar test items (e.g., putting all multiple-choice items together), directions to the examinee for answering items in each cluster, and arrangement of items for efficient grading.

Often enough, the staff who administer a test are not the same people who constructed the test. To ensure consistency in administering tests, it is advisable to develop a set of detailed and unambiguous directions. These directions could include how to identify students who should take the test, conditions for taking the test and how to check them (e.g., orientation of test takers, physical spacing of test takers, release to go to the restroom, agreement in using other resources such as dictionaries), test-distribution and -collection procedures, and what to do under unusual circumstances (such as cheating, utility problem causing lights to fail, missing pages of a test, test taker who becomes ill).

Once an evaluation instrument and its supporting documents have been generated, there is a need to establish their *validity* and *reliability*. When an instrument is valid it means that it is effective in measuring what it was designed to measure. When an instrument is reliable it means that it is capable of *consistently* measuring the knowledge level of students of the same group over the same instruction. Validity and reliability are complex concepts about which considerable is known. Experts recognize several types of validity and reliability. Common types of validity are: content, construct, concurrent, and predictive validity. Common types of reliability include: reader reliability, internal consistency, instrument stability, examinee reliability, sampling reliability, and congruence reliability. Mastering these concepts and their attendant techniques would require more than one course. Thus, the treatment of validity and reliability here will necessarily be limited. Some license will be taken to simplify their meanings as they relate to the job aids presented on the subject.

Validity   Discussion of test validity, here, is restricted to *content validity*. Gay (1976, p. 88) says that "**content validity** is the degree to which a test measures an intended content area." Determining content validity requires the application of both *face validity* and *sampling validity* techniques. According to Gay (p. 88): "**face validity** is concerned with whether the test measures the intended content area, and **sampling validity** is concerned with how well the test samples the total content area." Both face validity and sampling validity depend on the judgment of experts over the content area being tested. Both face validity and sampling validity applications have been included in the job aid on "Establishing Content Validity for Instructional Tests." There is no intent in this chapter to determine whether or not test items follow appropriate rules of test development. Relevant rules for these are included in the section on "Generating Criterion Test Items" in Chapter 4.

Job Aid / Establishing Content Validity for Instructional Tests

Description This technique lists the steps in acquiring judgments from content experts on how well they think a test measures what was intended, and the degree to which its items sample relevant areas of the instruction. Basically, it requires content experts to compare a test against the table of specifications for the test and the performance objectives of the instruction. The content experts render a report that identifies any elements that need to be modified, reasons for any inadequacies, and recommendations for their correction.

Use Rationale The generation of instructional tests is fraught with opportunities for error. Often the people who develop the instruction also develop the tests over it. While this is good in terms of their familiarity with the instruction, it creates problems in that they have gotten so close to the instruction that they may make inaccurate assumptions in their test writing. Clearly, if a test is not valid or reliable, its results cannot be used with any confidence in correcting problems within the instruction. Since it is very difficult for an instructional developer to become expert in all of the fields in which he or she helps develop instruction, the most efficient means of determining whether the right content is reflected in a test is to get the assistance of experts in that content.

Critical Tasks

1. **Acquire or generate a table of specifications and a test over specific course or unit content.**

2. **Check the test items against the table of specifications.** Make certain that there are test items included that cover each of the instructional objectives for the course or unit.

3. **Identify content expert(s).** Get agreement from knowledgeable persons in the content area to check the test's validity.

4. **Have the content experts assess the test's validity.** Ask the experts to apply the following criteria to the items of the test as they relate to the instructional objectives: (1) the items test *only* the intended content area, and (2) items are included that sample *all* appropriate subsets of the content area.

5. **Ask the experts to report inadequacies, the causes of the inadequacies, and any recommendations for correction.** This is done in reference to both the table of specifications and the instructional objectives, using a format such as that presented in Figure 9.6.

FIGURE 9.6 / Example of part of a report by content experts on the validity of a test over an instructional unit on media production

---

To: R. Belling, Project Manager
From: P. Major and L. Smith, Content Consultants
Date: June 14, 1991
Subject: Report on validity of test over media production

Conclusions: In our opinion the items of the test adequately measure and sample the content areas intended, based on the table of specification and the instructional objectives provided for the content area of media production, with the following exceptions:

continued

| Establishing Content Validity for Instructional Tests, continued |

A. Items not matching instructional objectives:
   1. Test item 23 refers to psychological concerns rather than media production. Recommend it be replaced with a production test item.
   2. Item 24 is testing a concept rather than the skill explicitly asked for in the objective. Recommend it be dropped.

B. Specific instructional objectives for which items were lacking:
   1. Items 32–37, 48, 52, and 61 only cover photographic aspects for production of slides. Need also to determine whether subjects know how to storyboard the sequence of slides. Recommend 4–5 test items be written covering storyboarding.
   2. No test items were listed for objective 5 on setup of media hardware. Recommend 3–4 items be written sampling among setups for slide/tape, motion picture, and video.

Reference

Gay, L. R. (1976). *Educational Research: Competencies for Analysis and Application.* Columbus, Ohio: Charles E Merrill, pp. 88–96.

Reliability   Gay (1976, p. 92) says that **reliability** "is the degree to which a test *consistently* measures whatever it measures." Imagine a yardstick that measured an object as being 20 inches long one day and a day later as being 30 inches! We expect a yardstick to measure the same object consistently. Similarly, if a student is tested over his or her knowledge of the Bill of Rights today, and takes the same test again next week, the two scores should be very close, given that the test is reliable and that the student had not been studying the topic in the interim.

Errors and ambiguities in a test are the biggest offenders of test reliability. Poorly written items and directions are examples of factors that may reduce a test's reliability. While no test is perfectly reliable, the object is to reduce the errors and ambiguities to a minimum.

The internal consistency of a test can be determined by using a statistic such as *split-half reliability*, where a test is administered to a group, then the test is divided into two halves to form two separate test scores, one from all of the odd-numbered test items and one from all of the even-numbered items. The scores of each examinee for each half are determined, giving each examinee two test scores: one from the odd items and one from the even. Finally, a **correlation** is run on the two sets of scores, to determine to what degree they are related. If the correlation coefficient is high, then the test has good split-half reliability.

The job aid on "Establishing Reliability of Instructional Tests" describes another popular procedure for determining the reliability of a test, one that does not use the split-half method or the correlation statistic.

Carrying Out the Evaluation

The logistics of successfully carrying out a proposed evaluation of instructional units depends on the completion of several tasks. The first task is to arrange for, or to select, an adequate testing site. Usually, this is at the

Job Aid / Establishing Reliability of Instructional Tests

Description   This involves a set of steps for determining how reliable a test may be, that is, how well it consistently measures what it was intended to measure. It uses the Kuder-Richardson formula 21. The standard deviation and the mean of the test scores must be calculated and then plugged into the formula.

Use Rationale   Instructional developers often work with clients who have little formal preparation in constructing test items or tests. Although they may have picked up a lot of skills over the period they have been instructing, they may not know whether their tests are reliable. Instructional developers depend on these tests to tell them whether or not the instruction is doing its job. They base their decisions on test results. Clearly, they cannot have a good reading of how successful the instruction is if the tests are defective.

Critical Tasks

1. **Administer the test to a group.** They should have finished the instruction recently, and they should be representative of the population for which the test was designed.

2. **Score the test.**

3. **Apply the reliability procedure.**

   a. Count the number of items on the test.

   b. Calculate the standard deviation of the test scores with the following formula (Gay, p. 235):

$$SD = \sqrt{\frac{\text{sum of } X^2 - \frac{(\text{sum } X)^2}{N}}{N}}$$

where:

SD	= standard deviation
N	= number of test subjects
sum X	= sum of the test scores
(sum $X)^2$	= square of the sum of scores

Example:

where:

N	= 5
sum X	= 15
(sum $X)^2$	= 55

$$SD = \sqrt{\frac{55 - \frac{(15)^2}{5}}{5}} = \sqrt{\frac{55 - \frac{225}{5}}{5}} = \sqrt{\frac{55 - 45}{5}} = \sqrt{\frac{10}{5}} = \sqrt{2}$$

Look up the square root of 2 in a square root table (found in most math books).
$$SD = \sqrt{2} = 1.4$$

   c. Determine the mean of the scores ($\overline{X}$) with the following formula:

$$\overline{X} = \frac{\text{sum } X}{N}$$

continued

Establishing Reliability of Instructional Tests, continued

Example:

where:

sum X = 15

N = 5

Therefore

$\overline{X} = \dfrac{15}{5} = 3$

d. Put the variables into the Kuder-Richardson formula 21 (i.e., number of items, standard deviation, and mean):

$$r = \frac{(K)\,(SD^2) - \overline{X}\,(K - \overline{X})}{(SD^2)\,(K - 1)}$$

where:

K = number of test items

SD = standard deviation

$\overline{X}$ = mean of test scores

Example:

K = 50

SD = 4.0

$\overline{X}$ = 40

$$r = \frac{(50)(4\{2\}) - 40(50 - 40)}{(4\{2\})\,(50 - 1)} = \frac{(50)\,(16) - 40\,(10)}{(16)\,(49)} = \frac{400}{784} = .51$$

Reliability for achievement tests should be .90 or above, so the test in the example would have an unacceptable level of reliability at the .51 level.

4. Revise the test, if necessary, as many times as it takes to establish an acceptable reliability coefficient.

Reference

Gay, L. R. (1976). *Educational Research: Competencies for Analysis and Application.* Columbus, Ohio: Charles E Merrill, pp. 88–96, 235–237.

same site where the instruction is given, and tests may be given before, during, and after the instruction. There are occasions when the instructional site is not appropriate for testing. Examples would be where the space is tightly scheduled for other activities, or where the time frame doesn't match that needed by subjects to complete the test. Or it may be that the means of testing calls for special equipment not available at that space.

The sample to be tested is usually the group of learners who have just finished the instructional unit in question, so they are easily identified. However, because some aspects of a particular evaluation may exceed what is normally done in the school or training program, it may be necessary to get permission from the test subjects or from those responsible for them. Permission forms such as the one presented in Figure 6.3 may have to be used to get permission not only for subjects to take the test but for developers and others to use the data from the tests (e.g., in reports and in published documents).

When there are a large number of subjects to be tested, or when several groups are to be tested at the same time, more than one person will be needed to administer the tests. At this point, it becomes necessary to select and train test administrators. A technique called *Oral Walk-Through* is one means designed for training test administrators. It is presented in detail in Chapter 7. This technique is used to familiarize or train individuals in the use of some system when they will not have an opportunity to practice with its intended subjects. For example, it is often used to prepare someone to run a part of a workshop or to prepare to take over someone else's course. It is also used to prepare individuals to operate special equipment or to administer tests. It can be used to prepare individuals for any task not too complex, and where it is difficult to have the person interact with subjects who are the object of the task. The process basically requires trainees to listen to a talk/walk-through of the tasks by the trainer, then to observe one of their fellows orally walking through under guidance of the trainer, followed by pairs orally walking through the tasks, where the demonstrator member of a pair is corrected and confirmed in his or her actions by the observer member. Members of each pair switch roles. The trainer then debriefs the group.

While the "Oral Walk-Through" job aid teaches a decent bare-bones approach to preparing personnel to carry out an evaluation, there are many other techniques that can improve the process. For example, it is desirable to control temporal and environment variables as closely as is practical, to reduce the effect of their differences on test taking. Having some students take the test early in the day while they are fresh, and others late in the day when they are tired, may cause differences in test scores of the groups. By the same token, large differences in the spaces used for test taking may affect student scores, e.g., temperature, lighting, noise level, and table space for test materials.

Once students have finished, the tests or inventories must be collected. The best rule is to collect them from individual students rather than having them passed forward. A cover sheet identifying them should be placed on top of the tests by the test administrator, and all tests should be secured by some means so that they don't become inadvertently mixed with others (e.g., rubberband, paper clip, marked manila envelope). Close security needs to be kept on the tests, usually by locking them away in a designated area. Any copies made should be signed out to those taking them, along with clear directions about maintaining test security. Once the individuals' work with the copies is finished, they should be retrieved and destroyed, or stored securely.

Reporting Results and Conclusions

The use of Stake's model as a guide is sufficient as a procedure for acquiring and treating the data that would go into an evaluation report on a course. It is important to keep ever in mind, as the report is being generated, what and whom it is for, so that extraneous material is kept to a minimum. In other words, tailor the report to fit the user's needs.

Determine how data and results will be presented (tables, graphics, etc.). As a rule, the initial paragraph should lay out what outcomes were sought by the evaluation (e.g., effectiveness, efficiency and relevance of instruction), and whether to maintain as is, revise, or eliminate the instruction.

Summary

This chapter provided instructional developers with some basic knowledge about processes and techniques for evaluating ongoing units of instruction. It presented a modification of Robert Stake's evaluation model as the major procedure for carrying out an evaluation. It also presented selected techniques for determining the validity and reliability of tests.

It is important to note that evaluation of instructional programs made up of several interacting courses is much more complex than is evaluating a single course. Evaluation of programs or interacting courses were not dealt with. Nor did this chapter deal seriously with the costs of an evaluation or with the costs that revision of instruction might entail. Refer to Chapter 13 to learn about means of determining such costs.

References

Gay, L. R. (1976). *Educational Research: Competencies for Analysis and Application.* Columbus, Ohio: Charles E. Merrill.

King, F. J., and Roblyer, M. D. (1984). Alternative designs for evaluating computer-based instruction. *Journal of Instructional Development* 7(3): 23–29.

Mellon, C. A. (1984). Group consensus evaluation: A procedure for gathering qualitative data. *Journal of Instructional Development* 7(1): 18–22.

Popham, W. J. (1974). *Evaluation in Education: Current Applications.* Berkeley, Calif.: McCutchan.

Stufflebeam, D. I., et al. (1971). *Educational Evaluation and Decision Making.* Itasca, Illi.: F. E. Peacock.

Tyler, R. W., et al. (1967). *Perspectives of Curriculum Evaluation.* Chicago: Rand McNally.

Wittrock, M. C., and Wiley, D. E. (1970). *The Evaluation of Instruction: Issues and Problems.* New York: Holt, Rinehart and Winston.

CHAPTER 10

Project Management

Process by which resources are controlled, coordinated, integrated, and allocated to accomplish project goals

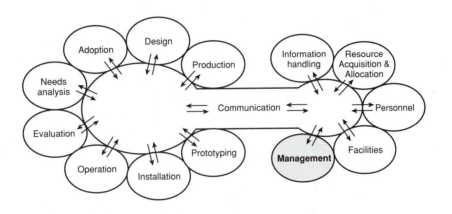

Learner Objectives

1. List common sources of funds for support of ID projects.

2. Describe an established technique for estimating project costs.

3. Discriminate between *tall* and *flat* administrative models.

4. Describe how to avoid common pitfalls in running project meetings.

5. Relate two established techniques for sequencing project tasks.

6. Compare PERT and flowcharting as work-breakdown techniques.

7. Match techniques presented in the chapter with specific management tasks.

8. List common problems in closing out projects.

9. Recall definitions of major terms.

Introduction

This section of the text begins a series of chapters on six ID support components: management, communication, information handling, resource acquisition and allocation, personnel, and facilities. These components are intimately entwined; but to reduce content to reasonable chunks for learning, they are presented in separate chapters. The focus of this chapter is *ID project management*, a system for controlling and facilitating the activities of instructional development projects. Several management techniques (e.g., PERT) were presented at points in preceding chapters for the sake of continuity and convenience. They will be referred to again here when appropriate.

A major responsibility of project managers is to guide staff in the process of carrying out the activities necessary to complete a project successfully. A *project* may be defined as a specific, finite task with a well-defined set of predetermined outcomes. Thus, projects differ from other activities of an organization in that they are temporary. As soon as the purpose of a project is met, it is dissolved, with its remaining resources reallocated to other projects or organizational needs. Models like the *Instructional Project Development and Management (IPDM) Model,* presented in this text, can assist managers in determining "what" project activities should be completed. But managers must also be knowledgeable in the application of a range of project management techniques if they are to answer "how" activities are to be completed.

Since instructional development is essentially a problem-solving process, it follows that an ID project manager must be skilled in problem solving. Many ID project problems and their solutions become routine because they are dealt with so regularly. But even when problems and their solutions are routine, variations in client, subject matter, and budget will make adjustment necessary. However, it is the more complex and nonroutine problems that consume so much of the manager's time, because their mismanagement can drastically affect project time and cost factors. This chapter addresses the use of some of the techniques that ID project managers have found reduce the effects of both routine and nonroutine problems.

Project Management Process

Managerial tasks important to the successful completion of ID projects include the following:

1. Employ procedures for analyzing, costing, and bidding ID projects.
2. Employ established policies and procedures for acquiring, allocating, and reallocating resources.
3. Employ established policies and procedures for interacting with clients.
4. Establish and organize the ID project team.
5. Establish project personnel motivation policies and procedures.

6. Establish policies and procedures for project team meetings.
7. Establish an efficient, accessible information-handling (IH) system for the project.
8. Establish efficient lines of communication within the project and with other relevant systems.
9. Establish a reporting system.
10. Establish a project monitoring system.
11. Maintain an up-to-date work breakdown of the project.
12. Establish contingency plans for dealing with project problems.
13. Establish policies and procedures for project evaluation.
14. Establish policies and procedures for project wrap-up.

Analyzing, Costing, and Bidding Projects

Most instructional developers base their cost estimates for new jobs on previous work done by them or their company. In other words, the development of skills of estimating costs for projects has been acquired by instructional developers more through trial and error than through any formal learning process. Unfortunately, only when there is a high degree of similarity between proposed and completed projects can a project manager be reasonably confident that basing the estimate on a previous project gives a reasonable estimate for a new one.

The actual searching out of potential agencies that might fund ID projects is discussed in Chapter 13. Any college or university library will maintain several directories of funding agencies around the country. These sources include corporations, government agencies, public and private foundations, unions, trusts, and professional associations. Organizations that want others to carry out a project for them usually send out an **RFP (request for proposal)**, which describes what they want done and asks for interested parties to respond with a plan and a bid, following a prescribed format. The requesting organization then examines the plans and the bids and chooses the one they think is most suitable. Factors included in their decision go beyond cost. It may include the reputation and experience of the bidders, when they can deliver the product, and their plans for validation of the product. Often, the logical sequence is reversed, with costs determined first, and tasks for a project's accomplishment determined second. That is, the client will say, "Here is what I want done and this is what I'll pay for it." At that point the instructional developer goes through the estimating process to determine whether the proffered amount is sufficient. If not, the options remaining to the instructional developer are to convince the client to increase the amount, to drop out of the project (if that is an option), or to build in a lot of cost-cutting measures, which may make questionable the validity of the final product.

An effective means of estimating the cost of a proposed project is found through the use of a variation on the *Program Evaluation and Review Technique (PERT)*. For a fuller understanding of PERT details, the reader is referred to Chapter 5, where it was recommended as a work-breakdown and management technique for carrying out production tasks. The job aid on "Bidding a Project" lists the major steps for using PERT to estimate the time and cost to complete a proposed instructional project. This PERT variation also assists in the important initial decision of whether or not to bid on a proposed project.

Job Aid / Bidding a Project

Description   This technique is a variation of the *Program Evaluation and Review Technique (PERT)*. Costs for a proposed project are determined by first generating all tasks (activities) that an individual or team thinks must be carried out to complete the project. These are sequenced, graphically, into a logical network; ordered on the basis of whether a task is predecessor to, successor to, or concurrent with other tasks. Times and other resources (e.g., personnel, facilities, equipment, materials) are estimated for each task in the network. Then costs associated with each task are estimated. From these data, accumulated time and cost estimates can be made for the total project and, if desired, for clusters of tasks within it. This provides the necessary data for a bid on a project.

Use Rationale   Bidding a contract for a project can be a make-or-break situation. A fairly common discouragement for instructional developers is discovering at the end of a project that they have run over their budget. Cost overruns have all too often sounded the death knell for fledgling ID companies. Time and cost factors for each instructional development project are different, and survival depends on the degree to which developers are able to use techniques such as PERT to anticipate such differences.

Critical Tasks

1. **Propose or identify a project.** That is, one that you or your organization would like to have funded.

2. **Generate the tasks that are essential to completing the project.** Staff members *independently* generate all of the tasks they can think of as necessary to complete a project. These may be written on 3 × 5 cards, with one task per card. Consultants may have to be hired to identify some of the tasks for areas in which staff expertise is lacking.

3. **Arrange all of the task cards in predecessor, successor, and concurrent sequence.** Use a large surface, e.g., table, floor, wall.

4. **Revise the sequence of tasks.** Add any additional activities or tasks, collapse activities, or break down activities into subactivities, as you sequence. Throw out duplicate activities.

5. **Generate a PERT network, using the established format and symbols.** See Figure 10.1. Capital letters represent tasks, and numbers represent events that begin and end those tasks. Do the network manually if necessary, but it is preferable to use a PERT computer program such as *Expert* by Dekker, Limited, that has versions for Macintosh and for IBM-PC and compatibles.

6. **Add dummy activities as appropriate.** These are indicated by dashed arrows, using zero time and resources. The line between events 3 and 5 in Figure 10.1 is a dummy task. This is used when an activity in one path must be completed before an activity in a concurrent path can begin.

continued

Bidding a Project, continued

FIGURE 10.1 / PERT application showing a critical path

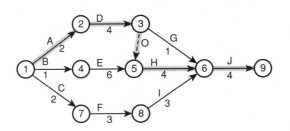

Key:
events (circles) = beginning and/or ending tasks
arrows = activities
dashed arrow = dummy activity
numbers = time, in weeks
letters = specific tasks

7. **Estimate the time to complete each activity.** Use the following formula:

$$t_e = \frac{o + 4m + p}{6}$$

where t_e is the estimated time; o is the time expected if everything goes without a hitch, i.e., **o**ptimistic time; p is the time consumed when whatever can go wrong does, i.e., **p**essimistic time; and m is the developer's best guess, i.e., **m**ost likely time. Continue to add or delete activities, as appropriate.

8. **Estimate all direct and indirect costs for each activity.** Use experienced people for estimating. Continue to add and delete activities during this process, as appropriate.

9. **Identify slack periods in the network.** This will be where work groups on one path are expected to finish sooner than groups on a concurrent path. Plan on shifting resources from idle work groups to busy ones, and estimate how much this will cut time and cost on the project. Readjust the network, accordingly.

10. **Identify the critical path through the completed PERT network.** This is done to estimate how long it will take to complete the entire project. Do this by adding the times for each of the possible paths through the network. The critical path is the one that consumes the most time. See the heavy line in Figure 10.1. As a safety buffer, experienced developers should increase that time estimate by 10%, and those inexperienced by 15%.

11. **Reassess the cost estimate for each of the activities.** Do this in the context of the completed network; e.g., throw out any duplicate costs, make equipment rental versus purchase decisions.

continued

Bidding a Project, continued

12. **Determine the overall cost of the project.** Do this by accumulating costs for all of the tasks. If you plan on subcontracting some of the work or assigning work to teams, accumulate subcosts for different parts of the network.

13. **Organize and reaccumulate activity costs by budget categories that fit the funding agency's budgeting format.** E.g., salary, telephone, travel, copying, equipment rental.

14. **Add a buffer percentage to the total cost to protect against estimation error.** 5–10% for experienced instructional developers, and 10–15% for less experienced developers.

15. **Add a reasonable profit margin.** It should be reasonable for the developer and reasonable to the client, i.e., what the market will bear.

16. **Compare the total to any limit previously set by the funding agency or client.** Remember, whatever the funding agency said was their limit may be negotiable.

17. **Make the final decision to submit or not to submit a bid on the project.**

18. **If the decision is affirmative, incorporate the PERT-derived delivery times and costs into your formal bid for the project.**

19. **Be prepared to negotiate with the funding agency.** Invariably, it will be necessary to compromise. Being aware of what can best be given up and still do the job puts the bidder at an advantage.

References

Meridith, J. R., and Mantel, S. J. (1985). *Project Management: A Managerial Approach.* New York: Wiley, pp. 209–248.

Moder, W. C., Phillips, C. R., and Davis, E. W. (1983). *Project Management with CPM, PERT, and Precedence Diagramming.* New York: Van Nostrand-Reinhold.

Wiest, Jerome D., and Levy, Ferdinand K. (1977). *Management Guide to PERT/CPM.* Englewood Cliffs, N.J.: Prentice-Hall, pp. 87–102.

A number of the steps in the "Bidding a Project" job aid could certainly be done more precisely through the application of traditional PERT formulas. The means for estimating the critical path and the buffer percentages for time and cost are examples where this would be true. But again, the modification presented here will be sufficient for most estimates. Remember that renegotiation will probably occur once the agency receives and favors a bid. At that time instructional developers need to consider how much additional risk they are willing to accept, given the potential value of the job. Concessions on the developers' side may include earlier delivery and/or reduction of buffer percentages. The client may agree to drop some bells and whistles, reduce the objectives to be met, and/or extend delivery time.

There are, of course, additional bases that will need to be covered before submitting a bid on a proposal. For instance, it is important that provisions in a contract are included that cover possibilities of variables that may affect the developer's cost estimates (e.g., inflation). For externally funded projects, using attorneys with contract expertise is a cheap investment for the protection that well-written contracts give.

In Chapter 6 it was mentioned that a PERT network developed for timing and costing projects could also be used for assisting the manager in making decisions while the project is ongoing. It is very useful for adjusting activity time and resources as the project progresses. Those readers unfamiliar with techniques such as PERT and CPM (critical path method), should realize that the PERT variation presented here is an adaptation from far more complex and powerful techniques that use a range of sophisticated formulae for purposes beyond those served here.

Acquiring and Allocating Resources

A crucial part of the bidding process is the negotiation of final costs. There is a basic conflict between funding agencies that want the best product for the fewest bucks and developers who want top dollar for doing the job in the shortest period of time. A saying among the cynical is that "the man with the gold, has the control," which is another way of saying that instructional developers often have to make concessions if they want projects to be funded. The three primary tasks for any project manager is to finish his or her project on budget, on time, and at product criteria. Starting a project with inadequate resources is starting with two strikes against the developer. Despite that fact, many instructional developers do start projects with inadequate resources, usually with the hope of finding additional resources elsewhere, if necessary.

Certainly, getting all necessary funds allocated in the first place is the most desirable alternative. When that is not possible, application of techniques such as *Proactive Requisitioning* (Chapter 8) may prove useful for acquiring additional funds.

Another way of approaching the problem is by figuring out means to reduce costs. A source for reducing costs not tapped nearly as often as it should be is the broad array of existing instructional materials. Much of this extant print and nonprint instructional material can be adopted or adapted to new projects. Unfortunately, a common organizational bias says, "If it wasn't made here, then it won't work here." This bias gets in the way of acceptance of such materials. Another obstacle to the use of such materials is a lack of knowledge on the part of developers of what to look for, or *where* to look. There are a number of excellent directories to these materials that can be acquired at nominal cost, including directories from the *National Information Center for Educational Media (NICEM)*, the *Educational Film and Video Locator*, and the *Educational Products Information Exchange (EPIE)*. These organizations catalog literally thousands of print and nonprint items, and can give leads to promising material and to persons or organizations owning the rights to the material. Usually, the costs of getting permission and adopting or adapting extant materials will be far less than the costs of original production.

As mentioned earlier, the best form for a project budget is not necessarily the form desirable for submitting to a funding agency, whether the agency be internal or external to your organization. To illustrate, consider

FIGURE 10.2 / Project budget, by task and month

Task	Estimate	Monthly Budget							
		1	2	3	4	5	6	7	8
A	7,000	5,600	1,400						
B	9,000		3,857	5,143					
C	10,000		3,750	5,000	1,250				
D	6,000		3,600	2,400					
E	12,000				4,800	4,800	2,400		
F	3,000				3,000				
G	9,000			2,571	5,143	1,286			
H	5,000					3,750	1,250		
I	8,000						2,667	5,333	
J	6,000								6,000
	75,000	5,600	12,607	15,114	14,192	9,836	6,317	5,333	6,000

Source: Meredith, J. R., and Mantell, S. J., Jr. *Project Management*. New York: Wiley, 1989, p. 242.

the abbreviated budgets presented in Figures 10.2 and 10.3. Figure 10.2 shows a *task-oriented* budget, where the budget is broken down by task. The estimate for task A, for example, could have been drawn from PERT cost and time estimates for task A. The total cost for task A, $7,000, is to be spent in the first two months of the project: $5,600 in the first month, and $1,400 in the second month. This is a desirable budget form for project managers, because it gives tighter control over costs for specific parts of the project. However, most funding agencies tend to use a *line-item* budget, as shown in Figure 10.3 In this particular budget, the major line items are: personnel, fringe benefits, travel, equipment, supplies, and other. *Direct costs* are those actually spent on the project, while *indirect costs* are those used to recompense the home organization for the use of space, utilities, and other costs borne. The particular breakdown of a budget as presented in Figure 10.3 happens to be for the life of a project, but it could be broken down by month, as well. In this example, the funds for the project are contributed by two separate agencies; USDE (United States Department of Education), and MSU (Michigan State University). The salary basis for personnel is for academic year (AY), summer school (SS), or annual (AN). Most funding agencies insist that instructional developers translate their task-oriented budgets into a line-item format similar to this one.

The procedures listed in the "Bidding a Project" job aid are satisfactory for getting the data to plug into a budget. But, with the wide variation in how organizations expect to be approached, it is wise to get the best advice possible from those in the funding agency as to their preferred budget format.

Dealing with Client Policies and Procedures

The relationship between the project manager and the client or clients who fund an ID project needs thoughtful tending. Conflicting expectations

FIGURE 10.3 / Project budget, by line item, for 2-year project life

		Salary	Basis	% USDE	Cost USDE	% MSU	Cost MSU
Personnel							
Wiggins, H.	88–89 AY beg. 10/1/88	48,500	AY	10%	4,580	30%	13,741
	Summer school '89	48,500	SS	40%	5,820		
	89–90 AY thru 3/31/90	50,925	AY	10%	3,397	30%	10,190
Perkins, G.	88–89 AY beg. 10/1/88	49,549	AY	10%	4,680	10%	4,680
	89–90 AY thru 3/31/90	52,026	AY	10%	3,470	10%	3,470
Beck, G.	88–89 AY beg. 10/1/88	33,708	AY	10%	3,184	10%	3,184
	89–90 AY thru 3/31/90	35,393	AY	10%	2,361	10%	2,361
Kirkland, K.	10/1/88–9/30/89	18,656	AN	5%	933		
	10/1/89–3/31/90	19,589	AN	5%	490		
Olrich, W.	10/1/88–9/30/89	18,656	AN	5%	933		
	10/1/89-3/31/90	19,589	AN	5%	490		
Clerical (hourly)	1,500 hours	5	hr	50%	7,500		
Grad. Assts.	10/1/88–9/30/89	1,016	mo.	200%	48,768		
(4 @ ½ time)	10/1/89–3/31/90	1,067	mo.	200%	25,608		
					112,214		37,626
Fringe Benefits							
24% for AY & AN					5,884		
7% summer school					407		
					6,291		
Travel							
Project director's meeting ($500 transportation plus $100/day lodging and meals for 2 days)					700		
Person site visits—Michigan (20 trips at $100/ea transportation)					2,000		
Person site visits—national (4 trips at $500/ea transportation plus $100/day lodging and meals for 2 days each)					2,800		
Presentations at 3 regional and national conferences ($500 transportation plus $100/day lodging and meals for 2 days)					2,100		
					7,600		
Equipment							
1 Mac II computer w/color monitor, 2MB RAM min., extended keyboard, and 40-meg HD							5,000
1 TV producer board							1,000
5 LD-V4200 videodisc players w/serial interface ($1,200 ea)					6,000		
1 VO-7600 ¾" videotape player							4,200
1 BKU-761 serial interface for videotape player							480
1 SGN-1203 frame code gen.							2,800
1 KTU-190 video monitor for composite video							500
					6,000		13,980
Supplies							
Software					1,500		
Paper					150		
Computer disks					75		
Videotape					100		
					1,825		

continued

FIGURE 10.3 / Project budget, by line item, for 2-year project life, continued

	Salary	Basis	% USDE	Cost USDE	% MSU	Cost MSU
Other						
Advisory council meeting (2 mtgs. for each of the 5 advisory board members—ea. mtg. based on $250 transportation, $75/day lodging and meals, and $100/day consulting fee per member)				4,250		
Interpreter services for above mtgs. ($65/day for 2 days)				130		
Professional studio time				1,000		
Mastering and duplicating videodisks				3,000		
Copying/printing				1,000		
Communication costs						
Postage (site mail)				300		
Phone				500		
				10,180		
		Direct costs		144,110		51,606
		Indirect costs @ 42%*		58,006		
		TOTAL		202,116		

*42% of total direct costs ($144,110) less $6,000 for equipment.

during development and at the end of projects commonly occur. Obviously, a major responsibility of project managers is to avoid or reduce such conflicts. During the run of a project, the project manager will have to meet with the client several times to assess the project's progress. As a result of these assessments, the manager may need to make new decisions or modify old ones. Sometimes the decisions will have to do with proposed changes in the course design, initiated either by the ID project manager or by the client. Or it may be to get client sign-offs at prescheduled checkpoints in the project, e.g., acceptance of the set of behavioral objectives completed by project personnel. A most desirable condition of the ID contract is that there be just one person from the client group designated to make decisions and sign-offs. This reduces the likelihood of misunderstanding and shortens the time it takes to come to agreement. When such a policy is not set up, instructional developers often find themselves being bounced from one member of the client system to another or, worse yet, from one committee to another. It is very difficult to satisfy multiple masters.

Both client and ID project personnel are subject to their organization's respective policies and procedures. Problems arise when an ID project manager fails to identify policies and procedures of the client's organization that may affect the project. Formal policies and procedures of client organizations may all be contained in a single manual of personnel, policies, procedures, and operations, or they may be in a separate document, e.g., hiring manual, employee's handbook, or purchasing manual.

The policies and procedures used to guide a project are of three kinds: those that the project's client organization imposes, those imposed by ID project management, and those adapted for working with a specific client. Once policies and procedures are known, it is very important that the manager make project personnel sensitive to the ones relevant to the project. This is to prevent, among other things: dispensing of inappropriate information to clients, disruption of delicate negotiations, or asking the wrong decision maker to make an important decision affecting the project. To this end, policies and procedures for interacting with clients need to be clearly spelled out in a document available to all project team members. Developers may find that needed policies have yet to be adopted by a client group. When that occurs, it may be necessary to initiate the client policy-making processes. *Policy Setting*, a technique useful for examination of client systems policies and for encouraging the development of new policies, was presented in Chapter 3.

Forming ID Project Teams

There is a tendency in organizations having large instructional development units to use an indiscriminate approach to forming new project teams. That is, when a project comes up, the first question most often asked is "Who is available?" rather than "What skills are needed?" Usually, personnel and job titles are listed in the initial project proposal, but they don't always include job descriptions. Staffing of ID projects is facilitated by having clearly stated job descriptions. The job descriptions for project personnel and the amount of personnel time needed can be satisfactorily determined by first performing a PERT and then analyzing the network tasks in terms of the skills and hours required to complete the tasks.

The administration of project team members once they are hired or assigned is usually based on a **flat (systems) hierarchical model**, where there are usually no more than two layers of decision makers over project staff. This administrative model satisfies the need for quick turnaround on decisions. A **tall (bureaucratic) hierarchical model**, with its many layers of decision makers, is too cumbersome for administering such problem-solving ventures, where turnaround decision time of a few days or even hours may make the difference between black ink or red ink in the ledger. Organizationally, a team may be made up of a project manager and staff, or the team may have a project manager acting as a general manager over a second layer of middle managers heading up smaller, specialized teams within the project. Of course, there may be several specialties represented among the project team members themselves.

Motivating Personnel

When well-trained, well-paid professionals work on a challenging project with adequate resources, in a friendly environment, and under competent management, there is seldom a problem with motivation. However, it is unusual for all of these conditions to be at the desired level at the same time. Inadequate conditions need to be either corrected or compensated for by changing variables such as salary and working conditions. There are times when project team members may be willing to work in a hostile environment for more money, or they may be willing to work for less money if the job is challenging enough. Manipulation of such variables to ensure project member satisfaction while maintaining productivity is one of the project manager's most important balancing acts. The manager must always keep in mind that the project must be brought in on time, under or at budget, and meeting prescribed objectives. Additional details on project staff motivation are dealt with in Chapter 14.

Handling Staff Meetings

Someone once said that "a camel is the result of a committee trying to make a horse!" The committee technique is one of the most misused, and least efficient, means of getting effective work out of a group. Part of the inefficiency of committee work is due to inherent design weaknesses in the technique, but a larger part is due to its inept use. Committee work is strongly affected by the actions of dominant, highly verbal individuals who often redirect the intended agenda or who may cause the group to dwell on some small or tangential aspect to the detriment of the overall agenda. Committee meetings are also viewed by some members as forums for complaint about issues unrelated to committee purpose. The size of the group and the scheduling of meetings are examples of other factors that affect the productivity of committees. A more useful technique for getting the best judgments out of a group in the shortest period of time is the *Nominal Group Process*, presented in Chapter 3. However, the use of the Nominal Group Process technique requires some preliminary work with the people involved, in cases where it is alien to their previous practices. Also, the technique's restrictive requirements, as compared to the familiar and free-wheeling conditions of committee work, may initially cause resistance to its use.

Given the low probability of project managers' abandoning committee work, it is useful for them to know some of the better techniques and attendant rules for handling committee meetings. The techniques presented in the next four job aids have proven to be reasonably effective means for running meetings. Almost all of the rules and procedures presented transfer to the committee setting as well as to other types of meetings. The first job aid, the "Broadwell/House Team Meeting Technique," focuses on the committee meeting's purpose and the logistics of handling a meeting.

Job Aid / Broadwell/House Team Meeting Technique

Description   Rules for conducting successful meetings are applied. They include rules for preparing for the meeting, conducting the meeting itself, drawing closure, and following up on conclusions and decisions made there.

Use Rationale   Meetings seem to be necessary for any team effort. However, project team members often resent meetings that take them away from their busy schedules, especially during prototype production. Therefore, making productive use of meeting time is essential to the instructional developer. To ensure this, it is important that one person lead the meeting. This strategy provides suggestions for that person.

continued

Broadwell/House Team Meeting Technique, continued

Critical Tasks

1. **Determine the purpose of the meeting.** Without a clear purpose, meetings tend to deteriorate into complaint sessions. The following list presents common reasons for holding team meetings:

   a. To inform or report on the activities of team members

   b. To persuade team members to take some action

   c. To lead the team in solving a problem

   d. To meet for some purpose mandated by higher authority.

2. **Develop a meeting agenda.** A manager without a plan is akin to a ship without a rudder. Don't pad the agenda. Have only those items on the agenda that can reasonably be gotten through in the time available.

3. **Prepare members.** Provide members with the agenda ahead of time. Assign roles or tasks so that members are prepared to participate.

4. **Prepare the meeting place.** E.g., water, refreshments, lights, heating or air conditioning, phone, visual aids.

5. **Conduct the meeting.** Begin positively. Use participants as notekeepers, timekeepers, and summarizers. Watch for hidden agendas. Be open-minded, but do not allow participants to deviate totally from the agenda.

6. **Conclude the meeting.** Let the agenda items run out before time runs out. Summarize the meeting's outcomes. Be specific about any action steps to be taken, assign people, and establish a timeline for their completion. Thank the group.

7. **Follow up on the meeting.** Summarize the notes, action steps, deadlines, and the next meeting date in writing, and circulate the summary to participants.

Reference

Broadwell, Martin, and House, Ruth. (1986). *Supervising Technical and Professional People.* New York: Wiley, pp. 203–229.

The "How to Run a Meeting" job aid focuses on the needs of individual members and the differences among them.

Job Aid / How to Run a Meeting

Description A skilled manager must deal not only with the structure of discussion during a meeting but also with the idiosyncrasies of individuals in attendance. These are guidelines for managing members during a meeting to help ensure productivity and cooperation.

continued

How to Run a Meeting, continued

Use Rationale   Properly managed meetings are necessary for efficient and effective movement toward project completion. Meetings help to define the team and greatly increase the speed and efficiency of communication among members. They also help individuals to understand the collective aim of the group, and instill in those present a commitment to decisions made and objectives pursued.

Critical Tasks

1. **Always start the meeting on time.** This is appreciated by those who get there on time, and may reduce lateness on the part of others at succeeding meetings.

2. **Insist on brevity.** If necessary, interrupt ramblers by picking up on a phrase they uttered and offering it to another, e.g., "That's an interesting idea. What's your opinion, Sam?"

3. **Draw out the nontalkers.** Ask the opinions of silent members. Express interest in suggestions made by reluctant individuals in order to encourage continued participation.

4. **Protect the junior members.** If disagreements occur between junior and senior members, junior members may be reluctant to contribute further. Therefore, the manager should support the value of everyone's contributions.

5. **Encourage discussion and debate.** Act as a guide, mediator, stimulator, and summarizer. Keep your own comments brief, and preferably make them after others have commented on the same issue. Do not let debate escalate into an argument or a clash of personalities. If this starts to happen, draw in a neutral member by asking him/her a question.

6. **Work up the pecking order.** To gain a wider spread of views and ideas, start off with junior members and gradually work your way up. Avoid starting with high authorities, because less senior members will feel uneasy about disagreeing with someone more senior.

7. **Close on a positive note.** If possible, end by commenting on an item that has been resolved. Thank the members for their help.

8. **Schedule a time and place for the next meeting.** It is much easier to schedule at that time than later.

Reference

Jay, Antony (1976). How to run a meeting. *Harvard Business Review.* 54(2): 43–57.

The "Oppenheim Meeting Management Theory" job aid is based on control theory, where meetings are treated as part of a management control process.

Job Aid / Oppenheim Meeting Management Theory

Description This technique is based on the theory that meetings should be viewed as management control processes. It takes a four-step approach to the control of meetings that includes techniques of scheduling, preparation, discussion, and follow-through to achieve priorities set for a project.

Use Rationale Productive team meetings are crucial to project success. Meeting productivity depends as much or more on what happens outside the meeting as what transpires in the meeting. The advantage of a meeting management control technique is successfully showing project team members what the project objectives are, and effectively communicating those prioritized objectives so that they can be met with the least amount of time and energy.

Critical Tasks

1. **Determine a meeting schedule.** Meeting dates corresponding to the estimated date for completion of each significant project milestone should be included, along with interim meetings.

2. **Send a copy of the meeting schedule to each team member.** This is to ensure that members can reserve meeting times on their respective calendars.

3. **Set up a specific agenda for each meeting.** The meetings should be structured for maximum effectiveness.

   a. Keep to a consistent meeting format (such as: present update reports, discussion, development of action plans, and adjournment).

   b. Specify a time limit for the meeting.

   c. Have each meeting focus on a specific topic or task. Assigned team members should be expected to report any developments up to the current milestone, and any problems encountered getting there.

4. **Develop a specific plan of action for each team member.** Do this by the end of each meeting. Set specific guidelines for their completing the assigned actions.

5. **Do not deviate from the schedule of meetings.** That is, unless the project timeline changes.

References

Cole, Diane (1989). Meetings that make sense. *Psychology Today* May: 14–16.

Conlin, Joseph (1989). Management strategy: Get control. *Successful Meetings* June: 37–42.

Another means for preparing for a meeting, avoiding pitfalls, and concluding meetings is presented in the job aid on "How to Use Management Meetings."

Job Aid / How to Use Management Meetings

Description   Well-run meetings are planned in advance. A leader capable of mobilizing the group toward established objectives is chosen. Details of participants, location, equipment, etc., are worked out. Care is taken to avoid common pitfalls. The flow of the meeting is crafted ahead of time, including a good introduction, a means of carrying proceedings forward, and a planned conclusion that involves a summary of what has transpired and what is yet to come.

Use Rationale   Poorly conceived and poorly run meetings are a waste of time. Meetings generally tie up several costly personnel hours and must therefore be run efficiently and productively. Management meetings can be the backbone of organizational communication and effectiveness if they are planned and executed properly. Proper methods not only can save time but can prove to be very constructive in morale building, problem solving, decision making, and training.

Critical Tasks

1. **Select or be a qualified leader.** Capable leaders mobilize the group toward achieving desired objectives. They are qualified if they have the respect of the group, and if they can effectively carry out the following steps.

2. **Prepare for the meeting.** Examples of preparations are:
   a. Be clear on objectives.
   b. Eliminate unnecessary attendees from the roster, and make sure that key people are available.
   c. Have the size of the meeting reflect its purpose. Large groups may be more efficient when making announcements or giving information, but decision making and problem solving work best with small, odd-numbered groups. Creativity is helped by maximum freedom and cooperation with *five* members.
   d. Prepare the meeting place. E.g., reserve the space, check the need for a public address (PA) system, and provide essential supplies, and see that extraneous materials are removed.
   e. Check the state of presenters, e.g., for readiness, time needed, and whether they will be fielding questions.
   f. If guest speakers are planned, choose ones that can inject vitality. Consider inside talent as well as those from outside the organization.

3. **Avoid Pitfalls.** Examples are:
   a. Avoid mystery agendas. These irritate people who do not want to be there or who resent not being able to prepare for the meeting.
   b. Identify appropriate problems. Misidentified problems can create confusion and resentment.
   c. Don't chastise members at the meeting. Public punishment will not likely lead to improvement.
   d. Don't deal with confidential or controversial matters at the meeting. Such matters may be handled best in writing or in private.

4. **Structure meetings for effectiveness.** Provide a direction-setting start, a logical on-track development, and a constructive wrap-up. Avoid both laxity and rigidity. In problem solving, identify the problem, analyze and search for causes, and probe for solutions.

continued

How to Use Management Meetings, continued

5. Conclude meetings effectively. Examples would be:

    a. Summarize what has been accepted, rejected, or postponed, and provide important points in a written record.

    b. Clarify any follow-up that is to be done.

    c. Make provisions for progress reports to be presented at future meetings.

    d. Set the scene for the next meeting, e.g., by a good preview.

References

Kerzner, H. (1989). *Project Management: A Systems Approach to Planning, Scheduling and Controlling.* 3d ed. New York: Van Nostrand-Reinhold.

Uris, A. (1986). *101 Greatest Ideas in Management.* New York: Wiley, pp. 134–148, 204–206.

Techniques of hiring, firing, motivating, censuring, and training project personnel are dealt with in greater detail in Chapter 14.

Handling Project Information

The effective and efficient management of any system, including instructional development systems, is dependent on essential information being available at the right time in the right form, and with the right credibility behind it. Often a manager may not know that a system function requires a particular piece of information until it is time for its use. This can mean time and other resource loss while that information is being generated or sought. There are techniques that enable a manager to be proactive to the information needs of a project staff.

Besides being able to search out relevant information, it is important to be able effectively to store and retrieve project information. The most desirable way of doing this is through an electronic database, but manual systems can also serve that purpose. In fact, the large majority of management systems use a combination of the two. Both electronic and manual systems are discussed in Chapter 12.

An example of the processes important in a project information-handling system were mentioned briefly in Chapter 9. Generically, they may be stated as:

Selection: process by which content selection criteria is determined for some project informational need

Collection: process by which information is acquired that meets content selection criteria

Organization: process by which print and nonprint information is arranged or packaged to meet a particular project need

Storage: process by which information can be effectively, efficiently, and securely stored

Retrieval: process by which information can be effectively and efficiently retrieved

Transmission: process by which information is distributed or circulated

Assessment: process by which the effectiveness of information is determined

A technique incorporating these processes is presented in the "Information Handling" job aid in Chapter 12.

Storing and retrieving information through electronic databases has done much to speed up the processes of information handling for a project. A number of excellent databases have been developed for personal computers that would work very well for storing and retrieving project information. Again, a much more in-depth discussion of information-handling systems is presented in Chapter 12.

Communicating Information

Receiving accurate, timely information is crucial to the success of any project. However, messages that should be sent are sometimes not sent, some messages arrive in the wrong form, and other messages arrive too late to be useful or they arrive too early and are forgotten. The way in which a project communication system is designed, what policies are formulated for it, and what procedures are set up for implementing those policies can affect the efficiency of the project. An "open-door policy" on the part of the manager is one policy that could facilitate communication (with the trade-off being that the overall efficiency of a manager may be affected by having to attend to a lot of trivial items).

Information can be exchanged through many means, ranging from face-to-face meetings to very formal written reports. To the degree practical, the formats for exchanging information should be consistent. The consistent use of formats reduces confusion about the purpose of specific messages. Figure 10.4 shows a sample format of a *staff weekly report* that team members submit to their project manager.

**FIGURE 10.4 / Example of a weekly report
from part-time staff**

IVDS STAFF WEEKLY TASK REPORT

Name: Jim Galin
Date: August 28, 1991

Description of tasks currently working on:

This is a report on my search for appropriate graphic systems for our project. In speaking with Phil Smith of Adobe Systems, we were offered a 50% discount on the purchase of "Illustrator '88" ($495 list, $247.50 discounted). In addition, we were informed that a special package, "Classroom in a Box," is available that includes ten original and unflawed copies of "Illustrator '88," along with teaching aids, for the price of $500, complete.

continued

**FIGURE 10.4 / Example of a weekly report
from part-time staff, continued**

I contacted Aldus Corporation to see whether a similar deal might be available in the purchase of "Free-hand." Their special incentive program, formerly offered to owners of "Pagemaker 1.0," was no longer active. After informing the sales rep of the deal offered by Adobe, I was informed that the best discount we could get would be 20% off the list price of $495 ($396). They did carry a "Classroom Package" for $500, but each of the ten copies provided would print out all work with the message "for training purposes only." A definite minus. In further inquiring into the purchase of the program, I was informed that processing our purchase order would take four weeks, minimum. I contacted InaComp Computer Centers, in East Lansing, and was told that they had the program in stock and could sell it to us through the university for $321.75.

Letraset USA, the makers of "Image Studio," were contacted next. Early reviews give it an edge on its competition, Silicon Beach Software's "Digital Darkroom," but only in the number of extra paint tools. The company only deals through dealerships and gave me the names of two dealers specializing in educational sales: Chambers of Boqua Rey in Florida, and Campus Technology in Leesburg, Virginia. I contacted Campus Tech and they offered a $250 price (retail $495). I then contacted Silicon Beach and was offered a price of $95 (retail $395, introductory $295).

In attending the computer show at the MSU Union on Saturday, I spoke with local company representatives. One company (Datalus, located in Okemos) displayed the new touch screens available for the Macintosh. A scanned-in-face on the screen was able to mouth certain words and phrases realistically when touched. Another company rep was able to answer my question concerning the ability to export images between "Freehand" and "Illustrator '88." Clipboarding was possible, but lost something in translation; whereas use of EPS (encapsulated postscript) was possible in both programs.

I discussed my findings with Dr. McLeod, and he directed me to go ahead and order some of the software so as to allow more time to get acquainted with the programs. As of Wednesday, October 26, four programs had been ordered: "Illustrator '88" graphics, "Fox Base" database, "Digital Darkroom" graphics, and "Freehand" graphics.

Problems:

No specific problems to report at this time.

Proposed Next Steps:

I will continue my present research on "Videoworks II" and "Videoworks Interactive," looking at articles concerning their use and capabilities.
Upon arrival of the software, I will spend most of my time learning to use them and working with Cynthia and Fai to see how certain elements can best be utilized in production.

Long-Distance Phone Calls Made:

Thursday, Oct. 20:	2:00p?	(415) 962-2122	Adobe Systems, Inc.
	2:35p	(415) 962-2122	
	2:55p	(415) 962-2122	
Friday, Oct. 21:	2:15p	(415) 962-2122	
	2:25p	(206) 622-5500	Aldus Corporation
Tuesday, Oct. 25:	12:15	(415) 962-2122	Adobe Systems, Inc.
	12:39p	(415) 962-2122	
	1:32p	(415) 962-2122	
	1:40p	(206) 628-2320	Aldus Corporation
	2:20p	(703) 777-9110	Campus Technology
	2:37p	(619) 695-6956	Silicon Beach Software

continued

**FIGURE 10.4 / Example of a weekly report
from part-time staff, continued**

Wednesday, Oct. 26:	2:00p	(419) 874-0162	Fox Software, Inc.
	2:15p	(619) 695-6956	Silicon Beach Software
	3:00p	(619) 695-5956	
	3:05	(619) 695-6956	

Weekly report sheets from the team members, such as the one in Figure 10.4, combined with the project manager's own observations, can be used to work up a *weekly agenda and task sheet* (Figure 10.5) for the staff. The weekly agenda and task sheet would control the weekly team meeting and provide opportunity for modifying task assignments as new information surfaces during the meeting. These sheets, along with oral reports by the team members, can keep team members up to date on what others are doing, especially as the activities relate to their respective tasks. In addition, minutes of the meeting can record any decisions made that amend the agenda and task sheet.

**FIGURE 10.5 / Weekly agenda and task sheet
for an ID project**

IVDS PROJECT STAFF MEETING

Room 452 EH, Monday, February 12, 1990, 4:00–5:30 pm

Agenda

1. Allen
   a. Report on criterion checklist graphic prototype
   b. Report on plan for completing orientation graphics

2. Cynthia
   a. Report on time estimation for program
   b. Report on plan for peer evaluation of signing

3. Linda
   a. Report on status of revised flowchart
   b. Report on revision of compiled program to match revised flowchart

4. Lauren
   a. Report on status of orientation storyboard revision
   b. Report on proofing of completed system flowchart

5. Pat
   a. Report on status of revised flowchart
   b. Report on outline of User's Guide
   c. Report on plan for criterion checklist

continued

**FIGURE 10.5 / Weekly agenda and task sheet
for an ID project, continued**

6. Randy
   a. Report on revision of compiled program to match revised flowchart
   b. Report on procedure to globally search and change numbers on compiled program
   c. Report on schedule for burning EPROM chip

7. Ellen
   a. Report on proofing flowchart of the program, and provide a list of any errors or anomalies

Task Assignment

1. Lauren
   a. Complete arrangements for formative evaluation #3, February 16–21
   b. Work with Allen on criterion checklist

2. Randy
   a. Complete revision of compiled computer program to match revised flowchart
   b. Test procedure to globally search and change numbers on compiled program
   c. Report on number of computer dumps necessary for disc

3. Linda
   a. Complete revision of compiled program to match revised flowchart

4. Cynthia
   a. Get feedback from Brundle on latest orientation videotape storyboard, and revise again
   b. Get VHS copies of elements from "Sign Connection" video footage that will also be used in the orientation tape
   c. Set up logistics for orientation video shoot

5. Allen
   a. Develop graphic plan for orientation tape
   b. Begin graphics production for orientation video
   c. Work with Lauren on criterion checklist

6. Pat
   a. Meet with Cass on new draft of User Guide
   b. Assist Randy and Linda in compiled program revision
   c. Make certain the option to practice signing with a peer is included in the program

7. Ellen
   a. Proof revised flowchart of the program, and provide a list of any errors or anomalies

The *format* for information is itself information, in that it tells the recipient what type of information to expect when he or she sees that format. In other words, it sets up expectations and enables the user to consume the information more quickly and with less chance of misunderstanding. Various techniques for communicating messages are presented in Chapter 11.

Reporting

Reporting is a crucial activity, and one often either slighted or overdone by instructional developers. Long, poorly written, and/or complicated reports tend to be avoided by those who are expected to read them. Nowadays, with the advances in word processing and graphic systems, reports can be made more interesting and informative.

Proponents of the value of reports continue to seek ways to make them more palatable to readers. The *Eisenhower Brief* is a technique that can be used effectively with long reports. The story is told that General Dwight Eisenhower, responsible for Allied efforts in the European theater during the Second World War, refused to accept any report from his aides that was over one page long. This forced his aides to be very selective and very precise in what they wrote. This type of well-thought-out abstract is a good device to use in conjunction with a long report. It provides the report reader with an advance organizer that puts the report into perspective, and alerts him or her to particular sections that need to be read in depth. Today the more popular term for abstracts such as this is "executive summary." The "Eisenhower Brief" job aid describes one procedure for writing such an abstract.

Job Aid / Eisenhower Brief

Description   Essentially, the Eisenhower Brief is a technique for abstracting essential data from a longer document. The use of this technique makes it necessary for the writer to choose the messages going into a report very carefully, and to write skillfully.

Use Rationale   A major problem with reports is that many of them are never read. Most reports are written in dry, technical language that make difficult reading. By providing a concise abstract of the report, readers get an advance organizer that enables them to decide either that they don't need to read the longer version or that they need to search out specific parts of it.

Critical Steps

1. **Acquire or write a report for which a one-page abstract is to be written.**

2. **Write a brief descriptive heading for each section of the report.** Use action words to denote the contents of a section, e.g., "*Reduce* Overhead," instead of just "Overhead."

3. **Choose the headings to be incorporated in the report, based on their criticality to the receiver.** How necessary is this information for the receiver?

4. **Write a concise summary for each section heading.**
   a. Use simple or complex sentences rather than compound sentences.
   b. Use key terms and phrases from the report.
   c. Edit out figures of speech, digressions, and discussions that are not essential.
   d. State the summary in a form relevant to the need of the receiver.

5. **Add context data.** E.g., date, source of report, and report target. Supply a brief title for the report that makes clear the report's purpose, e.g., Cost-Cutting Procedures.

continued

Eisenhower Brief, continued

6. **Edit the sections for coherency.** E.g., use the same terms throughout the brief. Have one or more individuals read it for understanding.

7. **Continue editing until the brief is down to one page.**

8. **Attach the brief to the report, and submit copies to the appropriate receivers.**

References

Legget, G., et al. (1982). *Handbook for Writers.* Englewood Cliffs, N.J.: Prentice-Hall, pp. 484–486.

Tuckman, B. W. (1972). *Conducting Educational Research.* New York: Harcourt Brace Jovanovich, pp. 189–190.

Witt, Paul (c. 1975). The Eisenhower Brief. Unpublished memorandum to the Instructional Development and Technology Faculty, Michigan State University. East Lansing, Mich.: the University.

Monitoring

The contention of the poet that the best-laid plans of mice and men often go astray is nowhere more true than with plans for ID projects. Keeping track of the progress toward these predetermined plans is a continuing managerial responsibility not to be shirked. The means for keeping track range from the casual to very systematic techniques. The monitoring of a program's progress may be carried out by the manager, the client, accountants, independent assessment teams, or some combination of these.

Peters and Waterman (1982) in their book *In Search of Excellence* tell us that an important characteristic of the superior managers they studied was that they did not depend solely on their assistant managers for information about how well projects were going, but, rather, themselves found some means of sampling the system for possible trouble spots or ways to improve their businesses. One of the techniques they present is called *Walking About.* The "Walking About" job aid operationalizes the concept.

Job Aid / Walking About

Description   This technique serves both troubleshooting and preventive maintenance purposes. It involves having the manager wander around within the boundaries of the system for which he or she is responsible. It is viewed as a facilitative approach rather than as checking up on personnel. It is done on an informal and spontaneous basis, but it is important to cover the whole territory, over time.

Use Rationale   Once a project begins operation, it is important for managers to keep it progressing according to plan. Periodic monitoring on a semirandom basis (wandering around with intent

continued

Walking About, continued

eventually to cover the whole system within a specified time) gives the manager a good reading on whether or not the system's operations are on track. It also lets personnel know that you are serious about the project plan, gives opportunities to keep personnel informed about the status of those things relevant to their tasks, and makes you accessible to them.

Critical Tasks

1. **Set a time cycle for visiting, unannounced, on the job, with all levels of project personnel.** Keep a log after each walk-about, indicating who you saw and at what level. There may be several walk-abouts in a single time cycle. Check the log before beginning the next walk-about, to keep in mind those you have already seen in the cycle so that you are sure to visit others.

2. **For all persons approached, observe and discuss the operation in which they are currently involved.** If you are unclear about what they are doing, seek clarity from them. Ask a general question like "What kinds of problems crop up in this process?" If you know something about the operation that they don't, then tell them.

3. **Briefly inform all persons about what is going on in the system.** Especially about those things that may directly affect them or their tasks, but also in terms of the larger activities, to encourage the sense of belonging. Encourage their constructive reactions to operational decisions or policies.

4. **After each conversation, jot down any relevant observations by you or comments by personnel.** This is important because short-term memory tends to fade fast.

5. **At the completion of each walk-about and each time cycle, analyze the log data.** See if any of the items from different persons are related. Determine which items need action, and who should be involved in correcting or preventing any problems.

Reference

Peters, T. J., and Waterman, R. H. (1982). *In Search of Excellence.* New York: Harper & Row, pp. 287–291.

A second useful means for monitoring certain aspects of the system is through the old standby, the *Suggestion Box.* This technique depends on monitoring by others in the project, and their willingness to submit their ideas or concerns. Usually, the technique is more useful in gathering anonymous comments about failing parts of a system, rather than comments about means of improving it. The "Suggestion Box" job aid presents a typical version of the technique as used to identify problems.

Monitoring resource expenditures, i.e., determining that resources are being expended at a rate commensurate with planned project progress, can be assisted by PERT, our workhorse technique. *MacProject*, an electronic application of PERT presented later in this chapter, is able automatically to reconfigure the PERT network as resource timelines, task cost entry and resource cost entry tables, and cash flow tables, among others. These timelines and tables make very clear what resources were planned

Job Aid / Suggestion Box

Description   This technique serves to capture problems and concerns of staff members, particularly those who would like to remain anonymous. Basically, its operation depends on announcement of the purpose and the conditions under which it operates, its placement, and the collection and analysis of the suggestions.

Use Rationale   All systems have their critics, but some people, for whatever reason, are reticent about speaking up. Since their input may be of value to improving the system, it is desirable to collect their input. The suggestion box technique is one way of doing that.

Critical Tasks

1. **Decide that suggestion boxes are appropriate.** In those situations where communication appears to be effective, where channels are open and people feel free to offer constructive criticism, it is probably not worth the bother.

2. **Select the most appropriate locations for the boxes.** They are best put in places where individuals will have privacy in dropping in their suggestions.

3. **Buy/design/produce the suggestion box.** Basically, these are lockable, wooden or metal boxes with a slit in the top that can accommodate the size of the sheet on which the anticipated suggestions will be written.

4. **Announce the intent to set up the suggestion boxes.** Do this through either a meeting or a memo. Include:
   a. Reason for having suggestion boxes
   b. Criteria to be applied to suggestions, e.g., must benefit project, be practical
   c. Respect for suggester's anonymity
   d. Where they will be located
   e. When the suggestion boxes will be operative

5. **Place the suggestion boxes.** Put them in the preannounced locations.

6. **Collect suggestions.**

7. **Analyze the suggestions.** Apply predetermined criteria, e.g., must be job related, ignore unsubstantiated vilification of personnel, must be logical.

8. **Get secondary verification of the problems or need for proposed changes.** What is a problem or an improvement for one may not be for others.

9. **Make the appropriate changes.** Often, choices will have to be made among competing goods, with choices scheduled as resources allow.

10. **Announce the changes, giving appropriate credit for the ideas.** This helps motivate individuals to continue providing constructive criticisms and ideas for correcting problems.

Reference

None

FIGURE 10.6 / Sample of an ID project cash flow table abstracted from MacProject

Starting	Costs	Income	Ending	Cumulative
1/9/89	1,032.00	900.00	1/16/89	−132.00
1/16/89	764.00	800.00	1/23/89	−96.00
1/23/89	342.00	500.00	1/30/89	62.00
1/30/89	2,340.00	1,500.00	2/6/89	−778.00
2/6/89	800.00	640.00	2/13/89	−618.00
2/13/89	1,140.00	2,040.00	2/20/89	282.00
2/20/89	656.00	1,000.00	2/27/89	626.00
2/27/89	1,457.00	1,500.00	3/6/89	669.00
3/6/89	2,018.00	1,600.00	3/13/89	251.00
3/13/89	1,873.00	1,200.00	3/20/89	−422.00
3/20/89	1,238.00	1,600.00	3/27/89	−60.00

for tasks, at what costs, and over a specified period of time. Figure 10.6 shows a sample *cash flow table* reconfigured from a MacProject PERT Network to show the cash resources expended, as contrasted with cash resources available, during specific periods. The first row of the table shows the first time period from January 9, 1989, through January 15, 1989. Project costs for this period were $1,032.00, but income was only $900.00. The last column for this time period shows the cumulative costs, which can be either positive or negative. In this case they are negative, because more was spent to complete the tasks for that period than was budgeted. Reconciling those costs and times with resource billing receipts will keep the manager aware of how closely planned expenditures follow actual expenditures. When a group of tasks is completed at less than planned cost, the project is that much ahead; however, when some tasks or clusters of tasks cost more to complete than was planned, previous saving may have to be expended to make up the differences. And when the costs exceed the planned income and any accumulated savings, managers must scurry around and try to find additional funding to cover the deficit, or sacrifice additional profits. In a worst-case scenario, developers may have to pay money out of their own pockets to complete a project. Clearly, that event cannot happen very often.

Another useful means for monitoring the progress of a project is the technique *Key Indicator Management (KIM)*. This technique was presented in Chapter 8 as a means for continuously monitoring the progress of an ongoing course or program, but with a little adaptation it can be used for monitoring ID projects as well.

Preparing Project Work Breakdown

A companion technique to PERT is *analytic flowcharting*. Both PERT and analytic flowcharting are methods for identifying and sequencing project tasks. Analytic flowcharting differs from PERT in that it shows *alternative* sequences of tasks based on project decision points that need to be considered.

Analytic flowcharting is a procedure for identifying and graphically representing the sequential and alternative relationships among processes and decision points, relevant to completing a project.

One application of analytic flowcharting found useful by instructional developers is to apply flowcharting to the more critical individual tasks listed in the PERT network. That is, take an individual activity or task, such as "get agreement from decision makers," and flowchart it. This application will ensure that the manager is constantly sensitive to alternative sets of tasks that may need consideration as the project progresses. The type of PERT discussed here does not permit the use of decision points in its network, although a variation of the critical path method, called *Decision Critical Path Method (DCPM)*, does attempt to incorporate alternative paths through a network. At the time of publishing, the author had not found computer software designed for DCPM.

There are a number of excellent computerized flowcharting programs available. These are much easier to use than is the process of manually drawing and redrawing a flowchart. An example is *MacFlow*, used with Macintosh computers. The "Analytic Flowcharting" job aid assumes that the developer will be doing the flowcharting manually, but the skills learned here easily transfer to use of the several excellent computer programs for flowcharting, such as MacFlow.

Job Aid / Analytic Flowcharting

Description   Analytic flowcharting is an efficient means of graphically representing project tasks in terms of their sequence and alternative decisions. Specific symbols are used to indicate tasks, decision points, and their connections. The first step is to identify the major project tasks. Then these tasks are broken down into specific subtasks and are sequenced as labeled graphic symbols. The flowchart may have to be drawn several times during its development as new information surfaces.

Use Rationale   Flowcharting is relatively easy to do and is generalizable to any process, although it is particularly useful in analyzing complex processes. A flowchart assists the developer in identifying, clarifying, checking, and sequencing processes or tasks and concomitant decision points. In converting project tasks into a flowchart, instructional developers will be able to check for gaps or other defects in their original concepts regarding the necessary tasks and their sequence in the instruction.

continued

Analytic Flowcharting, continued

Critical Tasks

1. **List all the major tasks necessary to completing a project.** It is wise to have experienced people list the tasks, or at least critique them. If flowcharting is being used in conjunction with PERT, usually flowcharting is limited to the most critical tasks in the PERT network.

2. **Analyze each major task.** It may be necessary to break broad tasks down into smaller tasks, or to collapse simple tasks into a broader one.

3. **Show the sequence of tasks in a graphic form.** Use an *oval* symbol to start and end the flowchart, a *rectangle* symbol to show a task, and *arrows* to connect all symbols and to show the direction of task flow.

4. **Determine and insert any major questions into the task sequence as decision points.** Redraw using a *rhombus*, or diamond-shaped symbol, to show a decision point. Normally, all arrows leading from a decision point will indicate yes or no decisions. See Figure 10.7.

5. **Check the yes/no decisions for each path.** For decision points that indicate repeated tasks, loop back to the starting point for that task, when practical, as shown in Figure 10.7. In extreme cases, more than two arrows may be used to indicate alternative paths from a single decision point.

6. **Check that all paths through the flowchart begin and end appropriately.** The rule is that all tasks and decisions come from somewhere and all go somewhere; there are *no* dead ends except for the Enter and Exit symbols.

7. **Check for the correctness of all feedback and feedforward loops.** Have them show appropriate connections to earlier or later tasks or to decision points.

8. **Check for the correctness of all on-page and off-page connectors.** The on-page symbol is used when it would be confusing to draw an arrow across several others to get to a task. The *circle* symbol is used to connect elements on-page; the *house* symbol is used to connect paths off-page.

References

Bertrand, P. A., Terpstra, D., with Manual by Greenwood, S. (1989). *MacFlow: Fast, Clear Flowcharts on the Macintosh.* Agora Hills, Calif.: Mainstay.

Delp, Peter, et al. (1977). *System Tools for Project Planning.* Bloomington, Ind.: Program of Advanced Studies in Institution Building and Technical Assistance Methodology, pp. 107–112.

Enrick, N. L. (1972). *Effective Graphic Communication.* New York: Auerbach Publishers, pp. 56–72.

Lenher, John K. (1972). *Flowcharting: An Introductory Text and Workbook.* New York: Auerbach Publishers.

continued

Analytic Flowcharting, continued

FIGURE 10.7 / Flowchart of the PERT task "get agreement from decision makers"

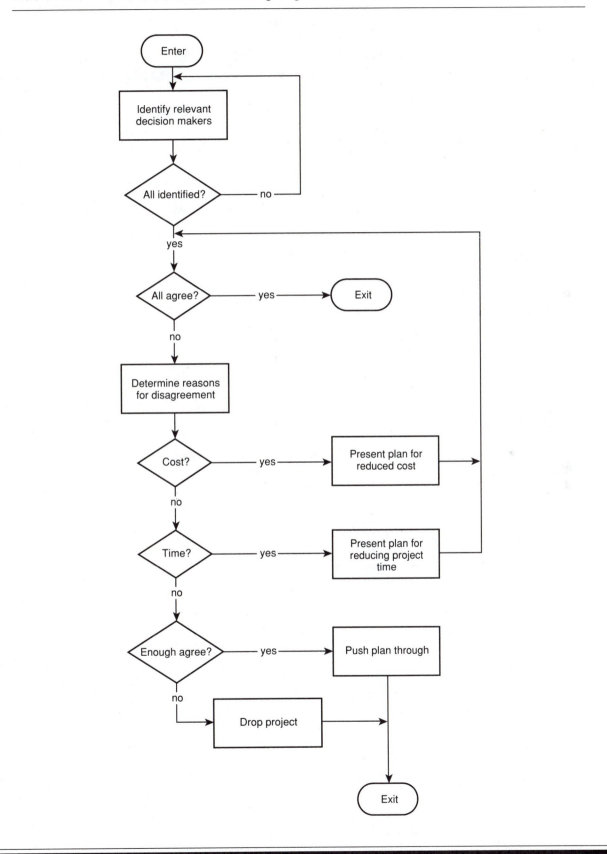

Computerized work-breakdown and sequencing programs take much of the tedium out of generating and revising task networks. The "Mac-Project" job aid teaches the use of a computerized version of PERT. This is a particularly user-friendly technique.

Job Aid / MacProject (PERT)

Description   *MacProject* is a computer program for assisting in the systematic management of project resources, including personnel. It requires that all pertinent tasks be laid out in their proper sequence to form a network (see Figure 10.8). Time, costs, personnel, and materials can be tied to specific tasks in the network. Once done, accumulated times for tasks on different paths through the network indicate the *critical path* of the project (i.e., the one path through the network that consumes the most time). Network data can be automatically reconfigured into other report forms, including resource and task timelines, resource and task costs, cash flow and project charts. Changes in the network are automatically carried through the network and to related charts.

Use Rationale   ID project management is a balancing act because of the variety of activities going on simultaneously. Tasks and resources require constant adjustment as the project progresses, and some means, such as PERT, are needed to keep the manager and staff aware of the effects of individual changes on their respective parts of the project.

Critical Tasks

1. **Generate an initial list of project tasks.** Often, this is initially done on 3 × 5 cards and rearranged on a large surface to determine their logical sequence.

2. **Boot up the MacProject program on the computer monitor.**

3. **Enter task and milestone descriptions to form a network from left to right.** Descriptors need be short, but sufficient for clarity. Task boxes are formed by depressing the mouse button and dragging until the desired-size box is formed. These boxes can be made smaller or larger as needed by clicking on the box and dragging one of the little knobs attached to the box. The first and last boxes of a network are usually in the milestone shape. These are formed by clicking on a box and going to the Task column of the menu bar and releasing on Change to Milestone.

4. **As task boxes are formed, place them in their logical sequence.** Tasks are sequenced according to whether they are concurrent or predecessors or successors to one another. Concurrent tasks will follow different paths. See Figure 10.8, where Start–Talk to realtor–Visit locations–Decide on location forms one path, and Start–Arrange financing–Decide on location forms a concurrent path.

5. **Connect the task boxes with lines.** Start with the first task, and pull the cursor from the center of one box to another, with the mouse button depressed, before releasing. Continue until all dependent tasks are connected. Boxes can be added, deleted, or moved. To delete, click on the box and cut it from the Edit column of the menu bar. To move a box, set the arrow on the box's side, depress the mouse button, and move it.

6. **Connect any dependent tasks in concurrent paths.** Connect the arrow from the earlier task in one path to the dependent task in the other path. The dependent task box must be positioned slightly to the right of the task on which it is dependent for the dates to be correct.

continued

MacProject (PERT), continued

FIGURE 10.8 / Simple PERT network showing times and the critical path

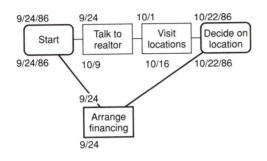

7. **Enter time and resources required for each task.** Choose Show Task from the Task menu. Enter under "Days" the time, in days, it will take to complete the task. Press Tab key, and enter up to six resources required under "Resources." The Task Info window shows data only on a selected task.

8. **Enter the estimated duration of the project.** Choose Dates from the menu bar, and open the calendar. Click on the appropriate parts of the time wheel to limit the workday, and click on the days in the calendar that will not be workdays, e.g., Saturday and Sunday. The manager can change these times as appropriate, with the system feeding through changes that affect other estimates.

9. **For each task, enter the Earliest Start Date or the Latest Finish Date.** Go to the Dates column of the menu bar to select task start or finish dates, then click on Set button. To remove a date, select the Clear button. The dates will appear at the upper left of the task box. Updates will occur automatically for tasks that follow.

10. **Calculate backwards from the project deadline to the latest time to begin a task.** Choose Show Dates from the menu, click Latest Start, and click OK button. Show at the bottom of the boxes the latest possible dates that tasks can be begun and still meet the deadline.

11. **View the critical path.** This is the longest path through the network and is indicated by dark lines between boxes. If changes are made in the network that creates a longer path, that path will then become the critical path.

12. **Enter all fixed costs and fixed income related to each task in the Task Cost Entry form.** This is found under the Chart column of the menu bar. These estimates can be changed with new information.

13. **In the Resource Cost Entry form, enter any costs incurred from using each resource.** The unit of measurement is based on the selection you made when setting task duration. You must indicate whether the cost is divided among tasks in a single day (single) or whether the full cost is applied for each task assigned on a single day (multiple).

continued

MacProject (PERT), continued

14. **Print to another application.** Select All from the Edit column of the menu, select Copy, quit MacProject, call up the desired application document, place the cursor at the desired point, and choose Paste from the Edit column of the menu bar.

FIGURE 10.9 / Simple PERT network showing the relationship between the top path and the middle path

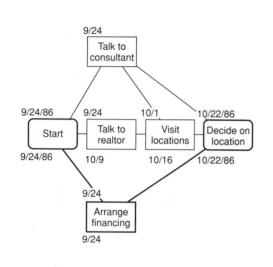

FIGURE 10.10 / Sample task cost entry for network

Task	Name	Fixed Cost	Fixed Income
1	Start	0	0
2	Talk to realtor	10	10
3	Arrange financing	5,000	5,000
4	Visit locations	30	40
5	Decide on location	10	10

References

Kaehler, C. (1984). *MacProject: Program Users' Manual.* Cupertino, Calif.: Apple Computer, pp. 41–56, 82–89.

Meridith, J. R., and Mantel, J. S. (1985). *Project Management: A Managerial Approach.* New York: Wiley, pp. 209–228.

Developing Contingency Plans

No ID plan is ever followed exactly. Invariably there will be unanticipated problems arising that slow a project and/or increase its cost. Successful managers keep escape routes available in case the unexpected happens. The general types of problems are: cost and time overruns, client requests for changes, dissension among project team members—including disciplinary problems, staff members leaving the project, and ailing software and hardware.

The first step is, of course, to recognize that a problem or potential problem exists. Earlier, analytic flowcharting was described as a good adjunct technique to PERT because it would show alternative possibilities in a process, whereas PERT was not designed for that. These alternative paths may be thought of as *contingency plans* for dealing with a problem. Consider the decision points in the flowchart at the end of the "Analytic Flowcharting" job aid, presented earlier in this chapter. Each decision point presents an alternative to what was originally planned. Another technique serving to alert developers to an alternative or contingency plan is *Cost–Benefit Analysis* (Chapter 3). This technique speaks to **trade-offs** among resources, which also represent choosing among alternative plans.

The value of contingency planning is that developers are prepared to move quickly in a positive direction when a snag occurs in the original plan. At the time problems arise, there is usually pressure to make a quick decision, either because a particular window of opportunity is brief or because of pressure from clients. Lack of careful thought at this point can result in a decision that later costs too much.

Unfortunately, a manager cannot always follow the perfect plan, because of conditions that have been imposed, such as restrictive limits on money and time to complete a project. Under these circumstances contingency plans must be considered if the project is to continue. A technique that has proven useful for this purpose, presented in Chapter 3, is called *Successive Approximation*. This technique is based on the idea of using a process or product in less than an ideal state (i.e., an approximation), but with the understanding that progressive improvement will be made over a prescribed period of time. Its value lies in the fact that the use of the technique permits project personnel to get past an initial sticking point so that they can work on successor tasks.

Evaluating Project Processes and Products

There may be several forms of evaluation going on over a project's lifetime. These range from initial validation of the project idea, through efficient use of project funds, formative and summative evaluation of the project product, and client assessment of the project, to name some of the more common ones. Most instructional developers prefer to keep control of the evaluation process themselves, and to report the results to clients and other decision makers. However, there is no doubting the instructional developer's bias in terms of his or her own product. Ideally, an outside agency, with no axes to grind, should be assigned the task of evaluating the products of the project. Unfortunately, instructional developers have found that when the responsibility is placed in the hands of outsiders, the criteria used for making the evaluation are often not well matched with project objectives. Given that outside evaluation is to take place, the instructional developer should insist on providing, or signing off on, the criteria used to evaluate the project. The *Modified Stake Evaluation Management Technique* (Chapter 9) has proven effective for those instructional developers who do retain responsibility for evaluating project products and processes.

Closing Out a Project

The period concluding a project is often hectic. With client deadlines to meet, few remaining resources, and the boss breathing down the developer's neck about that next project, it is little wonder that instructional developers have difficulty in finding time for the niceties involved in closing out a project. However, past practice has demonstrated that this period can have a strong effect on the instructional product's future. If the right conditions are not provided at the time of installation and beginning of ongoing operation, there is a good chance that the instruction will be rendered less effective, and may even begin the process leading to elimination. Another reason to spend more time assisting the client in shaking down the instruction, is that neglect on the part of the instructional developer at a time when the client feels a great need can affect the possibility of future projects from the client. An important rule is "Never poison your own well." Chapter 7 discusses these problems in detail. One technique recommended is that of *Gradual Disengagement* (Chapter 1), which has the instructional developer maintain a certain level of contact with those operating the product or process until they have successfully integrated the innovation into the parent system. Successful integration of an instructional innovation usually requires some modification of the policies and procedures of the parent system. In some cases, if the new instruction is to be integrated, the organization's policies have to be changed (e.g., a distance-education video package is ready to go, but the organization has a policy not to give credit for off campus self-instruction). Application of the *Policy Setting* technique (see Chapter 3) may be useful at that point.

Summary

Management of instructional projects is still more of an art than a science, but there are established processes and techniques that have proven effective over the years. Rationale and techniques were presented in the chapter for carrying out management functions. The techniques ranged through the overall processes necessary to ID project management. Included were techniques for costing proposed projects, setting up policies and procedures for acquiring and allocating resources, for interacting with staff and clients, for handling client and staff meetings, for maintaining lines of communication, for monitoring a project, and for project evaluation and wrap-up.

References

Anthony, R. N. (1965). *Planning and Control Systems: A Framework for Analysis.* Cambridge, Mass.: Harvard University Press.

Clyment, E. W. (1984). The project-oriented matrix and instructional development project management. *Journal of Instructional Development* 7(1): 14–18.

Consortium of College and University Media Centers (1990). *Educational Film and Video Locator.* 4th ed. New York: Bowker.

Craig, R. L. (ed.) (1987). *Training and Development Handbook: A Guide to Human Resource Development.* New York: McGraw-Hill.

Durzo, J. J. (1983). Getting down to business: Instructional development for a profit. *Journal of Instructional Development* 6(2): 2–7.

Educational Products Information Exchange Institute (EPIE) (1990). *Educational Product Report.* New York: the Institute.

Frantzreb, R. B. (ed.) (1991). *Training and Development Yearbook.* New York: Prentice-Hall.

Green, E. E., and Mills, G. E. (1978). Putting together an instructional development team. *Journal of Instructional Development* 2(1): 29–33.

Levesque, J. D. (1986). *Manual of Personnel, Policies, Procedures, and Operations.* New York: Prentice-Hall.

National Information Center For Educational Media (1987). *Film and Video Finder.* 1st ed. Albuquerque, N.M.: the Center.

Osguthorpe, R. T. (1985). Conducting literature searches for instructional development projects. *Journal of Instructional Development,* 8(4): 20–24.

Piper, Amy J. (1990). An Analysis and Comparison of Selected Project Management Techniques and Their Implications for the Instructional Development Process. Unpublished dissertation in Educational Systems Development. Michigan State University. East Lansing, Mich.: the University.

Plunkett, W. R., and Attner, R. F. (1989). *Introduction to Management.* Boston: PWS-Kent.

Rutt, D. P. (1979–80). A framework for investigating consultation in instructional development. *Journal of Instructional Development,* 3(2): 9–16.

Tessmer, M. (1988). Subject specialist consultation in instructional design: Higher education. *Journal of Instructional Development* 11(2): 29–36.

Walter, S., and Earle, R. S. (1981–82). Contracting for instructional development. *Journal of Instructional Development* 5(2): 26–31.

Weist, J. D., and Levy, F. K. (1977). *A Management Guide to PERT/CPM with GERT/PDM/DCPM and Other Networks.* Englewood Cliffs, N.J.: Prentice-Hall.

CHAPTER 11

Project Communication

Process by which essential information is distributed
and circulated among those responsible for,
or involved in, the activities of a project

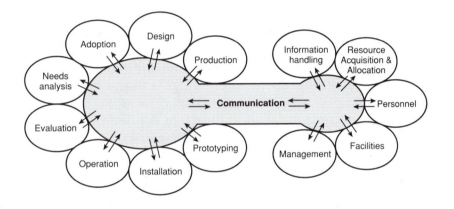

Learner Objectives

1. Recall the names and the sequence of components of the Shannon-Weaver communication model.

2. Explain how use of the Shannon-Weaver communication model can reduce errors in project communications.

3. List two or more techniques for identifying personnel who should be included in a project's communications network.

4. List and explain major factors affecting the communication process.

5. Describe the four elements necessary to the structure of a formal communications system.

6. Recall definitions of major terms.

Introduction

A central task of project managers is to ensure effective and efficient communication of essential information among those involved in a project. Instructional development projects, like all other types of projects, are fueled by information. This chapter does not deal in any great detail with the selection, collection, or creation of information. Those tasks are the subject of Chapter 12. Instead, this chapter focuses on processes and techniques that are important in running a project *communication system*. Such a communication system enables the effective and efficient distribution of essential information among project members, clients, vendors, and consultants.

A major attribute of human beings, when contrasted with other species, is their superior ability to communicate among themselves. Verbal and nonverbal language permits the exchange of an almost infinite range of concepts, facts, and feelings. A problem with human communication is that it is fraught with the possibility of error. For example, the inadvertent recording of the wrong delivery date for critical materials may set an ID project back for months. Typographical errors in design specifications can do the same thing. The function of the communication component in the Instructional Project Development and Management (IPDM) Model, presented graphically in Figure 11.1, is to provide means for reducing communication error in ID projects. The IPDM model in Figure 11.1 has arrows going in and out of each of the development and supporting components via the communication component. These arrows indicate the flow of essential information among the fourteen components. The assumption is that each of the components has or will have essential information needed at some point in the instructional development by the other components. As mentioned earlier, responsibility for determining, collect-

FIGURE 11.1 / Exchange of essential information among IP model components

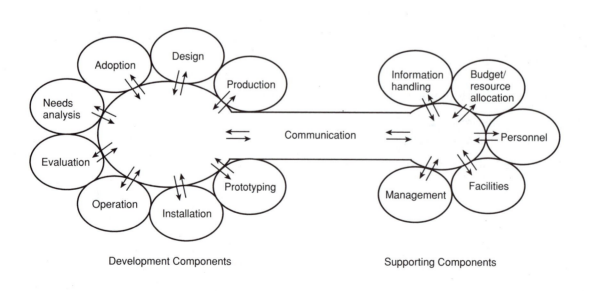

Development Components   Supporting Components

ing, and creating information resides in the information-handling component, but the process of getting the information to persons needing it, at the right time and in the right form, is the function of the communication component. In that sense, the communication component relates all of the other instructional development and management components to one another.

The accomplishment of some tasks, regardless of the system, requires more precise communications than that of others. There are many situations where the need for precision in communication is readily agreed to. Examples would be when members of a bomb squad are defusing a potential explosive device; when a surgical team is involved in a delicate operation; and when government interpreters are translating messages during a crisis between countries. For critical situations such as these, considerable effort is expended to ensure *precise* communication of *precise* information. However, for other, less critical situations, such as those found in instructional development projects, there seems to be a basic assumption that the necessary precision in communication will automatically take place. Unfortunately, there is little evidence supporting that assumption. From the author's observation, inadequate communication occurs about as often as adequate communication. As a result, poor or imprecise communications are likely to affect the performance of ID project teams negatively, reducing both their effectiveness and their efficiency.

To compound the problems of communication, it is now becoming increasingly important that instructional developers (along with the rest of society) be able not only to communicate with one another but to communicate effectively with "intelligent" machines, as well. Interesting changes in responsibility have taken place as computer use has evolved. Early on, computer designers created rather cryptic programming and application languages that users had to learn in order to communicate with computers. But in more recent times, designers have switched the responsibility around so that computers are more and more able to respond to commands made in ordinary language. This switch was partly motivated by the desire of manufacturers to encourage the mass use of personal computers. At this point in the evolution of the personal computer and its software, user-friendly systems are becoming the rule rather than the exception. The range of possible uses of computers on ID projects continues growing at an impressive rate. Broadly, these uses include management, production, and instructional delivery. From a communication perspective, computers can be programmed to deliver whatever is stored in their systems, on demand, in a variety of forms. They are also becoming more and more useful as messaging systems that permit those taking part in a common endeavor to communicate when it is convenient. Even with all of the advances in the interface between users and computers, a degree of computer literacy is necessary for effective communication between the two.

If information is what fuels an ID project, then a major task of the manager is to set up conditions so that essential information is communicated to project members when they need it, where they need it, and in the form they need it. To accomplish this, a manager needs to know some of the basics about group and interpersonal communication. **Communication**, put simply, "involves the transmission of information from senders to receivers and from receivers to senders" (Thompson, 1969, p. 4). The main elements of communication are, as Harold Lasswell (1948, p. 37) so succinctly put it, "*who* says *what* in which *channel* to *whom* with what *effect?*"

A Communication Model

In the late 1940s, an important model of communication grew out of the work of two scientists: Claude Shannon and Warren Weaver. A graphic variation of their model is depicted in Figure 11.2. The symbol at the top left of the figure represents the point where a message is created in someone's mind. That person is the **communication source**. The actual process of creating a message is hidden among the electro-chemical reactions that take place in the brain of the message source. Once created, a means for *transmitting* the message to others in a form they can understand is chosen (e.g., through speech or through writing). The means chosen to transmit the message determines the *channel* that will carry the message. That is, if the voice is chosen to transmit the message, then the channel carrying the message will be sound waves, and the *receiver* of the message will be the hearing apparatus of the person for whom the message was intended. If the message is encoded in writing, then the channel that carries the message will be light waves, which will stimulate the targeted person's visual apparatus (receiver). The receiving apparatus (ear or eye) in turn translates the message back from light or sound wave form into the electrochemical form decipherable by the brain of the person targeted for the message. The mind that receives the message might then change to become the source (lower right symbol) of a new message, in response to the one received, and the new message will go through the same process as did the first, and so the cycle continues. The point is that the message may be transformed several times before it gets to its destination, and each point may provide conditions causing message distortion.

One use of the Shannon-Weaver communication model, for project managers, is as a reminder to check for errors among the elements of communication, i.e., source, transmitter, channel, receiver, and destination of the message. As examples, consider the possibilities of error in a message written on the chalkboard by an instructor (source):

FIGURE 11.2 / Modified Shannon-Weaver model of communication

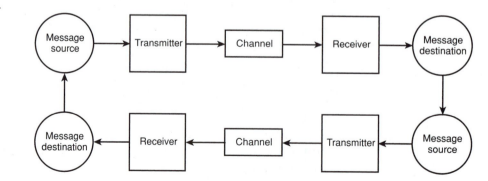

source   The message created contains inaccuracies.
transmitter   The handwriting is difficult to read.
channel   Light glare on the chalkboard distorts the message.
receiver   Some of the students have faulty vision.
destination   Some students are biased toward the instructor.

If any one of these errors occurs, it could impair the intent of the instructor's message for some students. To generalize, a manager can reduce the likelihood of such errors by searching out conditions that might cause a message to be distorted at any one of these points in the communication process and taking preventative measures.

Many other factors, besides errors originating among specific communication elements, may contribute to confusion or misinterpretation of messages. There are also questions about to whom a message should go, when it should go, and in what format it should be couched. In addition, communication problems may arise among ID project staffs and their parent organizations, client systems, resource systems, and other related systems. Again, the effectiveness with which communication takes place within and across these systems can affect the successful development of instruction. Good communication among individuals and groups does not occur by chance. To quote Severin and Tankard (1988, p. 47): "Communication networks must be established and maintained if a group is to function." Communication systems of ID projects are critical, because communication is the central means by which management controls the activities of projects. Before considering the formal structures and techniques relevant to project communication systems, it is important to look at specific tasks essential to communicating within a project.

Project Communication Process

The following is a set of tasks important to the effective performance of a communication system for instructional development projects:

1. Determine who should send and receive information through the project's communication system.

2. Determine the positive and negative factors affecting communication in the project environment, and the means for their control.

3. Determine the appropriate means for communicating specific project information.

4. Determine the means for providing feedback on the effectiveness of individual communications.

5. Establish policies and rules for communicating with individuals and groups, internal and external to a project.

6. Formalize procedures for the project communication system.

Identifying Senders and Receivers

The answer to the question of who should be involved in sending and receiving project information can be important to a project's success.

Identifying *all* of the persons in a system who might provide useful information, and those who should be receiving information, is not always easy, particularly for project personnel coming from the outside. As pointed out in Chapter 7, most of the individuals in an organization who may be important to a project can be identified through examination of organizational charts and through applying techniques like *Communications Network Analysis*. Of course, the simple expedient of querying those in charge will surface most of the individuals who might affect a project; but often, significant individuals slip through that net. Key individuals among those identified through these and other means will require selected information at different times during the life of a project. They may also act as sources for some of the information essential to the project. Of course, much of the information needed by a project is generated by the project manager and staff, along with designated subject matter experts. The latter source of information, the subject matter expert, is usually drawn from the client system. Other information needed by a project may require the expertise of individuals not found in the ID or client systems. At any rate, sources of essential information must be identified, and their information communicated, if a project is to be carried out effectively.

What and how much of the project information should be shared, and with whom, depends primarily on three variables: who needs to know, project and client security needs, and competition for resources. It is somewhat ironic that information in one person's hands can be detrimental to a project while the same information in another's can be beneficial. Information important to a project may be readily available, or it may be withheld for some reason, and once received it may or may not be used. The reasons for sharing and not sharing information are many. For example, no one is surprised that businesses try to maintain an edge by keeping proprietary knowledge from their competition. But it is sometimes forgotten that most projects, especially those funded internally, are competing with others in the parent system for the same limited resources. For these and other reasons, information is often restricted or filtered by those controlling it. Usually, control is accomplished through "need to know" rules and secured-access procedures that have been established by an organization's hierarchy.

Certainly, there are occasions when a "need to know" rule, for security reasons, should be enforced. But more often, a better reason for being selective in sending information is to avoid inundating staff or clients with unnecessary information. Projects are managed more effectively when those involved are provided with just the essential information rather than being overloaded with all of the information available on a task. This does not mean that other information should necessarily be withheld from those involved with the project, only that such information would not be shared unless asked for specifically.

Overload is not the only reason information is not used by receivers. In fact, the reasons for project members' using information or not using it are numerous. Not trusting the source of the information is one reason. This condition causes many personnel to search out alternative sources of information rather than go with the ones officially designated. Poor timing of information is another reason information is not used. Information sent too late is of little use, and information communicated too early is often lost or forgotten. Factors like these are considered in more detail in the next section.

Factors Affecting Communication

Identifying other systems that must cooperate with project personnel if the project is to be completed in a desirable fashion is a fairly simple task, as is the identification of the respective subsystems of those systems. And generally, it is not terribly difficult to determine the information that must be exchanged among systems and subsystems, or which individuals control the information. What is difficult is determining ahead of time where the problems will lie in moving the information from the source to the user.

One technique for assisting in that determination is called *interface analysis*. Interface analysis is a spin-off of general systems theory, which looks at all organized entities as systems made up of interdependent subsystems or components. The effective operation of system components, working together, permits the system to function according to its design. As an example, the automobile component of a transportation system depends on its own components (motor, transmission, drive shaft, wheels, electrical system, and so on) operating together in order to function. The automobile, in turn, must interface with other components (e.g., drivers, roads, traffic signs, traffic rules). Each of these components has information that is essential to the functions of the other components in the transportation system. Information essential for the functioning of the components must travel across their common boundaries, called **interfaces**. Sometimes these interfaces are *closed* to the passing of information. For instance, a defective gear shift will not permit the driver to inform the car which transmission gear to connect to the drive shaft.

The concept of **closed systems** and **open systems** extends beyond things mechanical. Social systems may also be closed to information from other social systems. For example, many nations at different times in their history have closed their borders to foreigners and prevented their citizens from traveling, thereby inhibiting the ready exchange of information with the rest of the world. In an example closer to home, instructional developers, in order to carry out the tasks of production and prototyping, will need information that has been generated by the design group, and they in turn may have important information needed by the design group. An important task is to determine what variables or factors are operating that affect the sending and receiving of information essential to a project. The "Interface Analysis" job aid demonstrates how this technique is applied to such a task.

Experience of developers has surfaced a number of additional factors that often affect the communication process. Immediately next are listed and discussed four of the factors that commonly *inhibit* communication. Following those are three factors that tend to *enhance* the communication of information.

Noise   In communication theory, **noise** is anything that distorts a message. For a phone message, static on the line could literally be the noise

Job Aid / Interface Analysis

Description **Interface analysis** is a technique that helps analyze common boundaries between systems, and between components making up a system, including those of instructional development systems. Interface analysis helps determine which interfaces are effective, or ineffective, in transporting essential information from one component to another across their common boundaries. In this process, system components and their functions are identified, and interfaces of the components are identified and compared in terms of eight characteristics important to the effectiveness of interfaces. The interfaces are then rated as to how critical they are to the instructional development process, and modifications are recommended for correcting defects.

Use Rationale The assumption is that each component of a system has varying amounts of information relevant to its other components. This information travels from one component to another across the natural or artificial "interface(s)" between them. If the interfaces are defective, or closed, then essential information may not get to appropriate components, or the information that is received may be distorted or misleading. These conditions can reduce the effectiveness and efficiency of the individual components and of the ID process as a whole.

Critical Tasks

1. **Delineate components of the ID process used.** E.g., administrative, design, production, prototype testing, training, budget.

2. **Plot the interfaces between the components.** E.g., any mechanisms for exchanging information between the design component and the production component.

3. **Determine the information functions of each interface.** For example, the interface between the design and the production components deals primarily with design specifications and how they relate to the requirements, capabilities, and/or limitations of the production component.

4. **Identify the potential generators and receivers of essential information.** E.g., individuals who generated the storyboards and other specifications, with receivers being individuals who must translate the storyboard into a video production.

5. **Rate each interface in terms of eight general characteristics.** I.e., permeability, selectivity, directionality, visibility, deprivation, stability, dependency, and capacity. See Figure 11.3.

6. **Determine the performance potential of each interface.** Relate the minimal essential information required, with its general characteristics.

7. **Prioritize the defective interfaces in terms of criticality.** This is mostly a judgment call, sometimes ameliorated by the manager's ability to get essential information to a component through some other interface. See Figure 11.4.

8. **Determine and list the modifications required to correct the defective interfaces.** An example of a modification might be to get a policy change that would permit release of needed information.

continued

Interface Analysis, continued

___

FIGURE 11.3 / Interface characteristics*

___

There are certain general characteristics of interfaces that may be used to guide our analyses of them. A listing and a brief description of each of these characteristics follows.

1. **Permeability:** the ease with which information can travel across an interface from one component to another. The permeability of an interface may depend upon any number of factors. The organizational or administrative models controlling the interacting components is certainly a major factor. For example, a democratic administrative structure permits much freer access to information than does a militaristic administrative structure. Factors of language, values, and culture may either inhibit or facilitate the exchange of essential information across an interface.

2. **Selectivity**: the constraints placed on access to information in a system or subsystem. The Great Wall of China, the former Iron Curtain, government and corporate secrecy, privacy laws, all are indicative of systems that limit access to information. Knowledge of the rules that govern such access for client systems becomes necessary if instructional developers are to acquire the essential information to complete their tasks.

3. **Directionality**: the predominant direction in which information flows across an interface. The direction of information flow also depends to a large degree upon the administrative structures imposed upon an organization. Where militaristic or bureaucratic models of administration are used, it is expected that information would flow primarily from the top down; information would tend to flow equally in both directions in democratic models. Early knowledge of the administrative model used by a client system could reduce false starts at acquiring information.

4. **Deprivation**: the effect on information flow resulting from inadequate resource support for an interface. It is rare that interfaces have access to either sufficient resources or sufficient skills for ensuring adequate information handling. As a result, the anemic condition of most interfaces affects the amount and quality of information that can be transported across an interface.

5. **Visibility**: the readiness with which an interface can be identified. In every organization there are both formal and informal communication and information-handling systems operating. Some of the most valuable are found among the informal; however, their identification is not always easy. Techniques for identifying informal liaisons and communication links are available.

6. **Stability**: the degree to which an interface is well established and dependable in providing a consistent level of information. As a general rule, older systems have more stable interfaces, while newer systems have less stable ones. By the same token, interfaces of the former type are much more difficult to change than those of the latter type.

7. **Dependency**: the degree to which a system or subsystem depends for its survival on the information provided by other systems or subsystems. Some systems are so dependent that the closing down of a single interface could render the system ineffective in some critical operation.

8. **Capacity**: the quantity of information that can travel across an interface in a prescribed amount of time. There are peak periods in any system when the information needs are greater. If the information is not delivered in the appropriate quantity at the appropriate time, then the system's effectiveness and efficiency may be seriously affected. Part of the problem, in many systems, is that there is poor discrimination between essential and nonessential information. The nonessential information tends to clog the interface, slowing the essential.

___

*From Gentry and Trimby (1984, p. 97).

continued

Interface Analysis, continued

**FIGURE 11.4 / Sample rating report
on the characteristics of an interface**

Rating Key: S = sufficient
I = insufficient

Characteristic   *Rating*

1. Permeability   I
   a. Information required would necessitate a change in their computer program.
   b. They don't want to make the change out of concern for having to provide the same
      service for others.

2. Selectivity   I
   a. They are concerned that they may be liable to privacy laws if they give us the information.
   b. They were not able to show the section of the privacy law that legislated against their
      providing this information.

3. Directionality   I
   a. Their practice has been to send out information that they see as valuable rather than to
      respond to requests.

4. Deprivation   S

5. Visibility   S

6. Stability   S

7. Dependency   I
   a. It is very necessary to identify these students.
   b. The information will continue to be needed on a regular basis, even after development is
      complete.
   c. The assistant director is sympathetic to the need.

8. Capacity   S

Reference

Gentry, C. G., and Trimby, M. J. (1984). Interface analysis of ID systems. In *Instructional Development: The State of the Art*, Dubuque, Iowa: Kendall/Hunt.

---

that distorts the message. But dislike or disrespect for the person sending a message on the part of the person receiving it may also distort the message. Obviously, under this meaning, a poorly worded message is also a source of noise that can affect the transfer of an intended message.

The function of the communication component in the IPDM Model is to effectively and efficiently get project-relevant information from the source to the destination. The message can be distorted at any point in the communication process, i.e., at the source, the transmitter, the channel, the receiver, and/or the destination of the message. Consider the potential for noise in an ordinary classroom. The sounds of traffic outside of a classroom window may make it difficult for students to hear the lecturer. Ambient light striking the chalkboard so as to cause glare may prevent students from reading the message put there by the instructor. The instructor's squeaking chalk on the chalkboard makes it hard for some students to concentrate. Poor adjustment of the mimeograph machine makes handouts hard to read. The garbled sound of the motion picture projector distorts the message, as does "snow" in a video presentation. Similarly, opportunities for distortion of communications of an ID project are many. However, noise can be reduced significantly by knowing at what points in the communication process it can occur, and by taking steps to reduce its likelihood.

Access Limitations   Information is a form of power, and may be withheld for reasons having little to do with the project that needs it. Sometimes information is withheld because of competitive paranoia among organizations or of parts of organizations. Even when a project or individual can demonstrate the right to information, it may prove difficult to come by. One way of negatively controlling the effects of information is to send it too late to serve its purpose. The *Law of Delay*, propounded by Parkinson (1957), declares that delay is the deadliest form of denial. As an example, if help for a drowning man arrives several hours after he goes down for the last time, it does not serve the purpose of saving him. Similarly, if project members don't receive essential information when needed, time and other resources may be irretrievably lost.

There are many horror stories about information being withheld from ID staff who were unable to proceed effectively without it. One instance had to do with developing an instructional program to train Army personnel to maintain a new military tank. A group of instructional developers and content experts from outside of the organization contracted to develop the instruction. Serious problems arose when gatekeepers in the system decided that the members of this outside project group were not cleared to receive certain information necessary to developing the instruction. This standoff lasted almost 6 months. During this time, the ID team members were put in the position of attempting to design instruction without access to the essential information necessary to the task. As a result, there were several undesirable outcomes: some project team members quit out of frustration, resources were wasted from false starts, and the instruction was not delivered until much later than was necessary or desirable.

As would be expected, managers have less control over external communications than they have over communications within their projects. However, anticipating when information will be needed by project personnel enables the manager to focus early on both internal and external sources of the information. This increases the likelihood that the information will be made available by the time needed. Again, a regularly updated *PERT* is an excellent device for determining when project members will need specific information in order to carry out assigned tasks.

Information Overload   Communication theorists claim that the mind is limited to dealing with seven (plus or minus two) bits of information at any one time. Too much information is, indeed, hard to handle. In these times when Western society is being inundated with information, no one person could begin to keep up with all of the information generated for a single profession, even if the person worked at doing so full-time. In an attempt to alleviate the problem of information overload, electronic databases have been designed to store and retrieve information by key term. Using key terms, or descriptors, a person accessing an electronic database is able more efficiently to sort through the mass of data stored, to obtain only that information most relevant to his or her work. Database search techniques are discussed in Chapter 12.

An error commonly made by managers is to provide too much information too fast to project members. Much of the information is interesting or nice to know, but may not be really essential to the project. When project members lack the time or inclination to sort through masses of information, they tend to make decisions unsupported by data, and projects suffer. Thus, it has become a major responsibility of managers to see that essential information is filtered from the mass and provided to users in a digestible size, in the form needed, and at the time needed.

Uncertainty   The opposite of too much information is too little. Filling in the blanks may be very difficult, and result in errors that can create serious problems for a project. Besides the affects of too little information on *uncertainty*, there are also problems due to *ambiguity* of the special terminology used by different groups. To gain precision and efficiency in communicating among their members, all professions have developed their own particular jargon, having special and shortcut meanings for concepts and relationships. This is equally true for street corner gangs, rap groups, plumbers, and politicians. For example, engineers have devised blueprint symbols that communicate a great deal of information to those who know the meanings of the symbols. Instructional developers also have special ways of communicating among their members, but too often their special terminology confuses and irritates clients ("How do you say that in English?"). The degree of uncertainty in a message will influence the efficiency with which it is understood and responded to by clients and staff.

To illustrate how too little information can cause decision makers to suffer uncertainty, consider the following example. A real estate broker bought a large tract of land, zoned industrial. He divided the tract up into 100 lots, and put them up for sale at $100,000 each. He soon became concerned when the lots failed to sell. After some analysis he decided that the reason no one was buying was that they didn't want to make that kind of investment without seeing some evidence that others were also interested in buying lots in the tract. Their reasoning was that they needed to be sure that the area would become an active industrial area, and thereby protect their investment. To stimulate initial buyers, the broker decided to lower his price on two of the lots to $89,000 each. The two lots sold quickly, but then a serious problem arose. Because the broker had failed to make clear to his sales personnel that only two lots would be sold at the $89,000 price, he suddenly found himself inundated with buys for several other lots at that price, some of which he had to honor, at a considerable loss to his company.

The concept of *uncertainty* has had a long and interesting use in the hard and the social sciences. The Heisenberg and Garner statements of the uncertainty principle are well represented in the literature (Berrien, 1968). For purposes of analyzing communication systems, the principle can be stated as follows: All open systems are probabilistic systems. Be reminded that a system is *open* when information flows readily between it and its suprasystem, related systems, and/or its subsystems. Projects are basically problem-solving endeavors in which instructional elements are in a continuing flux of development, testing, and revision. To get the necessary information for such problem solving, projects are in constant need of information external to themselves. This means that there are always variables operating in projects whose values may be questionable for the needs of the project. The range in precision of available information essential to a project's processes makes it probable that results will vary somewhat from intentions.

Given the uncertainty of whether or not messages are interpreted satisfactorily by the persons receiving them, the question remains as to how project managers can best reduce the uncertainty in message transmission among those involved in their projects. The set of factors that follow are ones found to *reduce* uncertainty and error.

Redundancy One of the strengths of the English language is that it abounds with different ways of saying the same thing. If a message can't be gotten across in one configuration of words, then there is usually a number of other possible configurations that have the same meaning. This is called **redundancy**. As an example, consider these alternative ways of giving directions for getting to a particular location:

> Left on Elm, go to third stoplight, turn right, third house on left

> Take Venice Avenue to Elm and turn left, go 3 miles to Beech and turn right, find 817 Beech in middle of first block

> Take Halstead east to Beech and turn right, go one-half block past Elm to 817 Beech on left side of street

> Follow my car

Another way of saying the same thing would be to combine graphic and verbal signs as in Figure 11.5. As with verbal directions, there is a variety of ways of visually presenting the same information.

Not only may a manager verbally or graphically state the same message in different ways, he or she may also package it differently, that is, send it through different transmitters, e.g., face-to-face delivery, memo, phone, another person, a newsletter. The "Memo Writing" job aid gives some tips about one of these transmitters, i.e., how to write a memo that communicates effectively.

Care must be taken in not overusing memos. There is a tendency to ignore them if they become too profuse. For longer communiqués, abstracts of various types are used. An example of an abstract, or summary, would be the *Eisenhower Brief* technique presented in Chapter 10. Abstracts are basically summaries of longer reports. For some purposes,

**FIGURE 11.5 / Visual
directions to a location**

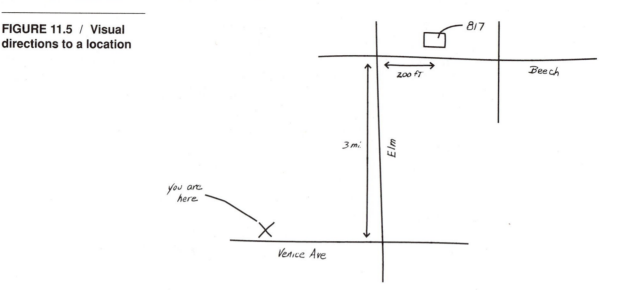

abstracts may serve in place of longer reports, or they may be used by readers as an advanced organizer for their study of the longer report.

Job Aid / Memo Writing

Description   The written memorandum is one of the most common communication techniques for providing information to individuals or to members of a group. It is usually short (one or two pages), and written in a consistent format. The concerns of memos usually are immediate, although they may serve the purpose of documenting conclusions or decisions of meetings or of phone conversations.

Use Rationale   A problem with passing brief, spoken messages on to project members is their ephemeral nature, and the difficulty of recalling what was said and decided at the time. Written memos are a formal means of communicating limited information and of keeping a record of such communications.

Critical Tasks

1. **Choose the memo to communicate a relatively short message.** E.g., reminder of a meeting's purpose, time and date; documenting a decision made at a previous meeting.

2. **Determine the target for the memo, and who it will be copied to.** This may also help decide whether the memo should be on letterhead or not. A letterhead gives a memo an appearance of official sanction.

3. **Determine if sending a memo must be cleared through higher authority.** If yes, get permission to send it out under your name or someone else's.

4. **Divide the memo into three parts.** Include identification, body, and reference sections.

   a. **Divide the identification section into four parts:**

continued

Memo Writing, continued

To: (target's name, and title)
From: (sender's name, and title, followed by verification initials)
Date: (date sent)
Re: (subject of memo)

b. Divide the body of the memo into three parts:

Orienting statement
        —provides reference point for reader
Message
        —limit to one topic
        —refer to any attached documents
Closing statement
        —Request for action
        —dates for action
        —sender telephone number for response to any questions

c. Complete the reference section:

Typed initials of sender and typist, e.g., CGG/jls
List names of those to whom message is copied.

5. Distribute original and copies.

6. File personal or office copy.

References

Ficker, B. (1975). *Effective Supervision*. Columbus, Ohio: Charles E Merrill, pp. 95–104.

Kalsem, P. J., and Johnston, N. M. (1945). *Practical Supervision*. 1st ed. New York: McGraw-Hill, pp. 119–120.

Scheer, W. E. (1982). *Personnel Administration Handbook*. 3d ed. Chicago, Ill.: Dartnell Press, pp. 265–271.

Feedback Part of determining whether information has been correctly understood and used is providing and receiving *feedback* on user understanding and application. **Feedback** is information received that assists in confirming or correcting project actions. Automatic feedback devices are common in our technological environment. The workings of a household thermostat are often used in illustration of the concept. The thermostat is a device whose purpose is to keep an even range of temperature in a house. The thermostat receives information that tells it whether the lower or the upper limits of the desired temperature range have been reached. Say that the desired temperature is between 65 and 70 degrees, Fahrenheit. If the temperature drops below 65 degrees, the thermostat activates a switch that causes the furnace to generate heat. When the temperature rises above 70 degrees, the thermostat throws a switch that shuts the furnace down. In an analogous way, standards of instructional development can be maintained by managers of projects by confirming or correcting the actions of team members. Feedback given by managers to project members is usually stimulated by questions, observations, or reported information, such as the staff weekly task report presented in Chapter 10.

Getting valid feedback from information users requires some skill on the part of the manager. It is better to get feedback *proactively* than *reactively*. That is, get the feedback at a point in the instructional development process before serious mistakes are made, when costs for correction are relatively low. For example, it is better to give clients a chance to match a new video script or storyboard against their expectations *before* the video crew begins shooting the scenes for it. Again, it is a question of who receives information and when it's received.

A common maxim among instructors is never to ask students questions to which they may answer simply "yes" or "no." The logic of this maxim is that all a yes-or-no response communicates is that students *think* they understand! Thus, if a student is asked, "Do you know what pages in the text you are to read?" and she responds "yes," the instructor still doesn't know if the student knows for sure. But if the instructor asks, "What pages are you to read in the text?" and the student responds "pages 331 to 367," the instructor will definitely know whether the student knows or not. Similarly, if a project staff member is asked if he has received information on a new graphics software package, a yes or a no doesn't tell much. But if he is asked what information he has received on the new graphics system and he responds that he received the manual for the *Adobe Illustrator 88* graphics system, the manager will really know whether or not he has received the desired information. One of the ways of getting feedback on whether certain information has been received or not is to attach a *return sign-off memo* to the communiqué or item sent to a staff member. An example of a return sign-off memo is presented in Figure 11.6. In this instance, C. Jones sent a manual through the local mail system to Bill Olrich, with a return sign-off memo attached. Olrich signed and dated the memo and sent it back to Jones, thus confirming that the manual had been received.

FIGURE 11.6 / Example of a return sign-off memo

Return Memo To:	C. Jones, Project Director
	Room 14
	Allison Hall
Item(s) Sent to You:	
	item: *Illustrator '88 manual*
	item:
	item:
Date Sent:	*February 13, 1988*
Date Received:	*February 17, 1988*
Received By:	*Bill Olrich*

Formating   In Chapter 10, the point was made that the format used to present information is itself information, because, based on knowledge of that format, the recipient can anticipate the type and location of information that is forthcoming. The memo format presented in the "Memo Writing" job aid gives clear indications to the reader in which section to look for the immediate information desired. Such knowledge of formats enables users to consume information more quickly and with less chance of misunderstanding.

Robert Horn has developed and tested several formats for presenting information effectively and efficiency. These formats, which he terms *information maps*, have been carefully researched and have proven effective. This technique is presented in Chapter 12 as a means of organizing information, but it is also an excellent means for presenting information.

The job aid on "Anticipating Communication Problems" covers many of the factors inhibiting or facilitating communication.

Job Aid / Anticipating Communication Problems

Description   This is a proactive technique that involves checking a communiqué against a set of criteria and then correcting those factors that do not meet the criteria. The technique does not tell *how* to correct the factors. An assumption is made that either the skills for making such corrections are available within the communicator or he or she has access to them elsewhere.

Use Rationale   Communiqués delivered to those involved with an instructional development project do not always adequately serve their intended purpose. Means for making them adequate are important to a project's progress.

Critical Tasks

1. **Determine how critical the information being communicated is to the project.** The more critical the information in the communiqué, the more attention should be paid to the following tasks.

2. **Determine whether project members already have access to the information to be communicated.** If they already have it, refer them to the information in the context of its importance.

3. **Determine whether the designated source of the information is credible to the receiver of the information.** If not, choose a more credible source, e.g., through the *Communications Network Analysis* technique.

4. **Determine if there is too much nonessential information in the communiqué.** If so, remove the nonessential information.

5. **Determine if additional information needs to be added to the communiqué.** If so, add information; e.g., use *PERT* as a guide to determining if additional information is required for the specific tasks in question.

continued

Anticipating Communication Problems, continued

6. **Determine if the information is in the best form for efficient and effective use.** If not, change to a more suitable format; e.g., use *Information Process Mapping*, *Memo Writing*, or other communication techniques.

7. **Determine if there are more cost-effective means of delivering the information.** If so, choose another means of delivery; e.g., through variations of the *Cost-Effectiveness* technique.

8. **Determine if the value of the information to the receiver is clear.** If not, find a means of relating the information directly to the team member's task at hand, usually by cover letter or memo.

9. **Determine if this is the appropriate time for the information to be delivered.** If not, change the time of delivery. Information is most likely to be used when it is delivered within 4–5 days of when it is to be applied.

10. **Send or deliver the corrected communiqué to the appropriate receivers.**

Reference

Gentry, C. G. (1978). Unpublished ID workshop communication exercise.

Means for Communicating Messages

A regularly updated *PERT* is a useful device for communicating information about where different members of a project are in their work, and what is coming up next. A PERT network also serves project managers by enabling them to anticipate what, and when, information is needed by each of the project members as they move from task to task. Similarly, the *Analytic Flowcharting* technique enables a manager to anticipate information needs covering alternative tracks through a project. Weekly task reports (see Chapter 10) written by project members on their activities also keep a manager sensitive to informational needs. *Troubleshooting* and *Walking About* techniques are other means by which a manager garners an understanding of informational needs. Once aware of the needs, the manager can consider the most appropriate means of collecting and communicating the information to those involved in the project. One means for doing this is through the weekly agenda and task sheet.

There are occasions when time and distance affect the choice of the communication technique. For example, if certain information is needed about new software that can only be obtained from a software producer several states away, the choice, depending on the time bind, might be regular mail, telephone, fax, or computer modem.

Meetings are another means for collecting and communicating information. Techniques used include committee meetings, *Nominal Group Process*, and one-on-one meetings. Within these meetings, several techniques may be used to communicate information, including lecture, overhead transparencies, discussion, simulations, and games.

Communication Effectiveness and Efficiency

How can the effectiveness and efficiency of a communication system be determined? One way would be to analyze the elements of a project communications system via the Shannon-Weaver model, to identify potential sources of message distortion and to make appropriate adjustments to prevent distortion from occurring. Questions that could be raised about information being communicated include: Did it arrive on time? Did it arrive in a format appropriate for the person receiving it? Was the information germane to the task? Was the information used as intended? Before the fact, members could be asked what information they think they need that they don't yet have. After the fact, a simple expedient would be to ask recipients if the information received was sufficient for the intended purpose. Clearly, these communication tasks take planning, resources, and execution. Often, managers are able to catch most of the problems at weekly meetings or in everyday contact with their project members. Even with problems that are caught late, corrections can still be made, and notes can be taken on how to avoid similar problems in the future.

Formalizing the Communication System

The factors, processes, and techniques discussed thus far provide the groundwork for the formal structure of a project communications system. The next few sections discuss the elements constituting a proposed structure for an ID project's communications system. The elements include: (1) a function statement, (2) system policies and rules, (3) network description, and (4) operational procedures.

Function Statement The function statement basically presents the central purpose that guides the project communications system. In this case, the function of an ID project's communications system is to ensure effective and efficient delivery of essential information among those involved in a project.

System Policies and Rules Policies are the general directives that guide the operation of an ID project's communications system. Policies define the broad limits and options in a system. Policies should not be confused with rules, which are more specific directives for guiding behavior in an organization. The communication policies developed for an ID project are usually very few, but should be enforced rigorously. Examples of such *policies* are:

1. Only designated persons will communicate with clients.
2. Information cannot be shared outside of the project without authorization by the manager.
3. Project personnel communications must follow the chain of command.

Examples of *rules* for a communications system are:

1. All project documents will be labeled with the names of the writer(s) of the document, the authorized receiver(s), and the date struck.

2. All personnel will submit a weekly report of their activities, following the prescribed format.

3. Any significant internal memo or report generated by project members should be copied to the manager.

In addition to the communication policies and rules formulated and enforced within a project are those of clients and other organizations that are relevant to the project. Often, their policies and rules relevant to the project are similar to the ones listed for the project.

Network Description   A description of a communications network can be simple or complex. Simply put, the network can be described in terms of the relationships among information users (by position or by name), lines of communication, and information sources. It can also be described in terms of its constituent hardware and software.

Information users include project members, selected members of the client system, and special consultants. In addition, software and hardware vendors and funding agents, external to both the project and the client system, may have some access to project and client information. These users may be listed by position and/or name.

Lines of communication are laid out to show who needs to talk to whom. Usually this discrimination is made for the sake of the efficient use of project members or to restrict the inadvertent dissemination of privileged or sensitive information. As mentioned earlier, two means for determining who should be communicating with whom, especially in large organizations are the organizational chart of a system and *Communications Network Analysis*. Many organizations are very proprietary about information regarding what is being developed and about information generated during development.

In most bureaucratic organizations the chain of command roughly parallels their lines of communication. For example, the organization's CEO (chief executive officer) talks to division managers, who talk to plant managers, who talk to assistant plant managers, who talk to building supervisors, who talk to assistant supervisors, who talk to workers. The kinds of information shared are dictated by policy and by need. There are exceptions and variations on this *bureaucratic* model theme from organization to organization. Even in large bureaucratic organizations, some persons at the bottom of the hierarchy may, under special conditions, speak to the ones at the top, e.g., by appointment, through a *Suggestion Box*, through *Walking about*. On the other hand, in small organizations it may be practical for everyone to communicate freely with everyone else. ID projects are usually organized on a *flat* model of administration, with few layers of administration between the top and the bottom groups. This is due to the problem-solving nature of instructional development projects, where time does not permit going through several layers of bureaucracy to get answers that are needed right away. Particularly sensitive is communication between project members and client members. The wrong thing said at the wrong time to the wrong person may jeopardize the continued relationship between the two groups. Experienced managers usually make very clear who on the project team may and may not converse with the client, and on what limited subjects.

Sources of information will vary with the needs of a specific project, but generally sources will include other project members, client personnel, organizational and commercial databases, materials and equipment vendors, and consultants. Designation of responsibility for garnering information from, or distributing information to, these groups, may be formal or informal. Managers have found it very important that responsibility for critical information be designated formally.

Hardware and software used to run a communications system are becoming increasingly sophisticated as computer-based systems are incorporated. This includes the more common local area networks (LANs), which are private communication networks connecting several personal computers by cable within a limited area, such as a building or a group of buildings. But it could, and often does, include the use of modems, which permit information in remote databases to be communicated electronically to the personal computers of staff personnel. Other common devices for communicating at a distance are by U.S. and private mail services, fax machines, and, of course, the telephone.

Operational Procedures   The procedures necessary to an ID project communications system's operations include budgeting, coordination, monitoring, maintenance, and assessment. *Budgeting* may include costs of such mundane items as copies from the copy center, or of having a graphic rendered for a report. At the other extreme, costs may soar when the decision is made to install a computerized network with individual work stations for project members and some client members, with all of the equipment and software that could entail. There are many related costs associated with running computer networks, such as access through modems to internal and external databases. Regardless of the sophistication of the communications system, each must be backed with sufficient economic resources if it is to be effective.

For smaller projects, the project manager alone is usually responsible for *monitoring* the communications system, making sure that the right information is accessible to those who need it when they need it. However, in larger systems there may be several individuals or groups with responsibility for monitoring. Monitoring of a communications system can be guided by the triple-threat PERT, in that the project's PERT enables managers to predict what types of communications should take place in order for specific tasks to be completed. Knowing that, they are able to check whether or not communications have taken place. For example, was a sign-off on proposed changes obtained from the client? Does the responsible project member have the 800 help number of the vendor who provided the new software? Was information on formative evaluation received and acted on?

Coordination of the procedures involved in an ID project's communications system also tends to fall on project managers. This can include taking responsibility, or assigning responsibility to others, for toot-our-horn activities that send newsletters and brochures to selected audiences, generally communicating the value, activities, and progress of a project. The coordinator also spends time gaining access for other project members to sources of information, and making sure that essential information is distributed appropriately. Other means of disseminating critical information inside the project group, mentioned earlier, are weekly task reports and meeting agenda and task assignment sheets.

Maintenance of a communication system can include the care and feeding of the computers used in a communication network, and reconciling personal or professional differences among project members. It often means finding alternative sources of information for project tasks. *Interface analysis* is a sophisticated means of identifying the flow of information in and related to an ID project.

The *assessment* of a project communications system draws most of its data from the monitor or from concerns broached by project members and clients. The intent here is to assess how well the communiqués serve the needs of the targeted users.

From a project manager's point of view, his or her involvement could generally be represented by the flowchart in Figure 11.7.

**FIGURE 11.7 /
Communication tasks
of project**

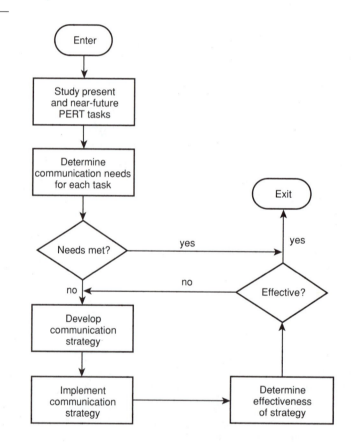

Each member of an ID project staff comes to the project with her or his own personal communications system intact. How does each interface with a communications system designed to facilitate the purposes of an ID project? A major way is to set up common *formats and schedules* for sharing information among members. As mentioned more than once, the weekly agenda and task sheet is one way that managers can communicate with staff members. A weekly meeting, where progress, problems, and changes in assignment are made, is another means by which the manager can pass on as well as receive important information. A cautionary concern is that meetings tend to perpetuate themselves, occurring whether important information is communicated or not. Managers should be sensitive to wasting time in meetings. Remember that an hour-long group meeting per week for twenty people consumes twenty man-hours per week, eighty per month, and almost a thousand hours per year. And that doesn't include preparation time for meetings. Several efficient techniques for running meetings, such as the *Broadwell/House Team Meeting Technique*, were reported in Chapter 10. Other means of improving communication include keeping to consistent formats for the memos and reports being sent to project members and clients. The consistent formats provided by other documents, such as those of a project's PERT, also help project members keep a common perspective.

Summary

Ensuring that project communications are sent to the proper persons, on time and in the appropriate format, is a major task of project managers. A position was taken in favor of maintaining a consistency in terms and formats used for communicating. The chapter looked at models, processes, factors, and techniques relevant to effective communication among those involved with a project.

References

Berrien, F. K. (1968). *General and Social Systems.* New Brunswick, N.J.: Rutgers University Press, pp. 48–54.

Lasswell, H. D. (1948). The structure and function of communication in society. In *The Communication of Ideas*, ed. Lyman Bryson. New York: Institute for Religious and Social Studies.

Parkinson, C. N. (1957). *Parkinson's Law.* New York: Ballantine Books.

Severin, W. J., and Tankard, J. W. (1988). *Communication Theories: Origins, Methods, and Uses.* New York: Longman.

Shannon, C. E., and Weaver, W. (1949). *The Mathematical Theory of Communication.* Urbana: University of Illinois Press.

Speer, D. C. (1972). *Nonverbal Communication.* Beverly Hills, Calif.: Sage.

Thompson, J. J. (1969). *Instructional Communication.* New York: American Book Company.

Vinsonhaler, J. F., Wagner, C. C., and Gentry, C. G. (1989). *People and Computers: Partners in Problem Solving.* New York: West.

CHAPTER 12

Information Handling

Process of selecting, collecting/generating, organizing, storing, retrieving, transmitting, and assessing information required by an ID project

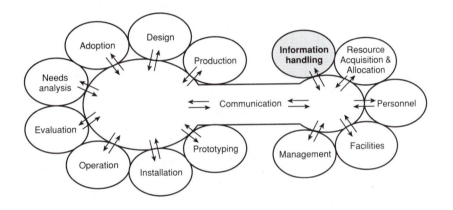

Learner Objectives

1. Describe and sequence components of the information-handling system model.

2. Describe the structural elements making up a database for an ID project.

3. Contrast advantages and disadvantages of electronic and manual databases for instructional development.

4. Justify the use of commercial databases for ID projects.

5. Describe the use of the ERIC educational database in ID projects.

6. Discriminate between *databases* and *database vendors*.

7. Recall definitions of major terms.

Introduction

As demonstrated in the last chapter, there is a close relationship between information handling and communication. **Information handling** has been defined as the process of selecting, collecting/generating, organizing, storing, retrieving, transmitting, and assessing information. The transmitting step in information handling is the central task of the communication component of the IPDM model. This step is included here in the information-handling process for the sake of continuity. The relationship between the communication component and the information handling component is another reminder that, while for instructional purposes these components are presented separately and largely in a linear fashion, there is, in fact, a dynamic interaction among them that leaves their operation far from linear.

The statement that information is what fuels the instructional development process has been repeated several times throughout this text. Naisbitt (1982), in his book *Megatrends*, makes the case that Western industrial society is rapidly evolving into an information society, and that Western man is suffering a deluge of information. In fact, there is such a mass of information being generated for every profession, no single individual could possibly read more than a fraction of it. A most important task for all professionals is to learn how to sort through this mass to find the most useful information for their purposes. This skill is certainly valuable to educational technologists, because of the broad sweep of information necessary to their generalist role.

Part of the solution for handling the flood of information has been to set up massive electronic databases designed to facilitate the search for relevant information. But before considering the use of databases, the information-handling process needs to be put into some kind of conceptual context.

Information-Handling Model

The simplistic model in Figure 12.1 is an attempt to look at information-handling systems in terms of their structure. Each of the eight elements making up the model is considered necessary to effective information handling. The purpose of the *selection* element is to determine what information is needed to complete a task, and to generate specifications for the needed information. For example, specifications could be written for a set of behavioral objectives needed for each of the instructional modules to be developed by a project. These specifications are written in terms of *what kind* of information is sought, not the actual information. Acquiring the information specified, e.g., written performance objectives, is the function of the *collection* element of the model. It is possible that the objectives sought already exist, or it may be necessary to contract or assign someone to *generate* them before they can be "collected." The *organization* element follows next, because, rarely is the collected information in the desired final form or sequence for its intended purpose. Having organized the information, it is usually important to preserve it for later use or, more perfunctorily, to put it in *storage*. Storage is intimately related to the process of *retrieval*, or accessing information. The *maintenance* element is concerned with keeping the information updated and in good repair, regardless of its format (e.g., printed documents, video, audio, photographs, graphics, computer discs).

FIGURE 12.1 / Information-handling system model

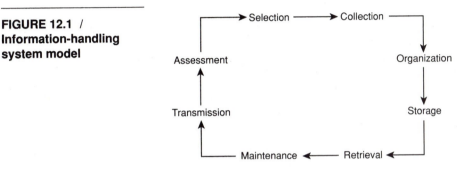

At some point in the ID process, essential parts of the stored information are delivered to those who will use it to forward development of the instruction. This is the function of the *transmission* element, and includes both distribution and circulation of information. In the *distribution* process, the receiver does not have to return transmitted information. However, in the circulation process, a document, or whatever was circulated, eventually will need to be returned to storage. Again, this is the focus of the communication component. The last process of the model is *assessment*, which concerns itself with the degree to which specific information has served the user's purpose. Based on that assessment, additional selection decisions may have to be made to satisfy a project's information needs. Thus, the cycle begins again, as shown in the figure.

Information-Handling Process

The steps in the information-handling process closely follow the steps of the model presented in Figure 12.1:

1. Determine and specify the information needed.
2. Acquire or generate the required information.
3. Arrange and/or refocus the information so that it more closely fits a specified need.
4. Categorize, store, and retrieve information in the project database.
5. Maintain information stored in the database.
6. Distribute or circulate information to appropriate individuals.
7. Assess the effects of the information in terms of its intended purpose.

These steps are the subject of the next sections of this chapter.

Selecting and Specifying Information

The range of information required by an ID project of any size is considerable. Determining exactly *what* information is needed is the function of the selection process. Of course, if the project staff is made up of experienced professionals with ready access to content specialists, much of the information required will reside among them. However, despite the level of experience and knowledge brought to bear, information-handling problems invariably crop up in a project during its run.

While there may be a dearth of some information, usually there will be an overabundance of other information. The latter is partially the result of a tendency among project staff to collect "nice to know" information that may "some day" be useful. Not only does such information clog up the system, but its collection and maintenance is costly and time-consuming. All of which supports the conclusion that the search for information is best restricted to what is directly applicable to a project. One way of questioning the need for the information is to ask "How does this particular information assist in meeting objectives of the project and of the instruction?" Or more specifically, "How does the information contribute to completing a particular project task?" If the information can't be demonstrated as clearly necessary for those purposes, then the collection of such information can be foregone.

Once it is clear in the requester's mind what information is needed, it is important to provide a few guidelines to the persons who are to collect or generate the information. For example, they need to know when the information is to be delivered, how accurate and complete it must be, and in what format. In a real sense these are also *design specifications* for the information. To illustrate, assume that behavioral objectives for instructional modules need to be acquired or written. A set of specs for this informational need might look like the data element specification document in Figure 12.2. The headings in the document are not exhaustive, and other headings may be pertinent for different information requests.

Acquiring/Generating Information

The process of collecting (i.e., acquiring and/or generating) information needed for an ID project is not without pitfalls. For example, care must be taken when collecting data within a client system to determine whether the information collected is viewed as proprietary or as subject to limited access. Every organization has policies and rules about access to their information. The developer should go through proper channels of the organization to get information and to get sign-offs, especially for use of sensitive information. Another problem that collectors have is ensuring that information is accurate. Often, there are errors in in-house information. When possible, the collector should check the data with a second source. A third problem that collectors endure is verifying ownership and getting permission for use of information coming from external sources (e.g., books, journals, documents, and nonprint materials). A number of cases where copyright has been ignored created serious embarrassment and sometimes considerable cost to the violator, even though the violation may have been unintended.

FIGURE 12.2 / Example of specifying needed information

DATA ELEMENT SPECIFICATION DOCUMENT

Date: December 28, 1991
Requested by: C. B. Kappan, designer
Authorized by: J. P. MacMillin, project manager
Date needed: February 15, 1992
Project: Sex education instruction for third-graders

Information Requested: A set of behavioral objectives for teaching a module on sex education for third-grade students.

Completeness: Write only the *behavior* part of the objectives, excluding *conditions*, and the *criteria* elements. Objectives should be focused on the following topics:

1. relevant definitions
2. purposes of sex
3. morality of sex
4. process of sex
5. problems of sex
6. responsibility of sex

Readability: At the second-grade level

Accuracy: Without error, within the bounds of readily accessible knowledge

Format: Place the objectives in a list under the six topic headings, above, and sequence them by number in the order to be taught. Report them on 8½ × 11-inch sheets of paper, three-hole punched.

Other: No

Experienced collectors check first to see if the desired information already exists, either in the system or outside of the system, before making a decision to generate it. Unfortunately, there is a bias that says, "If it wasn't created here, it won't work here." This bias has historically obstructed the use of existing information, despite its suitability, and has unnecessarily cost untold numbers of dollars for the regeneration of information. The job aid on "Acquiring Project Information" is an effective procedure for instructional developers to follow. Cost-minded instructional developers are constantly on the lookout for items to build up a database of information that can be used across many different ID projects.

Organizing Information

Information when first collected is seldom in the most useful form for those seeking it. Major reasons for this are that the information may contain portions not useful for the intended purpose, may come from several sources and need to be synthesized, may need to be resequenced, may

Job Aid / Acquiring Project Information

Description   This technique presents guidelines to be followed in a basic search for project information. The technique directs the searcher to look for existing materials that might serve the purpose when to do so would be less expensive than developing the information anew. It also presents steps for carrying out the search.

Use Rationale   Having a straightforward process to follow in searching for materials can reduce the time and cost of such searches.

Critical Tasks

1. **Determine the information needed.** Check with requesters or specifiers. A precise statement of the information needed should be made, e.g., "information on applications of interactive videodisc technology."

2. **Determine if the information already exists in-house.** Sometimes, because of the format or context, it may not be easy to recognize the relevance of existing information already in the system.

3. **Determine if a search must be made outside of the system.** Do so when the information is not found in-house or if costs of generating the information are prohibitive.

4. **Generate specific descriptors for the search.** For example, in a search for information on the use of computers in elementary education, the four descriptors *elementary, school, computers,* and *applications* might be used singly or in combination.

5. **Carry out the search for the desired information.** Complete the following tasks:
   a. Check for alternative materials.
   b. Check for alternative sources.
   c. Collect the data.
   d. Keep complete references on all information collected.
   e. Note any materials that require copyright release.

6. **Make arrangements for internal or external generation of information.** This is done if it is not otherwise available.

7. **File the generated or collected information by topic.** This ensures easy retrieval for future use, and creates safe copies, in case others are lost.

8. **Deliver the information files to the requester.**

Reference

Hussain, K. M. (1973). *Development of Information Systems for Education.* Englewood Cliffs, N.J.: Prentice-Hall.

Job Aid / Organizing Project Information

Description This technique provides a set of tasks for organizing information found and/or generated internally and/or externally so that the information more closely fits a project's requirements.

Use Rationale Information, particularly when parts come from different sources, often needs to be edited and resequenced to fit the new purpose.

Critical Tasks

1. **Receive the information that was generated and/or acquired.** Check with the requesters or specifiers.

2. **Organize the search result into a rough draft.** Complete the following tasks:
   a. Place the information in the desired format.
   b. Ensure the completeness of the information.
   c. Ensure the accuracy of the information.
   d. Ensure compatibility, e.g., language, equipment, readability.
   e. Remove any nonessential information.
   f. Resequence materials as appropriate.
   g. Modify the linkages or interfaces between segments, to ensure continuity.

3. **Check the rough draft of the document.** I.e., against client need. Revise as needed.

4. **Seek the release of any copyrighted materials.** This should be done early, before too much dependence on the information occurs, so that if refused, alternative sources can be sought.

5. **Finalize the information product.** Do this in appropriate format, fully documented.

6. **Deliver the product, and get a sign-off from the client**.

References

American Psychological Association. (1983). *Publication Manual of the American Psychological Association.* 3rd ed. Washington, D.C.: the Association.

Hussain, K. M. (1973). *Development of Information Systems for Education.* Englewood Cliffs, N.J.: Prentice-Hall.

need adjustment of its readability or vocabulary levels, may need to be put into a context that fits other information used by the project, or may need to be put into a different format. A process for making these modifications is presented in the job aid on "Organizing Project Information."

A technique developed by Robert E. Horn for organizing information into clarifying formats is called *Information Process Mapping.* This version of information mapping is the subject of ongoing research. Some of the research results are very impressive. As an example, in one piece of research, subjects using the Information Mapping version made 54.5%

fewer errors than did subjects using a conventional method (Shaffer, 1982). The preparation of information maps is time consuming and requires some training, as well as a certain amount of commitment on the part of team members. The "Information Process Mapping" job aid presents a much shortened version of Horn's technique. This job aid is an adaptation using merely one type of block in one type of map. Horn's mapping formats are extensive and capable of dealing with much more complex information than the one presented here. For a more in-depth understanding of his information mapping model, readers are encouraged to check the references.

Job Aid / Information Process Mapping

Description   Information Process Mapping is part of a larger technique called *Information Mapping.* Information Mapping was developed by Robert Horn for the U.S. Air Force, for purposes of making communication of project information easier and quicker. It is constituted of a set of rules for placing data in formalized information blocks. There are six different types of information mapping formats: structure, procedure, process, classification, concept, and fact. *Only the process mapping format is considered here.* A *process* is some structure changing through time, usually for some identifiable purpose. An information process map describes such changes. See the example in Figure 12.3.

Use Rationale   One of the most serious problems in any endeavor is ensuring accurate communication among project members about aspects of processes. The use of information process mapping has been demonstrated to increase efficiency as much as 50% in different projects.

Critical Tasks

1. **Determine that the data to be communicated are concerned with a process.** This includes any information that can be divided into time chunks, such as stages, or where there are changes of structure, or where words like *cause-effect, functioning,* and *action* are included, or where there is description of movement.

2. **Gather the specific data that are to be included in the information process map.** E.g., data on the operation of a gasoline engine.

3. **Sequence the data in blocks according to the information process map format.** There are two types of blocks used in information process mapping, as shown in Figure 12.4: those that are common to all information maps, and those that are specific to information *process* maps only. In the figure the *common blocks* are listed in the sequence as they would occur in a map. Usually, only one or two of the *specific blocks* are used in any single process map. The example in Figure 12.3 uses a stage table block.

4. **Refine the information process map blocks by applying appropriate rules.**
   a. Make sure the topic of the map is clearly limited.
   b. Make sure the data, in appropriate blocks, are complete.
   c. Make sure that each block is correctly labeled in terms of the function or content of the block.

continued

Information Process Mapping, continued

FIGURE 12.3 / Sample of an information process map

OPERATION OF A GASOLINE ENGINE

Introduction | The gasoline engine gets its power from the burning of a mixture of gasoline and air in the cylinders of the engine

Process

Stage	Description	Diagram
A	During the first stroke, the inlet valve is opened and the descending piston sucks the gas-air mixture into the cylinder.	
B	During the <u>compression</u> (second) <u>stroke</u>, the valves are closed. The piston rises and compresses the gas-air mixture.	
C	The third stroke is called the <u>power stroke</u>. The spark plug causes a very small, hot spark to ignite the gas-air mixture. This makes the mixture expand rapidly and forces the piston downward.	
D	During the <u>exhaust stroke</u> (fourth stroke), the exhaust valve is open and the piston moves upward to push the burned gases from the cylinder.	

---

d. Make sure that long series of words or phrases are tabulated in a column.

e. Make sure appropriate words, such as <u>not</u>, are underscored.

f. Do not refer within a block to previous maps or blocks.

g. Use letters (A, B, etc.) to sequence state and stage tables, and use bullets for all other lists.

h. Start each new map at the top of a page, to reduce confusion.

continued

Information Process Mapping, continued

FIGURE 12.4 / Examples of possible blocks common to all information maps, and to those specific to information process maps only.

Common Blocks	Specific Blocks
Name of map	State table
Introduction	Stage table
Comment	Parts-function table
Synonym	Block diagram
Diagram	PERT chart
Analogy	Cycle chart
Related page	

5. Distribute the new information process map to the appropriate persons.

Reference

Horn, R. E. (1976). *How to Write Information Mapping*. Lexington, Mass.: Information Resources, pp. 1–33, 76–86.

Storing and Retrieving Information

Systems for storing and retrieving information serve several purposes: to ensure ready access to the information; to ensure that environmental conditions are adequate for preserving the print and nonprint information; to protect proprietary information; and to ensure the information is not lost for later use. Probably, the most desirable way of setting up in-house storage and retrieval for *printed material* of a project is through an electronic database, but manually operated databases can also serve that purpose. Both will be discussed. There will also be a presentation on the use of commercial databases. The job aid nearby describes "Implementing an ID Project Database."

Job Aid / Implementing an ID Project Database

Description   This technique provides a generic set of steps for using any of the several excellent database software programs to store and retrieve ID project information and to generate reports. The actual steps in using a database will depend on the specific program chosen. This job aid focuses on database objectives for the project, design of the database, development of the project database, storing and retrieving data, report generation, and evaluation of the project database.

continued

Implementing an ID Project Database, continued

Use Rationale   ID projects require information in order to function. Much of the information used is specific to a particular project, thereby requiring its own database. Most of the relevant information is verbal and graphic in nature, and can be easily stored and retrieved electronically in a computerized database.

Critical Tasks

1. **Select appropriate database software.** Choose software based on how compatible it is with the project's computer systems, and how easily it permits data entry, storage, retrieval, and report generation.

2. **Determine the database objectives.** Specify the different ways the database will help instructional developers meet their goals and solve their problems.

3. **Design the database.** The design should be based on objectives. List all record types, all fields in each record, and characteristics of each field. Create a set of prototypical records for purposes of periodically testing the database as development proceeds.

4. **Develop the database.** Start up the database program, choose *record definition* mode, and enter all information regarding the form of records.

5. **Enter and edit the database records.** Start the *data entry/edit* mode, and begin entering data into the system, and then save to disc.

6. **Retrieve the records for deletion or alteration.** Retrieve them using appropriate search commands, make any changes, and then save to disc.

7. **Prepare to generate reports from the database.** Complete the following steps:
   a. Determine the objectives of the specific report (since many reports can be generated from the same database, the user's purpose must be considered in each case).
   b. Design the report: determine the records to be used; the form of the report, including what existing fields, computed fields, and text labels should appear; and the order in which the records should be placed for report generation.
   c. Develop the report: start up the database, call up *report definition* mode, enter information regarding the form of the report, the fields included in the report, and other details. Save the report definition to disc.

8. **Generate reports from the database.** Access the database, retrieve the desired records, sort the records into desired order, access the proper report definition, and start the report process. Send the report either to print or disc file.

9. **Evaluate/edit the report.** Have users inspect the report to see if they agree it serves the intended purpose. Edit in any appropriate modifications.

10. **Evaluate the database.** Do this initially at different times during development, by running the prototypical records developed earlier through the database. After the database is satisfactorily implemented, maintain a log of project and client members' reactions to the reports generated, as evaluation data pointing to revisions in the database.

continued

Implementing an ID Project Database, continued

Reference

Vinsonhaler, J. F., Wagner, C. C., and Gentry, C. G. (1989). *People and Computers: Partners in Problem Solving.* New York: West, pp. 354–356.

There are also a number of inexpensive, manual database systems available. One technique that attempts to combine the better qualities of several different manual database systems is taught in the "PIFS" job aid.

Job Aid / Personal Inverted Filing System (PIFS)

Description   This is an effective technique that educators and other professionals have used to store and retrieve information. Its major advantages lie in its capacity to retrieve by more than one key term (e.g., one could retrieve all articles that deal with the combined terms of *elementary education, media,* and *mastery learning*) and to find rapidly any document in the system. Each document or article going into the PIFS is given its own unique accession number, which is entered onto one or more matrix sheets, which in turn make up the physical part of the storage-and-retrieval system. Each of the matrix sheets is labeled with an individual key term; by matching the sheets, relevant documents are identified that contain the desired key terms. Documents are kept in a second folder, in the sequence of their accession numbers so they are easy to find.

Use Rationale   All professionals have the problem of finding information that they have filed away. Most systems are catch-as-catch-can and are not terribly effective or efficient. This system enables the user to store and retrieve information with minimum hassle and consumption of time.

Critical Tasks

1. **While reading a document, identify and circle potential key terms in the document itself.** This will make them easy to spot later. E.g., select key terms out of an article for evaluating short-term training programs, such as: *evaluation, faculty development, workshop, seminar, simulation, method, instrument, rating scale, debriefing,* and *standards.* When finished reading, write all of the key terms at the top of the document. This will save searching for them later when you begin entering them into PIFS.

2. **Write the full bibliographic reference at the top of the first page of each document you read.** This ensures that you will be able to reference accurately the document or article later, when you pull it from storage.

3. **Reconcile the potential key terms in the document against the ones in your current thesaurus.** You may be using a commercial thesaurus, e.g., ERIC, or you may begin your own. Your own **thesaurus** would consist of only the list of key terms from your documents, in alphabetical order. Don't include several terms in your thesaurus meaning the same thing. E.g., don't use both *video* and *television;* use one or the other. Add any new terms to your thesaurus as you go along.

continued

Personal Inverted Filing System (PIFS), continued

4. **Label a new matrix sheet for each new key term.** Each key term or descriptor must have its own matrix sheet. Matrix sheets are usually $8\frac{1}{2} \times 11$-in., and are oriented the long way (see Figure 12.5). The matrix consists of ten columns and twenty-five rows. The columns are labeled 0 through 9. The key term identifying each matrix is written on a tab at the top of the sheet. The matrix sheets are kept together, in alphabetic order, in a folder next to the document folder.

FIGURE 12.5 / Example of matching up matrix sheets using three key terms

Training

0	1	2	3	4	5	6	7	8	9
30				54	25		47	18	
40				(84)	65			(58)	

Interactive Video

0	1	2	3	4	5	6	7	8	9
50		12		34	15			28	39
60		32		(84)				(58)	
				104				78	

Self-Instruction

0	1	2	3	4	5	6	7	8	9
10		22		14	5		17	(58)	
20		52		24	45		27	98	
70				(84)			77		

5. **Assign an accession number to the document being entered.** The identifying number of the document will be the next one available. If, e.g., the last article entered was given the number 75, then the next one will be assigned 76. All documents will be stored in a folder, by their respective accession numbers for easy retrieval.

6. **Enter the accession number in the appropriate matrix sheets.** Using the key terms appropriate for the article, pull the matrix sheets for those terms, and enter the article's unique number into each matrix. Enter a number onto the sheet according to its last digit. E.g., if the accession number is 135, that number would be entered in the column under 5, 50 would be under column 0, 38 would be under column 8, etc. See Figure 12.5. Note that the article with accession number 52 is entered under column 2 of the Self-Instruction Matrix sheet.

continued

Personal Inverted Filing System (PIFS), continued

7. **Store the documents by accession number.** A separate file folder is used for the actual documents. These are kept in the order of their accession numbers so that they can be easily found. If documents are thrown away, their accession number can be given to a new document.

8. **Retrieve the documents by key term and accession number.** When you decide what key terms or descriptors you need data on—say, *training, interactive video,* and *self-instruction*—pull the appropriate matrix sheets and match them up to find any common accession numbers for relevant articles. Note the three overlapping matrix sheets in Figure 12.5. In this instance, documents 84 and 58 are found entered on all three matrix sheets, meaning that the three key terms are related in the two documents with accession numbers 58 and 84. These documents can then be quickly pulled from the document folder by their respective accession numbers.

9. **Remember to return the documents to the storage folder when finished.** The system only works if the documents are there if needed. Experience shows it is best not to loan the documents, but rather to make copies for distribution and return the originals to the folder.

References

Holmes, T. F., and Gentry, C.G. (1979). A foolproof personal filing system. *Audiovisual Instruction* May: 40–42.

Sheets, K. J. (1985). Evaluating short-term training programs. *Journal of Instructional Development* 8(1): 26–32.

Since the advent of readily assessible electronic databases, the use of manual database systems has been in decline. However, elements of manual systems, such as that of filing articles and other informational formats by accession number, will probably continue to be used for some time. It would certainly be desirable to be able to retrieve all information electronically, whether it be documents or video, or any other format, but currently it is simply not cost-effective to put all information into electronic form.

Electronic databases are proliferating rapidly. Universities have certainly been leaders in development of large databases for student and faculty use. Most North American universities provide student access to the services of the On-line Computer Library Center (OCLC). Its central computer holds over 7 million documents, available to students and faculty.

One of the many commercial databases from which information can be retrieved electronically by subscribers is the **Educational Resources information Center (ERIC)** database. It stores only printed matter. Its application is presented in "ERIC Search" job aid. The ERIC database can also be accessed through other technology. It can be purchased on a CD-ROM disc, called the Silver Platter, which plays on a CD-ROM disc drive attached to a personal computer. These are laser discs. Currently, these can be read from but not written to. Their value is that they can store a great deal of data on a small disc. Increasingly, libraries are making this form available to students and the general public.

Job Aid / ERIC (Educational Resources Information Center) Search

Description   ERIC is the largest of the electronic databases serving education. It holds over half a million citations that cover research findings, project and technical reports, books, and journal articles. The information in the database can be retrieved at different levels of abstraction, from a reference citation to full text. References are also provided for articles in major educational journals that refuse to have their works entered in ERIC. ERIC also has a manual counterpart, found in most large libraries, with the information stored on microfiche. Microfiche collections are updated monthly by about 3,500 citations.

Use Rationale   The searching of libraries for information is often unsatisfying to the researcher, for a variety of reasons: the book or document may be checked out, it may be on limited reserve, it may be floating somewhere in the system (e.g., waiting on a cart to be reshelved), it may be lost, or the library may never have acquired the document in the first place. Electronic data searching has a cost. But compared to the search time, often futile, spent in a traditional library, the money is usually viewed as a cost-effective option. Also, much of the information stored in electronic databases cannot be found in the library, since it was generated for the databases in the first place.

Critical Tasks

1. **Determine the information needed.** A precise statement of the information need should be made, e.g., "information on applications of interactive videodisc technology toward the teaching of science to sixth-graders."

2. **List the descriptors to be used in the data search.** In the example in task 1, major descriptors or key terms could be: *applications, interactive videodisc, teaching, science,* and *sixth-graders.*

3. **Consult with the ERIC search specialist on a search strategy.** ERIC search specialists are usually reference librarians with an understanding of a variety of ways to approach the database. From past experience and training they are able to match up your descriptors with those recognized by the database. For example, *interactive videodisc* may be stored under the larger descriptor of *computer-assisted instruction.* The specialist will also understand how to sequence various combinations of your descriptors to get the maximum information out of the system.

4. **The ERIC search specialist carries out the search.** The options available are to provide the information in decreasing levels of abstraction, because of the cost. The first run is usually just bibliographical references, a second level could be a brief abstract, a third level could include a comprehensive abstract, and finally, the complete text of a document could be ordered up if desired. Since the cost varies according to these levels, the specialist will usually consult with you about which ones to run.

5. **Analyze the preliminary search readout.** The initial run will probably be a list of bibliographical references, ordered according to the combinations of descriptors used. Their titles usually provide enough information that you can choose the most likely candidates for running at the abstract or the full-text level. In addition, new combinations of descriptors may be used; e.g., *sixth-grader* may be too narrow a descriptor, and can be replaced with *primary* or *elementary school student.* Or perhaps a term narrower than *science,* e.g., *biology,* might bring you closer to the information you seek.

continued

ERIC (Educational Resources Information Center) Search, continued

6. **Run the primary search.** As indicated, different levels can be run. Full text can be run or if cost is a factor, one of the abstract levels can be chosen. Then you can go to the ERIC microfiche section in the library and study the documents for free, using a microfiche reader. Most libraries will also have the means to generate hard copies of the documents from microfiche, if desired.

Reference

Barnett, Lynn (ed.) (1980). *Thesaurus of ERIC Descriptors*. New York: Macmillan.

There are a number of other commercial databases available through vendors. Bibliographic Research Service (BRS), for example, has well over 150 separate databases, including ERIC, that users can subscribe to for a relatively nominal fee. Other similar vendors of databases are Compu-Serve, Dialog, Nexus, and The Source, to name four. The vendor databases are stored in main computers some distance away from their users. Access to the databases in the vendor's main computer is through the use of a telephone modem attached to the user's personal computer. Users simply dial a telephone number that connects their computer with the vendor's main-frame computer, and then enter a predetermined identification code, where upon they are presented with a menu of databases from which to select. Specific databases can then be searched by whatever key terms are appropriate for the particular task. Whole documents or references and abstracts of documents can be saved to the users' computer and/or printed out.

Maintaining Information

The maintenance element is concerned with information in its various media forms. The element's function is to check all information coming into storage (electronic or manual) to make sure it is in good repair. The range of repairs to be made could include replacement of missing pages in printed matter, the repair of a broken strip of 16mm instructional film, and the replacement of a damaged video segment or computer disc. The maintenance element is also responsible for **weeding (purging)** the database of information that is outdated or no longer in use.

Transmitting Information

As mentioned earlier, the transmission element is concerned with how project information is communicated by and to appropriate individuals involved with an ID project. The communication component is dealt with in detail in Chapter 11. This component serves to: ensure a consistent adherence to a system's communication policies; provide rules and procedures for the distribution and circulation of information; ensure that information gets to the client where and when needed; ensure security of information in transport; and ensure retrieval of information on temporary loan to users.

Assessing Effects of Information

Delivering information is one thing, but ascertaining its effectiveness is quite another. An assessment component in an information-handling system provides data relevant to several of the system's features: it periodically assesses the validity of its policies, objectives, and processes; it determines whether the broad and specific goals of the system have been met; it determines new informational needs of the users to be incorporated in the system; it provides data on the state of repair and obsolescence of materials in the system; it determines its level of efficiency and effectiveness; and it provides information on attitudes of users toward the information-handling system. Many of the same processes and techniques presented in Chapter 9, on evaluation, are relevant for assessing the effects of information on project tasks.

Model Synthesis

All of the elements in the information handling model detailed in the preceding sections are brought together in the "Information Handling" job aid. The skills and knowledge of information-handling processes and techniques is one of those areas in which educational developers should continuously update themselves.

Job Aid / Information Handling

Description The model presented in Figure 12.6 was adapted from the work of Khateeb Hussain (1973), and includes seven steps in handling information, each of which requires quite different skills. Each step deals with a specific information-handling process, i.e., selection, collection, organization, storage, retrieval, transmission, or assessment.

FIGURE 12.6 / Information-handling system model

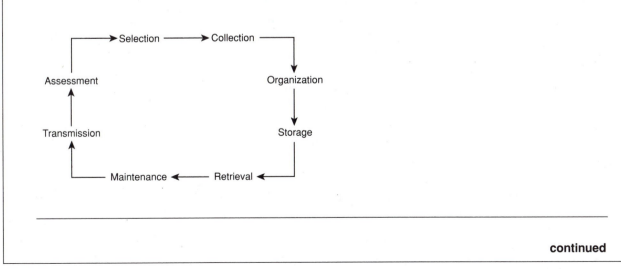

continued

Use Rationale The development of instruction, like many other human endeavors, requires a great deal of information. Knowledge of the concepts, processes, and skills necessary to the acquisition, treatment, storage, retrieval, and assessment of information is becoming increasingly important to instructional developers.

Critical Steps

1. **Select the appropriate information for the tasks.**
   a. Establish what objectives the information is to meet.
   b. Establish criteria for assessing the information in terms of its value to the project.
   c. Determine the priority level of this request for information in terms of resources available.
   d. Determine whether the information use is ephemeral or long-range.
   e. Determine the information format requirement.
   f. Determine how accurate and complete the information must be.
   g. Provide an information specification document for those responsible for collecting or generating the information.

2. **Collect the specified information.**
   a. Determine the information elements that exist and those that must be generated.
   b. Determine the potential sources for the information.
   c. Compare the costs for buying existing information, and for generating new information, through alternative sources.
   d. Compare existing and generated information in terms of the criteria provided by the selection component, to be sure it falls in the range of acceptability.
   e. Get copyright release on existing or generated information acquired, if appropriate.

3. **Reorganize, as necessary, the data collected to meet project needs.**
   a. Remove nonessential print or nonprint elements.
   b. Sequence the data appropriately for their purpose, when the data are drawn from more than one source.
   c. Resequence print or nonprint information from a single source, if appropriate.
   d. Provide linking information between the resequenced sections, as appropriate.
   e. Modify the format and vocabulary to match the project/client requirement.

4. **Process the information for storage and retrieval.**
   a. Storing the information:
      1) Classify, catalog, and write descriptors for all incoming new or old information.
      2) Inspect incoming old and new information for completeness, before storing.
      3) Refer print and nonprint for maintenance, replacement, and repair, as appropriate.
      4) Maintain proper environmental conditions to preserve the information in storage.
      5) Store information by descriptor or key terms.
   b. Retrieving the information:
      1) Receive a request or recognize a need for information from the project information-handling system.

continued

ERIC (Educational Resources Information Center) Search, continued

    2) Ensure that persons requesting information are cleared for access.

    3) Access information from storage for circulation or distribution by using descriptors.

5. Distribute and/or circulate (transmit) the information.

  a. Package the information for ease of transport and delivery.

  b. Schedule personnel to deliver and/or recover the information.

  c. Report overdue, lost, or damaged material.

  d. Notify the information user of the delivery-and-retrieval schedule.

7. Assess the effectiveness of the information.

  a. Collect data from users on how useful particular information was for their purposes.

  b. Determine information gaps in the system, and report them to the selection component.

  c. Weed out inadequate or inappropriate information.

  d. Collect data from users on the effectiveness and efficiency of the information provided and on the information-handling processes.

References

Gentry, C. G. (1978). Information Handling Systems. Unpublished class handout (CEP 833). East Lansing, Mich.: Michigan State University.

Hussain, K. M. (1973). *Development of Education Systems for Education.* Englewood Cliffs, N.J.: Prentice-Hall.

Vickery, B. C. (1973). *Information Systems.* London: Butterworths.

Summary

A specific information-handling model and its seven elements were discussed. The elements are selection, collection, organizing, storage, retrieval, transmission, and assessment. The relationship between information-handling systems and communications systems was explained. The transmission element in the information-handling model is presented as equivalent to the communication component, which has primary responsibility for delivering or transmitting information to users. The information-handling processes relevant to the model's seven elements were discussed in turn, and related to specific techniques.

References

Bass, R. K., and Dills, C. R. (eds.) (1984). *Instructional Development: The State of the Art.* Dubuque, Iowa: Kendall/Hunt.

Hawkridge, David (1983). *New Information Technology in Education.* Baltimore, Md.: Johns Hopkins University Press.

Helvey, T. C. (1971). *The Age of Information.* Englewood Cliffs, N.J.: Educational Technology Publications.

Hicks, W. B., and Tillin, A. M. (1970). *Developing Multi-Media Libraries.* New York: Bowker.

Horn, R. E. (1974). Information mapping. *Training in Business and Industry.* pp. 27–32.

Horn, R. E. (1972). *Developing Procedures, Policies and Documentation.* Waltham, Mass.: Information Mapping, Inc.

Naisbitt, John (1982). *Megatrends: Ten New Directions Transforming our Lives.* New York: Warner Books.

CHAPTER 13

Resource Acquisition and Allocation

Process of determining resource needs, formalizing budgets, and acquiring and distributing resources

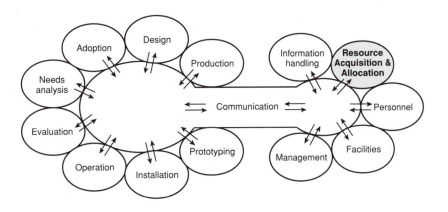

Learner Objectives

1. Discriminate among the four general budget types.

2. Explain the value of the four budget types to ID projects.

3. Explain how electronic spreadsheets support developing and maintaining budgets.

4. Explain and provide examples of *direct* and *indirect* costs.

5. Recognize major directories listing external sources of project funding.

6. List factors that assist in prioritizing potential funding sources.

7. Explain the process for developing and submitting a proposal for project support.

8. Describe the process of allocating and reallocating project resources.

9. List common steps for closing out a project.

10. Recall definitions of major terms.

Introduction

Careful selection of the means for obtaining and allocating resources is critical to the success of any ID project. Sources of funding for projects are varied, and the means by which they are acquired are just as varied. Once resources are acquired, managers are responsible for their allocation and reallocation to project activities. The budget is an essential instrument for carrying out these processes. Remember, the three primary tasks for project managers are to meet project objectives, on time, and *within the budget.*

What is a budget? A **budget** can be viewed as the financial statement of the objectives, programs, and activities of a system. A more specific definition is proposed by Wildavsky (1964, p. 1): "In the most literal sense a budget is a document containing words and figures, which proposes expenditures for certain items and purposes." In other words, it is a formal statement of anticipated revenues and expenditures for a given period.

Budgets are supportive of organizations in terms of both policy and administrative perspectives (Mosher, 1968). From the policy standpoint, budgets provide regular opportunity to reexamine the goals and objectives of an organization. It also expedites cost–benefit and cost-effectiveness analyses of alternative plans. In addition, it assists communication between administrators, who set funding limits, and project managers, who apply the funds to project tasks. Budgets may also assist in establishing **accountability**, i.e., making specific personnel responsible for their portion of the budget. For some organizations, such as governmental agencies, budgets may provide the legal basis for expenditures.

How budgets are categorized varies across organizations, but most of them fit under one of four general types. The first, and simplest type is the **no-budget budget**, which really represents incongruities in the main budget type used by the system. Most organizations leave some slack in their budgets, allowing for discretionary movement of funds in and out of certain accounts. The amount of slack depends on how stringent are the rules for shifting funds among the accounts of the budget. Sometimes, special line items are deliberately included in a budget for the very purpose of covering unforeseen needs. One name for such budget lines is the **contingency account.** Another budgeting practice that provides a clue to some available funds are those budgets that have revolving accounts. **Revolving accounts** are basically accounts for holding transitory funds that are earmarked for specific tasks and are being held there temporarily until needed. Few questions are asked of revolving accounts as long as the amounts in them are the same at the end of the fiscal year as at the beginning (usually close to zero). This provides enterprising individuals with the opportunity to bring in funds from different endeavors, and pay out for others, without having to account for their actions at a higher level. For example, the revolving account in a media center at one university known to the author would buy and sell to students for their class projects items such as photographic film and processing. The media center built in an overhead cost, plus a small profit on each item that was paid into the revolving account. This gave media center personnel a source of contingency funds for themselves for which they did not have to account. Often, home organization administrators are aware of what is going on but turn their heads the other way, unless of course there is a serious disparity between the beginning and ending amounts for the year.

Such budgets or accounts are the target of entrepreneurs seeking funds through the no-budget budget window. While these funds are seldom extensive or dependable, some instructional developers have become quite adept at ferreting them out and convincing those in control to allocate some of their funds to ID projects. Another common source of no-budget budget funds are those budgets written when the costs for certain activities were not known or were uncertain. When budgeting in strange territory, budgeters may write in funds for a particular resource about whose need they are uncertain, and later discover that the resource is not needed, providing a surplus of funds. Such accounts may be responsive to outside requests. Another opportunity to gather in funds from others' budgets comes at the end of the fiscal year, when any budget moneys not spent are expected to be returned to the general fund of the central administration. Managers try to avoid returning unspent money, because not only don't they get to spend the money returned, but in all likelihood their budgets will be trimmed the succeeding year, based on the amounts they previously turned back. To avoid such cuts, there is a general scurrying around at the end of the fiscal year to find a respectable place to spend the excess. A job aid teaching how to take advantage of the end-of-fiscal-year budget shuffle is the *Proactive Requisitioning* technique, presented in Chapter 8.

A second type of budget is called the **object–function budget**. Here similar expenditures are clustered under a general category. Typical categories are shown in Figure 13.1. For example, all moneys paid to hourly or salaried personnel in a project might be accumulated under the category of "salaries." Similarly, moneys used by different personnel for transportation would be accumulated under the "travel" category. In the budget, these broader categories may be broken down further. For example, under "salaries" may be listed the names or titles of personnel, along with their respective salaries. While this type of budget is popular, because it is easy to understand and manage, it does not assist in determining how effective the expenditures were in terms of specific project objectives. In their critique of budget types, Gillespie and Spirt (1973, pp. 85–86) argue that object–function budgeting is based on a faulty assumption, that "certain resources are needed to perform certain functions, based on the belief that

FIGURE 13.1 / Typical object–function budget categories, with cost examples

Categories	Costs
Salaries	$37,626
Travel	7,600
Communication	1,200
Maintenance	900
Equipment	6,000
Supplies	1,825
Other	2,180

certain activities always produce certain results." They point out that this assumption is rarely true because of the variation in human behavior. Nevertheless, object–function budgeting is the most popular budget type among organizations today.

A third type of budgeting is the **performance budget**. This budget also clusters moneys to be allocated by general category, but these categories are put in a matrix that enables a manager to see what specific task or unit of work is supported by what expenditure within each category. Note an example of a performance-budget matrix in Figure 13.2. This particular budget matrix example is focused on the design step in instructional development. The first column lists the general budget categories, which are matched, in the other columns, with basic units of work necessary to the design process. Clearly, the headings for the column to the right would change depending on the work being funded. While the performance budget ties funds to specific units of work or tasks, it still does *not* tie funds directly to the specific objectives of projects.

FIGURE 13.2 / Example of a performance-budget matrix for design [adapted from Gillespie and Spirt (1973)]

Accounts	Writing Objectives	Writing Test Items	Selecting Strategies	Selecting Media	Writing Design Specifications
Salaries	(Time needed for each design activity, converted to dollars)				
Equipment	(Cost of equipment for each design activity, in dollars)				
Supplies	(Etc.)				
Communication					
Travel					
Maintenance					
Etc.					

The fourth type of budget expands the concept of performance budgeting, and is termed the **Planning, Programming, Budgeting, Evaluating System (PPBS).** "Evaluating" is left out of the acronym to ease memory. This budget type *does* relate the expenditure of funds to the specific objectives of a project. While desirable in concept, it has been difficult to apply. To this point, the major users of PPBS have been governmental agencies, and they have used it with questionable success.

Most budgets in large organizations fall under the object–function type. Instructional developers usually translate their final budgets to the form used by their respective funding agencies. However, in working up initial project costs, something like the performance type of budgeting is more useful to developers in arriving at accurate estimates of project costs, and for allocation and monitoring purposes. The next section shows how budgeting fits into the overall process of resource acquisition and allocation.

Resource Acquisition and Allocation Process

The following processes are important to **resource acquisition and allocation**. This process begins after instructional developers have satisfied themselves that the project in question is worth doing and that it falls within their area of expertise.

1. Determine the resource needs of a project.
2. Write up a trial budget.
3. Identify potential sources of resources.
4. Study procedures by which potential sources make their funding decisions.
5. Prioritize potential sources of funds.
6. Write up a proposal for the project according to the funding agency's format.
7. Submit the proposal for funds (to the most likely source).
8. Modify the proposal, as necessary, based on the response of the funding agency.
9. Repeat steps 3–8 until funding is obtained.
10. Allocate and reallocate resources according to need.
11. Close out the project.

While these steps may be logical in their sequence, the process is not as linear as is implied. Actual procedures and sequences vary, depending on the particular project and the person acquiring and allocating resources. For example, the instructional developer may have a specific funding source in mind before he or she ever begins this process.

Determining Resource Needs

The first step in the costing of projects requires a listing of the tasks that must be performed for the project's completion. Then the costs for performing individual tasks can be estimated, and they can be collated into general categories for budget format purposes. One of the most efficient and comprehensive methods of determining project tasks is through the *Program Evaluation and Review Technique (PERT)*. PERT has been discussed at length in Chapters 5 and 10. When responding to a request for proposal (RFP), a useful application of PERT is the *Bidding a Project* technique, also presented in Chapter 10. This technique lays out, in sequence, one set of the tasks for costing a project.

An example PERT network for completing video production, generated through MacProject software, is presented in Figure 13.3. This is a very simplistic example, serving merely to illustrate PERT's ties to the budgeting process. A real PERT network for such a project could run from fifty to several hundred tasks, depending on the complexity of the job. Each box

FIGURE 13.3 / Simplistic example of a video production PERT

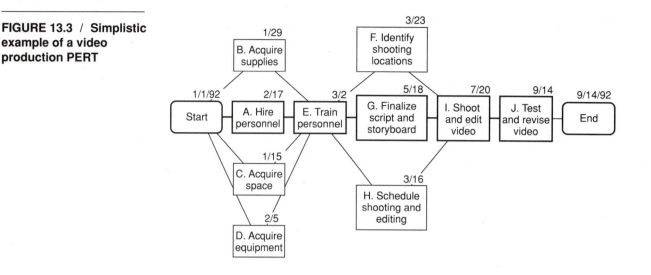

in the PERT network refers to a specific task. The tasks are put in sequence according to when they must be finished. In this example, the date that each is to be finished is presented at the top right of each task box. Refer to the PERT techniques just mentioned to get details of generating and sequencing tasks. The point is that generating this type of network provides a systematic way of determining what tasks must be completed for a project. After identifying and sequencing individual tasks, personnel, material, equipment, and facility needs can be estimated for each. These resources can then be costed out and organized according to budget categories.

Costing out resources of materials, equipment, facility use, and the time of personnel for the individual project tasks is tedious but very necessary. How much per hour does it cost to rent a video studio? What is the cost of the graphics software you will need? What are the personnel costs to take a camera crew and program talent to a shooting location 50 miles away, for 3 days? How much does it cost for 75 hours of a video editor's time? An illustration of one way of recording task costs is presented in Figure 13.4. Estimates of costs such as these have to be made and summed for each project task. The collection, collation, and reformatting of these data provides the dollar input for budget categories. Experienced ID managers will have much of the cost data available from previous endeavors. If they don't have the cost information, the data can be obtained from appropriate vendors and service personnel.

Creating a Trial Budget

Using the cost estimates for the resources required by our example tasks (A–J) in the PERT presented in Figure 13.3, the costs for each task can be determined as in Figure 13.4, and then their totals can be tabled in a budget format, by month, as shown in Figure 13.5. The example in Figure 13.5 is incomplete because it does not include salaries or **indirect costs** (overhead items such as utilities, rent, taxes, depreciation, insurance, facility maintenance, and accounting charges), but it illustrates how a manager can better relate project expenditures to task and time. For example, if the manager has spent $1,700 dollars

FIGURE 13.4 / Cost estimate for a specific ID task

COST ESTIMATE FOR TASK A

Task: Hire 5 project personnel

The items and their costs, listed below, cover the hiring of five project staff, including costs for searching, checking paper credentials, transportation, lodging, food, and interviewing.

Chargeable Item	Estimated Cost
1. Job descriptions development @ $15/hour	$ 150.00
2. Professional journals ad @ $75.00/month	150.00
3. Mailings @ $.50/mailing	200.00
4. Evaluating paper credentials @ $10.00/each	170.00
5. Screening telephone interviews @ $10.00/each	200.00
6. Interviewee transportation @ $100.00/each	1,000.00
7. Food and lodging for interviewee @ $140/2 days	2,800.00
8. Cost of interviewer time @ $15/hr	700.00
	Total: $5,370.00

on task B by the middle of January it could be a signal that something has gone awry.

The first budget written is invariably done with uncertainty (too little information). Several reiterations are usually necessary before the budget is at the point where it can be submitted, with confidence, to a funding agency. For this reason, instructional developers often use **electronic spreadsheet** programs for tabling their budget data. These are very efficient in manipulating tabular data such as those found on an accountant's ledger sheet. Figure 13.5 is an illustration of how data might be organized

FIGURE 13.5 / Spreadsheet showing project budget by task and month

Task	Estimate	Jan	Feb	Mar	Apr	May	June	July	Aug	Sept
					Monthly Budget					
A	5,370	3,000	2,370							
B	1,900	1,100	800							
C	300	300								
D	8,060	3,460	4,600							
E	1,523	1,523								
F	400			400						
G	13,770			3,570	5,400	4,800				
H	200			200						
I	11,700			1,000	3,300	2,800	2,700	1,800		
J	3,785								700	3,085
	47,008	6,983	6,400	5,170	8,700	7,600	2,700	1,800	700	3,085

in a spreadsheet. A major value of a spreadsheet is that when new numbers are inserted into its tables, hidden formulas cause the tables to be automatically updated, changing all numbers that would be affected by the new numbers. The "Excel Spreadsheet Program" job aid teaches how to set up such a spreadsheet. The job aid uses only a few of the procedures from Microsoft's Excel spreadsheet application, primarily to illustrate the process. Most spreadsheet programs work similarly.

Job Aid / Excel Spreadsheet Program

Description   The Excel spreadsheet software for the Macintosh is user friendly and effective for small to large ID projects. This job aid barely scratches the surface of the capability of the Excel application, but it illustrates the technique of using spreadsheets for keeping track of a project's costs. The software contains a spreadsheet template into which numerical data can be inserted via the computer's keyboard and number pad. The spreadsheet is an excellent means of keeping track of a project's finances. It also can respond to "what/if" questions to see how changes in costs for one activity may affect others.

Use Rationale   Keeping track of a project's resources is one of the most important things that a manager can do. But the means chosen have to be reasonable, in terms of the amount of time expended keeping track. Spreadsheets are excellent for this purpose.

Critical Tasks

1. **Determine the objectives for a spreadsheet.** Examples of objectives: to keep track of costs and/or to see how entering varying costs affects other costs of the project.

2. **Determine the project tasks and their respective costs.** You could use *PERT* to determine tasks, then cost the tasks with assistance from vendors and service people.

3. **Complete a task cost report.** See Figure 13.6. This report is for an individual task and is made up of two columns: Chargeable Item, and Estimated Cost. The total of the estimated costs is the amount that will later be entered into one cell of the spreadsheet.

4. **Design the spreadsheet.** *Specify the spreadsheet output,* e.g., differences between Total Estimated Cost and Total Actual Cost of each task. *Specify the input needed,* e.g., monthly costs per task. *Specify the functions to convert input to output,* e.g., to find the differences between Total Estimated Cost and Total Actual Cost of each task, use =SUM(P8 – Q8).

5. **Boot up the Excel spreadsheet program.** This will present a blank worksheet into which data can be inserted. The cursor for the spreadsheet takes the form of a cross. When it is placed over a cell in the spreadsheet and the button on the mouse is clicked, it highlights the cell. Data can only be entered in highlighted cells.

6. **Name and save the new spreadsheet to file.** Go to the Menu Bar to File, and select Save, open desired folder from Dialog Box, then type in an arbitrary file name for the new spreadsheet, and save to the file. The working space where data are entered and changed is just below the Menu Bar. The first section lists the highlighted cell. Data are entered in the third section of this bar.

continued

FIGURE 13.6 / A cost estimate format for a single project task

COST ESTIMATE FOR TASK E

Task: Two-day workshop to orient and train ten new personnel in the procedures and techniques to be used in the project

The items and their costs listed below cover ten participants and the ID project manager for two days at a local conference center. In addition, the manager's supervisor, a presenter, and a simulation game team of three will attend for 1 day.

Chargeable Item	Estimated Cost
1. Conference center room at $125.00/day	$ 250.00
2. Video projector rental at $75.00/day	150.00
3. Portable projection screen at $10.00/day	20.00
4. Personnel workbooks at $10.00/each	100.00
5. Manager transparencies	25.00
6. Presenter transparencies	195.00
7. Presenter handouts	11.00
8. Overhead projector at $15/day	30.00
9. Coffee, soft drinks, and snacks for four breaks	115.00
10. Lunch at $7.50/person/day	202.00
11. Coordinator and monitors for diffusion game	425.00
Total:	$1,523.00

7. **Type in a descriptive heading as a document title.** For example, type in Arco Project Monthly Budget, after selecting cells G1, H1, I1, J1, K1, L1, and M1. See Figure 13.7. In this case, to select more than one cell, click on the first cell, then hold down the shift key and click on the other desired cells to highlight them, then type.

8. **Label the rows and columns of the spreadsheet.** Note in Figure 13.7, at cell coordinates A4, that "Task" is used as the heading label for the A column, below which are listed tasks A through I. The rest of row 4 lists the months for project operation and an estimate of what each task will cost, the actual costs, and a column showing the difference between the two.

9. **Insert numerical data into the appropriate coordinates.** E.g., click the cursor on cell B8, and type in the number 600. It will appear in the work space directly below the Menu Bar and in the highlighted space on the spreadsheet.

10. **Insert the formulas for treating the data.** See Figure 13.7. Click on the spreadsheet cell where the output of the formula is to appear, and type in the appropriate formula; e.g., click on R8 and type in =SUM(P8 – Q8). The formula directs the spreadsheet to find the difference between the numbers in cells P8 and Q8, and to record it in cell R8. Similarly, formula =SUM(B8:B16) directs that estimated costs for January, listed under column B, be totaled in cell B18. There are many other formulas provided by Excel for calculation purposes.

continued

Excel Spreadsheet Program, continued

FIGURE 13.7 / Example of a spreadsheet with estimated and actual costs entered

	A	B	C	D	E	F	G	H	I	J	K	L	M	N	O	P	Q	R
1	ARCO PROJECT MONTHLY BUDGET																	
2																		
3																Total	Total	
4	Task	Jan		Feb		Mar		Apr		May		June		July		Est.	Actual	Diff
5																		
6		Est.	Actual	Est.	Actual	Est.	Actual	Est.	Actual	Est.	Actual	Est.	Actual	Est.	Actual			
7																		
8	A	600	700	1000	1200											1600	1900	–300
9	B	1100	1000	6200	6000											7300	7000	300
10	C	300	400													300	400	–100
11	D	3460	3200	4600	4500											8060	7700	360
12	E			1197	1000											1197	1000	197
13	F					400	625									400	625	–225
14	G					3570	3500	5400	6000	4800	4500					13770	14000	–230
15	H					200	200									200	200	0
16	I					1000	1200	3300	2900	2800	2900	2700	3000	1800	1500	11600	11500	100
17																		
18	Totals	5460	5300	12997	12700	5170	5525	8700	8900	7600	7400	2700	3000	1800	1500	44427	44325	102

11. **Test the spreadsheet by replacing a few numbers.** When costs change because of problems or as a result of finishing early, they can be inserted in place of the old costs to see how they affect other costs. For example, in Figure 13.7, if the number 1200 in E8 were changed, it would trickle through to change the numbers in Q8, R8, E18, Q18, and R18.

12. **Save the spreadsheet to the file previously named.**

13. **Print out the spreadsheet.** Go to the Menu Bar and select File, and then Print.

14. **Option: Copy the spreadsheet to a Report in a word processing application.** For example, to copy a spreadsheet to a Microsoft Word document, first move the cursor to the lower right-hand corner of the spreadsheet section, press and hold the mouse button down as the cursor is moved to the top left of the spreadsheet to highlight the section to be copied, and release the button. Hold down the Shift key while selecting Edit/Copy Picture at the Menu Bar, then go to the Microsoft word process document, click its cursor at the point where the spreadsheet is to be pasted, and open up a space large enough for the spreadsheet. Then click on Edit/Paste from the Menu Bar.

References

Microsoft Excel User's Guide. (1990). Spreadsheet with Business Graphics and Database. Version 3.0. Apple Macintosh Series. Redmond, Wash.: Microsoft Corporation.

Vinsonhaler, J., et al. (1989). *People and Computers: Partners in Problem Solving.* New York: West, p. 302.

It is desirable to have some flexibility in shifting resources within an ID budget. Remember that developing instruction is basically a problem-solving venture. Too many of the variables that can affect budgets are out of the control of a project manager (e.g., inflation). Being able to shift resources from one budget category to another gives the manager the possibility of using funds saved in one area to bolster areas where there are shortfalls.

A final budget, in object–function form (for the benefit of the funding agency), might look like the one presented in Figure 13.8 (first presented in Chapter 10). *Direct costs,* stated in the budget, are those funds that are spent directly on project tasks, while *indirect costs* are for overhead items, including use of space, utilities, taxes, depreciation, insurance, facility maintenance, and accounting charges. ID teams, who are part of a parent

FIGURE 13.8 / Project budget, by line item, for 2-year project life

		Salary	Basis	% USDE	Cost USDE	% MSU	Cost MSU
Personnel							
Wiggins, H.	88–89 AY beg. 10/1/88	48,500	AY	10%	4,580	30%	13,741
	Summer school '89	48,500	SS	40%	5,820		
	89–90 AY thru 3/31/90	50,925	AY	10%	3,397	30%	10,190
Perkins, G.	88–89 AY beg. 10/1/88	49,549	AY	10%	4,680	10%	4,680
	89–90 AY thru 3/31/90	52,026	AY	10%	3,470	10%	3,470
Beck, G.	88–89 AY beg. 10/1/88	33,708	AY	10%	3,184	10%	3,184
	89–90 AY thru 3/31/90	35,393	AY	10%	2,361	10%	2,361
Kirkland, K.	10/1/88–9/30/89	18,656	AN	5%	933		
	10/1/89–3/31/90	19,589	AN	5%	490		
Olrich, W.	10/1/88–9/30/89	18,656	AN	5%	933		
	10/1/89–3/31/90	19,589	AN	5%	490		
Clerical (hourly)	1,500 hours	5	hr	50%	7,500		
Grad. Assts.	10/1/88–9/30/89	1,016	mo.	200%	48,768		
(4 @ ½ time)	10/1/89–3/31/90	1,067	mo.	200%	25,608		
					112,214		37,626
Fringe Benefits							
24% for AY and AN					5,884		
7% summer school					407		
					6,291		
Travel							
Project director's meeting ($500 transportation plus $100/day lodging and meals for 2 days)					700		
Person site visits—Michigan (20 trips at $100/ea transportation)					2,000		
Person site visits—National (4 trips at $500/ea transportation plus $100/day lodging and meals for 2 days each)					2,800		
Presentations at 3 regional and national conferences ($500 transportation plus $100/day lodging and meals for 2 days)					2,100		
					7,600		

continued

FIGURE 13.8 / Project budget, by line item, for 2-year project life, continued

Equipment

1	Mac II computer w/color monitor 2 MB RAM min., extended keyboard, and 40-meg HD		5,000
1	TV producer board		1,000
5	LD-V4200 videodisc players w/serial interface ($1,200 ea)	6,000	
1	VO-7600 ¾" videotape player		4,200
1	BKU-761 serial interface for videotape player		480
1	SGN-1203 framecode gen.		2,800
1	KTU-190 video monitor for composite video		500
		6,000	13,980

Supplies

Software	1,500
Paper	150
Computer disks	75
Videotape	100
	1,825

Other

Advisory council meeting (2 mtgs. for each of the 5 advisory board members—each meeting based on $250 transportation, $75/day lodging and meals, and $100/day consulting fee per member)	4,250
Interpreter services for above meetings ($65/day for 2 days)	130
Professional studio time	1,000
Mastering and duplicating videodisks	3,000
Copying/printing	1,000
Communication costs	
Postage (site mail)	300
Phone	500
	10,180

Direct costs	144,110	51,606
Indirect costs @ 42%*	58,006	
TOTAL	202,116	

*42% of total direct costs ($144,110) less $6,000 for equipment.

organization, may be charged for indirect costs, a standard percentage of the funding brought in from the outside. However, this amount is usually negotiable, depending on how badly the organization wants the external funding and/or how persuasive the ID project manager is. In universities, the "standard percentage" taken for overhead can vary anywhere from zero to 70%.

Locating Funding Sources

Funding sources for projects may be found within the agencies housing instructional development groups, and from a range of potential outside clients, including those in business and industry, governmental and military agencies, and educational institutions. There are a number of excellent directories to such external organizations. Next are listed some common sources for finding both inside and outside funding.

External Sources   Agencies such as the Education Funding Research Council and Government Information Services can assist in finding a wide range of funding for projects. The giant *Annual Register of Grant Support* is a good directory to funding from a broad spectrum of governmental, business, and professional agencies. Probably the most comprehensive listing of grant-making foundations in this country is found in the *National Data Book of Foundations*. Sponsored by The *Foundation Center* in New York, it is one of several directories put out by that agency. Others of its directories include the *Foundation Grants Index* and the *Foundation Directory*.

Most directories cover a wide range of funding areas, but a number of them lead to funding for specialty areas, e.g., Eckstein's *Handicapped Funding Directory*, and his *Directory of Computer and High-Technology Grants*. The *Grants Register* is a source of funding in support of graduate students and for projects involved in professional or advanced vocational training. Most college and university libraries have copies of specialty and general funding directories available.

Internal Sources   The saying that "money is where you find it" needs to be kept in mind, especially for smaller projects. To this end, the study of budgets and the policies controlling them in potential funding organizations is mandatory for those who would seek to gain funds controlled by others. In fact, the budget is, itself, a device for control, and, thus, is a means of power. Power in any organization is guarded carefully, and usually can only be approached through its formal mechanisms. Budgets are viewed proprietarily, with only those running the budgets privy to the range and details of budgetary processes. However, getting copies of past budgets or parts of budgets is usually not too difficult. Business and industry must provide annual reports containing budgetary data to their stockholders, and these annual reports can usually be accessed. Many institutions, such as public universities, are required by law to have their budgets available. A copy is usually on file in their libraries, which permit public access.

The type of budget used by an organization tells much about its operation. A companion technique of finding out its operational processes is to follow a paper trail of a request for funds through the system. This can be done by asking someone in the system (e.g., a secretary) about the steps that a requisition goes through from submission to payout. Knowing who signs off along the way, and why, tells the developer what gatekeepers need to be approached and what steps must be taken to present the best case for a request for funds. Earlier, in the discussion of the no-budget budget, the technique of *Proactive Requisitioning* was mentioned as an effective means for finding and requesting funds in other people's budgets.

Training programs in business and industry and in government and military units usually supply the necessary funds for their in-house instructional development teams. To a large degree this is done by educational institutions as well, but faculty are strongly encouraged to seek outside funding. The earlier discussion of vulnerable sources of funds, such as contingency and revolving accounts, suggested that they may be a source of supplementary funds from within an organization. Usually, if no external funds are available and the organization is convinced of the merit of a project, administration will find a way to include its costs in their budget, often by appealing to their own higher budgetary authorities.

Approaching Funding Sources

Each internal and external funding source has its specific procedures for releasing funds to projects. Therefore, as previously mentioned, it is wise to learn the appropriate procedures. Often, external agencies will provide a template or outline for any project proposals that they request. Some of the forms they require are to satisfy legal questions, particularly for governmental and military agencies soliciting proposals from ID groups. Business and industry and educational institutions vary considerably in what they require in terms of proposal formats and budget categories. This complicates the process, but it doesn't represent an insurmountable problem. The usual procedure is to ask for a sample proposal or one that has been accepted for a past project that meets their criteria, and then to use the sample as a model for developing the new proposal and budget. Some funding agencies are willing to critique initial drafts of proposals. When this is so, developers should take advantage of the offer.

Prioritizing Funding Sources

When there are several possible sources of funds, how does a manager prioritize them? A number of variables come into play, but an obvious one is the match between the needs of the funder and those of the fundee. One criticism of governmental agencies that fund educational projects is that they use their power to control the curriculum by selectively funding projects. On the other hand, the ID manager may also have a hidden agenda for getting funding that may not necessarily match up exactly with the reasons for which the source agency is providing funds. Usually, the fund seeker will attempt to search out the agency where there is the closest match between their respective objectives.

The small size of grants available from funding agencies may place some of the agencies lower on the priority list, particularly if the grant is too small to provide all of the necessary resources for a proposed project. However, it is not unusual to have two or more funding sources supporting the same project. But multiple funding sources can complicate the lives of ID project managers, because that means they will have to satisfy more than one master. The general rule is to avoid multiple funding sources for a project if single sources are available.

The level of accountability required is another factor that gives the fund seeker pause. If the requirements are extensive or very stringent, and the project manager has some question as to whether they can be met, this may place a potential funder at a lower priority. An example would be when a funding source arbitrarily imposes a less-than-practical timeline for finishing the project.

Another negative factor affecting consideration of a funding agency is when it demands a direct hand in controlling how the project is run. The project will need to conform somewhat to policies of the funding agency, provide periodic progress reports, and get sign-offs on the completed project, but the day-to-day operations should stay under the control of the project manager. Any recommendations to the contrary should be looked on with skepticism.

Still another factor affecting the choice of funding agency is the agency's willingness to provide ready access to subject-matter experts (SMEs). Given the range of projects ID groups engage in, it would be unreasonable to expect an instructional developer to have content expertise in them all. Instructional developers need to keep up front that their expertise is in ID, not in the client's field. If the client is to provide the SMEs, the project manager needs to spell out the requirement carefully, because nothing can slow down a project more than a reluctant or inaccessible SME. Operationally, this means that a written agreement should be obtained as to the amount of released time for SMEs being made available to the project.

Structuring Proposal to Fit Source

Earlier it was mentioned that managers might want to use a performance-budget model, because it more closely ties resources to project tasks, and it enables the manager to keep better tabs on running costs and profit margins than does the more typically used object–function budget. However, as was also mentioned, the funding organization will expect the final budget to be put in a format of their choosing, which usually means an object–function budget format. The translation of a performance budget into an object–function budget is tedious but not difficult. It merely requires the collation of performance-budget items under the appropriate object–function categories from task cost reports (see Figure 13.4). Some instructional developers have suggested that there is value in submitting both types of budgets to the client, with the performance budget as an appendix. This may help the client see what might be lost if the budget is to be cut by them. But others prefer not to submit both, since the ID project's profit structure can be more easily discerned in a performance budget.

There is, of course, much more to a proposal than just the budget. An *outline* of a project proposal is presented in Figure 13.9. Such outlines vary depending on the project and the funding agency, but the categories listed in Figure 13.9 are usually addressed in some manner in most proposals. Statements common to most proposals have the nickname of "boiler plate." An example of boiler plate might be to include the information that project personnel are hired on an "equal opportunity" basis.

Depending on the client, there will be certain expectations about rights to the products of a project. When it is an outright grant, say to a university project by a government agency, all rights to the product usually stay with the project's home organization. On the other hand, if the project products have been developed for an external client, that client may demand all rights to the products. Some are so specific as to say that the developers may not even have their name on the product. If it is important for a developer to have some rights where a project's products are concerned, this should be agreed on, in writing, at the beginning of the project.

FIGURE 13.9 / Example of an ID project proposal outline

Title page
Completed forms for the application
Budget and budget explanation
Abstract of the proposal
The proposal
    Section 1 Need for the project
       1.1   Purpose
       1.2   Rationale for methodology
       1.3   Rationale for subject matter
       1.4   Rationale for target population selected
    Section 2 Expected project outcomes
       2.1   Project goals and objectives
       2.2   Project product goals and objectives
    Section 3 Approach
       3.1   General plan
       3.2   Major project activities and timeline
          a. First year of operation
          b. Second year of operation
       3.3   Evaluation plan
       3.4   Key personnel
       3.5   Project organization chart
       3.6   Evidence of project team's ability to complete the project
    Section 4 Biographical sketches of key personnel
References
Appendices

Submitting Proposal

Submitting a proposal is not merely mailing it to the funding agency. When proposals are to be sent to an external funding agency, they must first pass approval of the administrators of the project's home organization, who may impose additional requirements. Home organizations usually keep tight control over what proposals may go to a funding agency at a particular time. They do this to avoid the problem of having more than one project from their organization vying for the same funds. They fear that the funding agency may choose the proposal that costs least. Whereas, if the organization were only submitting the larger project by itself, it might have a better chance of being funded.

Additional requirements of funding organizations can include the numbers of copies of the proposal to be sent. For many, timing is a problem for submitting proposals. Often enough, managers find themselves finishing up their proposals at midnight on the day before the deadline for submitting them. Usually, funding agencies will accept the postmark on the mailed proposal as evidence that the deadline has been met. There are other occasions when it is wise to hand-carry a proposal to the external funding agency, particularly if it is a complex or involved proposal. That way, questions about its contents can be answered by a knowledgeable person. As mentioned earlier, it is desirable to be able to send the proposal to a contact person with whom you have had communication previously (by phone and/or letter). Such personal touches keep a proposal from being just another one in the pile.

Check to make very sure that individual pages of all the copies are included, right side up, in sequence, and that there are no printing glitches on any of the pages. Copies should be sharp and professional-looking. If sent by post, the proposal should be sent by registered mail, to ensure it is received by the funding agency. It is not considered good form to send the same proposal to several different funding agencies at the same time. A more accepted procedure is to submit the proposal to the agency given the highest priority, and if not accepted, then to submit to the next-highest-priority funding agency on the list, until the project is funded.

Modifying Proposal

Usually, acceptance of a proposal by an agency comes with conditions, which may require modifications in the proposal and/or budget sent to them (usually through addendums rather than a rewrite of the whole proposal). Often enough, costs will be the major subject of the change. Agency personnel may say that they are willing to fund the project at a reduced level if it can be cut back without invalidating the original intent. The manager may come back with a counterproposal or may agree to modify the proposal following recommendations from the funding agency and resubmit. Usually, if a cut in funds is the major requirement, then a cut in deliverables is the obvious answer to reduced funding. At some point, the manager may decide it is unlikely that the project can be done at the funding level offered, and then choose to submit the proposal to the next agency on the priority list.

Allocating Resources

After a proposal is approved, there is often a period of time before the first allotment of funds comes through from the funding agency. During this period, managers will find plenty to fill their time but will also be frustrated because they lack the funds for ordering the resources needed for the project. Often, the home organization can be persuaded to provide start-up funds, to be repaid when the moneys begin coming in from the funding agency.

Again, a regularly updated PERT in conjunction with a spreadsheet provides assistance in keeping track of how resources are allocated. The spreadsheet gives an up-to-date readout on funds spent and funds available. This enables managers to know early if there have been cost overruns and/or if there have been savings on some tasks. The savings on one task can be reallocated to balance out cost overruns on another, or to tasks on the critical path, where additional resources will enable their earlier completion. Of course, if there are no cost overruns, and the project is running according to the contracted timeline, the saving can become part of the profits. This continuous monitoring of the use of resources has great payoff for the bottom line.

Certainly, project managers need to monitor their respective budgets regularly to make sure that funds are being spent appropriately and that changes in internal and external variables are not reducing the value of the funds, and thus putting the project in jeopardy. Managers are in a unique position to account for costs and to understand how to save on one part of the project to make up for cost overruns in another part, because they can also answer the earned-value question, which the organization's accountant cannot readily do. *Earned value,* an aggregate performance measure, is used to compare actual costs with projected costs, as they relate to project objectives (Meredith and Mantel, pp. 384–387). Independent ID project managers will have to develop their own cost accounting and cost control procedures. There are a number of software products designed to ease that process, including VisiSchedule, Microsoft Project, and Qwiknet.

To get at cost accounting and cost control, project managers need to determine **work-breakdown packages (WBPs)** from the project's PERT network. They can do this by clustering PERT network tasks so that they form logical packages to be assigned to different teams. For example, all the tasks in the design process of some project might be clustered to form three WBPs:

1. Design orientation videotape
2. Design interactive videodisc segments
3. Design workbook and teacher manual

Each of these WBPs could be assigned to a different ID team. Clustering tasks into WBPs enables teams to know far enough ahead what is expected of them, but also enables costs to be looked at in a broader way. For example, the tasks delineated in the PERT network in Figure 13.3 might form four logical or practical WBPs:

1. Start-up activities
   a. Acquire supplies.
   b. Acquire space.
   c. Acquire equipment.
2. Personnel
   a. Hire personnel.
   b. Train/orient personnel.
3. Production
   a. Identify shooting locations.
   b. Finalize script and storyboard.
   c. Schedule shooting and editing.
   d. Shoot and edit videotape.
4. Evaluation and revision

The costs in the WBP are accumulated, collated, and tabled, by the week, to form a miniperformance budget for that WBP. This minibudget is then monitored by the manager for signs of overruns and savings. This is done by comparing monthly expenditures planned and actual expenditures. The U.S. Department of Defense has developed a relatively simple way of relating time and cost variables of a project with performance and with each other. They use a modification of the earned-value procedure called *cost/schedule control system criteria (C/SCSC).* This method requires three types of data:

1. The *budgeted cost of work scheduled (BCWS)*, that is, the cost budgeted for specific tasks scheduled for completion as of a given date

2. The *budgeted cost of work performed (BCWP)*, which is the cost of the work done on the tasks by that same date

3. The *actual cost of work performed (ACWP)*, which tells whether or not the amount actually spent differs from the amount budgeted for the tasks carried out as of the same date

These data can then be used to determine variance in schedule and cost. That is, subtracting the BCWP from the BCWS tells the schedule variance, while subtracting the ACWP from the BCWP gives the cost variance, to that point.

Once data are derived through the comparisons, questions to be raised include: "Where was money saved, and how can such savings be encouraged in similar instances of the future?" and "What modifications should be made in situations to reduce or eliminate unanticipated costs and/or cost overruns?" The next thing that the manager needs do is to look across all of the WBPs and see how they compare in cost savings and overruns. The savings from some WBPs can be shifted to other WBPs that may be behind in either funds or time. This procedure enables the manager to see the degree to which the budget is out of balance, either positively or negatively. No one complains when the expenditures are under budget and the earned value is as planned or ahead of planning. But when the result is negative, and little can be done about it (e.g., graphics artists are hired away by another company, causing production to slow by 2½ weeks), then the manager may see serious unproductive inroads made in the budget. When the discrepancy becomes serious enough, some of the choices the manager may consider are to throw in the towel, petition the client for additional funds, seek funds from some other sources, or take the extra costs out of profits (or, if necessary to maintain credibility, out of pocket). What is serious enough? A rule of thumb is that when accumulated cost overruns exceed accumulated task savings by 15–20%, the manager should calculate the effect over the remainder of the project's life in terms of additional funds needed. As mentioned, the manager may have to adjust project resource shortages by reducing profit level and/or by acquiring additional funding. The manager may also begin a regimen of cost cutting to save the project. This usually means a watered-down product.

Because of the problem-solving nature of ID projects, it is not unusual for their completion to take more time and funds than was originally anticipated. Most funding agencies are reasonably understanding about time overruns, and tend to extend deadlines without charge to developers. However, that is not always so. When clients have deadlines of their own to get new instructional systems up and running, they are not hesitant to apply late charges to developers as a means of motivating speedy delivery.

Another factor that may cause cost overruns is inflation. Under an inflationary economy, the dollar will simply not buy as much as it would at the time the budget was agreed on. This problem can be circumvented by building in an inflation factor that gives the developer some protection from such changes in the economy.

Closing Out a Project

Not all projects are closed out successfully (Cleland, 1990, p. 230). Some projects suffer early termination because of clients' or developers' inability to complete their respective sides of the bargain. Bankruptcy and other unfavorable conditions can develop on either side. Having a section in the contract covering such contingencies is insurance well worth the attorney costs.

The steps in closing out a successful project vary, but will usually include: (1) getting a sign-off on the project deliverables from the client, (2) collecting final payment from the client, (3) generating a final report for the funding agency, and usually for the ID team's home organization, (4) closing out project accounts, and (5) providing some support to the client in initial operation of the new instructional system. In terms of this last step, a means of graceful withdrawal from responsibilities to a client for completed projects is the technique called *Gradual Disengagement*, presented in Chapter 1. An outline for writing a final report for a project is presented in Figure 13.10.

Having satisfactorily delivered the instruction, the remaining funds owed by the client are placed in the same account used to place previous

FIGURE 13.10 / Typical outline for a project's final report

FINAL REPORT OUTLINE

1. Cover sheet

2. Table of contents

3. Abstract

4. Introduction to report

5. Methodology
   a. Project management process
      1) Staffing
      2) Coordination
      3) Reporting
   b. Instructional development process
      1) Needs analysis
      2) Design
      3) Production
      4) Prototype testing
      5) Revision
   c. Validation process

6. Results
   a. Attitude effect
   b. Cognitive effect
   c. Skill effect

7. Recommendations
   a. Need for additional discs
   b. Switch to level III mode
   c. Test under regular time constraints for instruction

8. Appendices
   a. Needs analysis sample
   b. Management network sample
   c. Flowchart sample
   d. Storyboard sample
   e. Coordinator meeting agenda sample
   f. Staff meeting agenda sample
   g. Staff report sample
   h. Project budget

Send Client ten copies of each of the deliverables:

Videodisc
User's guide
Orientation videotape

installments of funds for the project. For those ID project teams working as a unit in their home organization, funds received and spent are all accounted for in the home organization's budgeting system. Independent ID organizations will, of course, have their own budgeting system and procedures for dealing with expenditures and revenues and with use of profits. Final accounting of the ID group to the funding agency for project funds is usually necessary, in the form of a budget showing how the moneys were spent.

Summary

This chapter discussed some of the basic procedures and understandings that ID Project managers and personnel use in acquiring and allocating resources for projects. A set of steps in this process were discussed, and techniques for their facilitation were presented or referred to. The writing of project proposals to funding agencies was emphasized, along with descriptions of some of the national directories leading ID managers to potential funding agencies. A significant section was dedicated to budgeting issues and procedures. The differences among major budget types were discussed and related to the instructional development process, as were the budget interfaces among the ID project, parent organization, and funding agency. Of particular interest is the means by which project objectives, tasks, skills, and costs are tied together. Means for shifting resources within a project to cover cost and time overruns were also discussed. The importance of acquisition and allocation of resources was strongly emphasized as a major responsibility of project managers, as was the point that basic understanding and skills in this process are necessary to the successful completion of ID projects.

References

Annual Register of Grant Support: A Directory of Funding Sources. (1991). 25th ed. Willamette, Ill.: National Register Publishing Co.

Cleland, D. I. (1990). *Project Management: Strategic Design and Implementation.* Blue Ridge Summit, Penna.: TAB Professional and Reference Books.

Eckstein, R. M. (1992). *Handicapped Funding Directory.* 7th ed. Margate, Fla.: Research Grant Guides.

Eckstein, R. M. (1991). *Directory of Computer and High-Technology Grants.* 1st ed. Loxachatchee, Fla.: Research Grant Guides.

Gillespie, J. T., and Spirt, D. L. (1973). *Creating a School Media Program.* New York: Bowker.

Education Funding Research Council (1990). *Government Information Services.* Arlington, Va.: the Council.

Meredith, J. R., and Mantel, S. J. (1989). *Project Management: A Managerial Approach.* New York: Wiley.

Mosher, F. C. (1968). The study of budgeting. In *Reader in Library Administration,* ed. P. Wassarman, and M. L. Bundy, Washington, D.C.: NCR Microcard Editions, pp. 228–238.

Murphy, C. E. (ed.) (1992). *National Data Book of Foundations: A Comprehensive Guide to Grantmaking Foundations.* New York: The Foundation Center.

Olson, Stanley (ed.) (1992). *Foundation Directory.* 14th ed. New York: The Foundation Center.

Schmid, W. T. (1980). *Media Center Management.* New York: Hastings House.

Foundations Grants Index. (1992). 20th ed. New York: The Foundation Center.

Wildavsky, Aaron (1964). *The Politics of the Budgetary Process.* Boston: Little, Brown, p.1.

Williams, Lisa (1990). *The Grants Register: 1991–2.* New York: St. Martins Press.

CHAPTER 14

ID Project Personnel

Process of determining staffing needs, hiring, training, assessing, motivating, counseling, censuring, and dismissing ID project members

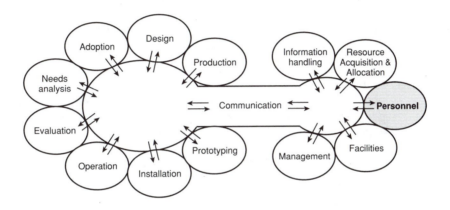

Learner Objectives

1. Contrast operating conditions that affect personnel, for project managers versus ongoing managers.

2. Describe a process for determining the staffing needs of an ID project.

3. Describe and justify the major tasks necessary to hiring project personnel.

4. Describe the steps in the interview process for hiring project personnel.

5. Explain how applicants are prioritized for an ID project position.

6. List the major employee training tasks that managers must complete.

7. Differentiate among techniques for training project personnel.

8. List the major reasons for on-the-job evaluation of project personnel.

9. List some common means of motivating project personnel.

10. Contrast counseling with censuring of project personnel misbehavior.

11. Explain how a manager prepares to dismiss project personnel.

12. Recall definitions of major terms.

Introduction

Managers of instructional development projects stand or fall on the basis of the competence and team work of their staffs. Therefore, it is not surprising that most managers are very concerned with finding and keeping the best people. Saying that competence and goodwill of project team members are critical factors in the success of ID projects is no doubt stating the obvious. These people, in all of their complexity, are the ones who must be managed in carrying out the tasks that make a project go. Managers, by definition, are the individuals who should understand enough about the needs, talents, and motivations of their personnel to coordinate their activities in such a way that a project is completed effectively and efficiently (i.e., at product criteria, on time, and within budget).

Projects, because of their relatively short-term nature, have personnel problems that differ in some ways from those of ongoing organizational programs. The amount of front-end time available for a project manager to hire and shake down new teams of workers is usually much shorter. New ID teams also lack the stability of having a history of staff interaction and problem solving found in ongoing organizational programs. Because the project does not promise ongoing security, there is also a greater worker turnover than is found in regular organizational programs. Finally, managers do not have as much useful information available about their new workers, in terms of factors such as skill, dependability, responsibility, and ability to get along with co-workers. This means that they are going to have to do proportionately more hiring, firing, assessing, counseling, censuring, and training.

Personnel-Handling Process

To be effective, managers must be able to carry out the following personnel handling tasks.

1. Determine staffing needs for a project.
2. Find and hire qualified ID project personnel.
3. Train personnel in appropriate areas.
4. Motivate personnel to meet project standards.
5. Council and/or censure personnel about inadequate or inappropriate on-the-job behavior.
6. Evaluate personnel effectiveness and efficiency.
7. Dismiss personnel not able or willing to meet project standards.

Determining Project Staffing Requirements

For the inexperienced project manager, there are some steps that can be taken that will assist in making staffing decisions. Laying out the project development strategy is a necessary first step to identifying staffing needs. A PERT network is an operational expression of the project development strategy. For the inexperienced manager, the PERT network can provide the data for identifying the kinds of skills needed on the job. By examining each of the tasks in the PERT network, a manager can determine both the range of skills and when and to what degree those skills are needed to complete project tasks. Once this information is obtained, the manager can collate the various skills into clusters that match the training of potential hirees. For example, the manager could cluster all skills relevant to graphics production. An examination of the time estimates for completing a cluster of tasks will assist the manager in determining how many graphics personnel would be necessary to complete the tasks on time. The job aid on "Determining ID Project Staffing Needs" lays this out in more detail. This procedure, though only beginning to deal with what could be done in human resource planning, will enable the new manager to lay out fairly quickly the kinds of qualifications and times required of specific professionals to carry out the tasks of a specific project.

Job Aid / Determining ID Project Staffing Needs

Description Human resource forecasting can be as complex as a manager wants to make it, but this job aid presents a fairly straightforward means for an inexperienced manager to determine what staff are needed for a new project. It entails the use of the project's PERT network. Personnel skills needed are interpreted from the network tasks. Closely related skills are clustered to match the training of professionals being considered, and an estimate is made of how many persons with a particular set of skills are needed.

Use Rationale Project managers want the right numbers of trained staff with the right skills to carry out the tasks of their projects. Inexperienced project managers can profit by a set of guidelines that help them avoid pitfalls in making staffing decisions.

Critical Tasks

1. **Complete a detailed PERT network for the life of the project.** The network tasks make clear what needs to be done, and from them the necessary skills and personnel time can be drawn.

2. **For each of the PERT network tasks, list the skills needed and the times to complete.** E.g., do needs analysis—40 hours; write video script—200 hours; storyboarding—250 hours; formative and summative evaluation—90 hours; generate sound effects—50 hours; video content expert—80 hours; computer programming—450 hours; video camera shooting—200 hours; video editing—170 hours; test item writing—80 hours; topic research—100 hours; select instructional media—20 hours; manual writing—90 hours.

3. **Cluster related skills and their times on a second list.** For example, a cluster of *instructional design skills* could include: do needs analysis—40 hours; write objectives—85 hours; select instructional strategies—40 hours; select instructional media—20 hours; and write design specifications—20 hours. If needed, the project manager may want to get an expert instructional designer's confirmation of the skills selected.

continued

4. **Adjust the clustered skills to fit realistic expectations of a professional's qualifications.** For example, for a graphics artist's position, only include those skills relevant to that professional's qualifications.

5. **Determine how many staff with particular qualifications need to be hired.** This is based on PERT network time estimates and the scheduling of those skills. This can include full- and part-time employee considerations.

Reference

Gentry, C.G. (1974). Determining ID Project Staffing Needs. In-house document for ID hiring committees. East Lansing, Mich.: Michigan State University.

Hiring Project Personnel

For training programs that have their own in-house instructional development groups, new projects may mean looking to see who is available that has the necessary skills, and then hiring any needed additional staff. But for many new projects, several people, including the project manager, may have to be hired. The new project manager usually takes an active role in hiring staff for the project. Most hiring of project personnel is done less than systematically, probably because of time constraints. After the hiring is finished, managers begin making an on-the-job assessment of new staff in terms of their respective motivation and capabilities in support of the project. Even when expectations are violated, acceptable adjustments by both management and staff can result in a harmonious and productive relationship. However, inability to successfully adjust may result in a liaison being painfully dragged out before the decision is finally made that a serious hiring error has been made. Then begins the equally painful process of dismissal and then going through another recruiting stage. This means that managers are wise to get to know the qualifications of potential employees as well as they can *before* contracting with them.

The major tasks necessary to the hiring of project personnel are: delineating the position, announcing the position, selecting applicants for interview, interviewing applicants, prioritizing applicants, negotiating with applicants, hiring the applicant, and orienting the hiree to the project environment. These tasks are elaborated in the following sections.

Delineating the Job   Most formal, written job descriptions are vague, and are seldom predicated on carefully thought out, predetermined criteria for hiring personnel. There have been many cases where a person has been hired to perform particular tasks, and then been assigned quite different ones. Sometimes this is to the employee's advantage, and sometimes not. Varying expectations of prospective employee and manager may result in problems. The likelihood that problems will occur can be reduced by being very clear about what the employee is expected to do once hired. That is not to say that every minute task must be listed; but certainly, general categories of tasks should be. In fact, it is wise for the employer not to be too task specific, because roles may need to be adjusted due to demands on the job, but an applicant should have a clear idea of the range of tasks he or she will be expected to perform, if hired. Concomitantly, the employer should have reasonable evidence that the employee can perform these roles at acceptable levels, or be willing to support an employee in acquiring the additional skills necessary to performing the tasks.

The job aid on "Writing Job Descriptions" describes an acceptable procedure. The job announcement presented in the job aid is merely an example. The organization, sequence, and format of job descriptions vary considerably. However, most of the elements included in this job aid are usually found in such announcements.

Job Aid / Writing Job Descriptions

Description   The **job description** is one of the most common means of announcing jobs for people in professions. Information required to write a job description includes: tasks to be performed, skills and qualifications required, salary and benefit range, when the job should start, directions for applying, and closing date for applications. The job-description writer also needs some knowledge of the different formats for job aids and of the means for checking their accuracy and completeness, as well as how best to distribute them.

Use Rationale   Unclear statements about what a new employee is to do in his or her role causes problems. Job descriptions clarify the position and can be referred to at a later date if disagreements occur.

Critical Tasks

1. **Analyze the staff position to be described.** Refer to the *Determining ID Project Staffing Needs* job aid (earlier this chapter) as one means.

2. **List the skills and other qualifications required by the job.** Refer to Figure 14.1. Avoid the tendency to list more qualifications than are needed.

3. **Establish the earliest starting time for the position.** Providing a time range for starting work reduces the chance of losing good prospects who might otherwise be cut out by time constraints.

4. **Determine the closing date for receiving applications.** This is done to stimulate timely application by potential employees. Obviously, if qualified personnel are not found by this date, the deadline will be extended.

5. **Determine the directions for applying.** This is basically a request for a letter of interest, a resume, and three or more professional references. There is usually a statement about confirming receipt of the applicant's materials, and when further contact will be made, and how.

6. **Determine what the market is paying a person with these skills.** This can be done partly on the basis of what the company is currently paying similar personnel, or by checking with university or private placement services or asking colleagues who hire for similar positions. Another source for determining the pay rate for beginning professionals is to ask heads of educational technology programs.

continued

Writing Job Descriptions, continued

FIGURE 14.1 / Example of a job description

POSITION OPENINGS FOR INSTRUCTIONAL DEVELOPERS

January 12, 1993

Position The AlphaBeta Corporation has positions available for three experienced instructional developers to work at their central training facility in Deerfield Center, Michigan. Persons accepted for these positions will be working on a range of instructional development projects, including the development of traditional course instruction, interactive videodisc instruction, and HyperCard self-instructional programs.

Qualifications A masters or doctoral degree in educational technology or closely related field, a minimum of 2 years' experience as an instructional developer in business/industry training programs, and having the full range of instructional development skills. These skills should include: needs analysis, task analysis, design, production skills (interactive videodisc and HyperCard), prototype development and testing, and prototype installation.

Starting Date June 3, 1993. Moving costs to Deerfield Center area, for employee's household goods, are covered by AlphaBeta Corporation.

Salary range and Benefits From $40,000 to $50,000, depending on experience and other qualifications. Benefits are highly competitive, including full coverage for health and dental insurance.

How to apply Send an up-to-date resume and at least three references to:

> Mr. Clarence L. Perkins
> Personnel Director
> AlphaBeta Corporation
> 3220 Fausett Road
> Deerfield Center, MI 48813

Please do not telephone. Receipt of applications and references will be confirmed within one week of receipt. All applications will be responded to within three weeks following the closing date for applications. Prior to that time, applicants may be asked to travel, at company expense, for an interview in Deerfield Center.

Closing date for applications Applications received must be postmarked by or before April 10, 1993.

---

7. **Write a statement about salary and benefits.** A salary range, e.g., $30,000—$40,000, or a statement that "salary will be commensurate with the applicant's experience and current market rate" is usually given to provide flex for both parties.

8. **Place the data in job description format.** See Figure 14.1. The law prohibits as discriminatory the requesting of an applicant's age, place of birth, religion, or race, or the requiring of photographs.

9. **Have others check the job description for completeness and accuracy.** Usually two kinds of knowledge are applied: that relevant to company format and policy, and that relevant to the position.

continued

Writing Job Descriptions, continued

10. **Determine how the job descriptions will be distributed.** They may be sent to heads of academic programs certifying such professionals. These people are also good sources of information about experienced people already in the field who may want to move. The descriptions are also sent to professional journals to be abstracted for their placement sections. National and state conferences for such professionals are good places to distribute the descriptions, if they are timely. Institutional rules may require that the position be posted within the hiring organization, as well.

11. **Distribute the job descriptions.** Hand-delivery, regular and computer mail, fax.

Reference

Gentry, C. G. (1974). Directions for Writing Good Job Descriptions. In-house document for ID hiring committees. East Lansing, Mich.: Michigan State University.

Distributing Job Descriptions Once project managers are clear about the type of skills needed and have written proper job descriptions for announcing the needs, they must deal with how best to let potential applicants know of the positions. Although most employers as well as fair employment laws require the posting of jobs to follow certain rules, the main strategy for searching out good applicants is an informal one making use of the ID project manager's network of colleagues and acquaintances. Telephone calls will usually provide not only names but also informal assessments of the abilities of prospects known to the searcher's colleagues. This is certainly the case in searching for experienced applicants. There are, indeed, some jobs on a project for which an educational technology academic program will prepare the beginning instructional developer well enough. But there are other jobs for which the manager would want someone with one or more years of experience on the job. For the former, sending the job announcements to heads of these academic programs and to journals in the field is usually sufficient to bring forth several applicants. Recruiting trips to schools graduating the type of professional wanted may also be appropriate. However, for project positions requiring more experience, professional and personal networks usually produce better results than the indiscriminate broadcasting of the job description.

Selecting Applicants for Interview The initial evaluation of applicants is done by comparing the collected data coming from resumes, from contacts with applicants and their former employers, and from other references. Usually, there will be some applicants at this stage whose lack of qualifications can permit them to be cut out. The reduced list of applicants can then be ordered in terms of their perceived strengths and weaknesses. The project manager uses this list to contact high-priority applicants by telephone and/or mail to set up face-to-face interviews. Reasons for an in-person interview are obvious. It is very difficult to make judgments about how well someone will fit a position just from his or her paper bona fides.

Managers are very wise to follow up on an applicant's work references. Usually, gathering such data from an applicant's former bosses is more effective through telephone conversation than through requesting a written statement. There is a tendency for the references about an employee to be more candid when given orally, as opposed to being held to comments in a written document.

Interviewing Applicants   The treatment of applicants who are viewed as prime choices may be very different from that given to those who are unknown quantities to the search committee. In the first case, the applicant is wooed by being presented the very best side of the organization. The process for the superior applicant begins with his or her being picked up at the airport and taken to a first-class hotel. He or she is introduced to power figures in the organization who will probably speak more personally to them then than ever again. Parties and fine restaurants may be attended in the applicant's honor. Pressure is low, and everyone is friendly and admiring. Those candidates not so well known can expect an arduous day or two. Usually they will have as many back-to-back interviews as can be scheduled. They will find themselves shuffled rapidly from one person to another in between interviews, with barely enough time to stop at the restroom. Some employers operate on the notion that constant bombardment by people will, by the end of the day, tire applicants to the point where they are less able to screen any of their defects. There is no empirical evidence that this tactic works.

To play an interview by ear is to provide the applicant with an opportunity to present a heavily one-sided view of his or her qualifications. The use of a simple interview guide can result in a more balanced assessment of an applicant. First, the guide should lay out procedures for *selecting interviewers*. Interviewers are usually of two kinds: those with job-related experience, and those responsible for administrative procedures affecting the potential employee. The former would be relatively expert in the skills and knowledge expected of the applicant; the latter are knowledgeable in the general criteria for company employees. Second, the guide should provide direction in *scheduling the interview*. There is the problem of matching applicant availability with interviewer availability, and of ensuring that sufficient time is provided for the interviews. Third, the guide should provide directions for *generating applicant questions*, and for assigning responsibility for them to specific interviewers. The fourth procedure, *setting up applicant demonstrations*, is optional, but is perceived as very valuable in discriminating the talkers from the doers for certain skills. The fifth procedure gives direction on *keeping a record* of the interview so that it can be easily compared with the records of other interviewers.

The essential elements in an interview are fairly simple. There should be a minimum of three knowledgeable people doing the interviewing (partly for tie-breaking purposes). The interviewers should meet with the applicant separately in the first round, so as to make maximum benefit of each interviewer's insights, uninfluenced by other interviewers. While someone else takes the applicant to lunch and answers questions about the organization and the locale, the three interviewers should come together and compare notes taken during their respective interviews with the applicant. They may design and assign new questions to deal with any differences of view, in preparation for a joint meeting with the applicant. There are three broad questions that should be answered in any interview: Does the applicant know what he or she is talking about? Can he or she interact well with both individuals and groups? And is this a position in which an applicant can be productive and grow professionally? The job aid on "Interviewing Job Applicants" lays out an acceptable set of procedures.

Job Aid / Interviewing Job Applicants

Description   The interviewer is asked to study and compare the available data on the position and on the applicant, to look for congruities and discrepancies, and to generate questions for the applicant from the analysis.

Use Rationale   Most instructional developers sooner or later are put in the position of hiring other instructional developers and specialists needed in their projects. The procedures for interviewing potential employees requires careful planning, because employees are usually easier to come by than they are to get rid of. Because of poorly applied interviewing skills, managers too often regret their hiring decisions. Basic procedures such as the following reduce the likelihood of poor hiring decisions.

Critical Tasks

1. **Accept the interview assignment.** Be sure to ask the project manager at this time for details about the kind of person he or she is looking for. Also ask for any constraints imposed on the hiring. If possible get a written statement of the project manager's expectations and requirements, including the job description.

2. **Study the skills and other qualifications required by the job.** As presented in the job description.

3. **Study the materials supplied by the applicant.** E.g., resume, written references, application letter, portfolio materials.

4. **Search for and record congruencies between the position description and the applicant's materials.** E.g., applicant's on-the-job experience meets or exceeds job requirement.

5. **Search for and record discrepancies between the position description and the applicant's materials.** E.g., where applicant claims a work experience that is not collaborated by the relevant reference.

6. **Generate questions relevant to any discrepancies.** E.g., "When you worked for the graphics department of the PHQ Corporation, what exactly were your task responsibilities?" Try to have questions that evoke knowledge, skill, and attitude responses.

7. **Generate questions to draw the applicant out.** E.g., in terms of his or her personal and group communication skills, and attitude towards work.

8. **Complete the interview guide.** See Figure 14.2 for an example.

continued

Interviewing Job Applicants, continued

FIGURE 14.2 / Example of an outline of an interview guide for judging an applicant

INTERVIEW GUIDE

Applicant's Name _____

Date of Interview _____

Directions Complete each of the sections below.

I.   Position Title:

II.   Job Description & Qualifications:

III. Applicant Data

    A. Resume

    B. References

    C. Date(s) available for interview

IV. Selection of Interviewer(s)

    A. Expertise needed:

    B. Agreement to Interview

V.   Schedule for Interview(s)

Interviewer(s)	*Room*	*Time*

V.   Questions for Applicant. Use a 1–5 response scale for how well applicant did on the questions, with 5 representing an excellent response on the part of the applicant, and 1 representing an unacceptable response.

Questions		**Scale**			
A. Knowledge:					
(1) (Question 1)	1	2	3	4	5
(2) (Et cetera)	1	2	3	4	5
B. Skills:					
(1) (Question 1)	1	2	3	4	5
(2) (Et cetera)	1	2	3	4	5
C. Attitudes:					
(1) (Question 1)	1	2	3	4	5
(2) (Et cetera)	1	2	3	4	5
D. Future plans:					
(1) (Question 1)	1	2	3	4	5
(2) (Et cetera)	1	2	3	4	5

continued

Interviewing Job Applicants, continued

VII. Demonstration by the Applicant

    A. Topic:

    B. Equipment:

    C. Observer(s):

    D. Criteria for Demonstration:

    E. Schedule (time, date, and place):

    F. Rating for demonstration: Excellent   Average   Poor

VIII. Record of Interview

    A. Overall rating: Excellent   Average   Poor

       Rationale: _____

       _____

    B. Recommendation: Hire   Don't Hire

       Rationale: _____

       _____

       _____

---

9. **Meet with the applicant on one-to-one basis.** Keep the atmosphere pleasant but business-like.

10. **Record details of the meeting with the applicant.** Recording should be done soon after the interview, to prevent data loss. All interviewers should, if possible, follow the same recording format so that their inputs can be easily compared.

11. **Generate and assign questions for the interviewers' group meeting with the applicant.** Questions are derived by having the interviewers compare notes from their individual meetings with the applicant.

12. **The group interviews the applicant.** Use the questions previously assigned. The responses by the applicant will stimulate other questions. This should not turn into a police interrogation. Be careful not to make the applicant defensive. Always close by asking the applicants if *their* questions have been answered.

13. **Each interviewer provides an independent critique to the project manager.** E.g., by filling out the last section of the guide in Figure 14.2.

Reference

Gentry, C. G. (1974). Interviewing instructional developers. In-house document for ID hiring committees. East Lansing, Mich.: Michigan State University.

Prioritizing Applicants   Without clear criteria for a position, project managers tend to use secondary criteria for making judgments about an applicant, eg., what their written references say, how the applicant looks, personality, what the applicant says he or she is capable of, instead of primary or objective criteria. Examples of objective criteria would be a performance checklist to assess an applicant's key skills and knowledge, and a product checklist to assess an applicant's portfolio. As they say, appearances can be deceiving, and hiring people solely on how they look or what they say can prove disastrous. To resolve this problem, it is important for a manager to list the qualifications expected of applicants, and the criteria by which the manager judges their qualifications. An example of such criteria for a project position is presented in Figure 14.3.

FIGURE 14.3 / Example of a set of qualifications and criteria for hiring a person to fill a graphics artist position on an ID project

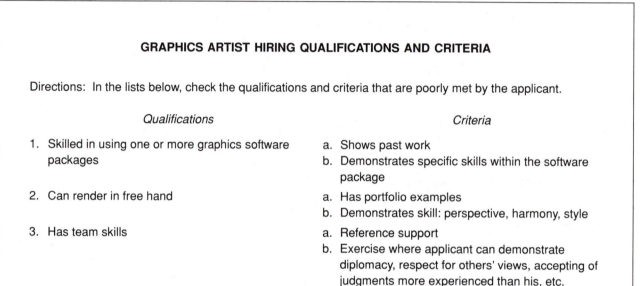

GRAPHICS ARTIST HIRING QUALIFICATIONS AND CRITERIA

Directions: In the lists below, check the qualifications and criteria that are poorly met by the applicant.

Qualifications

1. Skilled in using one or more graphics software packages

2. Can render in free hand

3. Has team skills

Criteria

a. Shows past work
b. Demonstrates specific skills within the software package

a. Has portfolio examples
b. Demonstrates skill: perspective, harmony, style

a. Reference support
b. Exercise where applicant can demonstrate diplomacy, respect for others' views, accepting of judgments more experienced than his, etc.

Once applicants have been assessed on predetermined criteria, the manager can compare the several qualified applicants in terms of how well they meet the job qualifications. Some more general questions that may help to choose among applicants include:

- When will the applicant be available?
- What other special qualifications does the applicant have?
- How costly is it to bring the applicant in for an interview?
- Does the applicant meet equity requirements, e.g., gender, race, handicapped?
- What is the state of the applicant's health?
- What does the applicant require as a salary?

Negotiating Position with Applicant Choice   The final step is to settle any remaining issues, including those of salary, benefits, work expectations, beginning work date, and contributions toward moving costs. In larger organizations, other administrators besides the project manager will usually be involved in the negotiation.

Hiring Applicant The final paperwork will usually be dealt with by higher echelons of the organization, including formal letters of acceptance and collecting administrative forms completed by the applicant. Whether done by a large organization housing training and development programs or by a small independent ID group, there will be a set of procedures to go through to bring a new hiree onto the payroll officially. These differ somewhat from group to group, but most of them depend on paperwork consisting of special forms for that purpose.

Orienting New Employee This is basically done to familiarize the new employee with the workplace and the policies and rules that guide its activities. The responsibilities of the parent organization and the services provided employees are usually explained. New hires are introduced to the people with whom they will be working. It is at this time that they are recognized by individuals and the group and made to feel relevant to the project. Often, it is a time for pairing them up with one or more individuals to assist them in acclimating themselves to the new environment.

Training Employees

Depending on the nature of the project and on the qualifications of project staff members, managers may find it necessary to provide training for some of their staff. The training of project employees is not a task embarked on lightly. It is costly, and it creates many management problems. However, the acquisition of certain new skills may be necessary to the project, and it can be rewarding to the employee. Factors important to consider once management assumes some responsibility for employee training include selecting employees to train, selecting the means for training, carrying out the training, and following up on the effects of training.

Selecting Trainees Who should be trained? Projects have finite objectives and a finite period in which they are to be fulfilled. This means that there is not a lot of time for training. Therefore, training decisions need careful consideration. The best of all possible worlds would be where employees came to the project already fully competent at their tasks, but this is seldom true. Even when new persons coming in are competent, they require orientation and time to become effective team members. Time is the important variable here, and each manager has to make judgments about the amount of time available for orienting and training new employees, and the cost of the training method in terms of pay-off to the project.

The problem is not just training those newly entering the project; there are also continuing circumstances that may make it necessary to train regular personnel in new skills. Suppose a project manager determines that a new computer graphics program is needed, and that training for it by the software company is for 5 days and costs $1,000 per employee. Besides this cost, there is also the cost of having someone fill in for employees while they are away at training. Before the manager decides to go with the training, he needs to consider whether an employee, once trained, can be expected to stay with the project to the end. What is the chance that this new training will increase the value of the employee to the point where she or he may be enticed away by better offers from competitors? Depending on the circumstance, managers may wish to get a commitment from the employee before sending him or her through training.

If the training is in-house, say where one graphics artist trains a peer, it may be less expensive, but will still slow the project down. There are other problems connected to techniques like peer teaching and apprenticeship that use in-house personnel to train others on a one-to-one basis. For example, graphic artists may be highly expert in their craft, but that doesn't necessarily make them good peer teachers. Further, the experienced graphic artist may not want to take time teaching the peer, resulting in frustration for both the artist and the peer when management forces them into these roles.

Selecting Training Methods   How employees will be trained varies with the subject matter and the preferences of management, all ameliorated by what is available. The effectiveness of most on-the-job training is questionable. Only with careful planning and follow-up are these procedures cost-effective. There are a number of techniques that are employed on the job. At the lower end of training adequacy is the use of techniques like the *Oral Walk-Through*, mentioned in Chapter 7. The procedures for this technique are to have a demonstration of a skill by an expert, followed by an explanation and then a supervised walk-through by the trainee, who also demonstrates and explains the procedure, with the rest of the learning being accomplished through trial and error.

Stopgap methods like these are quick, and certainly better than nothing, but other training techniques are preferred when time and resources allow (Goldstein, 1986, p.186). As *self-instructional packages* accumulate in a growing number of topical areas, they become more and more a cost-effective means of training employees. The flexibility of self-instructional systems lends them to adjusting to the schedule of the learner and the project in terms of time and other resources. Such systems are expected to become steadily more important. They are already very much manifesting themselves with the teaching of new software applications, as increasing numbers of these programs come with their own tutorials built in.

Four common training techniques used to train project personnel, are *Short courses, workshops, peer teaching*, and the *apprenticeship* method. The lengths of short courses and workshops range from a few hours to 2 or more weeks. These are supervised, tightly designed, instructional experiences, usually on very limited topics. Most projects have neither the time nor the resources to develop and run short courses and workshops, but managers can consider using a number of outside organizations that make their livelihoods by putting on such training. Peer teaching differs from the apprenticeship method: in the apprenticeship method, the teacher (journeyman) is usually more knowledgeable on several fronts, and the instruction is more extensive, and lasts for a much longer period. Except for very long projects, the apprenticeship method is not usually considered an appropriate on-the-job training technique. In contrast, the teacher in peer teaching is usually more knowledgeable in one or two skills, as compared to the person to be taught, and contracts for relatively short-term instruction. For example, a graphic artist skilled in a graphics software package might be asked, over a week or two, to train a co-worker in the package.

The "Peer Teaching" job aid presents a common methodology. Without following procedures such as those required in the job aid, there is serious question as to the effectiveness of peer teaching.

Job Aid / Peer Teaching

Description   Peer teaching (also called *peer mediated instruction, peer tutoring,* and *peer training*) is a useful technique for training for tasks that are limited in scope and in the time for learning. Basically it involves having a peer knowledgeable in an area that is not known to another peer teach a skill or a process. The process of developing a peer-teaching unit involves: specifying objectives, selecting an instructional strategy, specifying criteria for successful training, scheduling the instruction, and a follow-up assessment.

Use Rationale   Project managers often face periods when they know the available time of the person with specific skills will not be sufficient to get the job done on time. One solution is to train other project personnel in these skills through peer teaching.

Critical Tasks

1. **Identify a limited training task that is best done in-house on a one-to-one basis.** E.g., you need an employee to learn how to use a specific graphics software package.

2. **Identify the peer teacher and the peer student.** E.g., the peer teacher will be knowledgeable enough to teach a less knowledgeable peer how to use the software. There are occasions when one or both should have some extrinsic reward for this activity. They could be paid to do the peer teaching/learning activity on their own time, as well.

3. **Get the peer teacher and the peer student to accept the task.** Instruction goes easier if both are in agreement with their roles.

4. **Identify the specific objectives to be taught.** E.g., the trainee will be able to (a) boot up the program, (b) create images with paint tools, (c) select/move/cut/copy/paste images, and (d) deal with documents.

5. **Detail specific criteria for assessing trainee progress.** Usually this is done by laying out specific tasks or lesson elements for the trainee, with a standard established for each completed task, e.g., draw three separate images, described by teacher, and cut and paste the images to match a precise template, provided by the teacher; must show balance, harmony, and perspective.

6. **Detail the instructional strategy to be followed by the peer teacher and the peer student.** The peer teacher will explain and demonstrate a lesson element for a half hour in the morning and a half hour in the afternoon, each day for one week. Each lesson will be followed by a half hour of supervised practice relevant to the lesson element. The trainee will then be directed to practice lesson elements on his or her own for whatever time is available to the trainee for this purpose. During this latter practice, trainee will have limited access to the teacher for questions. In last stages of instruction, trainee should be doing real-time graphics assignments under the peer teacher. The peer teacher will complete two forms and submit them to the manager: an activity record, and a progress report. See Figures 14.4 and 14.5.

continued

Peer Teaching, continued

FIGURE 14.4 / **An example of a peer-training activity record**

PEER-TRAINING ACTIVITY RECORD

Peer Trainer: Peer Trainee:

Date/Time	Activity	Comment
6/22/92 8–9 am	Demonstrated and practiced booting up FullPaint software, using palettes, changing brush and pattern, saving and closing documents, quitting program.	OK on everything but using palettes. Needs practice.
6/23/92 4–5 pm	Demonstrated and practiced working in the Finder, use of painting tool: choosing shape of brush, using spray paint tool, drawing tools, patterns, and doing shapes and fills.	Needs practice on all of them. Gave appropriate practice tasks for him to do on his own. Showed good skill in using palettes.

7. **Schedule time and assignment.** The project manager must set up the instruction so that it has the least effect on the current progress of the project. This means that the sooner the process begins, the more opportunities there will be for scheduling so as to create the least number of problems.

8. **Assess the result.** Project manager meets with the peer teacher and the peer trainee to determine whether level of learning is satisfactory and to what degree the trainee can begin work on his or her own.

continued

Determining appropriate means of training for specific personnel depends on three variables: what is to be taught, the amount of time consumed in learning, and the cost of instruction. When what is to be taught is already being taught adequately as a short course in a local college or commercial workshop, the project manager may opt to use that resource. When the subject matter is idiosyncratic to special equipment or software and requires practice under supervision, the manager may choose *Oral Walk-Through* or the *Peer Teaching* method. When employees cannot be spared from regular tasks while learning, independent study or

Peer Teaching, continued

FIGURE 14.5 / Example of a peer-trainee progress report

PEER-TRAINEE PROGRESS REPORT

Key:
1 = excellent
2 = good
3 = satisfactory
4 = poor
5 = unsatisfactory

Trainer: Jones
Trainee: Smith
Skill: drawing

Date/Time	Skill or Process	Grade
6/24/92 9–10 am	Drawing rectangles	1
	Drawing rectangles with rounded corners	1
	Drawing ovals	3
	Draws free hand lines	4
	Draws free hand filled shapes	2
	Draws hollow polygons	2

References

Endsley, W. R. (1980). *Peer Tutorial Instruction.* Englewood Cliffs, N.J.: Educational Technology Publications.

Rosenbaum, P. S. (1973). *Peer-Mediated Instruction.* New York: Columbia University Teachers College Press.

self-instructional methods may be used, with employees learning on their own time, possibly being paid for it by the project. In the case of independent study, the topic and general objectives are usually mutually agreed on by the learner and facilitator, but the choice of materials to be studied is usually searched out by the learner. Self-instructional methods such as *programmed instruction (PI)* and *computer-assisted instruction (CAI)* are highly structured, automated learning systems where learners are given corrective and confirming feedback as they progress through the program at their own pace. Other variables, such as the time consumed in learning, may also affect the choice of training method.

During Training When employees are pulled out of their regular tasks for instruction, it may be necessary to have someone else assume their responsibilities on the project while they are gone This may be necessary to keep the project on its contracted timeline. Depending on the job, several alternatives offer themselves. Examples would be to hire a temporary person to carry out the tasks, and to spread responsibility among other project members. In some cases, time will permit the specific job to be put off while the person is being trained.

Follow-up   There is a basic assumption that persons trained in supposedly relevant skills will apply them when back on the job. Often, that is not true—partly because the skills are not immediately needed, and also because, unless immediately reinforced on the job, new knowledge tends to deteriorate rapidly until the employee no longer feels competent to apply the knowledge when the need does arise. Second, there is often an assumption that because a course is described in a way that would lead one to think it is directly applicable, what really is taught, and at what level, will affect its applicability. Thus, it is important to follow up on the effects of the instruction, to provide reinforcement of the importance of the new knowledge, and to establish how valuable or useful the knowledge is to the job.

Evaluating on-the-Job Effectiveness and Efficiency

A task periodically required of a manager in long-running projects is the evaluation of employees in terms of how effectively they are performing their jobs. This is done for purposes of salary increment decisions, for promotion, for determining training needs, and for dismissal purposes. Managers find it hard to carry out these evaluations effectively. This is partly because of a subjective view of the employee and partly because managers lack the skill or time to perform objective evaluations.

To perform an objective evaluation requires establishing several things, including baseline expectations for the job, what tasks to evaluate the employee on, and what criteria to use in evaluating the employee. The job description gives the general areas of competence to be evaluated, and the use of a PERT or of a task analysis can reveal the specific tasks to be evaluated. Two factors that need to be considered, are how well these tasks are done, and how long it takes to do them.

Take the instance where the task is to write behavioral objectives for an instructional module. How well this task was completed is judged by predetermined standards; e.g., the objectives match instructional goals; each objective is made up of behavior, conditions, and degree elements; objectives are correctly sequenced; and the employee was efficient in generating the objectives. The manager needs to go beyond these standards to ask if there were extenuating circumstances not attributable to the actions of the employee. For example, where employee efficiency is in question, the manager needs to know to what degree slowdowns were the result of the employee's not having ready access to content experts. It is useful to have some kind of baseline data on the production of objectives. Of course, it is important that employees have a clear idea of the expectations and the criteria used for evaluating them on the various tasks, *before* the evaluation period begins. Finally, employees should be given clear feedback on their evaluations, for purposes of counseling them to do better or to confirm their good work, or because they will find it difficult to improve if they are left in the dark about how they were evaluated and about the results of their evaluation. In some organizations, managers are expected to report evaluation results to other administrators in the parent organization.

Motivating Employees to Meet Project Standards

Employees who are reasonably paid, enjoy their work, and who see it as important have little need for external motivation. But part of the reason they enjoy their work is because someone has thought ahead to include the environmental conditions suitable to that employee.

What do project personnel need to make the workplace palatable? Among their needs would be to feel appreciated and recognized, to feel effective, and to have available the essential resources and conditions for carrying out the job, including clear expectations from management. Personnel have a strong aversion to being put in the position of playing guessing games about what the manager wants. On the other hand, they would like some flexibility to do things their way. The attitudes and style of management brought to a project can make a major difference. Every manager has her or his own theory for managing people. McGregor (1960), perhaps in an oversimplification, pointed to opposing management theories, called Theory X, Theory Y. Managers who support Theory X assume workers are lazy and irresponsible, and if not controlled, watched, directed, and coerced will be slackers on the job; to be productive they must be constantly pushed and motivated by fear of the negative consequences of wrong actions on their parts. On the other hand, Theory Y managers see their people as individuals who seek responsibility and personal growth and development, and who, with the proper support, will do the best job they can. Employees' commitment is related to the rewards associated with their achievement. Certainly, these polar views would make a difference in the way managers manage and workers work. Theory Y points toward a participative management style, where the manager engages the ingenuity, imagination, and creativity of staff members in solving project problems. Theory X points toward maximum control, where staff are expected to do what they are told, when they are told, and how they are told, with little variance. More likely, managers will use facets of both these theoretical positions. As Harrison (1981, p. 292) says, "It may be necessary to be detailed and autocratic with one individual, delegate with mild control with another group or individual, and be fully participative with others."

Going beyond these theoretical aspects is the more practical need to determine what will make the job important enough to the individual employee or group to get out the extra effort to go from mediocre to good or even great performance. The manager needs to ask what is professionally important to specific employees: Where do they want to go in their careers? What do they see themselves doing 5 years from now?

How can a project manager support high performance in participative management? For one thing, the manager needs to be sensitive to the motivators available, and vary their use with individuals or groups. The manager must also think in terms of the resources available to support the use of such motivators. Common motivators include:

a. Accepting employee input into the project decision-making process

b. Salary increases

c. Public recognition: giving employees credit when due

d. Giving employees a free hand in methods of accomplishing assigned tasks within appropriate resource limitations

e. Letting employees have a say in selecting the tasks or projects they take on

f. Provide employees with training they want or need

g. Giving employees perks, such as: trips to conventions, time off, office space, use of project equipment and software on and off job projects, and giving bonuses

These and other motivators should be parceled out with care, with the manager and the worker both having clearly in mind what performance merits such payoffs. In attempting to influence the performance of staff, the manager should also remember Maslow's first premise for the hierarchy of human needs: "Satisfied needs are not motivators, only unsatisfied needs motivate." Thus managers must keep aware of what it is that currently motivates a staff member. See the job aid on "Motivating Project Staff." As Harrison points out (1981, p. 300), an effective group "means working towards project objectives, without interpersonal or intergroup conflict, and with satisfied and involved members." He believes that to arrive at this state, a team goes through four stages: (1) development of mutual acceptance and trust, (2) open communication among members, (3) cooperation and sustained productivity, and (4) resolving of problems and control through mutual agreement.

Job Aid / Motivating Project Staff

Description   This technique lists a set of guidelines that, when followed, should increase the likelihood of employee needs being considered and the likelihood that appropriate motivations are applied in the workplace. It is based on providing staff with the information and incentives needed to complete their respective tasks, including: a clear statement of expectations on the part of management, an understanding of how the reward system operates, regular constructive feedback on progress, and a say in project decisions that directly affect them.

Use Rationale   ID project managers can expect to run the gamut of personnel problems, for several reasons, the main one being that allegiance to a finite project is not the same as that for an ongoing operation. Often, many of the personnel are transitory, in the sense they are brought in briefly to do their part and then leave the project. Managers need to remember that staff members have some needs that go beyond the project.

Critical Tasks

1. **Provide project personnel with a clear set of project goals and objectives.** Goals can come from a *Needs Analysis* done by the project or client group.

continued

Motivating Project Staff, continued

2. **Specify and sequence tasks that meet the goals and objectives.** A good means of accomplishing this is *PERT*.

3. **Assign the specified tasks to one or more project staff members.** Refer to the discussion of work-breakdown packages in Chapter 13.

4. **Inform project staff of the procedures to be followed in completing their assigned tasks.** These are basically controlling and coordinating directions for staff to follow.

5. **Specify the rewards for successful accomplishment of assigned tasks.** They may be intrinsic or extrinsic in nature, depending on the person and the accomplishment, ranging from recognition, paid time off, and bonuses, to a choice of tasks.

6. **Give project members periodic feedback on their task work.** This can be formal and/or informal, but should be consistent and constructive and clearly related to semicompleted and completed tasks. Positive feedback is done publicly; negative feedback is done privately.

7. **Follow up on the effects of feedback.** Establish whether the feedback was incorporated into staff behavior. Reinforce it if necessary.

8. **Provide rewards for successful completion of work.** This should be done immediately at completion, and publicly, for maximum reinforcement effect.

9. **Involve project members in project decisions that directly affect them.** This is useful because of the perspective staff can provide, and for getting them to buy into the project.

Reference

Bass, B. M., et al. (1987). *Motivation to Work: Advances in Organizational Psychology.* Newbury Park, Calif.: Sage, pp. 34–42.

Counseling and Censuring Inappropriate Behavior

Counseling should always precede censuring of personnel who are performing inadequately. Both counseling and censuring should usually be done in private. Public exposure of one's faults may be too debilitating for personnel, and may prevent them from listening appreciatively to recommendations for improvement. To the degree possible, managers should be friendly but objective in their counseling. The focus should be on the mutual solving of a problem that is hurting the project. Ground work should be laid by explaining the problem as seen by the manager, in terms of the problem's affect on the project, so that the manager's concern and responsibility to act is clear. At that point, a good next step is to ask the employee how he or she thinks the problem could be solved. More often than not the employee may propose a very adequate solution, to which the manager should readily agree. The manager should be sure that all of the conditions are in place for the solution to work, and then monitor to be sure it takes place. Problems that arise are not necessarily due to workplace factors, but may be due, among other possibilities, to problems in family or other extra-job relations, including financial or drinking difficulties. In some cases the best that the manager can do is to recommend that the employee seek professional counseling.

If counseling is unsuccessful in changing the behavior or performance of an employee, the manager may find it necessary to take a harsher step, that of censuring. *Censuring* is, basically, the process of pointing out discrepancies observed between satisfactory and unsatisfactory performance, and making employees aware that they can't continue an undesirable form of behavior without negative consequences. Data collected on undesirable behaviors may include inadequate completion of tasks, complaints from others involved in the project, or violations of organizational policies and procedures. Censuring should be followed by the manager's making means available to the employee for correcting the undesirable behavior. Censuring should be done when it is clear that counseling has not served the purpose, and before the problem gets out of hand. As mentioned, censuring should be done in private, but should be followed by a formal memo to the employee (see example in Figure 14.6), with copies to appropriate administrators. The latter procedure is both for keeping administrators informed and for documenting the undesirable behavior, as evidence should dismissal later become necessary.

Dismissing Personnel

Unfortunately, moments come in all managers' careers when they find it necessary to dismiss employees. This occurs when employees cannot, or choose not, to perform their roles with a project team adequately,

FIGURE 14.6 / Example of a censuring memo

To: Herbert H. Hobert, Instructional Developer
From: Harold G. Canfield, Gamma Project Manager
Date: April 14, 1993
RE: Attendance at project team meetings

I would like to be sure that we are both clear on the results of the meeting you and I had on Tuesday of this week. As you will recall, I stated my concern, and that of the general manager, about your *not* attending the last three project team meetings, of January 3, February 5, and March 1. While I sympathize with your desire to, instead, get regular project work done during those times, I do not agree with you that there is no benefit to your attending these meetings.

In fact, it is my strong view that the sharing of information by project team members during these meetings results in many problems being averted at a later date. While not demanding that you hold the same view, I do appreciate your agreeing to attend and actively participate in all future project team meetings.

Please let me know, at your earliest convenience, if your sense of the outcomes of our meeting do *not* concur with the statements above. Given that we are in agreement, no further action need be taken.

cc: Will Smith, General Manager

and where further training, counseling, or censuring does not appear to solve the problem. In these days of litigation, managers need documentation of an employee's inadequacy on the job. Examples of items to be documented could be: serious errors made in carrying out their tasks, slowness in completing tasks (may be due to incompetence, irresponsibility, emotional problems, or alcohol/drug addiction), or inability to get along with other team members. The accruing of documentation should be coordinated, with the manager facing the employee with the problems as they arise, and sincere attempts to assist the employee in modifying undesirable behavior. Satisfactory employees are ones who have the right balance between competence, and attitude. Clearly, to be effective they must have the knowledge and skills for the role for which they were hired. If they lack that competence or if it is economically unfeasible to develop it in them, then a mistake has been made in hiring them. Having competence and applying it consistently is a matter of attitude, of motivation, and of pride in one's work. If there is a lack of competency, and/or if the attitude is poor, and the usual means of training and motivation fail, then serious consideration must be given to the employee's dismissal.

Once the manager sees dismissal as the necessary recourse, he or she needs to stop and consider again the justification for the firing: is there appropriate documentation in support of the dismissal? Is the problem being viewed objectively by the manager? Has the employee been given fair opportunity to correct faults? If the answer to these questions is yes, then the next step is to make plans for the dismissal. This should be done in such a way as to create as little disruption of project activities as possible. If the decision to dismiss lies in the hands of those above the manager, then the manager must engage their agreement. Given their agreement, the manager needs to make plans for covering the employee's tasks in the interim before a new employee is hired. This is very important, because even a poor employee may be far superior to none, particularly when that person's dismissal may limit other members in doing their jobs. In many cases, other project members can pick up the dismissed member's duties until someone else is hired. In other instances, temporary help from outside can be accessed. The usual procedure in dismissal cases is to give the employee a 2-weeks' notice. Managers who have the choice prefer to give the employee the wages for the 2 weeks, and have them clear the premises immediately. This is particularly true when the employee, angry at being dismissed, might decide to perform some mischief. For example, in situations where computer operations are involved, employees upset at their dismissal have been known to do critical damage to programs and data during their last 2 weeks.

Careful records need to be maintained so that, should litigation rear its ugly head, evidence can be quickly produced to demonstrate justification for a dismissal.

For competent managers who are able to recognize and complement the needs of their project staffs, censuring and dismissal are relatively rare events. Despite the problems that are endemic to an ID project, under competent management and satisfied personnel, the work can be exciting and fulfilling.

Summary

Maintaining a highly motivated and productive project staff has to be a high priority for managers. Procedures and techniques for determining staffing needs and for hiring, training, assessing, motivating, censuring, and dismissing project employees were discussed in this chapter.

References

Chisholm, M. E., and Ely, D. P. (1976). *Media Personnel in Education: A Competency Approach.* Englewood Cliffs, N.J.: Prentice-Hall.

Craig, R. L. (ed.) (1976). *Training and Development Handbook: A Guide to Human Resource Development.* New York: McGraw-Hill.

Goldstein, I. L. (1986). *Training in Organizations.* Monterey, Calif.: Brooks/ Cole.

Harrison, F. L. (1981). *Advanced Project Management.* New York: Wiley.

McGregor, D. (1960). *The Human Side of Enterprise.* New York: McGraw-Hill.

Plunkett, W. R., and Attner, R. F. (1989). *Introduction to Management.* 3d ed. Boston: PWS-Kent.

CHAPTER 15

ID Project Facilities

Process for organizing and renovating spaces for design, implementation, and testing of elements of instruction

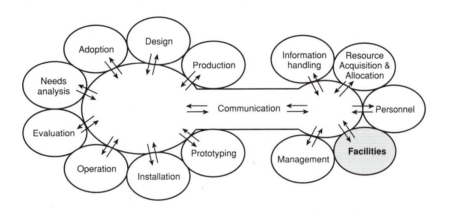

Learner Objectives

1. List the characteristics of projects that can affect the spaces they use.

2. List the common types of spaces required for ID project activities.

3. Describe common factors affecting the use of project spaces.

4. List common trade-offs considered in choosing among available project spaces.

5. Describe common types of modifications made to improve ID project spaces.

6. Describe basic maintenance needs of ID project facilities.

7. Recall definitions of major terms.

Introduction

People who run projects have special problems with the spaces in which they do their work. The main problem arises from the very nature of projects, since they are limited by finite objectives, time, and resources. This means that spaces taken on by projects will usually be temporary. The run of projects seldom exceeds 3 years, and may run for as little as a month or two. At the beginning of a project it is necessary to find and control spaces in which to carry out its activities; at the end, resources remaining must be redistributed, project members may be dispersed, and work spaces returned to the user pool. Professor John Tyo, a noted producer of instructional film and video programs from Syracuse University, long proclaimed the crucialness of instructional developers' having control of adequate work spaces. He contended that project managers without adequate space in their workplace for their various activities have two strikes against them. Arranging for temporary space elsewhere as needed is time-consuming and uncertain, making it difficult to schedule work any distance ahead. In addition, lack of adequate space tends to disperse project staff, making their management more difficult.

During the late 1950s and throughout the '60s, there was an increased concern for design of educational facilities in terms of how they affected people. Someone once said, "First we shape our spaces, and thereafter they shape us." Negative effects of facilities on people are easy to imagine: as extremes, consider the effects of a long prison term in solitary confinement, or the effects of a crowded tenement apartment on its residents. A popular area of study related to facilities design is called *ergonomics*. According to Ellington and Harris (1986, pp. 58–59):

Ergonomics is the application of anatomical, physiological and psychological knowledge and principles to the study of the relationship between people and all aspects of their activities.

Some time ago, Robert Sommer (1969) wrote a fascinating book called *Personal Space,* about the effects of the structures in which we live. His book is as relevant today as it was when first written. In his book, he revealed some of the more subtle effects of the spaces designed for everyday activities. In one example he reflected on the asocial effects of furniture in airport terminals (p. 121):

> In most terminals it is virtually impossible for two people sitting down to converse comfortably for any length of time. The chairs are either bolted together and arranged in rows theater-style facing the ticket counters, or arranged back-to-back, and even if they face one another they are at such distances that comfortable conversation is impossible.

Whether waiting for a plane, carrying out some work task, or attempting to learn a new skill, the structures in which these activities take place have their effect. The project manager needs to know enough about these effects to avoid the negative ones and to enhance the positive ones.

Spaces begin to change once people move in, even in the most restricted environment—the clandestine coffee pot, the visual barrier devised through placement of office file cabinets, placement of colorful posters, the green plant aficionados, the arrangement of office furniture, and so on. There appears to be a need to soften the institutionalized decor to satisfy human needs of body and spirit. Although, in the past, facilities required much adaptation on the part of the people who lived and worked in them, today, work spaces are becoming increasingly user friendly: automatic door openers for load bearers, and conveniences for the handicapped, including, width of doorways, ramps, and specially designed restrooms. Increasingly, spaces are examined and modified to accommodate the perceived needs of personnel. Included are concerns for adequate light, temperature, sound levels, color decor, seating arrangements, and patterns of traffic, to name a few.

To derive maximum benefit from the efforts of instructional developers requires that project spaces also be shaped to fit their needs. What then are satisfactory spaces in which instructional developers ply their trade? The processes discussed here do not include the more serious aspect of hiring an architect, as would be necessary in new construction or major modifications of existing spaces, but rather cover the kinds of changes ID personnel can themselves make or can contract out to workers such as plumbers, electricians, and carpenters.

Project Facilities-Handling Process

Steps for satisfying facility needs of instructional development projects include the following:

1. Determine the types of spaces necessary for satisfactory operation of a specific ID project.
2. List the conditions required for project spaces.
3. Locate one or more facilities that are available to the project.
4. Determine the degree to which a potential facility meets the conditions required by the project.
5. Given that modifications are necessary, draw up specifications for modifying the facilities.
6. Estimate costs for modifying the facilities.
7. Given sufficient resources, modify the facilities to meet the conditions necessary for the development of the instructional unit.
8. Maintain the space during ongoing operation.

Each ID project will be somewhat different in its spatial needs. There is no attempt here to provide a guide to the many possible spatial configurations; rather, through an example project, we show how such needs relate to the eight steps just listed.

The example project is one that the author managed with two of his colleagues at Michigan State University. Its major purpose was to develop a self-instructional unit to teach the hearing associates of deaf children to sign, and, thus, to enhance elementary and secondary classroom communication for the deaf. The medium chosen was a level II interactive videodisc. The completed instructional unit was named *The Sign Connec-*

tion. Two years were taken to complete the project. It was funded partly by a federal agency and partly by the Instructional Television and Computer Center units at Michigan State University.

Determining Types and Conditions of Spaces Required

Invariably, the acquiring of spaces to carry on project activities is the result of compromise. In many cases, spaces are allocated to instructional development teams with little initial input from either manager or team. Even so, it is wise to go through the process of determining what spaces are needed, so that judicious reorganization of the existing space is more likely to take place. Ideal conditions are seldom met specifically, and never generally.

The types of spaces needed depend on project variables. For example, when time is an important variable, it is unlikely that a great deal of effort will be put into modifying spaces for a project that must be completed in, say, 1 month. But for projects lasting 6 months or more, a number of advantages can come out of careful modification and reorganization of the spaces to be used by a project. But first, what are the general types of spaces required?

Generally speaking, the types of spaces needed by projects will include spaces to accommodate staff meetings and the planning, designing, producing, and pilot testing of instructional units. Projects may also require office and storage space. Of concern are the entrances and exits (including elevators) to the spaces, and placement of utilities such as restrooms, as well as traffic patterns, security, and office environment, including acoustics, lighting, temperature, and ventilation. The types of spaces that may be needed are discussed in more detail in the following sections.

Meeting Spaces   Because space always seems in short supply, spaces used for staff and small group meetings may have to serve other purposes as well. Universities usually have meeting rooms that project people can schedule, assuming their managers have faculty status. This was true for *The Sign Connection* interactive videodisc project. There was no problem as long as the spaces could be scheduled 2–3 weeks ahead, but on several occasions when emergency meetings needed to be called for the entire staff, there was difficulty in finding space. The manager's office was large enough to house a small table that would seat up to six people, and this was often used for smaller group meetings. In a number of cases, meetings had to be held in other buildings in less than desirable surroundings, and on a few occasions they had to be canceled for lack of space. In instances where cancellation was necessary, the manager had to call several smaller group meetings to cover the ground. This of course meant additional effort on the part of the manager, and that the messages given to one group varied somewhat from that given the others, and that information that would have resulted from the greater interaction of the whole project staff was missing. Basically, meeting spaces should be comfortable, large enough to accommodate the group, and readily accessible.

Spaces for Planning   As a rule, spaces used for project planning are not designated as such. Likely enough, spaces for planning meetings will include the staff meeting rooms, especially when they are controlled by the project. For *The Sign Connection* project, most of the planning occurred between the manager and his two coordinators in the ID project manager's office, and in the weekly staff meetings held in scheduled meeting rooms. Spaces for planning need to accommodate different-size groups, and flexible furniture is needed to work on a variety of material.

Spaces for Instructional Design   The type of space needed for instructional design can vary at different points in the design process. For instance, in the early stages of design, brainstorming, which proved to be a valuable tool, took place in a college conference room. One result of the brainstorming was the decision to collect needs analysis data on the importance of the proposed project from experts in deaf education, mainstream teachers, and parents of deaf children. The development of the needs analysis instrument took place in the home of the staff member assigned responsibility for developing the instrument.

In another instance, those staff members writing scripts and storyboards needed tables and chairs in a very quiet space. *Working walls* are also useful to designers applying techniques like *storyboarding*. A **working wall** is a plain wall to which sections of a storyboard or PERT network can be tacked for ready reference by those involved, flexible enough to permit rapid changes. For example, cells of the storyboard for *The Sign Connection* were tacked to a large section of cork board pasted to the wall of the ID project manager's office. This made additions and deletions of the cells by staff relatively easy, and enabled everyone to see where the storyboard was going and how their criticisms or comments could help. It also meant that the project manager had very little privacy. Much of the original scripting and storyboarding was done by project staff at their homes and on their computers. Many "make-do" spaces were used early on because *The Sign Connection* project did not get workspace assigned to it until 4 months into the project. During that time management was very labor intensive.

Production Spaces   The degree to which a project's instructional materials are produced by its members or, conversely, contracted out to others varies. To illustrate, of the production necessary to the interactive videodisc instructional unit for *The Sign Connection* project, graphics were done by regular project personnel using a computer workstation in the production room with software called the Director; the still photographs needed were done by a project staff member with a 35mm camera in a space temporarily loaned by the college media center; project and University Instructional Television (ITV) personnel shot the video segments with their camera and sound equipment, either on location or in one of their studios; and ITV also contributed time and expertise on special equipment in their editing suite, necessary for preparing the videotape used to make an interactive videodisc master. And, of course, the videodisc master itself was produced in the production facilities of a company in another state. As a further example, in order to get sharp and distinct photos for the instructor's manual, cooperation was sought through the Xerox Company, which had a special new copier that they used to provide our print masters. The budget available to *The Sign Connection* project could not have begun to cover the cost of facilities and equipment necessary to all of the production operations of an interactive videodisc instructional unit.

In contrast, larger instructional development units, particularly in business and industry, such as those of Arthur Andersen and Company, do most of their production in-house. Such units must bear the direct and indirect costs of graphics and photographics units (including darkrooms), studios and editing rooms for video and film production, and the specialized personnel for operating the units. Each piece or combination of production equipment in the respective spaces will have its own requirement for placement and electrical power.

Spaces for Pilot Testing   Depending on the stage and complexity of the testing of a new instructional unit, the need for space will differ. For example, when doing *one-on-one formative evaluation,* an evaluator and a representative learner might only need a small room that can house them and the instructional delivery system, whereas *small-group formative evaluation* or *summative evaluation* may use anywhere from 10 to 100 or more learners at a time, requiring larger spaces with or without special equipment. For *The Sign Connection* project, one-on-one, small-group formative, and summative evaluation were all done in spaces provided by the local schools from which learners were drawn. This meant that the interactive videodisc delivery system (i.e., hardware and software) had to be transported to and from the schools each time. When a project has only a limited amount of equipment, transporting it to several locations increases the likelihood of malfunction, and also takes the equipment out of reach of other staff who may need to use it. Usually, in business and industry training programs, pilot testing will be done in the company's regular training rooms. Spaces should be comfortable, and controllable in terms of external distractions.

Office Spaces   For a small project to furnish office space to its members is unusual, unless this was already a part of a permanent ID unit. University personnel who run projects may work out of their regular offices, but other personnel hired for the project will more often than not be assigned to a common workspace. In those cases where project space is acquired through rental or leasing, the manager will need to consider what furniture is necessary for office spaces, including desks, tables, and chairs. The acquisition and arrangement of communications system elements will have to be planned, including telephones, modems, interoffice computer networks, fax machines, and copiers. While *The Sign Connection* project used university meeting rooms and offices of the manager and coordinators of the project, a large production room was also assigned to them in which several workstations were set up for staff members. Among these workstations was a VHS video editing and video playback station, a computer graphics production station, a computer programming and laserdisc playback station, and a multipurpose computer station used for generation of project PERTs, flowcharts, scripts, storyboards, and reports. For the first 3 months of the project, a part-time secretary was also used. This person was already working for the university on a part-time basis and was able to do project work at her regular workstation. Interestingly, project members found that they made increasingly less use of the secretary because they were already composing most of their materials on the word processor before handing them to the secretary. Dispensing with her services was another form of savings.

Storage Spaces   There is rarely ever sufficient storage space for a project, particularly *secure* storage space. One of the storage needs for most ID projects is space for controlling applications software and project product masters. Another problem is the storage of equipment. For example, media hardware comes in varying sizes, so shelving needs to be designed to accommodate the variety of shapes and sizes. The rule of thumb is 8 inches deep for books, 10–18 inches deep for oversize material, and even larger shelves for equipment. *The Sign Connection* project used several cabinets that were procured one way or another. These were placed along two walls of the production space. The general rule is to take all of the storage space you can get and find a means of controlling access to it.

Restrooms   Among the codes for inhabited buildings are those for restrooms. In some cases, there must be two separate restrooms, one for men and one for women. There must be ready access to restrooms for handicapped workers and visitors. Fortunately, for *The Sign Connection* project the university building in which it was housed more than met code requirements.

General Factors Affecting Spaces

Additional factors affecting each type of space just discussed are presented in the next few sections.

Traffic Patterns   Entrances and exits from the building and the different rooms of the project space can be critical—not only in terms of causing the least disruption of activities going on in the space, but to satisfy fire and other emergency codes as well. Again, questions of handicapped ingress and egress is an important factor. Aisleways between workstations and other spaces need to be thought through; otherwise either there will be too little walking space, which will interfere with the project activities at the workstations, or there will be too much walking space, resulting in loss of valuable work area. Again, for *The Sign Connection* project, the university had already met exit, entrance, and elevator codes before this project came on campus. By careful arrangement of furniture and equipment, maximum use was made of limited space.

Security   Beyond the general securing of project space is the concern for limiting access to spaces used to store software masters and special documents controlled by designated personnel. Then there is the question of how best to protect project data stored in computers and on external tapes and discs. Data generated by computer for *The Sign Connection* project were stored on computers in the coordinators' separate offices and on a computer in the production room, with floppy-disc backup, which reduced considerably the chance of serious data loss through a system or disc crash. Later, when the final computer programming for the interactive videodisc was finished by a programmer in the university's computer center, a safe copy was preserved by the programmer as well as by several project staff. Passwords were used to protect the finished computer programs developed for and by the project. Also requiring security were the masters for application software that had been bought for various activities, e.g., graphics, flowcharting, and PERT. These were stored carefully in one of the coordinator's filing cabinets in his office, and were only used to make working copies. Original videotapes were kept for us by the instructional television division in their temperature-controlled video library. Safe copies were also kept in a cabinet in the project production room. The interactive videodisc instructional unit master was stored (at a price) by 3M, the company that did the mastering.

Having computers, videotape, and videodisc systems stolen is not an uncommon occurrence on university campuses. While such loss has happened in the past to several other projects on campus, it did not happen to equipment assigned to *The Sign Connection* project. The manager and coordinators are convinced that a major reason it did not was the care with which staff members both policed visitors and locked up the facility when leaving.

Staff Environment   People working in comfortable workspaces are, as a rule, more productive than those working in uncomfortable workspaces. It is easy to understand that staff members working under hot and humid conditions or under chilly conditions will lose some concentration on their tasks. Similarly, no one likes to work in a poorly ventilated room, for both health and comfort reasons.

Noisy rooms are distracting to workers. Examples would be noise caused by poorly maintained air conditioners, and the band practicing next door. There are ways of reducing the noise level in a workspace: cork tile flooring or carpeting, buying chairs that roll instead of scrape, and applying acoustical tile to ceilings and even walls.

Lighting that is too weak or too bright, that flickers, or that creates glare can be an irritant to workers. In modifying a space, thought should be given to the convenience of light control through effective window shades or blinds, and electrical switches in the right places, with rheostats to control brightness where appropriate. For example, brightness needs to be controlled in media preview spaces: sufficient light for note taking but not so bright that the media image is faded.

Worker access to electrical power outlets is another critical factor. Having five cords going to one electrical outlet is a fire hazard. Adding additional power outlets is not terribly costly, and the convenience and safety advantages are considerable. Ten electrical outlets were added to *The Sign Connection* production space in order to deal with all of the equipment that was being used.

What can a project manager do to make the project environment safe for staff? Posting signs for high voltage, modifying slippery floors, and providing the right kind of fire extinguisher are examples. Accidents do happen on the job. What is protocol if a staff member has a heart attack or some other serious illness that comes on suddenly? The posting of appropriate telephone numbers (including 911) to doctors, emergency services, etc., where everyone has quick access is one small step. What happens if someone has a minor accident? What should a manager be able to do in terms of first aid? Should there be a first-aid kit available, and someone who has had the basics in applying first aid or CPR? For small projects these are usually judgment calls. This concern is largely neglected in smaller projects. It certainly was in *The Sign Connection* project. In larger organizations, there may be a first-aid station with attendant nurse or even a doctor on call. But that is usually true only for organizations in which ID is just one of several components.

Facility Rules Any space where several people are working requires a few rules that will permit personnel to work effectively and in harmony. Examples are: rules covering smoking; protecting equipment (such as not drinking coffee or soft drinks at the computer—one that was bound to be ignored); the last person out at night turns off certain equipment and lights, and sets the alarm system; rules controlling whether, and under what conditions, people may work in the facility over the weekend or at night; who has access to certain areas, such as the supply cabinet or to the software master storage area; or who gets the best parking spots. As an example of one problem, it took almost 6 months to get everyone keys to *The Sign Connection* project production room, because of concern for rules prohibiting graduate students from having keys to certain rooms in the building. This was later compounded when keys to external entrances were requested so that night and weekend work could be carried on.

Assessing Existing Facilities

Usually, spaces available for a project include space recently released by personnel of completed projects, basements or upper floors of failed businesses, and decentralized spaces already available to project personnel. The manager needs to consider trade-offs among them, in terms of relative cost, availability, and how closely the spaces fit the more important conditions required of the different project tasks. Data collection on such spaces can be extensive. An example of a simple form for rating project spaces is presented in Figure 15.1. If copies of this form were filled out and then compared for the several available project sites, the manager would have a means to make a more objective judgment about their relative appropriateness to a specific project.

Specifying Facility Modifications

Once possible facilities have been assessed in terms of meeting the requirements of a project, the manager can consider what changes or modifications would have to be made in the one chosen to provide a satisfactory environment for carrying out project activities. The manager needs to divide the proposed changes into categories of "necessary" and "nice," with concentration on the necessary. At the same time, the manager should reconsider which of the project tasks might be more cost-effective to contract out, as opposed to doing them in-house. An example of such a trade-off for *The Sign Connection* project was the decision to use the university's instructional television unit's special editing equipment for the final editing of the videotape masters from which 3M would make videodisc masters. For the project to have bought the necessary equipment would have been prohibitive, to say the least.

FIGURE 15.1 / Example of a form for rating types of spaces and the conditions needed for a project

PROJECT FACILITY RATING FORM

Project: _____

Manager: _____

Rater: _____

Date: _____

Directions: List the conditions required for the specific spaces needed for the types of rooms to be used on a project. Then rate the spaces according to how well they meet the conditions, without modification, using the following scale:

6 = not appropriate or necessary
5 = very good
4 = good
3 = adequate
2 = poor
1 = very poor

Using the same scale rate the potential of the space, but assume that the resources are available to modify it to meet project conditions.

Spaces	Conditions	Value as Is	Potential
Meetings	Light control for media review	3	5
	Handle 16-ft. table with eighteen chairs	5	5
	Electrical outlets for media	4	5
Planning	Support small to medium-size meetings (10–15 people), and one workstation for computer flowcharting and PERTing	4	5
Design	Support two computer workstations used for storyboarding and computer programming	3	4
Production	Large enough to accommodate five production workstations and attendant equipment, appropriate lighting, electrical outlets, and ventilation	2	5
Pilot testing	Large enough to accommodate the twenty learners to be tested and the equipment used to deliver the instruction, along with concomitant furniture	3	4
Offices	One office for the project manager with desk, two chairs, two filing cabinets	2	4
Storage	Spaces to house cabinets for masters, supplies, and equipment not being used; should be able to lock up	1	3
Restrooms	Need two, one for women and one for men; should be designed for handicapped; desirable to have on same floor as working area	4	5

Another modification might make it necessary to remove and wall-up windows in order to get better light control. New doorways may have to be created to make maximum use of the space, including ensuring ready access to the facilities by workers and clients and/or to satisfy fire laws that require more than one exit per room. It may be necessary to string wires for video distribution or for computer networking, which is sometimes difficult when conduit was not run in the walls at the time of original construction. Often, the conduit will have to be run in the open, which, while not aesthetically pleasing, is certainly utilitarian.

Costing Facility Modifications

Resources for modifying project spaces are almost always very limited. Some changes, like painting, carpeting, and shades for light control, are reasonable in cost, as is the addition of electrical outlets. Given the changes that would need to be made among the facilities considered, the manager can determine their respective costs and do a trade-off analysis. To assess costs, managers can call on outside estimators who are knowledgeable about the costs of such renovations.

Facilities are never free of charge, but sometimes instructional developers who operate in public educational settings act as though they were. They are paid for through a system of indirect costs. For some projects, indirect costs may take 60% or more of a project's resources. Thus, it is not trivial to consider those costs with care. But more important, since a not insignificant slice is taken out of the project budget for overhead, it is worth approaching the parent organization to see if it will absorb some of the proposed modification costs.

Implementing Facility Modifications

Making changes in a facility may require releases and support from those controlling the spaces, which usually takes time. Lead time for getting a facility up and going is very important. Knowing early on what changes are needed, and making arrangements to get them done before project staff come on board, is desirable. Under less thoughtful planning, by the time modifications are begun, personnel may already be installed. Modifying a facility while staff are trying to work can make it difficult for everyone. To this end, the manager should get clear completion deadlines from workers carrying out the modifications, with penalties being established for exceeding the deadlines.

Ongoing Facility Operation

Without appropriate inputs of energy, all organized entities tend to deteriorate. For an instructional development facility this implies the need for continuing maintenance. From custodial service to equipment repair, none of these tasks get done by chance. If such services are not built in, then the manager will have to make arrangements for them. Keeping supply inventories up to date is another important task. The maxim "For lack of a horseshoe nail, a kingdom was lost" can translate into "For lack of a floppy disc, a program was not backed up, and *then* it was lost!"

Summary

This chapter has presented an overview of some of the elements that affect the spaces in which instructional development takes place and the steps a manager might go through to arrive at a satisfactory project facility. The types of spaces, along with some of their conditions, were examined, as were code requirements, traffic patterns, facility rules, security, and staff comfort. Included among the last were temperature, lighting, acoustics, and aesthetics. Recommendations were also made as to how a manager might compare and rate facilities being considered for housing an ID project.

References

Craig, R. L. (ed.) (1976). *Training and Development Handbook: A Guide to Human Resource Development.* 2d ed. New York: McGraw-Hill, pp. 7.1–7.26.

Ellington, Henry, and Harris, Duncan (1986). *Dictionary of Instructional Technology.* New York: Nichols.

Gillespie, J. T., and Spirt, D. L. (1973). *Creating a School Media Program.* New York: Bowker, pp. 119–128.

Knirk, F. G. (1979). *Designing Productive Learning Environments.* Englewood Cliffs, N.J.: Educational Technology Publications.

Sommer, Robert (1969). *Personal Space: The Behavioral Basis of Design.* Englewood Cliffs, N.J.: Prentice-Hall.

Thompson, J. J (1969). *Instructional Communications.* New York: American Book Company, pp. 185–191.

CHAPTER 16

Epilog

Man is unique, in that he creates his own future.

Anonymous

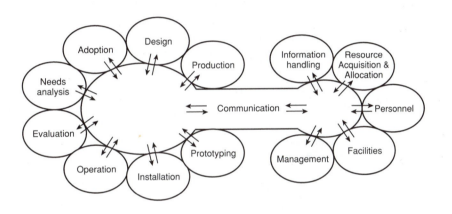

Learner Objectives

1. List advantages and disadvantages of professional jargon.

2. Explain the need for validating ID techniques.

3. Discuss means for identifying and documenting unreported ID techniques.

4. List advantages and disadvantages of using a common format for job aids.

5. Discuss the relationship among theories, models, processes, and techniques of instructional development.

6. Recall definitions of major terms.

Choosing a way through the labyrinth of possibilities found even in the simplest of projects can be daunting to those new to instructional development. The central purpose of this modest work was to bring together, in a coherent system, a set of basic knowledge and skills whose acquisition would enable beginning ID professionals to work at acceptable levels in the several environments in which they would be expected to practice. The knowledge learned here should be sufficient to enable inexperienced instructional developers to avoid major pitfalls common to ID practice while garnering important on-the-job knowledge and experience.

The *Instructional Project Development and Management (IPDM) Model* (see Figure 16.1) was used as an organizer for the basic knowledge and skills taught in the text. The relevant processes for each of the components in the model were discussed and related in a fashion intended to take some of the difficulty out of understanding the overall ID process and its management. The components on the support side of the IPDM Model are as essential as those on the development side. More needs to be known about their common interfaces. A reminder is made that the IPDM Model is only one of many instructional development models available to the practitioner. Whether readers choose to adopt this model or some other, they will find such a model to be very useful as a guide to carrying out instructional development and as an organizer for the plethora of ideas, facts, and other information that they accumulate over years of practice.

A unique quality of this book was the relating of the ID processes of the model to specific techniques for implementing those processes. These were presented in the form of *job aids*, i.e., shortcut formats for teaching technique application. Because the sources for these techniques are dispersed across the literatures of several professions and have not been

FIGURE 16.1 / Relationships among development and Supporting Components of the Model

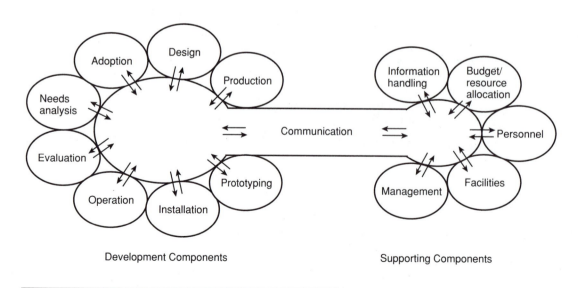

Development Components   Supporting Components

readily available before, it was thought that their compilation here would prove useful to the experienced ID professional as well.

Ultimately, it is the degree to which instructional developers find helpful the knowledge and skills taught here that determines the success of this work. Some of the ID techniques will be more useful to some professionals than to others, as they will be more useful in some projects than in others. Equally clear is that these techniques represent only a sampling of what exists and what is needed. The argument is not that these are necessarily the best techniques for specific ID tasks, only that they work and are generally cost-effective. Another important reason for writing this work is the belief that it might help stimulate further identification, collection, and reporting of ID techniques.

A task that has proved a struggle for the inexperienced instructional developer is understanding the special terminology of the field. Each profession has its own special language, or **jargon**. Jargon enables a short-hand communication that is efficient for practitioners who understand the many terms, but which is often confusing to those who don't understand those special meanings. While jargon is effective when communicating with fellow instructional developers, great care should be taken to use ordinary language when communicating with clients or with others not knowledgeable in the field. The use of jargon with such individuals or groups tends not only to confuse but also to alienate the uninitiated. A serious attempt was made in this work to clarify special ID terms in a language and context that would be helpful to the newcomer. In addition, these definitions have been gathered in a glossary at the end of the text, for easy reference.

Some may view this work as a somewhat mechanistic approach to instructional development, and there is some justification for that view. But this approach has proven, in the author's experience, to be a practical means of relating to learners the range of processes and techniques to the overall ID process. Again, a wider view of instructional development was sometimes sacrificed to the benefits derived from presenting a coherent system. Another criticism of the instruction in this text is that it is admittedly weighted heavily on the side of behavioral theory; but again, this orientation permits coherence of the system, and provides a basis for making ID decisions in a consistent and practical fashion.

Generation of Techniques

The reader will have observed an imbalance of techniques across the components of the IPDM Model. In some cases an instructional developer could choose among several techniques for the same task, as often with the design and the management components. In other processes, techniques were pulled out with excruciating difficulty, if at all, as with the facilities component. This doesn't mean the techniques aren't there, but rather that they have yet to be teased out of their users and originators.

Who are the originators of techniques? They are probably those instructional developers who find themselves dealing with problems for which they find no ready solutions. Necessity still remains the mother of invention! Many of the techniques reported are adaptations of techniques created for other purposes, that is, adjusted by imaginative instructional developers to fit their own purposes. Unknown numbers of useful techniques have yet to get into print, and are found only in the practice of instructional developers. Throughout his search, the author had only limited success in running down the originators of ID techniques. For the most part the techniques seem to be handed on by word of mouth, and only occasionally do they find their way into print, when someone thinks the version merits an article in a journal. Even in print, the technique's progenitors are seldom mentioned. Most of the techniques that could be traced have moved through an evolutionary process as they have been modified and remodified by several generations of users.

Instructional developers would like to think that there is both theoretic and scientific support for their processes and techniques. The development of some techniques do appear to be derived from scientific findings, but a distinction should be made between scientific findings and techniques making up a technology. As Hyman Rickover has pointed out (Gentry, 1987, p. 91):

> Science should not be confused with technology. Science dwells on discovering true facts and relationships of observable phenomena in nature, and with established theories that serve to organize masses of verified data concerning those facts and relationships. In contrast, ... technology cannot claim the authority of science, for technology deals with tools, techniques, procedures: the artifacts of and processes fashioned by modern industrial man to increase his powers of mind and body.

While the creation of most techniques seem to be without obvious theoretical or scientific stimuli, some educational technologists certainly do draw practical applications directly from the discoveries of scientists. Perhaps it would be profitable for educational technologists who have interests in specific areas of science e.g., physics, to monitor advances in those areas periodically for potential applications to the ID field.

Continuing Search for Techniques

The discovery that the majority of ID techniques used in some form by many different developers are largely undocumented is a disquieting comment about the field. There is a need for a systematic procedure for identifying and documenting what must be a wide range of techniques still unreported in ID and related fields. How best to tease these techniques out into a form that will be readily transferable to the field is not yet clear.

Researchers should look beyond the application of specific ID and training techniques to what their effects might be on the larger picture. Doctoral candidates and other researchers are a traditional group for carrying on such research, and, no doubt, some will see the search for and research on techniques as an appropriate challenge (Bennett, 1983). An important research concern is the *validation* of techniques. Do they really work? How does one technique compare to other, alternative techniques for the same purpose? How do alternative techniques differ in cost-effectiveness? The author's experience in seeking out and analyzing ID techniques for this book tends to parallel Goldstein's (1986, p. 290) strong statement that "there is a desperate need for high-quality empirical investigations that examine the usefulness of training techniques."

One important means of identifying and documenting unreported techniques might be to do longitudinal studies of ongoing ID projects, with the main question being "How did you do that?" National, state, and local educational technology associations are also groups that might set the collection of techniques as one of their organization's goals. Perhaps association journals as well as other education technology journals could reserve sections specifically for reporting on ID techniques. An appropriate stimulus might be to give prizes for the best techniques reported for the year, i.e., "Technique of the Year."

The author found no evidence that proprietary attitudes of those using the techniques affected access by others. Of the many professionals interviewed, all, without exception, were quick to share what they knew.

Categorization of Techniques

Categorizing techniques by the component processes of an ID Model, as was done here, seemed a logical procedure to follow. But the reader will note that a number of times the author violated the procedure by presenting some techniques in sections that would appear to fit more logically with other components, because it made intuitive and pedagogical sense to do so. Another complication is that many of these techniques can serve more than one purpose. Multipurpose techniques are generally viewed as more powerful than are single-purpose techniques. But what is the best way to categorize them? Perhaps, all techniques could better be categorized by ID problem. Would that make them more accessible to instructional developers? At any rate, determining better means for categorizing techniques should be subject to further exploration by members of the field.

Technique Format

This work has emulated earlier writers in various journals in adopting the job aid as an appropriate format for presenting techniques. A specific job aid format was adapted for this work. The reasoning was that a consistent format would facilitate communication, for the user, once familiar with the format, would not have to interpret the meanings of the sections of the formats each time. Still, there is some question about the validity of the decision to use only a single job aid format. On occasion, it proved a strain to force techniques into a single format.

As a disclaimer, the author is not suggesting that understanding a technique at the job aid level is superior to having an in-depth knowledge of the technique and its related concepts. The main justifications for using job aids are consistency of format, and the speed with which an instructional developer can learn to apply the technique to limited objectives.

Additionally, job aids are useful memory-joggers for those techniques that are seldom used. In many cases, busy instructional developers will not want to know more than they need to in order to apply the technique directly. In those cases where they would like to know more, it is assumed they will be motivated to search out appropriate information.

While the use of techniques in a job aid format has value in that users don't have to know a lot about a technique to apply it successfully, an additional value is that use of job aids can make people effective users of techniques without having to pay for the kind of training necessary to give an in-depth understanding. However, there is room for criticizing the blind application of techniques to limited objectives. Techniques, like other human endeavors, have interactive effects, some of which might cause instructional developers to preclude their use in certain circumstances if they understood the possible unplanned effects.

Predicting Technique Needs

The renowned educational technology prophet Marshall McLuhan (1967) said that most people go through life looking through a rearview mirror. That is, they are only concerned with how new technology can be applied to complement what already exists. A decided shift of mind is necessary to think in terms of the future. Decisions to adopt innovations are often made on neither logical nor practical grounds. For example, a common complaint of computer scientists is that people reverse the logical process when they purchase computers *before* determining the specific uses to which the computers will be put. An analogous concern is about instructional developers running around with their favorite techniques (i.e., solutions) looking for problems to solve. A future-oriented view would have instructional developers first identify problems that need solving, and then ask what would be the characteristics of techniques that could solve these problems. If none of the available techniques has the necessary characteristics, there would be motivation to invent ones that would. The goals of ID projects, i.e., to deliver products that are up to specification, on time, and on budget, are not necessarily the only focus for determining future technique needs. Instructional developers, as knowledgeable educators and trainers, might better be sensitive to the trends in learning and learning systems, and extrapolate technique needs from them.

Unfinished Business

Because the work that instructional developers do covers such a wide span of knowledge, they have had to become generalists. As one pundit put it: "Their knowledge is a mile wide and an inch deep." Instructional developers tend to be pragmatic, adopting or adapting with little question that which works. There is, no doubt, payoff in understanding the relevance to the ID field of certain theories, such as theories of general systems, learning, evaluation, communication, information, and cybernetics. These theories spawn ID models, and the processes derived from the models tell instructional developers *what* needs to be done. In turn, techniques tell *how* to accomplish the processes. This provides a logical connection between theory and practice, but still there is no coherent body of research that undergirds the field of educational technology.

Thus, the pragmatic instructional developer does not yet know what is owed to the researcher and theoreticians of the field. Perhaps this is a good time to reexamine the future of the instructional developer. The same question Thompson (1969, p. 226) so adroitly asked many years ago of media specialists can be asked today of instructional developers:

> He must decide if he belongs to education or technology, to people or to things, for he cannot long remain a generalist in a world of specialists. Yet he cannot help himself for he does not know who he is. Is he the prophet of a new kind of education just a little too early on the scene, or is he a relic of the past who has stayed a little too long?

Technology changes. While there is uncertainty about what the techniques of tomorrow are likely to be, there is an increasing suspicion that many of tomorrow's techniques will more and more serve objects that plug into walls, e.g., computers and laserdisc players. The concept of place utility will change at a faster rate, too, in the sense that students will be able to learn in many places, not just in classrooms (Gentry and Csete, 1991). What techniques are necessary to make that possible? Surely, there will be a need for techniques that permit the instructional system to respond to the learner, much as a personal tutor does. Minimally, this suggests interesting software and hardware combinations of computer-assisted instruction, optical technologies, and expert systems (McLaughlin, 1992). A continuing task is to give the development of instruction a deeper scientific basis without losing the creative aspects of development and product.

While the practice of ID has its fearful moments, most of the time it is enjoyable and rewarding. Success requires that practitioners recognize that to have fun at this game, they have to understand how the game is played, and how to change the game to the mutual advantage of developer and client. Understanding the limits of a system is more important than slavishly supporting the rules of play. The new instructional developer will find that there is an awful lot of ignoring of the rules that are presented here as important. For example, performing formative and summative evaluation of an instructional delivery system before full implementation is the exception in the field. What's the practical side of dealing with that type of problem? The most likely way of coping is at some level of *successive approximation* to evaluation; e.g., if the administration won't support twenty subjects to pilot test the instruction, get them to support one or two subjects. The careful use of the right one or two subjects will enable the developer to pick up on most of the glitches in the instruction. Pretty soon, responsible people will note that some team's instructional products are consistently more successful than those of others, and they will ask why. And thus inroads are made.

Summary

There is much to be done in the field of instructional development and its parent field, educational technology. This is a good time to be entering the field, with all of the technological breakthroughs in computer software and hardware. It is also a time when professionals will have to become more sophisticated in a number of areas relevant to the field, including processes and techniques of learning, communication, evaluation, and curriculum. The only limits are those of one's imagination and energy.

References

Bennett, T. L. (1983). A Study to Identify Major Field Techniques and Utilization Levels by Canadian Instructional Developers. PhD Dissertation. East Lansing, Mich.: Michigan State University.

Gentry, Cass (1987). *Educational Technology: A Question of Meaning.* In *Educational Media and Technology Yearbook 1987*, vol. 13, ed. E. E. Miller and M. L. Mosely, Littleton, Colo.: Libraries Unlimited.

Gentry, C. G., and Csete, J. (1991). Educational technology in the 1990s. In *Instructional Technology: Past, Present, and Future*, ed. G. J. Anglin, Littleton, Colo.: Libraries Unlimited.

Goldstein, I. L. (1986). *Training in Organizations: Needs Assessment, Development, and Evaluation.* Monterey, Calif.: Brooks/Cole.

McLaughlin, T. (1992). Combining Expert Systems and Optical Data Storage Technologies in Computer-Facilitated Learning. PhD Dissertation. East Lansing, Mich.: Michigan State University.

McLuhan, M. (1967). *The Medium is the Message.* New York: Bantam Books.

Thompson, J. J. (1969). *Instructional Communication.* New York: American Book Co.

The numbers, following each of the terms and their definitions refer to the chapters in which they are found.

Accept/reject decision: Process of clients' making go/no-go decisions about an innovation, based on trial data. (3)

Accession number: Numbers that are assigned to documents by which the documents are stored and retrieved. (12)

Accountability: Process of holding specific personnel responsible for their actions in a system. (13)

Adoption: Process of establishing acceptance of an innovation by decision makers, gatekeepers, and others affected, and of obtaining commitment of resources. (3)

Affective domain: The division of Bloom's taxonomy of educational objectives that references those objectives and test items demonstrating interest, appreciation, attitudes, values, and/or psychological adjustment. (4)

Analytic flowcharting: Procedure for identifying and graphically representing the sequential and alternative relationships among processes and decision points relevant to completing a project. (10)

Appraising proposed change: Process of clients' assessing fitness of a solution or change to their instructional problem, and of comparing it to other potential solutions. (3)

Behavioral hierarchy: The arrangement of educational objectives to graphically show their interdependence and the order in which they should be learned. (4)

Behavioral objective: A precise statement of intent that includes the *behavior* to be learned, the *conditions* under which the behavior is demonstrated, and the *degree* to which the behavior is to be learned. (4)

Budget: The financial statement of the objectives, programs, and activities of a system; the formal statement of anticipated revenues and expenditures for a given period. (13)

Closed system: A system that restricts the flow of information across the boundaries between it and other systems or between components of the system. (6, 11)

Cognitive domain: The division of Bloom's taxonomy of educational objectives that references those objectives and test items requiring recall or recognition of knowledge and the development of intellectual abilities and skills. (4)

Communication: The transmission of information from senders to receivers and from receivers to senders. (11)

Communications Network Analysis: A technique used to identify the relationships among individuals and groups possessing informal influence in a specific system. (7)

Communication source: The originator of a message. (11)

Content validity: The degree to which a test measures an intended content area. (9)

Contingency account: A special line item included in a budget for the purpose of covering unforeseen needs. (13)

Correlation: The degree to which a relationship exists between two or more quantifiable variables. (9)

Cost–benefit analysis (CBA): A technique designed to assist decision makers in identifying a preferred choice among possible alternatives. (3)

Criterion-referenced test items: Test items whose responses are compared with some objective standard rather than with other responses as in norm-referenced items. (4)

Critical Incident Technique: Procedure for collecting real-world examples of behavior that characterize either very effective or very ineffective performance of some activity. (2)

Critical path: The specific trail through a PERT network that consumes the most time; provides data for predicting the earliest time that a project can be finished. (5, 10)

Decision query: A technique that is useful in getting staff and administration to reexamine a decision about adopting an alternative that is competing with the one preferred by an innovator. (3)

Delphi Technique: Procedure for efficiently collecting informed judgments from experts who are anonymous to one another, and for gaining consensus about those judgments. (2)

Design (instructional): Process of determining and specifying objectives, strategies, techniques, and media for meeting instructional goals. (1, 4)

Direct costs: Those funds spent directly on project tasks. (13)

Distance education: An alternative to classroom education, with instruction being delivered at a distance from the providing institution. It has been known for years under such labels as *correspondence study* and *home study*, but is now a term more associated with learning applications of computer and video technologies. (7)

Dummy activity: A PERT activity represented by a dashed arrow used to show that an activity in one path of the network must be completed before an activity in another path can be started. Dummy activities do not consume time or other resources. (5)

Educational Resources Information Center: See *ERIC*.

Educational technology: The practical application of scientific and/or other knowledge to accomplish given educational tasks. (1)

Electronic spreadsheets: Application software that is very efficient in manipulating tabular data like that found on an accountant's ledger sheet. A major value of a spreadsheet is that new numbers inserted into its tables trigger hidden formulas that cause the tables to be automatically updated, changing all numbers that would be affected by the new numbers. (13)

Entropy: A general-systems principle stating that all organized entities tend to disorganize unless maintained. (8)

Environment: See *Suprasystem*. (1)

ERIC (Educational Resources Information Center): The largest of the electronic databases serving education; holds over half a million citations that cover research findings, project and technical reports, books, and journal articles. (12)

Ergonomics: The application of anatomical, physiological, and psychological knowledge and principles to the study of the relationships among people and all aspects of their activities. (7, 15)

Essay questions: Test items that require a constructed, written response for purposes of testing whether objectives from the higher levels of the cognitive domain (i.e., analysis, synthesis, and evaluation) are met. (4)

Evaluation: Process of collecting and analyzing data about, and assigning values to, an ongoing instructional unit, to help in making decisions on its maintenance, revision, and/or elimination. (1, 9)

Face validity: A technique used to collect expert opinion on how well a test measures an intended content area. (9)

Fault Tree Analysis: A technique for increasing the probability of success in any system by analyzing the most likely modes of failure that could occur within the system and then suggesting high-priority avoidance strategies for those failure modes. (2)

Feedback: Information received that is either confirming or corrective of some action. (11)

Flat (systems) hierarchical administrative model: A management model where there are usually no more than two layers of decision makers over project staff, making for quick turnaround on decisions. (10)

Flowcharting: See *Analytic flowcharting*.

Force-field analysis (FFA): A technique that can be used to generate and analyze forces that facilitate or hinder adoption of a proposed change. (3)

Formative evaluation: A technique used to identify design and production flaws *during* the process of instructional development rather than after completion of development. (6)

Gatekeepers: Individuals whose control of a system's resources may affect the adoption of an innovation. (3, 7)

Goal: A general expression of intent that is not limited in time or directly measurable. (2)

ID Model: A graphic representation of a systematic approach, designed to facilitate efficient and effective development of instruction. (1)

Indirect costs: Funds spent for overhead items of a project, including use of space, utilities, taxes, depreciation, insurance, facility maintenance, and accounting charges. (13)

Information handling: Process of selecting, collecting/generating, organizing, storing, retrieving, distributing,and assessing information required by an ID project. (1, 9, 12)

Innovation: A change that is new to the members of a targeted system. (3)

Installation: Process of establishing, testing, and ensuring the necessary conditions for effective operation when placing a new instructional package or process into a targeted educational or training environment. (1, 7)

Instructional design: Process of determining and specifying objectives, strategies, techniques, and media for meeting instructional goals. (4)

Instructional development: A systematic approach to the design, production, evaluation, and implementation of systems of instruction. (1)

Interface analysis: A technique for relating the components of a system in terms of their common boundaries; concerned with what information needs to flow across those boundaries, and the factors that affect that flow. (6, 11)

Interfaces: The common boundaries between components of a system. (6)

Jargon: Special terms generated, adopted, or adapted by members of a profession that enables a short-hand communication that is efficient for practitioners who understand the terms but may be confusing to those who don't. (16)

Job aids: Teaching devices intended to be self-explanatory and self-instructional; a formalized set of textual and/or graphical step-by-step directions for accomplishing a task through one or more techniques. (1)

Job description: Written format for announcing a position that is open for application. Information in a job description may include: tasks to be performed, skills and qualifications required, salary and benefit range, when the job should start, directions for applying, and closing date for applications. (14)

Lesson plan: A formal design for a particular instructional segment. (4)

Maintenance: The servicing, repair, and general upkeep of a system. (8)

Management: Process by which resources are controlled, coordinated, integrated, and allocated to accomplish project goals. (1)

Master: The final version of an instructional element from which copies are made. (5)

Matching-test items: Test items consisting of a stem that asks a question or gives a task, followed by two parallel columns (*premise* and *response*): an item in the *premise* column, through associated Arabic numbers or alphabetic letters, is matched with the correct item(s) in the *response* column. (4)

Media: The means by which messages are communicated. (4)

Multiple-choice test item: A test item that contains a stem setting forth a problem, followed by a correct solution randomly placed among several foils or distracters. (4)

Need: Any significant discrepancy between a desired outcome and an observed outcome. (2)

Needs analysis (assessment): Process of establishing the validity of needs and goals for existing or proposed instruction and for assigning priorities among them. (2)

No-budget budget: An informal budget type characterized by unplanned requests from personnel for funds, drawing from any discretionary funds found in the formal budget. (13)

Noise: In communication theory, anything that distorts a message. (11)

Nominal Group Process (NGP): An effective and efficient procedure for getting the best combined judgments from a group about some topic. (3)

Object–function budget: A budget type in which similar expenditures are clustered in a general category, e.g., salaries, travel, maintenance, equipment, supplies. These broader categories may be broken down further, e.g., under "travel" may be listed modes of travel, such as automobile, train, and plane. (13)

Objective trees: A technique used to hierarchically relate and to some extent generate objectives in terms of the desired ends of a project. Objectives and their relationships are portrayed graphically in the form of a tree, with the goal being at the top of the tree and levels of terminal and enabling objectives following in a hierarchy. (4)

Open system: A system that permits the ready flow of information across the boundaries between it and other systems or between components of the system. (6, 11)

Operation: Process of maintaining the ongoing use of an instructional package in a targeted environment after installation. (1)

Oral protocol: A technique in which, during a trial of a prototype, the learner is asked to talk his or her way through the instruction, to make clear what the student is thinking as he or she makes decisions and responses. The data are used to revise the instruction. (6)

Overhead projector: A device that can project the image in a transparent acetate sheet onto a screen usually located above and behind the presenter; used in place of a chalkboard. (5)

Overhead transparency: Clear acetate sheets on which an image is printed or drawn; used with an overhead projector to project images onto a screen for a viewing audience. (5)

Overlay transparencies: Where two or more sheets of acetate with images are put into register, hinged and overlaying one another, so that a presenter can build on preceding images. (5)

Performance budget: This budget type clusters moneys to be allocated by general category,

but these categories are put in a matrix that enables a manager to see what specific task or unit of work is supported by what expenditure within each category. (13)

Performance test items: Test items used to determine whether someone can directly apply specific skills in appropriate situations, usually taking the form of a checklist, where the evaluator checks off or grades appropriate items as the student performs them. (4)

Pilot testing: Procedure concerned with trying out a solution to see if it fits a specific environment. (3)

Planning, Programming, Budgeting, Evaluating System (PPBS): This budget type relates the expenditure of funds to the specific objectives of a project. "Evaluating" is left out of the acronym to ease memory. (13)

Policy: Broad, formally stated rules that guide managers in making decisions about recurring situations or functions. (3)

Policy setting technique: A technique for determining whether target system policies need to be deleted, added, or revised in order to accomplish the goals of a new process or product proposed for the system. (3)

Problem: A condition in which someone desires a certain state of affairs but does not immediately know how to attain it. (2)

Production: Process of constructing elements and/or revising existing elements for some system, as specified in a design. (1)

Product master: See *Master.*

Product validation: A procedure for providing evidence that a product is capable of delivering what was promised. (16)

Program Evaluation and Review Technique (PERT): A systematic programming, timing, and costing technique for measuring, monitoring, and controlling the development of a project. (5, 10)

Project: A specific, finite task with a well-defined set of predetermined outcomes. (1)

Prototype: A functional version of a new process and/or product, usually in an unfinished state, whose effectiveness and efficiency can be tested. (6)

Prototyping: Process of assembling produced and/or revised instructional elements, and of testing, revising, summatively evaluating, and preparing the system for marketing. (1, 3)

Psychomotor domain: The division of Bloom's taxonomy of educational objectives that references those objectives and test items demonstrating manipulative and/or motor skills. (4)

Redundancy: When alternative ways of stating the same message are included in a communication. (11)

Refreezing: Process of stabilizing a target system until clients have successfully integrated planned change or changes. (3)

RFP (request for proposal): An announcement by organizations that want others to carry out a project for them describing what they want done and asking for interested parties to respond, following a prescribed format, with a plan and a bid. (10)

Reliability (test): The degree to which a test instrument *consistently* measures the same group's knowledge level of the same instruction when taking the test over again. (9)

Request for proposal: See *RFP.*

Resource acquisition and allocation: Process of determining resource needs, formalizing budgets, accounting for resources, and distributing resources. (1, 13)

Revolving account: An account devised for holding until needed any transitory funds earmarked for specific tasks. Auditing is limited to reconciling beginning and ending totals for the account. (13)

Sampling validity: A technique used to collect expert opinion on how well a test samples the total content area being tested. (9)

Script: A written document that provides, for talent in a film or video production, details about their lines, where to stand, and the timing of their activities. (4)

Short-answer test items: Test items used for determining the degree of students' factual recall, where they respond to a question with a brief written answer in a designated space, usually below the question. (4)

Spreadsheets: See *Electronic spreadsheets.*

Storyboarding: A design technique for showing as individual scenes the proposed sequence of visual and audio elements in a production, using some form of optically projected media, e.g., television, slide/tape, interactive video. (4)

Strategy, instructional: An overall plan for attacking an instructional problem, as contrasted with *tactic* and *technique*, which tell *how* to accomplish the strategy. (4)

Structure: The framework of expectancies and limits that control a system's processes; consists of an organization's forms, procedures, and rules. (7)

Subsystem: One of two or more interacting components or elements making up a system. (1, 6)

Successive approximation: A technique for establishing what is necessary to implement a system initially, and then prescribing successive revisions of the system until it is up to original design specifications. (3, 10)

Summative evaluation: A technique used to collect evidence of the value of an instructional package, to demonstrate to prospective adopters that it teaches what it proposes to teach. (6)

Sunset review technique (aka sunset law technique): A technique that sets up the conditions under which an instructional unit will be reviewed at the end of a set trial period, for purposes of determining if it should be continued as is, revised, or eliminated. (3)

Suprasystem: A subsuming system that may affect the operation of a specific system. (1)

System: A set of interacting components arranged to perform some wanted operation(s). (1, 6)

Table of specifications: A matrix showing the relationship among, and values for, variables that are relevant to the object or objects to be produced; used as a guide to ensure that design criteria are met during production. (6)

Tall (bureaucratic) hierarchical administrative model: A management model with several layers of decision makers, usually with a strict chain of command for communication and decision making, i.e., a bureaucratic model. (10)

Task analysis: A process of identifying, sequencing, and relating the tasks and subtasks that should be performed in order to meet learning objectives. (4)

Technique: An established means for carrying out a specific task. (1)

Thesaurus: An alphabetical listing of key terms or descriptors, used singly and in combination, to locate relevant documents in a professional database. (12)

Trade-off: The choosing from among alternatives, so as to take a loss at one variable in order to gain with another, e.g., time versus cost. (10)

Troubleshooting: A technique for finding the cause of a problem, and a means for correcting it, through a process of systematically checking out the possible causes, beginning with the most likely and continuing to the least likely. (8)

True-false test items: A test item consisting of a short statement with which the person being tested indicates agreement or disagreement. (4)

Tryout: The testing of a prototype, or some subset of its elements, under actual or simulated conditions that are representative of those in the targeted system. (3)

Unfreezing: Process of clients' becoming aware of problems and becoming willing to consider potential solutions. (3)

Validity: The degree to which a test measures what it was designed to measure. (9)

Visitation: A carefully planned trip to some location to study some process or activity operating in another environment, usually for the purpose of determining the appropriateness of the process or activity for the visitor's location. (3)

Weeding (purging): The process of identifying and removing obsolete information from databases. (12)

Work-breakdown package (WBP): Unit of work formed by clustering related tasks of a project so the clusters can then be assigned to different teams. Clustering tasks into WBPs enables teams to know far enough ahead what is expected of them, but also provides managers with the data needed for tighter monitoring of costs. (13)

Working wall: A plain wall, used for project planning, to which sections of PERT networks and/or storyboards can be tacked for ready reference by those involved so they can be quickly modified to show recent changes. (15)

Workstation: An individual space dedicated to a particular project task, e.g., video editing, graphics production, computer programming. (15)

Acknowledgments

Chapter 2

p. 13, Fig. 2.1, Exhibit from Chapter 7 by Richard T. Coffing, p. 190 reprinted by permission of The Free Press, a Division of Macmillan, Inc. from *Dynamic Educational Change* by Gerald Zaltman, David Florio, and Linda S. Sikorski. Copyright © 1977 by The Free Press.

p. 13, Fig. 2.2, "Relating Needs Analysis, Program Development, Implementation and Evaluation," Roger Kaufman, et al, *Journal of Instructional Development*, 4(4), 1981. Reprinted by permission of the Association for Educational Communications & Technology.

p. 18, from *Group Techniques for Program Planning: A Guide to Nominal Group and Delphi Processes*, André L. Delbecq, Green Briar Press, 1986. Reprinted by permission of the author.

Chapter 3

pp. 33–38, from *Group Techniques for Program Planning: A Guide to Nominal Group and Delphi Processes*, André L. Delbecq, Green Briar Press, 1986. Reprinted by permission of the author.

pp. 47–50, from *Human Competence*, T. F. Gilbert, McGraw-Hill, Inc., 1978. Reprinted by permission of the publisher.

Chapter 4

pp. 88–91, "Alternative Methods of Task Analysis," W. R. Foshay and "The Process of Task Analysis," K. E. Carlisle, *Journal of Instructional Development*, 6(4), 1983. Reprinted by permission of the Association for Educational Communications & Technology.

pp. 92–95, adapted excerpts from *The Conditions of Learning*, Robert M. Gagne, copyright © 1965 Holt, Rinehart and Winston, Inc. and renewed 1993 Robert M. Gagne. Reprinted by permission of the publisher.

pp. 110–111, "Rapid Prototyping: An Alternative Instructional Design Strategy," Steven D. Tripp and Barbara Blichelmeyer, *Educational Technology Research and Development*, 38(1), 1990. Reprinted by permission of the Association for Educational Communications & Technology.

Chapter 6

pp. 169–171, from *The Systematic Design of Instruction*, 2/e by Walter Dick and Lou Carey. Copyright © 1985, 1978 Scott, Foresman and Company. Reprinted by permission of HarperCollins Publishers.

Chapter 8

pp. 199–201, from *Introduction to Management* by Warren R. Plunkett and Raymond F. Attner, PWS/Kent Publishing Company, 1989. Reprinted by permission of the publisher. From the exhibit "How A Key Indicator Report Can Promote Efficiency" in Robert L. Janson "Graphic Indicators of Operations," *Harvard Business Review* (November–December 1980). Reprinted by permission.

pp. 206–210, "Course Maintenance: The Problem and Solution," Charles F. Martinez, *Educational Technology*, 20(12), 1980. Reprinted by permission of Educational Technology Publications.

pp. 244–245, from *Supervising Technical and Professional People* by Martin Broadwell and Ruth House, John Wiley and Sons, Inc., 1986. Reprinted by permission of the publisher.

p. 247, "Management Strategy: Get Control," Joe Conlin, *Successful Meetings*, June, 1989. Reprinted by permission of *Successful Meetings* Magazine. Copyright © 1989 Bill Communications, Inc.

pp. 248–149, from *Project Management: A Systems Approach to Planning, Scheduling and Controlling*, 3/e by H. Kerzner, Van Nostrand Reinhold, 1989. Reprinted by permission of the publisher.

Chapter 12

pp. 300–302, from *How to Write Information Mapping* by R. E. Horn, Information Resources, Inc., 1976. Reprinted by permission of the publisher.

INDEX